John Work Garrett was born in 1820. He died at Deer Park, Maryland, in 1884. He was president of the Baltimore and Ohio Railroad from 1858 until his death. The railroad was responsible for this area's economic growth which included large summer resort business following establishment of the Deer Park Hotel by Mr. Garrett. When the county was created in 1872, Richard T. Browning, one of three men who had been most involved in creating the new county, was given the privilege of selecting a name. He chose Garrett. Photo courtesy of Mrs. Robert B. (Nelle) Garrett and John W. Garrett's great-grandson, Harrison Garrett, of Baltimore, Maryland

GARRETT COUNTY
A History of Maryland's Tableland

By
Stephen Schlosnagle
and
The Garrett County Bicentennial Committee

FIRST EDITION

McCLAIN PRINTING COMPANY
PARSONS, WEST VIRGINIA 26287

1978

This history as published is a revision of the author's original manuscript, *Garrett Green—A Bicentennial History of an Appalachian County*, by the History Editing Committee.

Standard Book Number 87012-310-6
Library of Congress Card Number 78-62435
Printed in the United States of America
for the Garrett County Bicentennial Committee
Copyright © 1978 by the Garrett County
Historical Society, Inc.
Oakland, Maryland
All Rights Reserved

CONTENTS

In Appreciation xi
I: The Land 1
II: Settlement 23
III: Destiny 186
IV: The Twentieth Century 334
Epilogue: Garrett County 353
Bibliography 357
Index 361

ILLUSTRATIONS

John Work Garrett	Frontispiece
Hon. William Pinkney Whyte	4
Deep Creek, U.S. 219, Bridge	7
Youghiogheny River	7
Grain field	8
The cove	8
Muddy Creek Falls	9
Forests of Garrett County	10
Famous Campers, left to right, Henry Ford, Thomas Edison, President Warren G. Harding, Harvey S. Firestone	11
Henry Ford at Muddy Creek	12
Four bridges over Casselman River	13
Casselman historic stone bridge (1813)	14
Washington Spring	15
Hoye Crest	15
B&O 17-Mile Grade	16
B&O Viaduct at Bloomington	16
Savage River Dam	17
Eagle Rock	17
Swallow Falls	18
Cranesville Swamp	19
Meshach Browning	20
Meshach Browning Cabin at Sang Run	21
Browning Roadside Marker	22
Grave of Meshach Browning	22
Mountain Lake—Boathouse and Icehouse	169
Mountain Lake Park Amphitheater	169
Sugar Maple Camp	170
C&O R.R. Station, Friendsville (1891)	171

Fuller-Baker Log House	171
The Braddock Road	172
Oakland Railroad Station	173
Compton Schoolhouse	174
Garrett County	174
Stone House Inn on U.S. Route 40	175
The Pennington Cottage, Deer Park	176
Friend's Graveyard	177
The Fenced Graveyard	177
Grave of Gabriel Friend	177
Grave of John Friend, Sr.	177
Deer Park Hotel	178
The Drane House, Accident	178
Drane Grave, Accident	179
The Oakland Hotel	179
The Glades Hotel, Oakland	180
Early Auto, International Harvester	181
Stanley Steamer	181
Bear Creek Iron Furnace	182
Bandstand, Deer Park	183
Mountain Lake Hotel	183
Courthouse, Oakland	184
Loch Lynn Heights Hotel	185
Narrow-gauge Climax	315
Forestry Operations	316
Woodsmen	317
A sawmill at Bear Creek	318
Crellin Sawmill	319
Autumn Glory Festival	320
Garrett County Fair	320
Garrett Community College	321
U.S. Route 48—National Freeway	321
Coal mine at Steyer	322
Strip mine	323
Richter Tannery	324
Skiing on Marsh Mountain	325
Boat Building, Gordon Douglass Boat Company	326
Old-fashioned winter	326
Boating on Deep Creek Lake	327

Golf, Oakland Country Club 328
Bausch & Lomb, Inc. 329
Altamont Spring Bottling House 330
Snow job at Keyser's Ridge 331
Garrett Memorial (Stone) Church 332
One-room school 333

IN APPRECIATION

The Bicentennial Committee wishes to recognize and express appreciation for the many contributions from persons in the past and in the present who have made it possible to publish this first history of Garrett County.

Seven persons were asked to be a History Editing Committee to help the author by reviewing and criticizing all materials submitted for this history. The bicentennial chairman was an ex officio member of this committee and others. The editing committee worked for many months to meet its responsibility. And its members realize there are omissions. It maintains, however, that its central purpose as a committee was to weigh the completeness of the author's work while encouraging him to tell the story of Garrett County and its people as accurately and interestingly as possible.

This book has been published with aid from the Maryland Bicentennial Commission. The committee also wishes to recognize the important support of the county commissioners in approving the use of federal funds to compensate Mr. Schlosnagle for his writing.

The Garrett County Bicentennial Committee has received continuous encouragement from Dr. Raymond O. McCullough, of Friendsville, in all its programs. Dr. McCullough has served his county and state as vice-chairman of the Maryland Bicentennial Commission. He has given his time to history committee meetings and has contributed directly to the contents of this book to bring it to completion. The committee has been able to achieve success because Dr. McCullough has helped to get funding for its program and the publishing of this book.

For the many courtesies extended to bicentennial groups

and the persons working on this history by Garrett Community College and the Ruth Enlow Library, we can be most grateful. Miss Edith Brock, librarian, has always been ready to help in any way toward the compilation and publishing of this history.

During the bicentennial program in Garrett County we have seen two projects undertaken and completed with financial and cultural success. These were the reprinting of *Miscellaneous Writings* by the late Jacob Brown, an important record of early area history, and the publication of an original Garrett County bicentennial calendar. We congratulate such leaders in these projects as Mrs. David Broadwater, Robert J. Ruckert, Mrs. Earl Opel, and Mrs. Wayne Fratz.

The Bicentennial Committee as a group and as individuals wish to record here a memorial of respect to its late members, Robert B. Garrett, of Deer Park; Daniel Hershberger, of Grantsville; and John S. Elliott, of Little Crossings. Their enthusiasm for publishing this history, their hard work toward accomplishing it, and loyalty to their heritage leave others indebted to them.

The people have been most fortunate to have B. O. Aiken, of Accident, serving as their Bicentennial Committee chairman. He has devoted much time and given material support during the past few years to help the people present and enjoy programs celebrating their heritage of freedom. He has continually supported this project of publishing a county history. And whatever shortcomings the book may have, his co-workers feel that Mr. Aiken speaks for them and himself regarding *Garrett County—A History of Maryland's Tableland* when he says: "It is presented with great pride."

I

THE LAND

> And you ordered me not to travel to the East, not to journey to the Indies by the land route that everyone had taken before me, but instead to take a route to the West, which so far as anyone knows no man had ever attempted.... So on Saturday the twelfth of May 1492 I set out from Granada, and I traveled to the seaport of Palos. There I fitted out three vessels and got crews for them and supplied them well with provisions. And on the third of August that same year, a Friday, I left Palos and stood out to sea, half an hour before sunrise....
>
> Christopher Columbus

Christopher Columbus discovered America on October 12, 1492, by moonlight.

In Europe, in 1492, the sun was beginning to shine. It first appeared in the Italian sky, then it moved westward. The Renaissance brought man from the darkness of the Middle Ages to the light of modern times. It gave him a new self-awareness, a new self-confidence, a new self-reliance, a new sense of identity. The warm sun of the Renaissance nourished new artists, writers, statesmen, and thinkers; it revealed new horizons; it beckoned new explorations and encouraged new explorers. *Renaissance* is French for *rebirth*.

"What a piece of work is man!" wrote Shakespeare for *Hamlet* in 1600. (The European Renaissance was at its height.) "How noble in reason!" he wrote, "how infinite in faculty! in form and moving how express and admirable! in action how like an angel! in apprehension how like a god! the beauty of the world! the paragon of animals!"

European man began to rediscover himself during the Renaissance of the fourteenth and fifteenth centuries. Then he began to discover, for the first time, whole new worlds. And within the course of a few hundred years of exploration the planet Earth would double in size.

Fired by the awakening spirit of the Renaissance, by religious fervor and dreams of riches beyond the horizon, men from many European nations voyaged far into the unknown and little known parts of the earth. Settlers quite often followed in their wakes.

Columbus, a Renaissance native of Genoa, sailed westward from the port of Palos carrying the flag of Spain and sixty-nine days later saw, in the dim light of a pale October moon, the shore of a new and unknown continent. He was quickly followed to North America by the French, English, and Dutch.

This inevitably led to conflict between the settlers and such Indian allies as each could acquire. By 1634 when Cecilius Calvert, Lord Baltimore, sent a small band of settlers to occupy the large proprietary grant of Maryland, this conflict was well developed. By mid-seventeenth century the English colonies along the Eastern Seaboard were threatened on the North and West by France and on the South and West by Spain, while the Dutch in New Amsterdam split the English colonial domains in two.

By 1763 the English had resolved the conflict with their French, Spanish, and Dutch rivals, leaving themselves supreme on the Eastern Seaboard. In the meantime the English king issued a proclamation forbidding English settlement west of the Appalachians. This appeased the Indian inhabitants of the region somewhat, but it didn't stop westward expansion.

Except for a single village of Indians living in a low, natural wide-open amphitheater of the Youghiogheny River in 1763, present-day Garrett County was uninhabited at the conclusion of the Great War for the Empire.

Spanning the continental divide of the Appalachian Mountains—its western slopes drain into the Youghiogheny, then the Ohio, then the Mississippi, then the Gulf; its eastern slopes drain into the Savage, which flows to the Potomac and thence to the Chesapeake Bay and the Atlantic Ocean—spanning the continental divide, high in the Appalachians, west of Fort Cumberland, Garrett County, in 1763 was still the extreme western frontier of Maryland's Frederick County.

Before the white men came to the mountains, the area was a favored hunting spot of the American Indian to the east and west. The natives came in the spring, like the herds of buffalo before them, from the lowlands of the great valleys that bordered the mountains. They paddled upstream in canoes; then they took to the traces and trails of the bison through rugged mountain passes and fertile valleys and marshes. On the cool mountaintop, swept by gentle breezes from the west, they established their camps in valleys and passed their summers on the hills in hunt while buffalo grazed in the lush, wide glades where grass grew tall as a man's waist. Then they returned to the lowlands for the winter. The buffalo followed.

White men first came to Garrett County in 1750, searching for a passage to the west. They built a road in 1752. They fought a war from 1753 to 1763. After the war the Indians left the mountain country forever.

In 1764, a year after peace was formally established, following Pontiac's uprising, a white man named John Friend walked up the mountains from the Potomac River on the trail of a fur trader which followed a buffalo trace. He crossed the crest of the Alleghenies, then descended to the sole Indian village of the area on the Youghiogheny. Here he bought land. He traded an iron pot for several cornfields and a few rough dwellings. Then he returned to the Potomac. A year later he came back. He settled on the land.

The Swedish John Friend was Garrett County's first permanent white resident. He moved to a land wild and high and secluded and free. Buffalo, deer, elk, and bears romped and roamed at will on the hills of his new home; trout and bass swam free in the streams. Wild grass grew tall and lush in the glades.

The mountains of Garrett stood eternal, quiet, serene, and still in 1764.

Garrett was very green.

HON. WILLIAM PINKNEY WHYTE
1824-1908

The Hon. William Pinkney Whyte, elected Governor of Maryland in 1871, signed the proclamation establishing Garrett County in 1872. In 1874 the Maryland Assembly elected Governor Whyte to the U.S. Senate. He resigned to allow the Assembly to elect his successor. He had formerly served in the Assembly and as State Comptroller (1853-1855). Governor Whyte was a graduate of Harvard Law School.

The former Governor was named for his grandfather, William Pinkney, eminent Maryland jurist and ambassador to England under President Washington. Governor Whyte was native to and lifelong resident of Baltimore.

We are indebted to the great-grandson of former Governor Whyte for the portrait we publish here. He is Mr. Edward C. Whyte who is employed by Allegany Ballistics at Cumberland. The portrait is one of four that Mr. Whyte has of his distinguished great-grandfather.—The *Glades Star*, Centennial Issue, vol. 4, no. 12, Oakland, Maryland, March, 1972.

Proclamation By Governor Whyte

The following copy of the proclamation that established Garrett County is to be found at the Court House in Oakland in Book No. 1, Page No. 1, of the Land Records of Garrett County in the office of the Clerk of the Circuit Court.

Proclamation by the Governor: State of Maryland, Executive Department, "Whereas by an Act of the General Assembly of Maryland passed at the January Session Eighteen hundred and Seventy-two, Chapter two hundred and twelve, Entitled an 'Act to provide for taking the vote of the people for or against a new County in certain Election districts of Allegany County at the election to be held in the fall of Eighteen hundred and Seventy-two' it is provided that all that part of Allegany County lying south and west of a line beginning at the summit of Big Back Bone or Savage Mountain, where that mountain is crossed by Mason and Dixon's line and running thence by a straight line to the middle of Savage River where it empties into the Potomac River, thence by a straight line to the nearest point or boundary of the State of West Virginia: then with the said boundary to the Fairfax Stone, shall be a new County to be called the County of Garrett: provided the provisions of this Act as to taking census of the people and the area of the new County and the sense of the people therein, shall be complied with in accordance with the Constitution of this State. And it is further provided that the proposition for such a new County shall be submitted to the voters residing within the limits of the proposed County, as above set forth, at the Election for President and Vice President of the United States in the fall of Eighteen hundred and Seventy-two, and that the returns of such Election shall be made to the Governor, and it is also provided 'that if a majority of the legal votes cast within that part of Allegany County contained within said lines shall be in favor of a new County, and the Governor is satisfied that the requirements of the Constitution and laws as to extent of territory and number of inhabitants have been gratified, and complied with, then said part of Allegany County shall become and constitute a new County to be called "Garrett County" and the Governor shall issue his proclamation to that effect and the inhabitants thereof shall henceforth have and enjoy all such rights and privileges as are held and enjoyed by the inhabitants of the other counties of this State'. And whereas the returns of said Election as held on the fifth day of November, Eighteen hundred and Seventy-two, have been duly certified to me by the judges of Election, and upon Examination of the Same, it appears that there were twelve hundred and ninety seven ballots for the new County and four hundred and five ballots against the new county and consequently a majority of the legal votes cast in that part of Allegany County within the said lines were in favor of a new County; And Whereas by the survey and plot (plat) made and returned to me by the County Surveyor of Allegany County and by the Census taken and returned to me under oath and now on file in this Department, it appears that the requirements of the Constitution and laws as to the extent of territory and number of white inhabitants have been gratified and complied with, Now Therefore I William Pinkney Whyte Governor of the State of Maryland in pursuance of the authority so vested in me by said Act of Assembly, Do by this my proclamation, declare and make known that all that part of Allegany County contained within the lines above set forth, has become and is now constituted a new County to be called "Garrett County" and the inhabitants thereof shall henceforth have and enjoy all such rights and privileges as are held and enjoyed by the other inhabitants of the other counties of this State. Given under my hand and the Great Seal of the State of Maryland at the City of Annapolis this fourth day of December in the year of our Lord one thousand eight hundred and Seventy-two.

By the Governor   Wm. Pinkney Whyte
   Jno. Thomson Mason
   Secretary of State

—The *Glades Star,* Centennial Issue, vol. 4, no. 12, Oakland, Maryland, March, 1972

The Deep Creek Bridge. This bridge carries U.S. Route 219 across Deep Creek Lake. The view is to the north a few miles south of McHenry.

The Youghiogheny River. This is a typical view of the "Yough" looking south from a point upriver from Friendsville.

Grain field. Shocks of grain like these were very common in Garrett County fields before combines came into use. Photo courtesy Robert J. Ruckert

The cove. A real beauty spot of Garrett County. Overlook on U.S. Route 219 south of Keyser's Ridge. Listed in some travel magazines as one of the seven most attractive scenes on a United States highway.

Muddy Creek Falls. Maryland's highest waterfall is created by Muddy Creek which has its source in Cranesville Swamp to the southwest. Falls plunge more than sixty feet from a ledge in Swallow Falls State Park. The stream empties into nearby Youghiogheny River. This popular scenic area was once a campsite for four famous Americans: Henry Ford, Thomas A. Edison, Harvey S. Firestone and John Burroughs. Photo by Ruthvan W. Morrow, Jr.

Forests. Garrett County has 292,000 acres of forests that cover about 65 percent of its total land area. Approximately 75,000 acres of the total is public owned. Paul Mateer of Oakland, a Maryland project forester, is here inspecting a stand of second growth hardwood timber. He states that the Maryland Forest Service directs its work toward the best possible use of woodland resources by both public and private owners.

Famous campers. This photo was furnished to Mrs. Lewis R. Jones by the Charles Edison Fund which identifies the men, *left to right*, as Henry Ford, Thomas Edison, President Warren G. Harding (Harding was not president in 1919), and Harvey S. Firestone on a campout picnic in Garrett County's Swallow Falls area in 1919.

Local accounts, local folklore and James A. Fowler, of the Henry Ford Museum, Dearborn, Michigan, do not agree that these men were here in 1919. These sources place Ford, Edison, Firestone, and naturalist John Burroughs here in 1918. In 1921 Ford, Edison, and Firestone (Mr. Burroughs had died earlier in 1921) returned, accompanied by their wives and members of their families, Edsel Ford, Mr. and Mrs. Harvey S. Firestone, Jr., and Russell Firestone. Before coming here the group camped at Big Pool, near Hancock, Maryland. While there, they were visited by President Harding. It seems plausible that this photo was taken at Big Pool in 1921. Note: See the *Republican*, Oakland, Maryland, August 22, 1918, July 28 and August 4, 1921, and the *Glades Star*, vol. 3, p. 452.

Henry Ford. A rare photo of Henry Ford doing his laundry in Muddy Creek, Garrett County, in 1921 when he, Thomas A. Edison, Harvey S. Firestone, Sr., and party were camping at Swallow Falls State Park. The three famous men had made a trip in 1918 to the area and were accompanied then by John Burroughs, well-known naturalist, who had died prior to the camping trip in 1921. Photo courtesy of the Henry Ford Museum, Dearborn, Michigan

Historic Crossing. Aerial photograph of the four bridges over Casselman River at the east edge of Grantsville. George Washington had named the place "The Little Crossings" in 1755 when he crossed the river there with General Edward Braddock's British troops. They had forded the stream, we assume, and between the stone bridge in the background and the steel one in the center. They had cut the Old Braddock Road through a wilderness from Fort Cumberland. The stone arch bridge in the background is the Old Casselman and it opened in 1813 to carry traffic on the National Road. The steel structure in the center was opened in 1933 to serve travel over Route 40. In the foreground can be seen two steel-and-concrete spans that mark U.S. 48, the National Freeway, which opened in 1976 to serve the heavy east-west flow of traffic. Photo by Ruthvan W. Morrow, Jr.

Casselman Bridge. This historic stone structure is a monument to masonry skill and design. A national landmark, the Old Casselman Bridge opened in 1813 to serve traffic on our first federal highway and continued for 120 years. It had the longest single stone arch in America when it opened. This vital link in the Cumberland or National Road stands at the east edge of Grantsville. Photo courtesy of Ed Price

Washington Spring. This spring, still marked by a pagoda, was located in the (park) grounds of the Oakland Hotel. An attractive walk through maples, pines, and oaks led to the spring. This was a popular attraction for guests of the hotel and local people. Tradition says that Washington stopped here in 1784 on a trip over the mountain. McCulloch's Path, one of the early trails, was nearby. (See *Glades Star*, vol. 2, p. 534.) Photo courtesy of Mrs. Robert J. Ruckert

Hoye Crest. This point, located near the West Virginia line about three miles from the Fairfax Stone, was proclaimed the highest point in Maryland (3,360 feet) by Governor Theodore K. McKeldin in 1952. It was named in honor of Captain Charles E. Hoye, founder of the Garrett County Historical Society. A state roadside marker was placed on this spot. (See the *Glades Star*, vol. 2, p. 160; vol. 3 p. 163.)

B&O 17-Mile Grade. This grade, beginning at Piedmont, West Virginia, and continuing to Altamont, Maryland, rises 1,626 feet in seventeen miles for an average rise per mile of 95 feet. In places the rise per mile is 116 feet, which became the standard maximum grade for railroad building. Building the railroad up this grade in 1851-52 was a tremendous undertaking. (See the *Glades Star*, vol. 1, p. 329; vol. 2, p. 351.)

B&O Viaduct at Bloomington. The stone viaduct at Bloomington which carries the B&O Railroad trains over the Potomac River was built in 1851. It still carries today's heavy trains and engines. An eastbound diesel-powered passenger train with dome car is seen crossing the bridge. During the Civil War, Captain John McNeill and his Rangers attempted to destroy the bridge (May 1864) but were driven off by Federal forces from New Creek (now Keyser). (See the *Glades Star*, vol. 3, p. 77.)

Savage River Dam. The Army Corps of Engineers impounded Savage River near Bond above Bloomington after World War I. The dam is 1,050 feet across and 184 feet above the stream bed. The corps operates the dam and controls its water flow through a concrete-lined tunnel 10 feet in diameter and 170 feet long. The dam is for flood control and water supply and provides good fishing. Photo courtesy Tim Dugan

Eagle Rock—elevation 3,160 feet. This high point located three and one-half miles S.E. from Deer Park affords an excellent view of mountain panoramas in all directions. It was formerly frequented by summer visitors who could drive there by horse and buggy. Source of photo and names of people not known. From Paul T. Calderwood collection

Swallow Falls. This picturesque cascade in the Youghiogheny River is near the public pavilion in Swallow Falls State Park. Downstream a short distance in this popular vacation spot is also found Muddy Creek Falls. Photo courtesy Robert J. Ruckert

Cranesville Swamp. This unique spot of sub-arctic environment which has existed since the Ice Age lies across the Maryland-West Virginia boundary line to the westward of Swallow Falls. It is named for a nearby Preston County village and McCulloch's Packhorse Path passed near it. Called "The Great Pine Swamp" by pioneers, the United States Department of Interior has designated it as a sanctuary of rare plant and animal life and placed a plaque at No. 18 concrete marker on the state boundary line. A small stand of larch or tamarack trees exist here at their southernmost location in North America. Photo courtesy Robert J. Ruckert

Meshach Browning. This illustration is the best known likeness of Meshach Browning, having appeared as the frontispiece of his autobiography *Forty-Four Years of the Life of a Hunter*. Edward Stabler edited the manuscript and drew the illustrations. This one is believed to have been made from an early photograph of Browning with the dogs and the deer being fanciful additions.

The Meshach Browning Cabin at Sang Run. The Sang Run cabin was built about 1820 and a nearby mill was built in 1821. This photograph was taken in 1920 after the cabin had been in disuse for many years. It is no longer in existence. Courtesy Mrs. Robert Browning Garrett

Browning Roadside Marker. Meshach Browning is buried in a small cemetery near the village of Hoyes, a rather central point in the area where he loved to hunt. This marker stands at the side of the cemetery along Route 42 near Hoyes. Courtesy Raymond O. McCullough

Grave of Meshach Browning. The shaft with the cross on top marks the grave of Meshach Browning. It is a recently erected gravestone placed there by his descendants. Courtesy Raymond O. McCullough

II

SETTLEMENT

> I say
> When night has fallen on your loneliness
> And the deep wood beyond the ruined wall
> Seems to step forward swiftly with the dusk
> You shall remember them. You shall not see
> Water or wheat or axe-mark on the tree
> And not remember them.
> You shall not win without remembering them,
> For they won every shadow of the moon,
> All the vast shadows, and you shall not lose
> Without a dark remembrance of their loss
> For they lost all and none remembered them.
>
> Stephen Vincent Benet

Mary Browning was the wife of a Garrett County pioneer hunter.

She was born in September 1781, at a place called Blooming Rose on a high bluff above the Youghiogheny River near the 1765 settlement of John Friend. Her parents were James and Rachel McMullen; she was the oldest of the family's five children.

When Mary was twelve years old, she met the visiting nephew of her family's closest neighbors. The boy's name was Meshach. He was hunting groundhogs near her house when she first saw him. She found the lad quite bashful.

About thirty or forty families lived at Blooming Rose in 1793. In the fall of that year the settlement organized a small one-room school for the education of its children. Mary and Meshach walked to the schoolhouse together each day. In class they rivaled for top honors. They became good friends.

Mary's father frowned on the friendship, so they often met secretly, or at the McMullen home when the father was away. Sometimes they attended dances and shooting matches together. Occasionally they exchanged presents. When Meshach was fifteen years old, Mary knitted a pair of woolen socks for him. In exchange Meshach presented the McMullen family with a string of one dozen fresh-cleaned trout.

In the year 1799, on the last day of April, at the age of eighteen, Mary McMullen of Blooming Rose married Meshach Browning, also eighteen years of age. Their wedding day dawned bright and clear. They were accompanied to Pennsylvania for the marriage ceremony by a group of young, high-spirited friends, all riding horseback. After a lengthy exhortation by the Presbyterian magistrate, they were pronounced man and wife.

Mary and Meshach Browning celebrated their wedding night at the McMullen home with music and dancing. The following night they passed at the home of Meshach's mother and stepfather, where, with friends, they again danced many a light-footed reel and jig. Then they returned to the McMullen home. The next morning they were thrown out of the house by the irate father. "Get up and go to your own home," James McMullen ordered his daughter, according to Meshach's later account, "for you shan't roost here any longer."

Meshach traded his horse for a small squatter's farm at Blooming Rose with fifteen or twenty acres of cleared land, three acres of wheat, and a small substantial cabin. Here the newlyweds began their life together on the frontier without a single dollar, without a cow for milk, without a pound of meat. Mary's mother gave the couple two plates, two knives and forks, two cups and saucers, two tincups, two spoons, and a woven basket. Meshach took to the thickets in search of game.

"I should be glad if you would keep out of the woods," a worried Mary soon told her adventurous husband. Meshach was destined to be a hunter for forty-four years. Once his uncle reprimanded him for his daring lifestyle, observing that "A pitcher which goes so often to the well will some day or other come back broken." When Meshach asked Mary early in their marriage to accompany him to the woods to hold a colt while he fastened a dead bear to its back she did not refuse, but merely remarked: "Is it not enough for you to hunt and kill bears, without making a squaw of me?" The young hunter often spent as much as a week at a time in the wilderness on the hunt, leaving Mary at home alone in the cabin.

Mary and Meshach Browning lived nearly a year at Blooming Rose, where the young wife gave birth to their first daughter, Dorcas. In the spring of 1800 an absentee claimant demanded immediate possession of their farm and threatened the family with legal ejection. The Brownings consequently moved southeast to the center of later Garrett County at a place then known as Bear Creek Glades at the headsprings of Bear Creek, a tributary of the Youghiogheny River. Here they squatted in the remains of an old cabin which had been partially torn down by hunters for use as firewood. Their possessions now totaled three cows, eleven sheep, one colt, and a dog named Watch.

When the Brownings arrived at their new home at Bear Creek they were greeted by a large rattlesnake which lay coiled up in a corner of the dirt floor of the abandoned cabin. Another rattlesnake was later discovered outside the house, which was immediately killed, as had been the first. The young couple soon learned to protect themselves from the attacks of the many snakes in the area by twisting hay or long grass into ropes and wrapping their legs to the knees.

On their first evening at the Bear Creek Glades, Mary was rushed by five wolves which she frightened from the thickets while dipping water from a spring. "You have got yourself into a hard-looking place," her father candidly commented upon his farewell after dinner that night.

"It is so," the daughter replied, "but outside this dreadful thicket, it is the most beautiful country I ever saw."

Bear Creek Glades in the early 1800s was a large level valley of land covered with wild meadows of waist-high, blue-tipped grass growing from a wet, marshy soil. The ridges between the meadows were heavily timbered with white and red oak, white and yellow pine, sugar and curly maple, wild cherry and birch, black and white walnut, wild cucumber and chestnut. The tall glade grass grew intermixed with wild flowers of all varieties and colors; song birds of many types—wrens, bluebirds, robins—flitted from tree to tree.

"It was a grand sight," Meshach wrote many years later, "to watch the tall grass, rolling in beautiful waves with every breeze which passed over its smooth surface, as well as the herds of deer, skipping and playing with each other. It was not a strange thing to see a great lubberly-looking bear forcing his way through the grass, when every deer which got a sight or scent of him would bound off, with tail erect, toward the nearest thicket. Sometimes a wolf could be seen prowling among the high grass, endeavouring to sneak on a fawn, or, if possible, even a grown deer. All that fancy could desire was here to be seen at a single glance. Our cattle and horses pasturing in grass reaching to their knees, the birds of different kinds, singing as if each was striving to outdo the other, and numerous turkeys roaming about, followed by large flocks of young ones. The country abounded with deer, bears, panthers, wolves, wildcats, catamounts, wild turkeys, foxes, rabbits, pheasants, partridges, wild bees, and in all the streams trout without number. The whole face of the country was like a beautiful sheet of wallpaper, variegated with all shades of color."

"We had everything in common," Meshach noted, "and, like the sheet which was laid down to St. Peter, we had nothing to do but 'Rise, Meshach, slay and eat.' "

Mary Browning had nothing to do during her four years' stay in the little cabin on Bear Creek Glades, two miles from the Lynns, their nearest neighbors, fifty miles from Cumberland, the nearest town, except raise a growing pioneer family on the Maryland frontier. She began by forking a bed quilt to the hole which substituted for a doorway in the cabin wall. Then she and Meshach made a table from a large sheet of maple bark tied down to two laths to keep it from curling at the sides. Meshach installed a split-puncheon floor in the cabin and covered the roof with clapboards. He also built a fireplace and chimney.

Mary Browning lived with her husband at Bear Creek Glades for four years. During this time she gave birth to two more children, Rachel and William. While Meshach provided the family with meat, Mary baked bread, churned butter, strained wild honey, milked cows, carded, spun, and knit wool, sewed buckskins into pants and hunting shirts, knitted socks, made soap from tallow and lye, made candles from panther fat, grew garden vegetables, chopped firewood, kept a blazing fire roaring in the fireplace to keep gnats and mosquitoes from biting her children, salted and dried meats and berries, boiled herbs—or "yarbs," as they were called by the mountain folk—into medicines, boiled maple water into syrup and sugar, bathed and nursed sick children and an occasionally hurt husband, bandaged cuts and bruises, grubbed and hoed and picked and burned brush, cooked meals over an open fireplace, cleaned poultry, fowl, and fish, salted and smoked wild flesh, washed clothes on a metal washboard, and tended the domestic animals. She also worried considerably about her husband. "I am afraid you will some day or other be found unprepared for the bears," she told him one spring before the annual hunt, "and be torn to pieces." Hers was not an easy life.

"This is the manner in which people lived in those times," observed Meshach many years after her death. "Yet at Bear Creek Glades," he noted, "I found my true pleasure—my wife, dressed clean, her beauty, in my estimation, unsurpassed, the children, as clean as water and soap could make them, a plenty to live on, and not an enemy on earth."

The Brownings had but three neighbors in the vicinity of the Bear Creek Glades. Moreover, they were connected to their neighbors only by rough packhorse trails through the thickets. The family of Colonel John Lynn, "a very prominent, and ... one of the most influential men in the county," lived within two miles. The family of William W. Hoye, "a very generous and kind neighbor," lived about three miles away, and the family of James Drane, "a very kind, gentlemanly, and truthful man," lived within five miles of the Browning home. "As I was a good hand at log-rollings and house-raisings," noted Meshach, "we all soon became acquainted, and really fond of each other."

In 1804, Meshach's mother and stepfather from Ohio visited the Browning family in western Maryland. After staying two months, they persuaded the young pioneers to sell out and return with them to Ohio. Meshach consequently sold his twelve cattle, six hogs, bulky household items, and the homestead at Bear Creek to a new settler, bargaining to receive the payment upon departure. When the time came to leave, though, he found he could not collect a single dollar from the sale, "and there I was," he reflected, "with not a living beast but that sick mare and one dog, for Watch had died of the distemper. I was completely ruined." The loss ended all hope of moving to Ohio and Meshach soon "became so dejected and out of heart, that I could do nothing but sit and fret, and I did not pretend to hunt or do anything for a week or two."

Meshach had Mary to thank for ending his period of despondency. The young wife rode to the Friend settlement, five miles away, and bought two pounds of powder and four pounds of lead on credit from a traveling peddler, promising payment by Christmas in skins or hams.

"Here, Meshach," she said to her husband when she returned, "is powder and lead enough to last you all the fall. Now do let me beg of you to cheer up, take your gun, and try your luck. You have been very successful in all your hunting; and if you give up this way, what will become of us all? You know that all depends on you, for I have no way of doing anything; and if you give up to your feelings, you may get out of your mind." She reminded her husband that "poverty was not treason, and that we could not be hung for being poor." Meshach subsequently rose early the next morning and once again took to the woods. Within four hours he killed three bears.

Having lost their home, the Brownings moved to a cabin on the Youghiogheny River near the mouth of Sang Run, a stream named by the Friends after the wild ginseng which grew abundantly in the area. In time, Meshach procured a new lot about a mile southeast of the old Bear Creek home, and in 1807 he began to clear the land there. The same year he moved his wife and three children to a new cabin, ten feet by twelve feet in size, located at a settlement near the new homestead, so that he would not have to walk every few days from the new lot the five miles to Sang Run to see his family. Then he began grubbing the Bear Creek woods just east of present-day McHenry in order to prepare the land for corn planting. Mary helped cut and burn brush during the day; in the evenings she tended a maple boiling camp about a mile away.

When spring came and the family ran out of meal, she loaded a horse and set out for a gristmill near the Friend settlement on the Youghiogheny; pitying the heavily laden horse, she herself walked more than half the way. The day was warm, and when she reached the mill she waded for a long time in the cold water, washing her face, her hands, her feet. By the time she got back home she could barely walk. She collapsed.

A local doctor pronounced her malady to be a paralytic stroke and advised the family to prepare for her death. Five months later Col. John Lynn, the nearest neighbor, learned of her condition, and, promising effective medication upon his return from a trip to Frederick, "galloped off like the wind." By the time he returned with fifty-two pills and a bundle of blister plasters, the Brownings had moved into their new home in the Bear Creek pines. On Christmas Day Mary rose from her bed for the first time since her journey to the gristmill the prior May, and, dressing, informed her husband that she felt as well as ever she did in her life.

"She had yet three pills to take," Meshach later wrote, "and as she felt so well, she consulted me as to whether she should take the other pills or not. I remarked that, as the medicine had done her so much good, and as the doctor had directed all the pills to be taken, perhaps the cure would not be perfect unless his directions were complied with. So she continued taking the pills until they were all used, when her face was drawn a little to the other side, and her eye sunk, and remained for the rest of her life smaller than the other." Eighteen months later Mary gave birth to a fourth child, a son, whom Meshach named John Lynn in honor of the man who had saved his wife's life.

The Brownings lived for nearly eighteen years in their new cabin in the Bear Creek pines. During this time Meshach supported the family by selling meat and furs in Hagerstown, Frederick, Georgetown, and Baltimore. Once, in 1823, he traveled to Baltimore with eighty-seven saddles of venison, three whole deer, seven saddles of bear meat, several buckets of butter and beeswax, and a large bundle of furs. Mary tended the home in the woods and gave birth to seven more children—James, Nancy, Allen, Thomas, Jane, Jeremiah, and Sally. One child—probably Thomas—was born while the father was in the woods on a bear hunt.

In 1826 Meshach traveled to Annapolis on legal business and took Mary along as far as Montgomery County, where a brother lived. Mary was more than a hundred miles away from home there; it was the farthest from home she had ever been. Before leaving the pines, she had made for her husband the most handsome hunting shirt he had ever owned. "Dressed in this, and a neat pair of moccasins," Meshach wrote after his return to the glades, "I appeared in the city, where I excited some curiosity; for everyone who saw me stared as if looking at an Indian chief."

The Browning family moved back to Sang Run in the early 1820s, where Meshach built a gristmill, a small barn, and a new cabin. Here Mary and Meshach Browning lived for the rest of their lives.

Mary Browning was the wife of a Garrett County pioneer hunter. During her lifetime in Garrett County she lived in seven log cabins, effectively managed a frontier household economy, and raised eleven children. She died on January 29, 1839, at the age of fifty-seven, three years after a crippling fall from a horse. Her grief-stricken husband later wrote a few lines of verse in her memory:

> I knew not if 'twas summer then,
> I knew not when 'twas spring;
> And if the birds sang in the trees,
> I did not hear them sing.
>
> If flowers came forth to deck the earth,
> Their bloom I did not see;
> I thought but on one whithered flower,
> The last that bloomed for me.

> Our sweetest hours glide swiftly by,
> And leave the faintest trace;
> But that deep mark that sorrow wears
> No time can e'er efface.

With such poetry as this a Garrett County pioneer hunter immortalized

> a loving wife,
> Who'd lived alone for him.

Native American Indians had hunted in Garrett County for at least four thousand years before John Friend settled on the Youghiogheny River near the mouth of Bear Creek in 1765. By this time they had established trails, campsites and burial grounds.

Before the white man came they paddled from the northwest up the Youghiogheny—(Waters-Flowing-in the Contrary-Direction)—from the east up the Cohongoroota—(River of Wild Geese), now the Potomac. When the waters became too shallow for the passage of their canoes, they took to land trails first traced by buffalo from the valleys on both sides of the mountains—animals which roamed each spring to the high Appalachian plateaus in quest of the tall, wild, blue-tipped grass which grew in abundance in the cool, marshy soil of the mountain glades. The early trails of the buffalo and the Indian avoided, as much as possible, the wet swamps and laurel thickets along the rivers and streams and generally followed the open forest regions of the high ground.

The major trails crossed the mountains from east to west. Nemacolin's Path, long used by Indians before the Ohio Company had it widened and cleared, connected the Potomac River at Wills Creek to the Ohio at the Forks, traversing the northern end of present-day Garrett County. The Great Warrior Trail passed through the southern part of the present-day county, connecting the North Branch of the Potomac at the mouth of Glade Run in the east with the Ohio River to the west. The Northwestern Trail, an extreme southern Garrett County east-west route, connected the northern and southern branches of the Potomac with the Cheat River above present-day Rowlesburg in West Virginia. A more central route, the

Glades Path, crossed the Great Youghiogheny Glades, and also connected the Potomac, near the mouth of Savage River, with the Cheat in West Virginia at Dunkard Bottom. Only one major route passed from north to south, the Seneca Trail, an important warrior path to the deep south running from New York to the Carolinas through the central part of present-day Garrett.

The ancient Mound Builders of the Ohio Valley were undoubtedly among the first Indians to visit the Appalachian highlands. They were followed, years later, by the Shawnees and the Iroquois, the Delawares and the Senecas. A total of sixteen scattered Indians lived in present-day Garrett County as late as 1800. Farmers today still find their arrowheads in plowed fields.

One of the members of Braddock's expedition against the French in 1755 described the native Indians living along the Potomac River near Wills Creek. "The Men are tall, well made and Active, but not strong," he wrote; "The Women [are] not so tall yet well proportion'd and have many Children; they paint themselves in different Manners; Red, Yellow & Black intermixt, the Men have the outer Rim of their Ears cut; and hanging by a little bit at Top and bottom: they have also a Tuft of Hair left at the Top of their Heads, drefs'd with Feathers. . . . Their Match Coat which is their chief Cloathing, is a thick Blanket thrown round them; and instead of Shoes wear Mokosins, which laces round the foot and Ankle . . . their manner of carrying children are by lacing them with a broad Bandage with a place to rest their feet, and Boards over their Heads to keep the Sun off and this is Slung to the Womens backs. . . . When it becomes dark they Return to their Camp, which is Woods, and Dance for some time with making the most hidious Noise."

The summer Indians of present-day Garrett County lived in circular wigwams and tent-shaped lodges covered with bark and skins. The men hunted and fished in the woods and meadows, while the women and children tilled the soil near the camps with sticks and grew corn. They lived at the junctions of rivers or in glades at the sites of natural springs. The Youghiogheny River Valley was the most heavily populated of all the Garrett County Indian camp areas; the Potomac Valley was the second most densely populated.

Along the Youghiogheny, Indians lived at the mouths of present-day Buffalo Run, Bear Creek, and Sang Run. They lived above the Youghiogheny at Blooming Rose and Indian Rocks. They also lived along tributaries of the Yough—at present-day Deep Creek near the Boiling Spring in Buffalo Marsh, in the Accident Valley near Bear Creek, at Cranberry Glade Marsh near Hoopole Ridge, in the Youghiogheny Glades around Pleasant Valley and in the Green Glades north of Oakland, along the Casselman River near Bittinger and northeast of Grantsville, and in the valleys surrounding Crellin. They lived on the Promised Land Camp about four miles northwest of Oakland, along Cherry Creek near the foot of Backbone Mountain, and at Clifton, near Elk Lick Creek. And they lived, at times, along the upper Potomac and Savage rivers, near present-day Kitzmiller and Bloomington. They quarried flint for arrowheads from rock formations near Buffalo Marsh and Meadow Mountain.

When the Indians of Garrett County moved west, they left behind a few stone axes, some scattered tomahawks and beads, a few clay trinkets and pieces of pottery, numerous arrowheads, and the bones of their ancestors. At Kitzmiller they left a primitive stone mortar and pestle for pounding corn into meal. Their burial grounds have been found at Buffalo Run, Sang Run, Blooming Rose, the Promised Land Camp northwest of Oakland, and at scattered points along the Youghiogheny. They buried their dead with weapons and trinkets at a depth of two or three feet beneath the surface of the soil in mounds of rock. An excavation of a campsite at the mouth of Sang Run in the summer of 1949 uncovered the post holes of a wigwam nine feet in diameter, two "house pits" containing numerous pieces of pottery, flint artifacts, animal bones, ashes, and several graves. Today, only the graves, the ashes, and the arrowheads remain. The legacy of the native American Indian in Garrett County—his deep communion with nature, his natural love for the wild, his annual life-supporting pilgrimage to the highland glades—has been lost forever to a trickle of time and a flood of change.

The first white men ever to visit present-day Garrett County were members of a surveying party under Captain Benjamin Winslow and Major William Mayo appointed by the king of England to determine, in 1736, the northwestern corner of the great Northern Neck land tract of Thomas, Virginia's Sixth Lord Fairfax. The party of seventeen surveyors and assistants left Harpers Ferry early in October and traveled by boat through bitter cold, rain, sleet, and snow, up the Potomac River to the headsprings of the river's northern fork, nearing their destination in early December. Here, near the mouth of a raging river, their food supplies were exhausted, and, threatened with starvation, according to one of the members of the expedition, they decided from necessity to kill and eat one of their own surveyors, John Savage, he being "the most worthless member of their party" as a result of failing eyesight. Supplies arrived in time to save the unlucky man, however, and the river by which they were encamped was named Savage in his honor. Savage River was thus ironically the first geographic feature of Garrett County to receive a white man's name. The Winslow-Mayo party completed its mission shortly before Christmas by blazing marks on trees near the supposed headsprings of the Potomac, the designated northwestern boundary of the Northern Neck tract, then returned east.

Ten years later, in 1746, Peter Jefferson, the father of Thomas Jefferson, and Benjamin Winslow, accompanied by the surveyor Thomas Lewis, commissioned by the king of England "to Run the dividing line Between His Majesty & Ld Fairfax from the head Spring of the Rappahanock to the head Spring of the North Branch of the Potomack," returned by an overland route to the area, found the blazed trees marked in 1736, and planted a stone marker at the site on October 22. George William Fairfax, a member of the expedition and eldest son of the Belvoir household of William Fairfax, a cousin and agent of Thomas, the Lord Fairfax, carved his initials in a tree beside the stone. Benjamin Winslow, meanwhile, mapped the tributaries of the Potomac in the region—Savage, Spruce, Indian, Dismal, Laurel, Flat, Moss, Gentle, and Cherry rivers and brooks. Only one of his designations remains on modern maps of the area—the Savage River. The Fairfax Stone, though, remains as the point designating the western-most north-south boundary line of Garrett County and the state of Maryland with West Virginia, though the line was a matter of major dispute until 1912. Several members of the 1746 expedition crossed the Great Backbone Mountain and explored for the first time the highland glades of present-day Garrett beyond.

Then, in August 1764, one year after the conclusion of the Great War for the Empire, John Friend, the descendant of a Swedish sea captain, accompanied by his brother, Andrew, and young son Gabriel, walked from his Virginia plantation along the Potomac River and crossed the continental divide of Western Maryland to the waters of the Youghiogheny in search of a new home. A devastating spring flood had ruined the fields of his Potomac farm, swept away his fences, destroyed his buildings; now he traveled west in the hope of finding new lands, new hunting grounds. The little party walked up the Potomac, passed Oldtown and Fort Cumberland, and then turned southwest. A few days' travel brought the hikers to the Great Warrior Path on the banks of the North Branch of the Potomac. Following the trail, three feet wide and a foot deep, they bypassed an Indian grave mound, forded present-day Glade Run, traversed present-day Ryan's Glade, and then ascended present-day Backbone Mountain to the crest of the Alleghenies. From here, they followed the path through dense trees to the foot of the mountain; then they left the trail and traveled north to the Deep Creek Glades, where a vast sea of blue-tipped glade grass, growing wild with a million clusters of brilliant Oswego tea, fireweed, foxglove, goldenrod, shooting star, and cardinal flowers caressed the shoulders of the men and swept the boy from sight. Only a few trees grew in the open glade: crab apple, willows, and some scattered scrub maples. At the edge of the glade they came to a big, seemingly bottomless boiling spring bubbling up through white sand, bordered by an ancient Indian campground. Then they passed over a hill thick with elderberry and threaded their way along a forest trace to the edge of a wide plateau from which their path fell a thousand feet in less than two miles. They descended the mountain to an inlet of level land where the Youghiogheny flowed wide and calm on its way to the Gulf of Mexico, and Indian cornfields, growing ripe in the late August sun, waved in the breeze before them.

At the crossings of the Yough, just south of a little island full of August greenery, in a natural outdoor canyon amphitheater surrounded by green leafy mountains, lulled by the rippling waters of the river, the Friends met a tribe of friendly Indians and remained in their camp as guests for several days before returning east. The Indians told them they were the first white men ever to visit the area and welcomed them with the festivity of the green corn dance in celebration of the harvest. With the red men the white visitors danced and chanted hymns of praise and thanksgiving to the mountains, acknowledging the bonds they all had with the universe, with its nature spirits, its Sun, and the one Creator who had created all. Before they left, they bought the river land and cornfields, paying with an iron kettle, promising to return the following year.

In the spring of 1765 John Friend, with two brothers, Charles and Andrew, accompanied by their families and a string of packhorses, moved their belongings west from the Potomac up the Braddock Road to present-day Keyser's Ridge, the highest point in the mountains along the old wagon road, once a buffalo trace, then an Indian path and a traders' route. From the ridge they followed an old Indian trail through the woods southwest to the valley of the Youghiogheny. On the west side of the crossings, at a place safe from flooding, near the old Indian village and cornfields he had discovered the prior year, John Friend built a small log cabin and settled on the land, naming his tract Friend's Fortune.

Brother Andrew settled downriver with father Nicholas in the Turkeyfoot area of Pennsylvania. Brothers Charles and Augustine later moved upriver into the heartland of Garrett County, Charles settling near the Big Boiling Spring in Buffalo Marsh, seven miles south of John; Augustine settling thirteen miles further up the river, near present-day Swallow

Falls on the Youghiogheny by a glade bordering the Great Warrior Path.

The "down-river" and "up-river" Friends had come to stay in 1765; Garrett County's first permanent white settlers had arrived. More than two and a half centuries of colonization, exploitation, greed, dreams, hopes, promises, and warfare since the discovery of America by Columbus in 1492 had brought European man to the crest of the Alleghenies. Garrett—all those lands encompassed by present-day Garrett County—would never again be the same.

The family of John Friend settled on the banks of the Youghiogheny in 1765 in direct violation of the proclamation of the King of England two years earlier at the conclusion of the Great War for the Empire prohibiting settlement and speculation west of the Alleghenies. Even before the proclamation was issued, in 1761, Joseph Tomlinson, of eastern Frederick County, had secured a state patent for a tract of land at Little Meadows along the Braddock Road, at the site of Braddock's fourth camp, naming the tract Good Will. His slaves were the first black people ever to visit the highland glades country; his land tract was the first to be surveyed in the land area of later Garrett County.

Garrett's second land grant was issued in 1768 through the Land Office of Maryland's Lord Baltimore to Captain Thomas Bassett, one of Braddock's engineers in his unsuccessful 1755 expedition against Fort Duquesne. Bassett chose a five-hundred-acre spread north of the Nemacolin-Braddock trail along the Casselman River, the eastern branch of the Youghiogheny, for his claim. He named the tract Grassy Cabin after an abandoned settler's dwelling on the partially cultivated, grass-grown fields bordering the river's ford in a valley then known as Martin's Cove after an itinerant settler. Bassett himself did not settle in the area.

Meanwhile, though, a pervasive feeling of security ensuing from a temporary restoration of peace with the Ohio Indians had lured a number of persons west from Maryland's eastern counties. Settlements gradually grew up after 1763 around Fort Cumberland and Oldtown and along George's Creek in later Allegany County, peopled chiefly by former residents of eastern Frederick County. At the same time, other settlers, including Halls, Fromans, Frazees, Spurgeons, Rutans, Van Sickles, and Coddingtons began to move to the extreme northwestern corner of Maryland along the Braddock Road near the Friend settlement on the Youghiogheny, squatting in the Sandy Creek Glades of Maryland, Virginia, and Pennsylvania. Then, in the spring of 1768, Maryland's Lord Baltimore, a direct descendant of George Calvert, the first royal proprietor of Terra Mariae, instructed Governor Horatio Sharp to select certain choice manors west of Fort Cumberland as part of his own private domain of Maryland lands.

(For over a hundred years the proprietors of Maryland had reserved for themselves at least two manorial estates in each newly formed county. They had also created other manors by granting large estates to certain favored individuals and conferring upon them the rights and privileges enjoyed by the manorial Lords of England, the most significant of which was the authorization to call and conduct certain criminal and civil court cases. The manor was an inheritance of English feudal custom which transcended the Renaissance and settlement of the New World, and usually comprised an area of land containing from one to fifteen thousand acres, on which lived the lord or his agent, as well as his agrarian tenants.)

Governor Sharp commissioned Francis Deakins, of Georgetown, the deputy surveyor of Frederick County, a well-known soldier and land speculator, to mark and lay out the tracts desired by the proprietor in 1768. Deakins plotted ninety-six thousand acres west of Fort Cumberland in March, including the Indian Old Fields on the Potomac and twenty-five hundred acres "near a place called Little Meadows," for his proprietor. On May 8 he completed a survey of the Great Glades Manor, over seventeen thousand acres extending from the mouth of the Little Youghiogheny to the foot of the Great Backbone Mountain in the southern part of later Garrett County. This survey included the later sites of Oakland, Mountain Lake Park, and Gortner. On May 16 he finished his plot of western Maryland's third and final proprietorial estate, the Green Glades Manor, forty-seven hundred acres located along Green Glades Run, a tributary of Deep Creek.

Before Lord Baltimore formally opened the Maryland lands west of Fort Cumberland in 1774 for patent and settlement by the general populace, he authorized four more private surveys in the highlands. Bad Is the Best of It, a 120-acre tract on Bear Camp Run, later Mill Run, a tributary of the Youghiogheny a few miles north of the Friend settlement, was surveyed on April 29, 1771, for Jacob Froman. In August of the same year John Head surveyed the 367-acre Arnos Vale estate in Ryan's Glade between the Great Backbone Mountain and the Potomac River. The glade had been first known as Warner's Glade after an early temporary squatter; it was later renamed after John Ryan, another short-term settler. Arnos Vale was patented to Norman Bruce on December 11, 1772. On June 10, 1772, Captain Evan Shelby, a noted Indian fighter, claimed Buffalo Run, a 149-acre tract on the west bank of the Youghiogheny between Mill Run to the north and the Friend settlement to the south. The stream of Buffalo Run itself had been so named by the Friends as a result of the killing of a bison near its mouth. The Buffalo Run tract was later the home of the Garrett County pioneers Jeremiah and Jonathan Frazee, and eventually became the site of Selbysport, Garrett County's first established town. The survey was patented to Shelby on September 29, 1773; it was the first Maryland survey made west of the Youghiogheny River. Shelby also received a final patent to land in western Maryland prior to the proprietorial opening of 1774, the Little Meadows tract, 100-acres—on May 26, 1773. This small estate bordered Joseph Tomlinson's Good Will along the Braddock Road and eventually fell into the possession of Tomlinson's daughter, Rachel Bruce.

Unauthorized settlement by squatters continued unabated in the highlands while the first surveys of western Maryland were conducted from 1761 through 1773. John McKane settled at Braddock's fifth camp along the Nemacolin Trail on a tract later named Cornucopia. Aaron Parker settled at the Bear Camp, the general's sixth camp, at a junction on the road with an old Indian path which ran southwest across the Youghiogheny near the mouth of Buffalo Run and into Virginia—the later Morgantown Road. He subsequently operated an inn on the site. At the same time, the first Amish and Mennonite settlers of Garrett County along the Casselman River (named for an early western Pennsylvania settler) began to establish homesteads of a few miles north of Maryland in Pennsylvania's Somerset County. Most of these soft-spoken, devoutly religious people came west over the Forbes Road, constructed by General John Forbes, of the British regular army, in his 1757 expedition to recapture Fort Duquesne, from settlements in eastern Pennsylvania, where they had been attracted from the Palatinate and Switzerland by the religious liberty earlier offered by William Penn. Some, arriving in the New World at Baltimore, traveled west over the Braddock Road, then north. By the turn of the century, they had crossed the state line into Maryland and began establishing productive farms throughout the Casselman Valley north of the Braddock Road.

Then, in the spring of 1774, William Wilton Ashby, with brothers Jesse, Peter, Henry, and George, accompanied by a party of forty-three families led by Uncle Jack Ashby, a military captain, ascended the Great Backbone Mountain on the Great Warrior Path, earlier trod by John Friend, from the South Branch of the Potomac in Virginia, on a westward migration to newly opened lands in Kentucky. They carried their possessions on packhorses; they drove their livestock in herds before them. In the grassy Youghiogheny Glades beyond the Allegheny heights their forward scout returned to the party with a stranger from the Ohio Valley bearing ominous news of Indian hostility in Kentucky. The scout advised delay until the restoration of peace. Captain Jack called a council of family heads; the council decided to remain for a time in the abundant grass of the glades before pushing onward. Within a few weeks the migrants built a stockade fort on Cherry Creek at the mouth of Douglas Run within the Great Glades Manor of Lord Baltimore, near the later town of Gortner. (Some unverified reports have since described the fortification as a large enclosure covering ten acres.) Fort Ashby served the Youghiogheny Glades region for years as a place of refuge during periods of recurrent Indian hostilities, then fell into disuse.

Most members of the 1774 Ashby party soon moved west of the Maryland line, which ran north from the Fairfax Stone, into the state of Virginia, thus avoiding payment of annual quitrents to either Lord Baltimore or Lord Fairfax. They settled temporarily in the Snowy Creek and Salt Lick regions of Virginia between the Cheat and Youghiogheny rivers, then they gradually migrated further west and south to Kentucky. Only the family of William Ashby remained on the Maryland-Virginia frontier; Sarah, William's wife, refused to proceed further. And with good premonition: "I gladly embrace this opportunity to inform you that we are still in the land of the living," her brother wrote from Kentucky in 1820, "though through affliction and infirmity we are tottering on the verge of eternity ready to drop into the house appointed for all the living."

The William Wilton Ashby family first lived in a cabin purchased from the trapper John Simpson and the Pringle brothers, deserters from the British army at Fort Pitt, on the banks of the Youghiogheny, just west of the Maryland-Virginia border. They later moved to a new stone house on Snowy Creek, and then, in 1781, returned to Maryland and the 1,000-acre Ashby Discovery tract near the later site of Gortner. In 1795 they bought Piney Bottom, 270 acres near the mouth of Cherry Creek on the Youghiogheny, making the site, about four miles southwest of later Oakland, the permanent Ashby home in western Maryland. Son Nathan remained in Virginia in the stone house on Snowy Creek.

In 1774 Maryland's Lord Baltimore opened all public lands in the state west of Fort Cumberland for survey and settlement by the general public. These lands comprised most of later Garrett County. Only the northern boundary of the newly opened area, the Mason-Dixon Line, established west of Savage Mountain between Maryland and Pennsylvania by the English surveyors Charles Mason and Jeremiah Dixon in 1767 under the escort of sixteen Indians (three Onondagas and thirteen Mohawks appointed by the heads of the Six Iroquois Nations), was clearly defined on contemporary maps of the time. The western boundary of the state was generally believed to run due north of the Fairfax Stone, but the southern boundary of western Maryland had long been a matter of major dispute, Virginia claiming the North Branch of the Potomac as the dividing line, Maryland contending that the South Branch was a more appropriate marker. In spite of the boundary discrepancies, however, some twenty land speculators and their agents swarmed to the mountains in the spring and summer of 1774, and, armed with land warrants and tripods, they speedily laid out sixty-five choice tracts of land west of Fort Cumberland, the tracts averaging about one thousand acres apiece.

Only eight years earlier the surveyors Charles Mason and Jeremiah Dixon had recorded their arrival at the summit of the Alleghenies: "Went to the top of Savage Mt. and about two miles from ye tents.... Between this Savage or ye Allegheny Mts. and ... little Meadow Mountain, runs Savage River, which empties into the north branch of Potowmack; this is the most westernmost waters that run to the eastward in these parts. Beyond the Dividing Mountain, the waters all run to the westward; the first of note ... is the little Yockie Geni (Casselman) running into the Monogahela.... At present the Allegheny Mts. is the boundary between the natives and strangers in these parts of his Britonic Majestic Colonies. From the solitary tops of these mountains, the eye gazes round with pleasure: filling the mind with adoration to the Prevailing Spirit that made them."

In 1766 the Allegheny Mountains separated European civilization, with its property ideas encoded in formal law, from that of the native American Indian. In 1774 the barrier was pushed aside. No longer was the white man hesitant to set his compasses west of the mountains in the open, as had been Christopher Gist during his 1750 mission to the Ohio Valley in behalf of the Ohio Company of Virginia. Now, in 1774, white men pressed eagerly across the mountains with complete self-assurance and abandon. They quietly surveyed huge parcels of land for purposes of speculation, and they left their axe marks on the trees. They later divided their tracts into smaller plots, which they sold to pioneer farmers at handsome profits. The farmers plowed the soil and grew wheat, etc.

The land speculators of 1774, including General John Swan, Samuel Chase, Colonel Francis Deakins, Governor Thomas Johnson, Rev. Jonathan Boucher, Thomas Beall, James Brooks, and William Paca, were wealthy and influential citizens of the state. Most hailed from Annapolis and Baltimore or Maryland's more established eastern counties. All were interested in personal profit. Two, Samuel Chase and William Paca, later signed the colonial Declaration of Independence from England in behalf of the state of Maryland.

The land speculators and surveying parties of 1774 chose choice estates in the virgin forests and glades of later Garrett County along the Braddock Road in the north, the Great Warrior Trail (or McCullough's Packhorse Path) in the south, and the Glades Path and other minor Indian trails in the county's central region. Cornucopia later became Grantsville, Swansylvania bordered later Gortner, Kindness became Hutton, Small Meadows became Crellin, Thomas and Ann became Herrington Manor, Deer Park was the future site of an exclusive eastern railroad resort village, Locust Tree Bottom later became McHenry, Look Sharp (the home of Gabriel Friend) became Friendsville, and Accident—so named because of an accidental double survey of the same area by two parties working independently of one another—developed into a self-sufficient agrarian community.

Blooming Rose, above the west bank of Youghiogheny, took its name from a verse in the book of Isaiah: "The wilderness and the solitary place shall be glad for them; and the desert shall rejoice, and blossom as the rose." The Castle Hill tract on the Glades Path near the summit of Backbone Mountain resembled from a distance an old castle's broken-down walls and battlements. John Swan, of Baltimore, a member of the Maryland militia and its general during the later Revolutionary War, named the Cocklefield and Dumfries tracts east of Backbone Mountain after towns in his native Scotland. Orme's Whim, located about one mile north of Little Meadows, was named in memory of Captain Robert Orme, General Edward Braddock's 1755 adjutant.

The names of other 1774 western Maryland surveys make biblical inferences and reflect the original surveyors' hopes, dreams, and ideals: Mount Nebo (on the Braddock Road), Chance (southeast of Red House), Covent Garden (west of Backbone Mountain), Kindness (the site of present Hutton), The Promised Land (in Dunkard Glade northwest of Oakland), Milk and Honey (near Swallow Falls), Eden's Paradise Regained (in the Deep Creek Glades), Peace and Plenty (the site of the late nineteenth century Deer Park Hotel and cottages), Good Hope (near Swallow Falls), and Pott's Adventure and Price's Choice (northwest of Oakland). Numerous parcels were named from geographic features or plant life predominating in the region: Fair Hill (at Little Meadows), Mount Airy (southeast of Mount Nebo), The Dunghill (along Bear Creek northeast of Accident), Sugar Point (between Big and Little Shade Runs), Spruce Spring (east of Little Meadows), Good Spring (east of Keyser's Ridge), Flowery Vale (in Ryan's Glade), Piney Bottom (southwest of Oakland), Mount Pleasant (the Gower settlement southeast of Gnegy Church), Sugar Tree and Walnut Bottoms (east of Backbone Mountain), Rich Glade (in the Deep Creek Glades), Crab Tree Bottom (near Hoyes), Wild Cherry Tree Meadow (along the Rock Lodge Road), White Oak Level (a few miles west of Accident),[1] Cherry Hill (on the waters of Buffalo Run), and Colemine Lick (in the Flatwoods neighborhood). Two others were named in light of renewed Indian hostility in the Ohio Valley in 1774: Shawnee War (a little distance south of Grantsville) and False Alarm (a few miles northwest of Oakland near the Cranesville Road). (The False Alarm tract was so named when its surveyors, desiring a holiday, falsely raised the cry of *Indians!* and abandoned their work for a pleasure-seeking scout in the woods, not returning to their superiors until after midnight.)

Of the sixty-five tracts charted in 1774, only one, Friend's Choice, extending from Bear Creek toward the slope of Elder Hill, was surveyed for an actual settler—Augustine Friend. Richard Hall later received 100 acres of Blooming Rose as a permanent squatter. The other tracts were all reserved and patented exclusively for purposes of speculation and profit.

1. *White Oak Level* was the site of the author's great-grandfather, Charles Schlossnagel's first home in America in the mid-nineteenth century.

The largest tract was Small Meadows near later Crellin, 5,025 acres, surveyed for Edward Lloyd and William Paca. Orme's Whim, north of Little Meadows, 24 acres, surveyed for Thomas Johns, was the smallest tract.

While land jobbers and their surveyors were plotting western Maryland tracts in the spring and summer of 1774, Virginia military troops to the east were mobilizing to march across the mountains to suppress an uprising of Shawnee Indians in the Ohio and Kentucky valleys. The conflict had long been an inevitable development between the opposing forces of two antagonistic civilizations. The Indians of 1774 wanted to retain Kentucky as a hunting ground; the Americans, mostly Virginians, desired the trans-Appalachia West for purposes of speculation and farming. The conflict began in 1773 with ruthless attacks by lawless frontiersmen on native Indian villages and homes west of the mountains. The hostility gradually escalated until the spring of 1774, when Lord Dunmore, governor of Virginia, formally declared war on the Shawnees and their Ottawa and Mingo allies under the Shawnee commander, Chief Cornstalk.

Though Lord Dunmore's War lasted less than a year, savage fighting immediately erupted throughout the frontier of the Ohio and Kentucky valleys, often extending as far east as the ridge of the Alleghenies. Alarmed settlers quickly built rude fortifications and shelters for defense against the disenchanted, marauding Indians. In western Maryland the William Ashby party, migrating to Kentucky, stopped in the Youghiogheny Glades to construct a rectangular stockade of upright logs on Cherry Creek. (Years later Sarah Ashby told her spellbound grandchildren stories of war-painted Indians lurking at night in the forest near the fort; she told how the frightened migrants hiding within the structure would throw buffalo tallow on the fires to create roaring blazes and the illusion of a large company within to minimize the possibilities of attack.) At the same time, the Friends along the Youghiogheny, with the aid of neighbors—Frantzes, Frazees, Freys, Spurgeons, Kaeses, and Whites—joined together to build three small defensive blockhouses on the west bank of the river. A third fortification serving settlers of western Maryland—Fort

Morris—was erected in the Sandy Creek Glades on Hog Run, just west of the Maryland-Virginia border. "The fort (enclosing about an acre of land) consisted of an assemblage of small hovels," wrote a contemporary resident of nearby Washington County, Pennsylvania, the Rev. Joseph Doddridge. It was "situated on the margin of a large and noxious marsh, the effluvia of which gave most of the women and children the fever and ague. The men were compelled to return home, and risk the tomahawk and scalping knife of the Indians, in raising corn to keep their families from starvation the succeeding winter. Those sufferings, dangers and losses, were the tribute we had to pay to that thirst for blood which actuated those veteran (white) murders who brought the war upon us!" A fourth local stockade was built near the Horse Shoe Bend of the Cheat River in Virginia, at the present site of Saint George, under the leadership of settler John Minear. None of the four structures was ever attacked.

In October 1774, Lord Dunmore led more than a thousand colonial troops into the Ohio country, and the native Indians, cowed and defeated, sued for peace. Though the subsequent Treaty of Camp Charlotte ended the war and officially opened the Kentucky lands to white settlement, pioneers of the Alleghenies east of the Ohio River were never totally safe from Indian attack and unrest until 1794, when General "Mad" Anthony Wayne completely defeated the Indians of the Old West at Fallen Timbers. As late as 1835 an Indian was found dead in later Garrett County below Puzzley Run. Some local settlers contended that the unlucky red man had died from a fatal fall. "Other opinions," later noted Jacob Brown, a Grantsville area historian, "were that he was thrown over, but that the fall did not hurt so much as the bullet. However, there was not much said about it and still less done." White resentment and prejudice against the American native died hard in the mountains after Pontiac's Conspiracy of 1763 and the Shawnee War of 1774. The fear was not so great as to preclude further settlement, however; by 1774 the white migration to the Allegheny highlands had just barely begun. By 1776, when the American colonists declared their independence from the English Crown, only about a dozen families lived in the mountains later to become Garrett County.

Men from five Garrett County families responded to a call of the Maryland Revolutionary Convention in 1775 and 1776 for the enrollment of militia companies throughout the province. Augustine Friend joined the Sandy Creek Rangers in western Maryland as captain; Gabriel Friend enrolled as lieutenant; Aaron Parker signed up as sergeant. John Friend, Jacob Froman, William Ashby, and Jesse Tomlinson simultaneously joined the Skipton Company of Frederick County at Oldtown, of which Garrett was still then a part, as privates. Sergeant Abijah Herrington was a member of the Sandy Creek Rangers. These "were men," later wrote the local Garrett historian Dennis T. Rasche, "toughened by frontier life who could endure hardship and privation and who could shoot a squirrel's head off at fifty paces." The Sandy Creek Rangers patrolled the countryside around the Big Youghiogheny, Sandy Creek, and Cheat River throughout the war. They planted fields, harvested crops, and protected the area settlers from English-inspired Indian hostility. Their headquarters were located at Fort Morris on Hog Run. The Skipton Company, with headquarters at Oldtown, composed of sixty-four men, meanwhile promised to "Respectfully March to such places within this Province and at such times as we shall be commanded by the convention or Council of this Province . . . in pursuance of said orders of the Convention or Counsell of Safety and there with our whole might fight against whomsoever we shall be Commanded." All seven Garrett County Revolutionary War rangers returned to their homes at the conclusion of hostilities unscathed. They were soon joined in the western Maryland mountains by other veterans of the war—Colonel John Lynn, Lieutenant James Drane, Jr., William Armstrong, Benjamin Duvall, Dudley Lee, Richard Tasker, Michael Paugh, John Jonas, John Simkins, Thomas Casteel, John Irons, David Seibert, George Reinhart, and William and Benjamin Coddington.

In 1775, just after the fighting had begun, Captain Michael Cresap of Oldtown, the son of Thomas Cresap, a member of the Maryland Sons of Liberty and an advocate of the first

Continental Congress, organized a special company of riflemen from Frederick County composed of a hundred and thirty backwoods frontiersmen. The company immediately set out on foot to supplement George Washington's army at Boston, armed according to T. J. C. Williams, a Frederick County lawyer and historian, "with tomahawk and rifle, dressed in deer skins and moccassins and treading as lightly as the savages themselves. They needed no baggage train nor equipments, save their blankets in which they wrapped themselves at night and then slept around their fires as contentedly as if they had been comfortably housed. As they marched to the field they could easily procure game in almost sufficient quantities for their support, and this, along with a little parched corn was the only provision they had."

At Frederick Town, before departing, the Cresap Company gave a public exhibition of their marksmanship. "A man would hold the target in his hand or between his knees for the others to aim at," recorded Williams, "—such was their confidence in their own skill." A contemporary Boston observer described the members of the company as "remarkably stout and hardy men, many of them exceeding six feet in height. They are dressed in white frocks or rifle shirts, and round hats. These men are remarkable for the accuracy of their aim, striking a mark with great certainty at two hundred yards distance. . . . They are now stationed on our lines, and their shots have proved fatal to British officers and soldiers."

The American Revolution spelled the final doom of the great Six Nation League of the Iroquois. The Mohawks, Onondagas, Cayugas and Senecas sided with the English; the Tuscaroras and Oneidas sided with the colonies. Thus, finally, the Iroquois divided against themselves in war, and the Great League, which had earlier struggled so hard to maintain a favorable balance of power between the English and French in the New World, at last split and fell asunder.

Though the battles of the Revolution never extended to present-day Garrett County itself, fighting in nearby Virginia, west of Maryland, erupted periodically throughout the war. In September 1777, and again in September 1782, British forces, reinforced by Indian allies, attacked Fort Henry at

Wheeling. Both times they were repulsed by the American inhabitants. More successful and threatening were small war parties of Indians ranging throughout the frontier woods. In the spring of 1778 one such party of savages surprised and killed a young squatter named James Brain at his new home on Snowy Creek just west of the Maryland-Virginia line. The Brain family had spent the prior winter in the Friend stockades on the Youghiogheny. Also killed in the rout were two women and two children; another woman and child were taken prisoner. One boy escaped by hiding. Another local settler Daniel Lewis, was killed by Indian allies of the British in 1778 while splitting fence rails near the Cheat River.

The Indians struck the Cheat region again in 1780 and 1783. In March of 1780 a large war party lurking near the 1774 settler fort at Horse Shoe Bend on the river killed Jonathan Minear, the community leader, when a group of whites left the fort to go to the river and surrounding farms. Minear's brother-in-law was captured at the same time, but managed to escape the following morning. Three years later another Cheat settler, John Green, fell under the blade of the tomahawk. His wife, baby, and two girls were made captive. The baby was murdered outright; the wife escaped four years later; the girls were ransomed after nine years of captivity. Sarah, a third daughter, was wounded but escaped and later married Joseph Friend of the Youghiogheny, a son of "Old John."

Though the autonomy of the American Republic was clearly established by the end of the Revolutionary War, the republic's indivisibility was not tested until 1794, when federal troops were dispatched by President Washington to quell a rebellion of western Pennsylvania farmers who refused to pay an excise tax collected on the sale of whiskey to help liquidate federal debts. Western discontent over the oppressive tax grew for three years until the possibility of open rebellion became a real threat. Then, on August 7, 1794, President George Washington issued a proclamation announcing his intention to enforce the laws by calling out the militia. On October 19 he appeared in full military uniform, for the last time ever, on the old parade ground at Fort

Cumberland to review the troops he'd assembled there. He dispatched the regulars northward into Pennsylvania; they quashed the rebellion.

In 1776 the Maryland General Assembly carved the western counties of Washington and Montgomery from Frederick, and pushed state political divisions over thirty miles to the west. Two years later it reserved all unpatented lands "westward of Fort Cumberland" for Maryland soldiers of the Revolution, voting as a special recruitment incentive a bounty of fifty acres to each soldier promising to serve at least three years in the Continental army. In 1780 it confiscated the property of all British subjects still living within the state, including the manors of Lord Baltimore in the Allegheny highlands. Then, in 1787, it authorized Colonel Francis Deakins, the Georgetown surveyor, to lay out 4,165 fifty-acre lots for war veterans in western Maryland, pursuant to the act of 1778.

Deakins began his work late in the summer of 1787, supervising ten assistant surveyors from Cumberland, each heading a separate party composed of surveyors, cooks, axemen, and chain carriers. He numbered the lots from 1 to 4,165, beginning near the mouth of the Savage River. The rougher mountain terrain was excluded from the survey—only the glades, valleys, and tillable hillsides, including the Lord Baltimore's former manor lands, were laid off. The surveyors also marked Maryland's western boundary (the Deakins or Old State Line) north to Pennsylvania from the Fairfax Stone. The surveying task was completely finished within three months, and Deakins filed his final report to the state on December 10.

The Deakins report listed the names of 323 squatters claiming 636 surveyed lots. Only about 50 of these settlers lived on military lots located within the land area of later Garrett County, the rest lived on the lands of later Allegeny. All, in 1787, lived in western Washington County. These settlers were given a preference to buy their claims at a rate ranging from five to twenty shillings per acre. Most refused to purchase their lots—many from lack of funds—and subsequently relocated.

Squatters living near the mouth of Savage River in 1787 included Charles Queen, Patrick Burns, Charles Boyles, Joseph Davis, George Fazenbaker, Moses Tichenal, Johanes and Michael Paugh, Henry Kite, Joseph Warnick, John Ryan, James Dennison, and John Streets. Charles Queen, claiming lots No. 1 and No. 2, was the first settler on the site of later Bloomington. Squatters along the Braddock Road at the time of the military surveys included Benjamin Coddington, Peter Crawl, John Kiser (from whom Keyser's Ridge takes its name), John Simkins, John Jonas, Matthias Barnstredder, Jacob Storm, Stephen Pierson, James McPipe, Joseph Mountain, and Jesse Tomlinson. Ezekiel Totten was allotted a parcel east of Savage Mountain. Along the Youghiogheny River, John Friend was allowed to buy three lots at reduced rates, David Robertson two (at the sites of later East and West Selbysport), and the Coddington brothers—William, Benjamin, and Samuel—and Frazee family—Jeremiah and Jonathan—were given preference for several other parcels. Sandy Creek settlers given special purchase preference in 1787 included Zachariah Van Sickle, James McMullen, Sylvester Ryland, and Robinson Savage, while Richard Hall and John Rutan were permitted to acquire lots on Blooming Rose Ridge at reduced rates.

Of the more than 4,000 military grants surveyed in 1787, only 2,575 were actually allotted to veterans. Most owners sold their lots at once to speculators. Only two, Dudley Lee and Richard Tasker, came west to live permanently on the reserved mountain lands. The plots sold for an average price of twelve dollars.

After 1787 it became the policy of the state to dispose of the remainder of its western lands as rapidly as possible under the belief that through private ownership the property would be developed, exploited, utilized, and added to the existing base for local and state taxation. The release of reserved lands initiated a ten-year period of rapid settlement. In 1789 the western districts of Maryland were sufficiently populated so that the General Assembly authorized the formation of Allegany from Washington County. At the same time, the northwestern half of present-day Garrett County was designated

Sandy Creek Hundred as a unit of local administration for levying taxes and organizing the militia (the hundred, like the manor, was an inheritance from the Old Country), and the town of Cumberland, composed of about thirty-five families living almost entirely on the west side of Wills Creek along the Braddock Road on lots laid out by Thomas Beall as Washington Town only four years earlier, was officially incorporated by an act of the Maryland state legislature. In 1790 the first federal census was taken and Allegany County was found to be populated by a total of 4,800, 258 of whom were black slaves. (Only a few score families then lived within the present domain of Garrett County.)

The final decade of the eighteenth century and the early decades of the nineteenth witnessed the growth and development in far western Maryland of Garrett County's first communities and neighborhoods. Six distinct communities began to take root during those years along the Youghiogheny: Blooming Rose, Friendsville, Sang Run, Selbysport, Oakland, and Sunshine (Crellin). Grantsville, Avilton, and New Germany meanwhile sprang up along and near the Braddock Road. Settlement of Finzel began a few years later. To the south, along the North Branch of the Potomac and in the midst of the rich Youghiogheny Glades, eight more communities were firmly established—Bloomington, Kitzmiller, Ryan's Glade, the Green Glades, Deer Park, Altamont, Pleasant Valley, and Sunnyside. At the same time, Accident, Bittinger, and McHenry took root in the county's central portion. A total of twenty-one pioneer settlements.

In 1791 the western Indians again went on the rampage against intruding white settlers. Meshach Browning, then a small boy, lived at Buffalo Marsh with his aunt and Uncle John Spurgeon in a cabin formerly occupied by Charles Friend, who had earlier moved from the Big Boiling Spring to the Youghiogheny Glades. "Things went on well enough," Browning later wrote, "until the news came to us that General St. Clair's whole army had been defeated and cut to pieces (in the Ohio country). This was such frightening news, that aunt was almost ready to leave all, and seek some better place of safety; and indeed I believe uncle too was a little frightened. Be that as it may, he continued but a short time until he took up his march again for the Blooming Rose. In that neighborhood there were some 30 or 40 families, who were not so easily frightened."

Blooming Rose, in 1791, was a rapidly developing farm community. Other families moved to the relative safety of the plateau neighborhood that year to avoid the dreaded tomahawk and arrow of the western Indian. In fact, most of the husbands and fathers of the area had once been soldiers or regulars who had long since tired of fighting the red man. One of these, James McGoffin, was probably the first Catholic settler of the neighborhood—most of his neighbors were Methodists. In 1790, John Enlow, ancestor of today's large Garrett County Enlow family, whose own ancestors from Holland had been naturalized in America in the late seventeenth century, moved from Turkeyfoot, Pennsylvania, to Frazee's Ridge, a little north of Blooming Rose. Four years later General "Mad" Anthony Wayne utterly defeated the western Indians at Fallen Timbers, and settlements east of the Ohio were finally forever safe from the Indian alarms. A traveler on horseback in the early 1800s described the peaceful Blooming Ridge Road: "Every mile or two was a farm just opening, generally white-oak land easily worn out, but can be kept good by lime-stone and stone coal after all the wood is gone."

While farmers were plowing fields and girdling trees in Blooming Rose, another settlement was gradually growing along the Youghiogheny about two miles to the east at the site of John Friend's first Garrett County home—Friendsville. Friend's Post Office was established there on January 7, 1830, with Gabriel Friend serving as the first postmaster. The name of the office was shortened two years later to Friendsville.

Friendsville Town itself grew with the development of the Allegany Iron Company, incorporated in 1828. Five years earlier John Brobst had opened the area's first iron furnace near the mouth of Bear Creek on the Youghiogheny, using local coal to melt the ore mined in nearby mountains. "He was without capital," though, observed Grantsville's Jacob

Brown, "and before long the business passed into the hands of a Baltimore company."

The Allegany Iron Company was incorporated by an act of the Maryland State General Assembly in March 1828. Local members of the enterprise included John McHenry, John Hoye, and Upton Bruce. The Allegany company was present-day Garrett County's first organized industry and its first incorporated company. "Its subscribers have already erected suitable buildings [at Bear Creek] for a furnace and a forge," noted the General Assembly in its 1828 proceedings, "and [they] contemplate prosecuting an extensive manufacture of pigs, castings and bar irons." The name of the business was changed to the "Youghiogheny Iron Company" in 1829.

The original furnace of the Allegany Iron Company stood near the mouth of Bear Creek about one mile above the town. Its forge and foundry, where some of the pig iron manufactured at the furnace was transformed into metal implements, tools, and kettles, was located about a half mile below the town on the west shore of the Youghiogheny. A wooden race carried water from the river to the forge to supply power for the forge's great hammers.

Most of the pig iron manufactured at Friendsville was hauled by wagon to Brownsville, Pennsylvania, from whence it was transported by boat to surrounding markets. Some was sold to blacksmiths along the National Road. An attempt was once made to ship the product down the Youghiogheny by flatboat, but it met with failure—the water was too shallow.

The iron companies at Friendsville provided work for over a hundred men. The company owners and managers built houses for their workers in town and operated company stores. For ten years the Friendsville iron workers mined ore from the clay and rock hills rising from Bear Creek. They smelted the ore into iron. Then, in 1839, the iron business in Friendsville died.

On October 10, 1839, the Allegany County sheriff sold at public auction all property of the heavily-indebted Youghiogheny Iron Company. "The reason assigned for closing," later explained the local Reverend D. A. Friend, "was due to the cost of transportation which consumed most of the profits."

Tableland historian Felix Robinson noted years later that, "competition with larger and better-equipped plants located on the Ohio in proximity to manufacturing centers assisted materially in the decline of this modest enterprise at Friendsville. Like other iron furnaces in the mountains of West Virginia and western Pennsylvania, the Youghiogeny Iron Company could not hope to succeed." The Mary Ann Furnace at Bear Creek had fully closed by 1845.

Tobacco was an early cash crop of the Friend settlement, but its production was soon halted, as it was elsewhere in western Maryland, after a few brief growing seasons, due to high costs of transportation to markets and depletion of the soil. The settlement nevertheless grew, not as an industrial town, nor chiefly as a farming village, but as a center for the work of pioneer tradesmen and a place of barter for the exchange of goods and services. By 1860 the goods and services offered in Friendsville were quite numerous and diverse. The town thrived with such tradesmen and professionals as mechanic, metalworker, founderer, and gunsmith, William E. Friend; painter, cabinetmaker, and wheelwright, John L. Hook; stonemason, Stephen Riley; carpenter and cooper, Jacob Herring; honey producer, Gabriel Forsyth; boot and shoemaker, Thomas Frantz; tanner, Jackson Frantz; merchant, Ralph Thayer; mail carrier, Richard Selby; miller and carpenter, David Kent; blacksmith, Abraham Welch; physician, William Frey; schoolteacher and merchant, Joshua Friend; carpenter and bridge builder, Abram Hoff; and miller, William Coddington. Area farmers of the time included John Slicer, Sylvester Ryland, James H. Rush, John S. Friend, John G. Friend, Jacob Friend, Andrew Friend, Jonathan Friend, Richard Frazee, Isaac Frazee, Abram Steele, Jacob Cuppett, John Hartman, John Liston, Adam Schroyer, Noah Humberson, George A. Fear, and Richard White. "These were all old gray-headed men when I was a boy," wrote the Rev. D. A. Friend just after World War I, "and some of them lived to a great age. But they have all long since gone to the great beyond, and happy are we their sons and daughters, if we be found living the pure and devout lives that they lived while here upon earth. Peace to their sleeping ashes, and joy and bliss to their immortal spirits!"

John Friend, Garrett County's earliest permanent settler, died before the end of the first decade of the nineteenth century at the town he had helped found. "According to the story handed down to us," a descendant later recorded, "it was on a winter's night, and all others of the family for some cause were absent except the old man and a granddaughter. In the evening he laid down on a deerskin with his feet toward the fire, as was his usual custom. When bedtime came the girl said to him, 'Grandfather, get up now, and go to bed, for it's getting late.' He replied, 'I believe I'll just lie here awhile yet.' Then he called her to him and said in a gentle tone, 'Daughter, if Grandfather should die tonight do you think you would be afraid?' She replied, 'O no, Grandfather, I don't think I would.' Her suspicions being aroused by this remark, she took an easy chair and sat by him for awhile when he seemed to go asleep. Upon his being so very still she investigated and found Grandfather had gone to the happy country beyond. She gently folded his hands across his breast and then retired to bed and slept as though nothing out of the ordinary had taken place."

John Friend died in the early 1800s. His settlement, though, lives on. "Friendsville," noted the Appalachian historian Felix G. Robinson in 1956, "is one of those American communities where the inhabitants are, with hardly an exception, all related to the original family from which the town derives its name. There is hardly a resident living in Friendsville today who does not trace his ancestory back to those hardy and prolific Swedes."

Shortly after they settled on the Youghiogheny at the future site of Friendsville in 1765, the Friend family discovered a hill about seven miles south of their home on which ginseng, whose medicinal roots had been highly prized by the Chinese for centuries as a restorer of waning vitality and virility, grew in abundance. They named the bluff Ginseng Hill, but the stream at its base became known simply as Sang Run. John Friend discovered the cave now bearing his name, John Friend's Cave, in the vicinity in 1765. At the same time, he found the remains of Indian cornfields in the area and watched buffalo graze in the local glades. His brother, Augustine, settled along Sang Run in the late 1700s before moving to the Big Boiling Spring at Buffalo Marsh. Another son, John, Jr., settled at the Sanging Ground in 1796. Two years later a party of federal surveyors presented John Friend, Jr., with a two-hundred-acre parcel of land at the mouth of Sang Run on the Youghiogheny in exchange for food and shelter. Friend was pleased with the bargain and named his tract Friend's Delight. The tract later became known as The Green of Sang Run; today it is simply referred to as The Community Park.

In 1799 William Waller Hoye, an Irishman from Frog Harbor Manor on the Potomac near present-day Williamsport, moved his family and slaves west from Cumberland over the Braddock Road, then south by packhorse to Crabtree Bottom at the foot of Ginseng Hill. Here he established an agrarian homestead, housing his slaves in the abandoned cabin of Augustine Friend. "A field was cleared, corn and vegetables planted," wrote descendant and historian of Garrett County pioneer families, Charles E. Hoye, in 1942. "Hay for the stock was made of the wild glade grass; the hogs fattened on chestnuts and acorns. Wild animals were abundant: bears, deer and turkeys supplied plenty of meat."

The families of Henry DeWitt, Andrew House, Meshach Browning, Robinson T. Savage, and Henry Sines moved to Sang Run during the first three decades of the nineteenth century. Though isolated from the rest of the world, the community slowly grew. "Your of January 17 was a long time before it retch me because of the snow," wrote William Hoye to a son-in-law in 1831. Deep snow drifts at Sang Run presented a problem common to all early settlers of the Allegheny highlands. "It was so deep all communication between this and Armstrongs (Oakland) post office was cut off," Hoye wrote. "Letters to me directed to Friend's post office retch me quicker than by Armstrongs," he suggested.

In spite of its awkward isolation, Sang Run was heavily enough populated by 1852 to be declared an Allegany County election district by the state's General Assembly.

"Owing at that time to the remoteness of the district," reported the *Cumberland Times* in 1908, "it was next to impossible to get the return (of votes) from Sang Run, and sometimes for many days after the election, especially in closely contested elections, the question would be: 'Have you heard from Sang Run?' So often was the question asked in those days that Sang Run became one of the most widely known districts in the county.... In one election remembered, the returns from Sang Run had to be heard from before it could be told who was elected, and it was many days before the result was known." In 1857 the Johnstown Post Office was established at a crossroads near the headsprings of Sang Run on military lots first owned by the Virginian, John DeWitt. The name of the office and crossroads was later changed to Hoyes after the area's early settler.

While the Sang Run settlement gradually grew during the early 1800s, another community—Selbysport, named after the Indian fighter Evan Shelby, who patented lands in the area in 1773 and then moved to Kentucky where his son, Isaac, became the state's first governor in 1792—suddenly sprang up on the banks of the Youghiogheny about two miles north of Friendsville. The first settler within the bounds of Old Shelby's Port was David Robertson, who later sold his holdings to the Frenchman, Peter Devecmon, of Westernport, a renowned local merchant and land speculator. Prior to 1798 Devecmon laid out a hundred building lots, joined by streets, on each side of the Old Morgantown Road from Braddock's Trail on the west side of the crossing. The organized town that grew up on the site was Garrett County's first. (Selbysport has since been flooded by the waters of the Youghiogheny Dam; the Old Morgantown Road now comes to a dead end at the lake front.)

In 1798 John and Thomas Pritchard, William Post, and Daniel Arnett were assessed with lots in Selbysport. The same year Aza Beall, of Cumberland, bought the remaining lots and moved with his family and slaves to a farm just west of the crossing, where he attempted to raise tobacco, while operating a general store for the local residents. Later storekeepers in the area included Ralph Thayer, Hiram Frazee, and Walter Lowdermilk. In 1799 Allegany County was divided into six election districts and Selbysport was designated polling place for District No. 2, Sandy Creek Hundred. Only one other polling place served the remainder of the residents of present Garrett County at the time—Ingman's Inn, near Swanton, on the old Great Warrior Path.

By 1800 fifty-four families lived in the Selbysport neighborhood. Later the families of David Hoffman, Daniel Smouse, Samuel Coddington, and George Matthews emigrated to the area. Finally, in 1833, the Selbysport Post Office opened, with Moses A. Ross serving as first postmaster. The mail office opening there followed by only three years that of the Friend settlement two miles to the south.

"This part of the country is much broken up by abrupt hills," wrote the hunter Meshach Browning of the Selbysport area in 1859. "The land, in places, is well adapted to the growth of Indian corn, wheat, rye, oats, and tobacco; and there are in this locality some fine farms, with excellent orchards of delightful fruit." The town of Selbysport served the surrounding countryside, much as did early Friendsville, as a place for the exchange and barter of goods and services in a rural setting. Ralph Thayer was but one of the town's several merchants who periodically wagoned products of the neighborhood to Baltimore over the National Road after 1838, returning after each trip to the highlands with merchandise to stock his store. Selbysport, now an underwater ghost town, flourished as Garrett County's largest and most bustling village until after the Civil War.

The community of Oakland, not so named until 1849, almost twenty miles directly south of Selbysport, a mile east of the Big Youghiogheny River on the north banks of the Little Yough, replaced Selbysport in the later nineteenth century as the county's most populous neighborhood. The first settler of later Oakland was "one named Boyle, and old Hollander," who lived for a time near an old buffalo and Indian ford of the Little Youghiogheny between the later-named Hooppole Ridge to the north and McCarty Hill to the south. Prior to 1798 Charles Friend had a tract of land surveyed in the area which he named Boyle's Sorrow.

In 1796 Eric Bollman, a German traveling west with the land speculator, General Irwin of Baltimore, spent a night with Boyle on the Little Yough. Bollman enthusiastically described the surrounding glades as "one of the most remarkable features of these mountains," noting that "there is not a tree to be found, but the ground is covered knee deep with grass and herbs, where both the botanist and the cattle find delicious food."

"Only lately have the Indians ceased roving in this vicinity," he observed, "which has done much to delay its cultivation, but now it is being cleared quite rapidly and in a short time will, no doubt, become a fine place for pasturage."

Oakland's first permanent settlers were William Armstrong, commissioned at the age of fourteen as an ensign in a Pennsylvania regiment of the Revolutionary army, and his wife Hannah, the widow of Peter Devecmon, the founder of Selbysport. In 1806 the Armstrongs were married and moved their family and slaves to the present site of Oakland, settling near the old Boyle cabin on the state road to Virginia. They soon erected a large log house, a substantial barn and other outbuildings, and a tavern or inn. The Yough Glades Post Office, Garrett County's first, was opened in the Armstrong tavern in 1812. For years post riders on their way to Clarksburg, Virginia, paused there to refresh and change horses. In 1819 the Armstrongs were assessed with six military lots and the Stewart's Delight tract, surveyed in the former Great Glades Manor of Lord Baltimore by Francis Deakins in 1787. Most of later Oakland—the west side—grew up on Stewart's Delight.

In 1815 George Loar settled on a military lot about a mile south of the Armstrong tavern. Over a hundred years later his grandson willed almost two hundred thousand dollars for the construction of Garrett County Memorial Hospital, Garrett's first and only large-scale health and medical center. The original Garrett County Loar lived at first in a one-story log house, later in a two-story log structure added to the original cabin.

Isaac McCarty, the son of an Allegany County Irish immigrant engaged in farming, business, and race horse breeding, the son-in-law of Hannah Armstrong through her first husband, Peter Devecmon, moved to the Yough Glades in April 1824, establishing a homestead for his family and slaves about a mile south of the Armstrongs on the later Aurora Road. In time, with slave labor, he built two log houses, two tobacco barns, a gristmill, and a sawmill. He served the community as religious, commercial, and social leader for over thirty years. In 1826 he patented a two-hundred-acre tract, The Wilderness Shall Smile—the present eastern half of Oakland—to his son Edward, then two years of age. Five years later he granted seven military lots south of the present town to his children, Peter and William. When William Armstrong died in 1848 the Yough Glades Post Office was transferred to the McCarty house.

Murray Thayer, a settler living south of the Yough Glades, named the Armstrong-McCarty neighborhood Slabtown after the slab-sided houses constructed in the area following the 1830 erection of the McCarty grist and saw mills. Slabtown later became McCarty's Mill, and, in 1849, when the first of sixty-four town lots were laid out, Ingabe McCarty, Isaac's daughter, chose the name Oakland for the area. Two years later the Baltimore and Ohio Railroad opened a station in the town, and the destiny of the community for over a half century was sealed. When a post office was established in the B&O station in 1854, the name Oakland became official.

The same year William and Hannah Armstrong moved to the Yough Glades, 1806, a nondescript John Smith established a homestead on All the Chances at Underwood Hill, a tract bordering Small Meadows, first surveyed in 1774. The Smith Farm, north of the mouth of Snowy Creek on the Big Youghiogheny, less than four miles southwest of the Armstrong settlement, overlooked the valley in which the town of Crellin would develop about eighty years later.

John Smith's son, Jacob, maintained the family farm at Underwood Hill until 1839, when he sold out to William Wilson and Thomas Ashby, sons of William Wilton Ashby, the pioneer immigrant. William Ashby lived on the Smith Farm with his wife Helen for over thirty years, raising a large family of nine sons and three daughters. (Thomas remained behind at the Ashby home in Virginia's Dunkard Bottom.)

Around 1850 the Ashby brothers constructed an up-and-down water-powered sawmill beside the Snowy Creek. The mill served early settlers of Crellin, first known as Sunshine, for over thirty years, providing the boards and beams needed for the construction of homes. A new sawmill erected by the associates of the Pennsylvania capitalist, Rolland P. Crellin, in the 1890s gave the area new life, new employment, new hope, and a new future in timbering and lumbering. The local post office, which opened in the store of one of William Ashby's sons in 1892, was consequently named Crellin.

While settlements gradually developed along the banks of Youghiogheny River in the early decades of the nineteenth century, three communities, Grantsville, Avilton, and New Germany, simultaneously took root and grew along the route of Braddock's Road in the northern part of present-day Garrett County.

Daniel Grant, a successful Baltimore innkeeper, proprietor of the well-known Fountain Inn, patented eleven hundred acres just west of the Casselman River (earlier referred to as the Little Youghiogheny), near the site of General Braddock's fifth camp, under the title Cornucopia in 1785. All of later Grantsville developed within the bounds of Cornucopia. Grant also took out patents to the nearby Good Hope, Clover Bottom, and Land Flowing With Milk and Honey tracts in 1785. Ten years later he left Baltimore with his daughter, Elizabeth, to reside in a log house at Cornucopia. He was one of the area's wealthiest men—in 1796 he was assessed in Allegany County with over five thousand acres of land, six slaves, four horses, four cows, and thirty-six ounces of silver plate. Financial reverses in Baltimore forced him to liquidate his mountain holdings through court order in 1804, however, and seven years later he returned to Baltimore. By 1815 he was living in a modest boarding house. Meanwhile a growing community bearing his name began to prosper in the mountains. Early Grantsville settlers included families with the following surnames: Yoder, Bittinger, Weimer, Bowman, Baker, Durst, Figgie, Stanton, Spiker, Miller, Maust, Engle, Hare,

Gnagey, Hershberger, and Layman. All of these were established in the area—most along the old Braddock Road—by 1785.

In 1801 John Sloan purchased most of the Grassy Cabin tract east of the Little Crossings below the Grant settlement and laid off four lots adjacent to the Braddock Road, naming his enterprise Sloan's Ville. Though he sold two lots to George Newman in 1812, the National or Cumberland Road (generally constructed along the route of Braddock's 1755 expedition) bypassed Sloan's Ville in 1815, Newman sold his two lots back to Sloan at a forty-dollar profit, and the settlement project on the site was abandoned. The old Grant Settlement likewise fell into decline through the ensuing years, while new Grantsville grew up along both sides of the National Road just west of the crossings.

Enough people lived in the Grantsville area by 1817 that Allegany County's election District No. 3 was then established there, with its polling place at Little Crossings. Three hundred and sixty-seven persons, including sixty-two slaves, inhabited the Little Crossings District by 1820. The population doubled within ten years.

Early in 1824 the Union Bank of Maryland purchased all eleven hundred acres of Cornucopia for speculative purposes. Eight years later it sold nearly half the tract south of the National Road, "except the ... six lots in the village of Grantsville," to Joseph Meyers. The following two years the remainder of Cornucopia, lying north of the National Road, was sold to Solomon Starner and Joseph Glotfelty. Though Grantsville was never planned or laid out as a town, it grew up on the three tracts through succeeding years.

Tomlinson's post office was opened in the Stone House Inn at Little Meadows to provide the Grantsville area with mail service in 1822. The postal address became Little Crossings in 1831, and in 1846 the office was moved to Grantsville, the address being changed accordingly. The town itself at this time consisted of at least four dwellings, one hotel, and one blacksmith shop. German Amish and Mennonite families from Pennsylvania—Benders, Millers, Gingerichs, and Kinsingers—continued to emigrate to homesteads north and south of the village throughout the 1830s and 1840s. By the middle of the century most of the land north of the town was occupied by the Amish; Amish farms continue to dominate the area today. Grantsville became the area's most important business and trade center, and in 1850 the polling place for the district was moved there from Little Crossings. The town was incorporated in 1864 by act of the Maryland state legislature.

A small settlement of German farmers had meanwhile grown up about four miles south of Grantsville at a place first known as Old Dutch Settlement. The community name was later changed to New Germany. Today it flourishes as a state park recreational center. A renowned state political celebrity, the "silver-tongued" Francis Thomas, secluded himself in a grove of white pines at New Germany in 1844 following a nationwide divorce scandal which undermined his once realistic hopes for being nominated Democratic candidate for president of the United States that year.

Francis Thomas served as delegate to the Maryland State House from Frederick County for three separate terms beginning in 1822, 1827, and 1829. During his last term he rose to the position of Speaker of the House. He was elected to the federal House of Representatives five times in succession from 1831 to 1841. In 1841 he won the governorship of Maryland following a heated campaign in which he engaged in a furious debate leading to a duel with William Price of Hagerstown. On the morning of his victorious inauguration, though, he announced his intention to seek divorce from his wife, Sallie McDowell, daughter of the governor of Virginia, his junior by twenty-two years, and his political star began to fade. He printed and distributed statewide a scandalous pamphlet divulging to the public his suspicions of matrimonial infidelity. The Maryland legislature subsequently refused to grant its jealous governor a divorce, but the Virginia legislature was more sympathetic to Mrs. Thomas, freeing her from the bonds of marriage while Thomas was still governor. In 1843 Thomas arranged a duel with his former father-in-law, Governor James McDowell of Virginia, but the duel was prevented through the intervention of friends. Sallie subsequently married a Presbyterian minister from Philadelphia, and Francis, defeated in the national Democratic convention of 1844 in Baltimore, largely through the efforts of the hostile Virginia governor, retired to the mountains of western Maryland where he owned nearly fifty thousand acres of land. For fifteen years he lived the life of a political and social recluse there.

Ross C. Durst, a later Grantsville-area historian, described Francis Thomas as "A Diamond of Many Facets," a man "of culture, education, wealth and great ability," who "often spent long hours (at New Germany) in The Slough of Despond." Though Thomas had once been noted for his keen wit, his frontier neighbors often spoke of him as "the man who never smiled." Not until the Civil War erupted did the former governor leave the mountains. In 1872 he was appointed minister to Peru by President Grant. He held the ambassadorial position until 1875, when he retired from politics and returned to a new home in western Maryland overlooking Savage River.

The Garrett County pioneer hunter Meshach Browning observed in 1859 that "Between the Savage Mountain and the Meadow and Negro Mountains is a country abounding in the finest pine timber, together with oak, curly maple, birch, and chestnut timber." As early as 1818 the area was known as the McKenzie Settlement after the homesteader Leo McKenzie. Other early settlers moving into the later-named Avilton area, about six miles east of Grantsville and New Germany, south of the Braddock Road, included the families of Christian Garlitz, Eli Whitzell, Patrick Dorsey, Christian and Andrew Blocher, and families with the surnames Wilhelm, Weimer, Broadwater, Fike, Turner, Camp, Miller, Crowe, Brown, Merrill, Robinson, Chaney, and Durst. Most all early residents of the McKenzie Settlement were farmers. "Wheat, rye, oats, and potatoes are the principal productions," noted Meshach Browning, "and timothy grows admirably in this region." A post office under the name Avilton was finally established to give the area mail service in 1885.

Meanwhile, to the northeast, high atop Little Savage Mountain near the source of the Savage River at Cranberry

Swamp, a boreal bog formed during the Ice Age, John George and Annie Margaret Finzel in 1858 established a homestead on the future site of the small town later to bear their name—Finzel, Garrett County's easternmost village. Early neighbors of the Finzel family included families of German and English origin with the surnames Fadely, Wolf, Rosenberger, Caton, Crowe, Warner, and Drees. Though Finzel was never formally incorporated, a post office was established in the town in the late 1890s. Many descendants of the founders, as is true with the rest of the county, still live in the area.

A number of settlers—Queens, Burns, Boyles, Davises, Fazenbakers, Titchenals, Paughs, Kites, Warnicks, Ryans, Streets, and Dennisons—already lived near the mouth of Savage River at the Potomac, sixteen miles south of its source in the Cranberry Swamp at Finzel, in 1787 when Francis Deakins surveyed the western Maryland military lots as soldier bounties. By the early 1800s additional families were living in the vicinity: Pritchards, Barnards, Gainors, Connellys, Turners, Magruders, Dixons, Guynns, Duckworths, Michaels, Wilts, Brandts, and Trubees. The settlement was named Bloomington in 1851 when the Baltimore and Ohio Railroad passed through the town. Two years later, after the opening of a local post office, it became Llangollen after a mining company operating in the area. An 1856 act of the state legislature restored the Bloomington designation, however, and this time the name stuck.

Thorton Offutt and Patrick Hamill served as early storekeepers in Bloomington. In 1811, when the United States government was preparing for war with Great Britain, John Brant, who had settled two years earlier a little over a mile above the mouth of the Savage, contracted with a Virginia based firm "to manufacture 2375 muskets with Bayonets compleat to be delivered at the United States armory at Harper's Ferry" within three years. The Brantsburg gun factory subsequently imported pig iron for its business from Pennsylvania furnaces up the North Branch from Cumberland. Black walnut, which grew abundantly in the vicinity, was easily utilized in the production of gunstocks. The completed muskets were shipped downriver to Harpers Ferry on flatboats.

Francis Thomas, the former governor of Maryland and secluded resident of New Germany for fifteen years, returned from Peru in 1875 where he had served a term as ambassador under the appointment of President Grant, to live in a new mansion he had earlier constructed north of Bloomington near Crabtree Creek. He brought with him a flock of twenty-five alpaca sheep from the Andes Mountains, a rare gift from the people of Peru. The following year he was struck and killed by a train near his home. Though Thomas himself was a one-time slaveholder, the epitaph over his grave at Petersville in present-day Frederick County notes that he was "the author of the measure which gave to Maryland the constitution of 1864 and thereby gave freedom to 90,000 human beings." The governor's ten surviving mountain sheep were sold after his funeral for a total of one thousand dollars, when his estate was settled, and all ten were transported to the Philadelphia Centennial World Fair for exhibition. All ten died soon afterward of exposure and inability to adapt to their new surroundings.

Kitzmiller, eight miles southeast of Bloomington on the Potomac, named after Ebenezer Kitzmiller, an early settler, was first inhabited by the families of Daniel Bray and Thomas Wilson. Subsequent settlers in the vicinity in the early nineteenth century were sturdy Scotch-Irish folk— Davises, Hamills, Harveys, Junkinses, Paughs, Pews, Rafters, and Taskers. Subsistence farming and stock raising were the chief occupations of the town's early residents. Ebenezer Kitzmiller established a woolen mill on the site in 1853 for the manufacture of the nationally known Poole shirt, which was worn by lumbermen and laborers from Canada to the Gulf of Mexico. The local post office opened in 1877 under the address of Kitzmillerville, the name having been suggested by Daniel R. Brant of Chicago, an annual visitor in the Kitzmiller home.

A third Garrett county settlement—The Ryan's Glade-Gorman community—was also established east of the Great Backbone Mountain, about ten miles southwest of Kitzmiller, by the early nineteenth century. Eric Bollman, the traveling German, dining at Castle Hill on Backbone Mountain in 1796, noted that "there are (already) many settlements in this vicinity. We were entertained in a beautiful, cool, roomy house, surrounded by oats fields, and rich meadows, where the sound of the bells told us that cattle were pasturing nearby. This is the 'backwoods' of America, which the Philadelphian is pleased to describe as a rough wilderness—while in many parts of Europe, in Westphalia, in the whole of Hungary and Poland, nowhere, is there a cottage (which) can be compared."

Alexander Smith, a Georgetown merchant, moved his family and slaves to a hill just south of the Great Warrior Path, a few miles south of Ryan's Glade, in 1793. Two years later the land speculator George Dickson deeded the Flowery Vale tract in Ryan's Glade to Colonel Norman Bruce of Maryland's Carroll County. Bruce's son, Upton, inherited the tract in 1810, settled in the glade, and established the Bruce home there. Israel Thompson bought the Bruce farm in 1849.

A free black family, John and Phoebe Davis, established a farm homestead in Ryan's Glade in the 1830s. John was the former slave overseer of Isaac McCarty of the Yough Glades, west of the Backbone Mountain; Phoebe was once a slave of Philip Bray of Kitzmiller on the eastern side of the western Maryland continental divide. Enough people lived in Ryan's Glade by 1835 that the Maryland General Assembly authorized the formation of an Allegany County election district there: District No. 10.

The first house in Gorman, a few miles south of Ryan's Glade on the Potomac, was built in 1840 by Jacob Shaeffer a few years after the Northwestern Turnpike was completed through the area. Shaeffer's dwelling doubled as a home and storehouse. Shaeffer later operated a tollgate at his settlement, learned cabinetmaking and established a tannery, and served the community—then known as Shaefferville—as its first postmaster. The surnames of early settlers at Shaefferville are reflected by the names of the seven hills surrounding the neighborhood—Althouse, Hoffman, Gilbert, Eger, Ridder, Rinker, and, of course, Shaeffer. The town was given its current name in the late nineteenth century to honor Maryland's Senator Arthur Pue Gorman. Its sister town across the Potomac, then Virginia, was simultaneously dubbed Gormania.

Four rural communities were established in the late eighteenth and early nineteenth centuries just west of the Backbone Mountain, south of the Savage River: the Green Glades, Deer Park, Pleasant Valley, and Sunnyside-Gortner.

The Green Glades, about ten miles due west of Bloomington, first visited by the family of John Friend on his 1764 trip to the Youghiogheny, was first settled in 1788 by a small party of travelers—two couples—migrating west from Hagerstown to the Mississippi Valley. The group met with disaster at Savage River and subsequently decided not to proceed further west than the glades. John Stauch (also spelled Stough) the leader of the migrants, recorded the event: "We attempted to cross the Savage Creek on Sunday morning after the heavy rain of Saturday night. My comrade got on the front horse, I on the saddle horse, the two women in the wagon. My comrade, when the horse commenced to swim, fell off and was swept away by the current. Thus I was alone, with the two women in the wagon, to behold the solemn scene, with the judgement of God resting on us."

The three survivors were soon joined by several other young couples moving to the Ohio Valley, and on Good Friday, 1788, they paused to rest in the Green Glades west of the continental divide: "We found a stopping place in the then called Virginia Glades." The migrants were delighted with their surroundings, with the fertility of the soil, the gushing springs, the natural meadows; they decided to stay.

On Saturday after Good Friday they "opened a sugar camp and when the Sabbath came we labored hard all day, gathering and boiling the water, thinking it right to save it if God made it to run on the Sabbath. When evening came we emptied the syrup into the trough, covered it with bark and retired to rest. During the night the cattle came and drank all the syrup. So we not only lost all our labor, but some of our cattle also. These two incidents, (the tragic fording of the Savage, the loss of the syrup) convinced us that no good would come from violating God's law of the Sabbath by travel and worldly labor."

The 1788 Green Glades settlers—Wagners, Deidricks, Wilts, Stemples, Rhinehards, Wotrings, Ridenours, and Harshes—chose John Stauch, the most educated member of the group, to serve as leader of informal religious services. In this capacity he performed one of the first white weddings of the Allegheny highlands when Yost Heck, a young frontier blacksmith, clad in animal skins and carrying a gun and some freshly shot game, strolled out of the wilderness with his young lady friend and requested a marriage service. "He with a manly countenance, she with a mischievous smile, asked to be married," recorded Stauch. "We told them we had no license to perform a legal marriage. Now they said they did not care, they intended to live together, and there was no minister in the country." The young couple argued that if Stauch could read sermons, he could just as easily read a marriage ceremony. Considering the couple's enthusiasm and avowed intentions, "We concluded we had better solemnize their nuptials," noted Stauch, "and did it backwoods style." The woods resounded with congratulations and best wishes for the young lovers.

Though the Green Glades never developed into much more than a farming community, Deer Park, four miles to its southwest, eventually became a bustling and exclusive railroad resort town of the late 1800s. In 1786 patents were issued to Charles Stewart and James McCullough for the Deer Park tract, first surveyed in 1774. At the same time, Thomas Johnson, Maryland's first governor, took the neighboring Peace and Plenty parcel bordering the old Glades Indian Path. Two years later Daniel Jenifer, George Scott, and John Swan announced in the *Maryland Journal* their intention to apply to the General Assembly for confirmation of their property rights to Deer Park.

Then, in December 1819, three families—two by the name of Thayer, one named Thompson—arrived in the Allegheny highlands from Massachusetts, and were persuaded by Captain George Calmes, Deer Park's original white settler, to remain and establish homes in the area. In 1851 the Baltimore and Ohio Railroad passed through Deer Park, and Emil Droege, emigrating from Germany to avoid military service, moved to the vicinity, and bought over a thousand acres of local land. He later established the Deer Park Distillery. Meanwhile, the town of Deer Park began to take root along the railroad.

A few miles southwest of Deer Park, almost directly south of Oakland, are the Youghiogheny Glades of Pleasant Valley. Just west of the Glades, northwest of Gorman across the Great Backbone Mountain, is Sunnyside. Pleasant Valley and Sunnyside developed concomitantly in the early 1800s.

On November 22, 1800, Thomas Johnson, owner of Peace and Plenty, Maryland's first governor, deeded The Glades at Sunnyside, almost three hundred acres, to George Rinehart, a German immigrant and Revolutionary War veteran who had settled in the area prior to 1798. Rinehart built a large two-story log dwelling in two sections, separated by a hallway and a kitchen on his homestead and served the community for many years as innkeeper, utilizing one large room of his house as a dance hall. Rinehart also expressed considerable interest in current civic affairs and was an influential leader in local religious, educational, and political events. His earlier neighbors included John and Robert Swan, sons of John Swan, Sr., Garrett County's most extensive land speculator.

George Rinehart was a guest at the home of Captain George Calmes, of the Deer Park area, on Washington's birthday in 1819 when the Thayers and Thompsons arrived on their journey from Massachusetts to Virginia. Both Rinehart and Calmes were influential in persuading the travelers to remain in the highlands. Stephen Thayer, with his wife and nine children, rented the Calmes farm for a year, then moved south to Pleasant Valley. Lewis Thompson, an expert blacksmith, settled nearby.

In 1820 another Thompson, Israel, a young herder from Virginia, met and married Catherine Lower of Sunnyside, a granddaughter of William Wilton and Sarah Ashby. "They squatted the day after their marriage to an abandoned cabin on a hill just south of the Little Youghiogheny River about two miles east of the Armstrong-Oakland settlement." In

1823 they paid two dollars apiece to attend school conducted by Nancy Thayer at the Rinehart home. Four years later they bought a tract of land in Pleasant Valley about one and a half miles southwest of their original home and began pasturing cattle on the fertile glades before moving east in 1839 across the Backbone Mountain to Ryan's Glade where they established their final homestead.

Around mid-nineteenth century about seventy-five members of the Old Order Amish and Mennonite churches moved south from Somerset and Cambria counties in Pennsylvania to later Garrett County and the fertile farmlands of Pleasant Valley. Their surnames included the following: Pfeil, Miller, Yutzy, Slaubaugh, Selder, Beachy, Gnagey, Schrock, Petersheim, Swartzentruber, and Lichty. The settlement of Gortner at Sunnyside takes its name from Peter and Barbara Gortner, who moved to the area by oxcart in 1849. Peter Gortner, like many of his neighbors, was a jack-of-all-trades: farmer, cabinetmaker, carpenter, mason, millwright, blacksmith. A progressive farmer, he owned the area's first mowing machine, reaper, horse-powered threshing machine, and covered buggy. The mid-nineteenth century Amish settlers of Pleasant Valley and Sunnyside transformed the local glades from an open cattle range to a farm valley of small, tidy homesteads. They remain in the area yet today, preserving their heritage and mild-mannered theology, inheriting the earth from their fathers and grandfathers.

The fertile Accident valley, about five miles southeast of Friendsville, named as a result of a surveying coincidence in 1774 and called Accident by mistake, also developed in the early nineteenth century as an Appalachian pocket of German farm settlement. "The cove and town of Accident," noted the pioneer Garrett County hunter Meshach Browning in 1859, "is decidedly the best part of the county; it has but lately engaged attention, is now a fine grain-growing neighborhood, and is settled by an industrious and enterprising class of farmers. The land is of good quality, level, well watered, and healthy. It is one of the best wheat-growing sections in Maryland. Indian corn is raised there; rye, oats, tobacco, and Irish potatoes all grow abundantly; and grass flourishes remarkably well."

The Accident tract was originally patented to William Deakins, Jr., in 1786. Deakins later sold the tract to Captain David Lynn, of Cumberland, who deeded Flowery Vale, 970 acres, which included most of the original Accident survey, to Colonel William LaMar of LaVale, descendant of a French Huguenot, in 1817. As early as 1798, however, Accident was "assessed" to Lynn but "charged" to LaMar. James Drane, Jr., LaMar's brother-in-law, a Revolutionary War veteran, became the first permanent settler of Accident around 1800. The Drane House, a log cabin built by the LaMars in the late 1700s, enlarged by the Drane family in the early nineteenth century, still stands today next to a farm pond and spring just east of Accident village as Garrett County's oldest existing structure.

Having earlier been tobacco planters in Maryland's Prince Georges County, the Dranes at Accident cleared the land surrounding their homestead with slave labor and successfully produced the crop for several years for the Cumberland market. Their plantation thrived on the edge of the wilderness. "One afternoon all the men were working in the fields," recalled a son at the age of ninety-four many years later, "when a ferocious bear came out of the woods near the house. Mrs. Drane shot and wounded the beast, and one of the negro women finished it with an axe."

Captain Truman West, of Frederick County, a first cousin of Governor Francis Thomas, settled on a large tract south of Accident, which he named Woodland Farm, in 1832. Like the Dranes before him, he operated a tobacco plantation with slave labor for a few seasons, but freed his slaves when it became apparent that the crop would not be profitable in the mountains, due to the cool climate and unavailability of markets. His son-in-law, Richard Fairall, later opened a large general store in Accident and operated a local sawmill.

German emigration, which began in the Accident area in the 1820s and 1830s and lasted beyond mid-century, transformed the agriculture of the fertile valley from that of the southern-type manor to that of the small, self-subsisting family-size farm. The Dranes of Flowery Vale and the Wests of Woodland Farm were the only English-speaking residents of the community for years. Richard Fairall, recognizing the future of the family-size farm in the area, as opposed to that of the slave plantation, himself made several trips to New York in the early nineteenth century to lure thrifty and industrious German immigrants arriving there back to the mountains. Among the first German settlers of the Accident-Cove region were the families of Jake Bowser, Adam and Joseph Spiker, Jonathan Frantz, George Ault, Melchoir Miller, Michael and Frederick Englehardt, Adam and George Goehringer, Frederick Schneider, Michael Groenmiller, Gottfried and Andreas Fuchs, Michael Menhorn, Valentine Kahl, John Eckhart, and John Reis. These were sturdy "Pennsylvania Dutch" people, Brethren, Mennonite, Lutheran, and Amish by religion.

"These new settlers were good farmers and skilled craftsmen, industrious and thrifty," noted the Garrett County pioneer historian Charles E. Hoye a hundred years later. "They soon made the neglected Accident neighborhood the most prosperous in Western Allegany."

"Accident, in its early period developed a finely-balanced community of handcraft, artisanship and farming," observed the Appalachian tableland historian Felix G. Robinson in the 1940s. "Flowery Vale became a beehive of industry," he recorded. "It was in most respects self-subsisting, as clothes, shoes, and furniture were home-made." Kathryn A. Speicher, a local schoolteacher and community chronicler, has suggested that "all the small industries found in the community accent the consistent record in making farming the chief vocation of the community. What industries were established were for the advancement of the farmer and in the interest of farming. Accident, like Friendsville, Selbysport, and Grantsville, developed as a trade and service center for an isolated rural community. The first post office was established in 1838 by William Drane. The area became an Allegany County election district ten years later.

Accident-Cove was perhaps the most self-sufficient of all early Garrett County settlements. Only two rough roads initially connected the area with outside civilization. The Engle's Mill Road wound northward over the hills from the town to Grantsville; another backwoods path descended a steep mountain slope beyond a hill west of the valley to Friendsville. Early Accident tradesmen included the following: tanners, distillers, millers, harness makers, coopers, cabinetmakers, stock breeders, hotel operators, carpenters, masons, and furniture makers.

German settlers at Accident often wrote home advising friends and relatives to emigrate to the area. After 1840 the families of the following came to the valley: Leonard Groemiller, Henry Richter, Leonhard Fratz, Jacob Schartzer, Leonard Burkhart, Christoff and Karl Schlossnagle, Konrad Spoerlein, Edward Margroff, Adam and George Stark, Frederich and Heinrich Kolb, Johann Georg, Michael Hobach, Leonhard Fischer, and Andreas Dietrich. In 1871 Joseph Buckel deserted the German army after the siege of Paris and stowed away on a ship to America, settling finally with friends at Accident, later moving to Bittinger.

Early merchants in the Accident village were J. W. Boyer and John Gnagey. Hotel owner was A. B. Reis. Harness makers were Eli McMillen and Christian Snyder. Blacksmiths included Adam Goehringer, Ferdinand Grouse, Frederick Grower, George Menhorn, and Abram Turney. Carpenters were Henry and Val Kahl. Boot and shoemakers were Alexander Haenftling, Edward Richter, George Vagdon, and George Burkhart. Tailors were William Hoffman and Bernard Zeptner. Frank McFadden was tinner. Milliners were Kate Ault and Mrs. Adam Richter. William Hinebaugh and John L. Richter tanned animal hides. Melchoir Miller distilled whiskey. (His product was distributed from a Westernport warehouse under the name Melkey Miller Rye Whiskey.) Henry Zinkin and Adam Goehringer made wagons and buggies. William Englehart made coffins.

Accident blossomed.

Meanwhile, a few miles east of the town, southwest of Grantsville, another agricultural community began to take root in the lush Bittinger Glades, named after the settler Henry Bittinger, who bought and lived on a tract of land called Briar Patch between two forks of the Casselman River around 1814. "His new neighborhood was typical of Garrett County," wrote descendant and community historian Wayne Bittinger in 1974. "There were few people; the land was hilly, rocky, fertile, and thickly forested; there were severe winters, and both late and early frosts."

"The wild animals that preyed in the close bordering dense forests and laurel thickets near Bittinger, Maryland, from 1840 into the 50's, were plentiful," recorded the contemporary Leo J. Beachy. "The large gray timber wolves were plentiful throughout the county, and in some localities they kept up such a hideous howling at night that some folks got out of bed, took a tin horn and blew a loud blast" to scare the predators away. Early nineteenth century settlers of the Bittinger region include Henry and Catherine Buckle, George and Francis Stark, Peter and Catherine Lohr, and the families of John Beachy and Joseph Buckel. The Bittinger pioneers were all of English, Irish, and German descent.

The post office at Bittinger was established in 1885, with Josiah Bittinger serving as first postmaster. The village at that time was comprised of a half dozen homes, a general store, a shoemaker shop, two blacksmith shops, a cooper shop, a church, a school, and a one-room building used for making commercial cottage cheese. Bittinger was then in its heyday. Successive storekeepers were Peter Lohr, Fred Snyder, Will Engle, William Stark, and Tom Turney. Clarence Brenneman ran a harness and shoe repair shop. "Professor" W. A. Althers taught singing and violin. The Bittinger Election District was created on April 8, 1890.

The same year Henry Bittinger settled at Briar Patch, 1814, a man from Cumberland, William Ridgely, bought nearly five hundred acres of the Resurvey of Shawnee War tract located about three miles south of Grantsville, a few miles north of the Bittinger Glades. Eli Ridgely, of Frederick County, William's brother, was the first white settler of the area. Ridgely Hill is located less than a mile north of present-day Jennings on the Casselman River. Early Jennings settlers were sundry farmers of English, Irish, and German backgrounds. Jennings itself was named in the late 1800s after the

Pennsylvania railroad and timber capitalists Cord H. and Worth B. Jennings, whose commercial enterprises in the vicinity gave birth to the town.

Meshach Browning, writing in 1858 of his life at the Bear Creek Glades in the 1820s with Mary McMullen, noted that "by this time [around 1823] we had several new neighbors—Captain Campbell, from Frederick County, with his family, and son-in-law, James Cunningham; as also Dr. James McHenry of Baltimore, and John McHenry, who settled at Buffalo Marsh." Buffalo Marsh, located about six miles southwest of Bittinger, nearly the same distance directly south of Accident, "took its name," recorded Browning, "from the fact that the carcass of a large buffalo had been found in the deep mud of the marsh by the first white men who . . . ever set foot in that beautiful glade." The first white visitors of Buffalo Marsh were the Friend brothers. Charles settled there, near the Big Boiling Spring, prior to 1784. His brother, Augustine, later lived in Charles's abandoned cabin before finally moving to the Cheat River in Virginia. It was at Buffalo Marsh that Nicholas, the father of John, Charles, and Augustine Friend, lived his last days. His sons buried the patriarch in a hollow chestnut log near the Boiling Spring. His grave is now covered by the McHenry inlet of Deep Creek Lake.

A number of influential and prominent eastern Marylanders began to patent lands and establish homes in the green fertile glades surrounding Buffalo Marsh in the early nineteenth century. The wealthy Colonel John Lynn, a Revolutionary War veteran and noted federalist clerk of the Allegany County Court and 1796 presidential elector for John Adams, was the first of the elite to move to the Deep Creek mountain glades, settling at Cherry Creek Meadows, two miles east of Buffalo Marsh, prior to 1800.

In 1802 Captain William Campbell, a Scotch immigrant, wealthy Frederick County landowner, acquired nearly twenty-three thousand nearby acres, including half of the Wild Cherry Tree Meadows estate, from the Washington speculators Benjamin Stoddard and William Marbury. He bought the remaining half of Wild Cherry Tree Meadows in 1806. Ten years later he acquired the old John Lynn place.

Meanwhile, though, in 1808, Dr. James McHenry, a close personal and political friend of Colonel John Lynn and frequent summer visitor at Cherry Creek, bought almost thirteen thousand acres near Buffalo Marsh in partnership with Robert and John Oliver of Baltimore from the speculators Stoddard and Marbury. Two years later he acquired Locust Tree Bottom at the site of the Boiling Spring and the abandoned Friend cabin. "I like this country," he noted, "its salubrious air, its mild summers, its interesting views made up of hills, woods, glades, streams, and mountains; above all it delights me as affording at my time of life a salutary retirement from the busy world and its cares." During the Revolutionary War the Irish immigrant had been a surgeon and secretary to George Washington; he had served on General Lafayette's staff as major until 1781. After the war he had served in the Maryland senate and had attended the Constitutional Convention of 1787. He had held the position of secretary of war under two presidents—Washington and Adams. Fort McHenry in Baltimore is today his namesake. "I do not feel disposed to wander further [than Buffalo Marsh]," he wrote in 1810, "or to quit it in a hurry. Indeed did it quadrate with the interest of the whole of my family to fix here I should never move from the spot I am now on."

Although he usually spent only the summers in the Glade Country, McHenry remained the entire winter of 1812-13 due to poor health. His son, Daniel William, had moved to a log cabin near the Boiling Spring the prior year, shortly after his marriage. In 1813 Daniel McHenry was assessed in Allegany County with eleven slaves, six horses, thirteen cattle, and fifty-six ounces of silver plate. Like his father, he bought and patented numerous tracts of land in the area. "My cousin, John McHenry," he wrote a brother in 1811, "has always attended with me on my survey and we have both taken field notes."

John McHenry moved to the Glades from Baltimore in 1813, settling initially at Cherry Creek Meadows north of Deep Creek. In 1814 Daniel McHenry died from internal injuries after being thrown from a horse, and John subsequently moved to Buffalo Marsh to take over the family property. "I shall have a very comfortable log house [at Buffalo Marsh] when it is finished," he wrote a cousin in 1818. "... it is thirty-six feet front, two rooms below, and the same above, a passage through it with a staircase ... I am also preparing logs for a cattle shed fifty foot long with a good joint shingle roof ... fewer will die and it will be more to my profit."

John McHenry lived at Buffalo Marsh most of his life. In 1816 he wrote the scholarly *Treatise on the Law of Ejectments as Practiced in the Courts of Maryland* there. His library included one of the most extensive private book collections in the state. He cleared and worked his farm chiefly with slave labor. He loved the Alleghany highlands genuinely. "I was in Cumberland on the 4th of July," he wrote his cousin John in 1818. "I thought I should have been stewed in an oven ... when I returned from France, I thought the summer climate of Maryland was intolerable. When a kind providence conducted me to the Glades, I thought I had discovered a hidden treasure."

Buffalo Marsh, he wrote in 1820, is "a country almost unoccupied ... [there are] no peculiar customs, prejudices or manners that a new settler is obliged to accommodate himself to except treating the original settlers with kindness and civility, which will be reciprocated and received without the rude forwardness so common among the under classes in other quarters ... it is all real, or like Don Quixote, I am enchanted. There is no society at all here," he noted in 1810, "unless at the distance of 15 or 20 miles."

"If you could manage to give the Glades some e'clat," he suggested prophetically to his cousin James in 1817, "and make it a place of resort for the idle of our cities and those who are immersed in business, dust, and smoke during the greatest part of the year. If you could people the country even in summer, with transitory beings, the Allegany mountains would soon become the favorite haunts of pleasure and hilarity."

Though the Deep Creek Glades did not become a "favorite

haunt" for over a hundred years when the Deep Creek Dam was built in the 1920s for the manufacture of electricity, a few scattered travelers did make their way west to the mountains in search of pleasure in the early nineteenth century. One of these was the French-educated Frederick E. Skinner, a friend of the Marquis De LaFayette family and son of the American agricultural press pioneer John Stuart Skinner, who edited at various times *The American Farmer, The Plough, The Loom and The Anvil,* and *The American Turf Register.* Skinner was a guest of the McHenrys and the Campbells during the summer of 1834. He traveled west over the old Braddock Road to Little Crossings, then south to the Deep Creek Glade country.

"What first struck me with surprise," he wrote for Baltimore's *Turf, Field, and Farm,* "was that it did not look in the least like a mountainous region, the surface only rolling enough to give life and motion to the numerous crystal streams all swarming with trout and much resembling the best farming lands in Maryland and Pennsylvania." Skinner breathed deep of the "elastic, exhilerating mountain air," and then met the McHenrys and Augustine Friend. "Mr. McHenry," he noted, "for some occult reason . . . [has] chosen to bury himself in this wilderness utterly secluded from the possibility of congenial companionship." Skinner nevertheless ate ravenously of the local foods at the McHenry household. "A Maryland jowl with cabbage and turnip sprouts eaten after a long ride through that ozone-laden air of the Allegany Glades," he later recalled, "becomes the peer of the finest *pate de foie gras* ever made in Strasburg." The memorable Glades meal was followed with "post-brandial pipes" and "charming conversation."

Skinner found his friend William Campbell living "the year through" on "an immense body of land adjoining the properties of the Olives [Olivers] and Swanns in the heart of the Maryland and Virginia glades . . . with his young family, an eccentric but learned old Englishman, named Yaulding, the family tutor, and a few servants. Here he had accumulated land," noted the young visitor, "had all the essentials of comfort and even the refinements of civilized life in the depths of a great wilderness and here with his excellent wife and promising children he dwelt in happy seclusion far away from the outside world and its annoyances, where he could indulge to the full his ruling passion for the sports of the field." Skinner himself hunted grouse, deer, squirrels, rabbits, and wild turkeys before returning east. He also fished trout from the streams.

In 1827 James Cunningham, Scottish immigrant and son-in-law of William Campbell, resurveyed and bought more than seventeen thousand acres of the Chevoit Dale tract about five miles east of the Deep Creek Glades, just south of Bittinger. In later years he added other tracts in the Savage River Valley to his holdings. Among these were Richlands and The Pink of the Alleghanies. The Cunningham family, one of the wealthiest of the mountains, lived in a house called Palo Alto on an estate now part of the Pleasant Valley Recreational Park and 4-H Center. They cleared about five hundred acres of Chevoit Dale timberland with slave labor. Mrs. Cunningham had inherited seventy-five slaves from her family before leaving the mountains forever in the 1840s.

Francis Scott Key wrote "The Star Spangled Banner" in 1814 at Fort McHenry in Baltimore harbor. Dr. James McHenry, after whom the fort was named, died two years later at his suburban Baltimore home. Just prior to his death he had had a tract of land patented in western Maryland on Marsh Hill under the name Vale of Avoca in memory of the valley and river of his native Irish home. (McHenry's son Daniel died the same year from injuries sustained from a horse fall.) In 1820 his nephew John wrote a cousin from Buffalo Marsh that "we have lost our neighbors, Mr. & Mrs. Cunningham. . . . Dr. Brooke too talks of moving. . . . We shall soon be left alone. . . . The widow Lynn's old mansion remains still without a tennant." The exclusive society of the Deep Creek Glades dissipated beyond the mountain horizon by mid-century.

"John and Martha McHenry had no children," recorded the Garrett County historian Charles E. Hoye in 1956. "Locust Tree Bottom passed into other hands. The graveyard where McHenry's neighbors and negroes [as well as Mr. and

Mrs. McHenry themselves] are buried became an unsightly place of bushes and briars; a later owner had it cleared and plowed, so today it is unmarked except by a few depressions in the green sod."

In 1848 the pioneer William Glotfelty, of Swiss descent, settled on the Wild Cherry Tree meadow tract north of the McHenry homestead and farmed the land. Today his descendants own farms from McHenry to Bittinger. The McHenry Post Office was established in 1875.

Garrett County pioneer settlers were farmers, hunters, and herdsmen. They established their homes in the woods, cut the trees, farmed the land. They supplemented the products of the soil in their tables with the wild game of the forest. They built sawmills and gristmills and pastured large herds of cattle in the open glades. Eventually the glades were fenced, the wild game was thinned, and the farms thrived. Communities were established; schools and churches were built. Towns became centers of trade and social intercourse. The frontier was tamed. The westward course of empire took its way.

Ivan J. Miller, a Grantsville-area Mennonite historian, has distinguished three types of American pioneer: "The monied speculators who took up land to sell later as the community's economy developed, the roving trapper or hunter, and the substantial settlers who acquired their lands where they lived with their families and developed useful farms, homes and business." Though all three classes were instrumental in the development of present-day Garrett County, none was more significant than that of the "substantial settler," for it was he who actually tamed the land, who transformed it. The homesteader lived at the edge of a wilderness frontier and brought a new civilization to an old world.

The Garrett County pioneer settler generally sought the fulfillment of at least three conditions for the establishment of a wilderness homestead: an abundant water source, tillable slopes, and fertile soil. "Many of the early settlers found an abundance of water in the innumerable fine springs flowing in many localities," recorded Elwood S. Groves for the *Glades Star,* a local historical publication, in 1965. "Often," he noted, "they built their habitations near one. Some, settling on land otherwise suitable but with no spring, resorted to the dug well."

The Garrett pioneer settlers built their cabins of logs and clay, utilizing the archetypal architectural pattern first developed by Swedes living along the Delaware River in the seventeenth century. "There was general, mutual helpfulness on the part of all toward each other," recalled the Reverend D. A. Friend in 1920 of his childhood in the mountains, "and at house raisings, and barn raisings or grubbing, or log-rollings, or corn-huskings and the like, all the people came together against sun-up; the men would do the outside work and the women would make a quilt within, and prepare the meals for the workmen, and when the day's work was done, all the people, both young and old, would remain for a general good time and a social that often extended into the small hours of the night." Occasionally the homesteader would merely squat in the abandoned cabin of an earlier settler, as did John Spurgeon at Buffalo Marsh in 1791. "We had an excellent log cabin to live in," remembered Meshach Browning, Spurgeon's nephew, years later. "Augustine Friend had left a fine potato patch and garden, which we took possession of as our own, and no person objected to our claiming the premises."

Usually, though, the Garrett pioneer bought his plot from an earlier speculator and cleared the land himself, often with the aid of neighbors. The larger trees were frequently girdled and allowed to stand until the roots rotted and the trees fell. The smaller trees and brush were cut and grubbed with ax and mattock. Sometimes vast fires were started to clear expansive tracts. "The Allegany, as well as the surrounding mountains, are ruined by the practice of setting fire to them," recorded as a traveler through western Maryland in the late 1700s. "The destruction of the vast Allegany forests done by fire is not to be described by a pen." The fires were later controlled by state regulations.

Some Garrett settlers, such as the Friends, Tomlinsons, and Ashbys, were spared the toil of clearing forests for fields by the presence of the treeless highland glades. Most, however, were not so fortunate. The hemlock forest at Sunnyside was still so dense, when Samuel and Elizabeth Gnegy moved there in 1856, that the midday sun was totally obliterated from view. The land was nevertheless cleared. Fathers and sons and grandsons picked roots from the fields for fences. With grubbing hoes, shovel plows, and mattocks they turned the soil. They planted crops: corn, oats, and buckwheat. Wilderness became farmland; cabins became homes.

"Wheat was grown by older settlers who had land that could be plowed with a shovel plow and harrowed," recorded Isaac W. Thompson in the 1940s, recalling events in the life of his pioneer grandmother in the Youghiogheny Glades over a century earlier. "A thorn bush ten or twelve feet in diameter made a horse a good load, and did a lot of scratching. A boy could ride the horse and the bush wouldn't get fast on the stumps and roots. It was customary in those days when there was land to be cleared, all the children big enough had to do their part. The father and older boys did the chopping and grubbing; the girls had to pick and burn brush; also burn the log leaps after they had been rolled together by the men. Fire was carried from the house, even if it was a half mile away. No matches were in use. When they had a log heap burning, by keeping it chunked up, there would be fire for days."

E. E. Enlow, in 1946 (age eighty-six): "Each year a few more acres were grubbed, plowed, fenced and sown or planted and we had more corn and more buckwheat and oats, and a small field of timothy or clover. Soon my father disposed of his ox team and secured a horse, and later had two horses, several cows, a few sheep, some hogs, some chickens, some ducks, some geese, and guinea fowls." Garrett County pioneers lived with thrift and utmost economy.

Home building served as a social function as well as a necessity for these early pioneer settlers. When John Wirsing, a Methodist preacher, moved to the Bear Creek Glades in 1803, "The neighbors turned out in force," recalled Meshach Browning a half century later. "There was plenty to eat, and plenty of whiskey to drink and all the hunters were there." Twenty-two men worked two days to build a barn for

Browning at Sang Run in 1825. When the log house of Peter DeWitt near the mouth of Laurel Run on the Youghiogheny burned down in the 1850s, neighbors helped replace the structure in three days' time. Storekeeper Cornelius Friend supplied the whiskey, suggesting each day that none be drunk until the day's work was completed.

"Groups of men would gather for house and barn raisings and other activities needing concerted effort," recorded Garrett historian Dennis T. Rasche in 1957. "They would bring their families for the day; it would be a social event. News and ideas would be exchanged. Other such gatherings would be for corn huskings and making maple sugar and syrup. In due time a log meeting house would be built in which to worship, and after the service the settlers would again meet as friends and neighbors."

The homes of early Garrett settlers were built of logs and chinked with clay. Roofing shingles were originally made from oak and pine with drawing knives. In the early 1860s Wright Thayer and William Frazee Enlow engaged in the business of making and selling handmade pine shingles from their homes near Deep Creek on the Oakland-Friendsville Road. Others also engaged in the business as communities grew and demand increased. Homesteads developed into farms complete with houses, barns, springhouses for the cooling of dairy products, and sundry other outbuildings. Sawmills were built for the cutting of timber.

Philip Hare opened Garrett County's first water-powered, up-and-down-sash sawmill in the 1790s on Meadow Run about two miles north of Little Meadows. Around 1815 Jesse Tomlinson built a mill at Little Crossings, and disposed of his lumber along the National Road. David Hoffman also built a mill in the early 1800s at the later site of Selbysport. Then, in 1820, Elias Kerr erected one equipped for furniture making near the Mason-Dixon Line on Bear Camp Run. Within a half century seven additional sawmills were founded along the stream by Abraham Miller, Benjamin Griffith, Hiram Guard, Hiram Griffith, John Speelman, John McCleary, and Adam Sembower. The stream itself became known as Mill Run.

Around 1825 Murray Thayer built a grist and sawmill for Isaac McCarty on the Little Youghiogheny at the foot of present-day Water Street in Oakland. Captain William Campbell erected a sawmill on Cherry Creek in 1826. In 1837 a Pennsylvania man named Williams built later Garrett County's first steam sawmill on Red Run about two miles north of the National Road. "A steam sawmill was then as much of a sight as [is] Barnum's big show now," suggested the Grantsville historian Jacob Brown in 1888.

At least four sawmills were built north of the National Pike in the 1840s by J. H. Hoblitzell, Meshach Frost (founder of Frostburg), Joshua Johnson, and a man named Kreebs. At the same time Frost and a man named Wright operated mills at the Shades of Death just east of Grantsville. In the 1850s John Swauger opened a mill at New Germany. Around 1870 William Ashby built one on Snowy Creek at Sunshine. The town of Crellin later grew up as a lumbering community on the site.

The white men came to Garrett County and built sawmills in the early nineteenth century. They left their axe marks on the trees. They founded farms and grew wheat.

"Rye, buckwheat, and corn were the staples," noted Jacob Brown. "Wheaten flour was reserved for holidays, pies, etc." The grain was sowed by hand in soil prepared by hoes and shovel plows, and spike and spring-tooth harrows. Horses provided extra power. The shovel plow eventually gave way to the moldboard plow, but the harrows remained.

"The cutting and curing of hay afforded us a fine frolic," recalled Meshach Browning in 1859. "I used to take two sons with me, and also one of my daughters to cook for us; and having two scythes, we would mow enough grass in the evening of the day we first went out, to make a good stack the next morning. I seldom killed less than from four to six deer during one haymaking trip while the boys would be fishing for trout."

Farmers sowed grain in the spring. They made hay in the summer. In autumn they harvested. They reaped their crops by hand with sickles and cradles, and bound their grain into sheaves and shocks for drying. They customarily served their farmhands and generous neighbors whiskey or hard cider in appreciation for harvesttime aid. They threshed their grains on open barn floors by hand with flails. "Our next step was to sweep the grain and hulls into a pile and place our windmill by its side," recorded E. E. Enlow, "and then while one of us turned the crank of the wheel on the windmill another would scrape up the grain and hulls and place them in the hopper of the windmill in which the chaff was blown out and the grain went through a sieve into a receptacle. Another way of threshing was to tramp the grain out. I was a mighty proud boy one season when one of our neighbors who had much buckwheat and a large threshing floor had me ride a fine stallion and guide several other horses around and around over his extra ripe buckwheat spread out over the barn floor while two or three men with forks were turning the buckwheat over and over. I felt that I was surely doing a major part of the work."

Water-powered flour mills were erected throughout the county in the early 1800s for the conversion of grain into meal. "These early mills were the center of the community activities," noted local historian Paul T. Calderwood in 1971. Not only were they "meeting places for the exchange of news, both local and distant," but they also served as area trading posts where local settlers exchanged part of their produce, as well as venison, bear meat, and animal skins, for manufactured goods, in the absence of abundant cash. Due to the scarcity of money, in fact, the Garrett millers of the early nineteenth century customarily retained a portion of grain from each bushel brought in as a standard "toll" for their services.

Dennis T. Rasche described the operation of early Garrett County gristmills in 1958. "The grain passed over two screens," he wrote, "one coarse, the other finer. There were shallow box-like frames screened on the bottom, geared to the moving machinery so as to be kept in a vibrating motion and slightly inclined to keep the ground particles moving toward the lower end. The screened meal was then carried to an upper floor and fed into a revolving barrel-shaped frame with sides of bolting cloth, this also turning on an inclined axis."

"Little was thought in those days of the time consumed and distance traveled going to a mill," wrote Rasche. "One instance is recorded of a young boy riding thirty miles each way leading a string of grain-laden pack horses." Flour mills were necessities to early settlers.

The earliest of the Garrett County gristmills was erected near the mouth of Bear Camp Run, later Mill Run, in the Sandy Creek Glades around 1774. Its builder was Jacob Froman, a Hollander, whose name had been Anglicized from the Dutch Vrooman. The Froman Mill, the first of two flour mills, eight sawmills, and one woolen factory to be built in the nineteenth century on Mill Run, featured an overshot water wheel and a mechanical blower for winnowing.

Jesse Tomlinson built the first gristmill near Little Meadows around 1795. This mill was rebuilt in 1856 by Perry Shultz and deeded to William Stanton in 1862. Stanton's son, Eli, later operated it for forty-three years. The Stanton enterprise at Grantsville is still in operation today; operated by Stanton descendants.

A gristmill was erected at the present-day site of Swanton in 1797. Moses Tichenal built one at the mouth of Savage River prior to 1800. Thomas Wilson built the original Kitzmiller mill in 1802. (The town itself was subsequently named after Wilson's son-in-law, Ebenezer Kitzmiller.)

David Hoffman opened the first Selbysport gristmill in 1805 on the south side of the Old Morgantown Road near the Youghiogheny River. The combined grist and sawmill opened by Murray Thayer around 1825 on the Little Youghiogheny at the later site of Oakland was the first in a succession of three gristmills to operate in the vicinity of present-day Water Street. (The most recent owner of a Water Street gristmill was Michael V. Kildow.)

The Ashby gristmill built near Sunshine in the 1820s or 1830s featured a unique undershot water wheel. A Mr. Hershberger built another Yough Glades gristmill around the same time along the Little Youghiogheny about a mile and a half west of Deer Park. Meshach Browning built a mill at Sang

Run around 1826. "Within six months I had my mill running," he wrote, "and grinding all the grain raised in the neighborhood. This was a great convenience to the people, whose children had formerly to go ten miles to mill, in all weathers." The Browning mill cost over four hundred dollars and was constructed only through an agreement with neighbor William Campbell to build a local sawmill at the same time.

"Lightfoot" John Durst built a Little Thunder gristmill in a pine woods at the headwaters at Blue Lick in 1831. Subsequent owners of mills in the area included John Layman, Jacob Swartzengraber, and Jesse W. Chaney. Engle's gristmill appeared near Accident on Bear Creek in 1835. A second Bear Creek flour mill was erected below Engle's in 1868 by Henry Kaese. (The Kaese mill still stands.) Weller's Flour Mill was built shortly afterward on the south branch of Bear Creek about one-half mile below present-day Route 219.

According to Jacob Brown, a number of gristmills were erected between the years 1835 and 1855 in the Grantsville area. At the same time, Peter Speelman rebuilt the Froman Mill on Bear Camp Run and became the first of its three generations of Speelman operators. Around 1850 Adam Sembower erected a gristmill about three miles upriver from the old Froman operation. In 1859 John Swauger opened a mill on Poplar Lick Run at New Germany.

Early nineteenth century Garrett County gristmills served vital functions in self-subsistent agrarian frontier communities. Forests were cleared, farmsteads were opened, fields were plowed, grain was produced, and the settlers provided their families with daily bread. Only trips to the gristmill required departure from the farm.

"The early settlers," recalled Meshach Browning in 1859, "being but few in number, had a hard time to maintain themselves; and had they not used the greatest economy, they could not have lived in the wilderness at all." Thus they built their own homes, grew their own grain, procured their own meat, produced their own clothing and furniture, shod their own horses, and paid for grist services with tolls from their own produce.

"All the settlers lived in cabins," noted Browning, "and fed their children on bread, meat, butter, honey, and milk; coffee and tea were almost out of the question." John McHenry, of Buffalo Marsh, wrote to a cousin in 1819 to describe the scarcity of luxury items. "The provision I laid in when I was in Baltimore," he observed, "of coffee, tea and sugar is now nearly exhausted. There is no means of getting a supply at Cumberland. I must depend on your goodness." Meat, nevertheless, "was generally plenty," suggested Browning, "for if the farmers could only keep the wild animals aways from their hogs, the nuts and acorns would make them very fat. Pork, beef, bearmeat and venison were easily obtained and on fair terms."

The Oakland merchant J. M. Davis reflected in 1906 on the innovative home economies necessitated by early Garrett County pioneer life. "The modern conveniences were unknown," he recalled. "For instance—matches were not manufactured, and fire was obtained by the use of flint and punk, or by shooting powder into a bunch of tow, or by going to a neighbor's house and carrying a chunk of fire to the home. The writing was done with a pen made from a goose quill. Envelopes were unknown; a sheet of paper was folded and sealed with wax. Sand was used to dry the ink instead of a blotter. Tallow candles supplied light for the home and church. Brooms were made from young growth hickory and known as split brooms. The introduction of cooking stoves was perhaps during the years between 1840 and 1845. Prior to this, our mothers cooked in an open fireplace."

Money currency was an especially scarce commodity in the early nineteenth century highlands. "In those times," noted Jacob Brown, "it is safe to say one-fourth of the currency was spurious—'bogus' as it was called." The pioneer farmer could fortunately produce nearly all his own food and the materials needed for the production of clothing. Commodities such as salt, tea, coffee, kerosene, and sugar, and services such as hired labor usually required payment in money, though. "Plain people in the country in most of their transactions would have some special understanding about the kind of money they were to receive," recalled Brown in

1896. " 'Hard money' would bring by 10 to 15 percent more than the soft stuff."

"If any man wished to hire help," recorded Meshach Browning in 1859, "the parties would have an understanding as to what the wages were to be paid in. Sometimes linsey, pork, beef, honey, or corn, and at others a calf, pig, sheep, deerskin, bearskin, coonskin, or a wolf's scalp, together with many other articles, were used as substitutes for money." Wolf scalps were redeemable for state bounties. Farm labor in the mid-nineteenth century cost about seven dollars a month. Harvest hands were usually paid fifty cents a day. Cows sold for ten dollars apiece, sheep for a dollar and a half, horses for thirty-five to fifty dollars. The price of wheat and corn averaged fifty cents per bushel; oats by the bushel sold for twenty cents.

Garrett County pioneer settlers lived frugal lives in a wilderness setting. They clothed themselves simply in buckskin and wool. They sheared sheep in springtime then carded the wool into rolls for spinning into yarn. They knitted their own socks, mittens, sweaters, scarves, caps, and rugs. They made their own shoes. "If a man wore a pair of boots," observed Meshach Browning, "he was considered a gentleman; and if a single lady had on a pair of calfskin shoes, or, by chance, a pair of morocco, she was at once declared a belle."

They ate the produce of their own toil, wild game procured from the woods, berries picked from the hillsides, honey from wild hives, maple sugar boiled down from sap. They washed their laundry on metal washboards and made soap from fat and water "leached" through wood ashes. They butchered in great iron kettles in the fall, smoked and salted their meat, and made apple butter in large copper kettles over open fires.

The early settlers were jacks-of-all-trades. John L. Hook of Friendsville manufactured hundreds of wool and flax wheels, weaving looms, and spinning wheels. Jacob Herring produced tubs, kegs, buckets, and barrels. William E. Friend, grandson of John Friend, operated a metal foundry in Friendsville in mid-nineteenth century composed of a large two-forge blacksmith shop, a general finishing shop, and several outbuildings.

He based his reputation in brass and copper, iron and steel, and produced, with the aid of journeymen, such goods as brass and copper castings, axes, hatchets, drawknives, and rifles decorated with silver and brass mountings. "I have stood by and watched him as he would be proving one of his new rifles," later recalled the Reverend D. A. Friend, "and he would fasten it in a vice that it might be absolutely steady, and fire at a target fifty steps away, and he would change and adjust the sights of that gun until it would drive the center at every shot, before it was allowed to leave his shop."

Pioneer farmers especially were proficient in the trades. Peter Gortner at Sunnyside made weather vanes, flax and spinning wheels, hand lathes, work benches, chairs, beds, sleds, plows, harrows, wagons, and coffins. Samuel Gnegy made wooden keelers for the collection of maple sap and pine shingles for roofing, as well as various pieces of furniture: bedsteads, tables, benches, and stools. His wife, Elizabeth, like Mary Browning and most other pioneer women, was proficient with the loom, spinning wheel, and knitting needles. She also cooked, washed, canned, butchered, and sewed.

Blacksmith shops and tanneries were almost as important to early Garrett County settlers as were gristmills. The Boyer tannery at Accident began producing cured hides around 1800. Subsequent Accident tanners included Daniel Hinebaugh and John and Adam Richter. Joseph Frantz began tanning at Selbysport in 1805. In 1853 Jacob Rhodes Schaeffer operated a tannery at Gorman. Blacksmith shops were common to all early Garrett County settlements.

Due to an extreme scarcity of trained doctors, the highland settlers of the early nineteenth century relied on "yarb" teas and home remedies for the alleviation of medical problems. William Wiland of New Germany enjoyed for many years a local reputation as a cancer specialist with a secret family remedy composed of twenty-one ingredients derived from wild roots and herbs. Settlers plaqued by goiter wore nutmeg around their necks in small bags; those bothered by leg cramps crossed their shoes one over the other under their beds at night. Small spiders sealed in thimbles with wax and worn suspended from the neck in cloth bags prevented, supposedly, respiratory ills, while cobwebs and chewing tobacco were known to be good astringents for cuts.

The pioneers relieved side pains by spitting three times on the undersides of flat rocks, and rid themselves of unwanted freckles by washing their faces with dew before sunrise on May Day. They applied dirty dishrags to warts, and then buried the rags under drips from the eaves of their homes in the dark of the moon. Parents also informed children that back peddlers had power to cure warts through purchase. Meshach Browning recorded an early remedy for snakebites. "Gather the weed called boneset, or St. Anthony's cross, boil a handful of it in new milk, drink the milk, and bind the weed on the wound. Also, drink from a pint to a quart of whiskey. The best preventive, however, is to wear strong boots, or coarse leggings, through which the snakes cannot sink their teeth into the flesh."

An 1834 advertisement in the *Maryland Advocate* made the following announcement: "Dr. William J. R. Brook, having located himself in the Flat Woods settlment [south of Accident], offers his professional services to the inhabitants of the surrounding country. He may generally be found at Mrs. Drane's or the vicinity thereof." Dr. Brook relocated in Petersburg, Pennsylvania, the following year. In 1856 Dr. David R. Welfly began practicing medicine at Accident. Dr. E. H. Glotfelty took up practice there in 1870. Dr. William Frye became the first general medical practitioner at Selbysport in the 1830s. The first doctor at Grantsville was John H. Patterson, who located there in 1842. "Never had $10 worth of medicine on hand at one time," noted Jacob Brown, "but he always had something as a remedy and never lost a curable case." Dr. Patterson died in 1852 and was followed in his Grantsville medical practice by Drs. M. A. and R. F. Carr and a Dr. Herman. Dr. Bayard T. Keller practiced medicine there for ten years in the 1860s, then relocated in Oakland before moving to Ohio. Early Garrett County doctors were few and far between.

The Garrett County pioneer settler lived under constant threat of injury or loss through natural calamity and wild animal predation. The year 1816 was known as the "year without summer" in the highlands. The *Baltimore Sun* reported frost or snow every month that year as far south as the Potomac River. More than nine feet of undrifted snow accumulated in February of 1852 in the Garrett timberlands. The month of June in 1855 was swept in on the tail of a severe snowstorm. In a remarkable display of ingenuity, a young Grantsville couple saved their wheat crop from destruction by frost in late June 1859 by rising before daybreak and crisscrossing their fields with a length of clothesline, brushing the frost from the tips of their plants. (Their harvest provided the neighbors with the necessary seed for the next planting season.)

Wild animals also threatened early Garrett settlers with injury and destruction. John McHenry noted in 1817 that "Since last fall seven of my cows died, and of forty-one sheep I can now only count twenty-eight; the wolves killed five of them." Meshach Browning concurred. "The sheep gave me more trouble than all the rest," he wrote, "for if they happened to be out of their pen only one night, it was ten chances to one that the wolves killed at least one of them." "Bears," noted McHenry, "were likewise very fond of fat hogs and kill many in the course of the summer." And, of course, there were always the rattlesnakes. Tom Paugh, of Elk Lick Run, a noted story teller and jester, often claimed that during a single day of haying in the early 1800s the snakes were so numerous in his fields that, even protected with a butcher knife held in each hand, he had returned to his home at nightfall with two bushels of snake heads still clinging to the protective ropes wrapped around his legs.

"The most dangerous [of the glade country reptiles]," reflected Meshach Browning in 1859, "is the rattlesnake; which lives by its cunning, and can charm birds, squirrels, rabbits, mice, chickens, etc. I have slain my thousands without even having been bitten by one. I was at all times prepared to receive their attacks; for before leaving home I always took hay, or long grass, and twisted it into a large rope, with which I wrapped my legs up to the knee; and this they would never bite through. When thus provided, I would go where I pleased in daytime; but being afraid they would creep to me in the night, if I was where I thought they were numerous, I would stuff leaves round my legs, inside of my pants, and sleep with my moccasins on; and making my dog lay down, I would lay my head on him; knowing that then no snake or animal could take me by surprise. Both ends being thus fortified, I could sleep as comfortably as if I had been in the most secure house and on the best bed in a city." Garrett County pioneers were a rough and tough breed of frontier settler.

They were also plagued—these settlers—at times, with vast flocks of grain-eating pigeons. In 1872 the passenger pigeons here were so numerous that they broke thousands of tree limbs at roosting time and darkened the sky in flight. They practically disappeared, though, by 1875.

Early Garrett game was much reduced by 1850 as a result of the development of farmland and extensive pioneer indulgence in hunting. Meshach Browning was perhaps the most renowned of all early Garrett highland hunters. In the fall and winter of 1858-59 he wrote the classic autobiographical *Forty-four Years of the Life of a Hunter* by candlelight at Sang Run with a quill pen. His great-great-great-great-grandfather, Captain John Browning, had emigrated to Virginia from England in 1621, only fourteen years after the founding of the first permanent English settlement in the New World at Jamestown. His grandfather, William, and father, Joshua, had served under George Washington's command in the 1755 expedition against Fort Duquesne and were present at General Edward Braddock's defeat. Browning himself moved to later Garrett County in 1791 as a small boy with an aunt and an uncle who squatted for a year in the abandoned cabin of Augustine Friend at Buffalo Marsh, before moving to Blooming Rose. He hunted in the highlands every season for a period of forty-four years.

"When the birds began to warble their sweet notes among the trees," he wrote, "the trap, the dog, and the gun, came freshly into memory. I set the boys at the ploughs, while I traversed the woods. . . .

"As I had no other way of procuring our winter's provisions, I went hunting. When the hunting season was over, which lasts till the first day of January, I took my skins and traded them for a sufficient quantity of grain to last until spring. I could sell deerskins at any time in the old settlement, for in those days many men, and almost all the boys, wore buckskin pants and hunting shirts, which made skins bring a good price. By this means I raised money, paid for my land and had something left over for the family, besides being able to hire a hand in a pinch of work."

Meshach Browning dressed much as did other early Garrett hunters after the departure of the native Indians. Neighbors and acquaintances usually found him clothed in homemade moccasins; hand-knitted woolen socks; trousers, and hunting shirts made of homespun cloth woven by hand from home-produced wool; and a fur cap of raccoon or bearskin. He was a tall, weathered, sturdy man with a firm chin and heavy dark brows. His hunting gear included the standard flintlock rifle (Browning's is now on display at the Smithsonian in Washington), powder horn, bullet pouch, hunting knife, punk, flint, and steel for making fires, and tomahawk. He estimated that during the course of his forty-four-year highland hunting career, which took him through the forests and glades of every section of present-day Garrett County, he killed from eighteen hundred to two thousand deer, from three to four hundred bears, about fifty panthers and catamounts, and scores of wolves and wildcats. "During this time," he wrote, "I think I found out as much about the nature and habits of the wild animals of the Alleganies as any other man, white, red, or black, who ever hunted in those regions."

"The harder the fight the better I like the fun," he noted. "In many cases I killed [bears] with my knife; but only when the fight was so close that I was afraid to shoot, lest I should kill a dog." Once, accompanied by Charles and John Friend, he killed a hibernating bear in its den in the Land Flowing with Milk and Honey glades near Swallow Falls. "Charley tied his rope to my ankles," he remembered, "so that he could pull me out when I shot, and I went down to the mouth of the hole [and] entered a large room with my wax candle on the end of a pole before me. I had to crawl on my hands and feet till I saw in one corner of the room a black lump, which resembled a large sugar kettle turned bottom upwards. This I knew to be the bear. I put the gun to his head and finished him."

In the fall of 1819 Browning killed a large buck with his knife in the swirling waters of the Youghiogheny after a savage hand-to-horn wrestling match with the animal in which he nearly lost his life. In later years he caught deer by hand in snowstorms for a park at his home near Sang Run. He often spent as much as a week at a time alone in the forest miles from his home and family. "It was dark," he wrote vividly of one night's particularly memorable experience, "and a heavy cloud was coming up with thunder and lightning, and every appearance of a dreadful storm. Seeing a large fallen tree, I took poles, and, laying one end of each on the ground, I placed the others on the log, and spread my bear's skin over them, with the greasy side upwards. . . . By the time I had seated myself under my shelter, the rain was pouring down in torrents, accompanied by vivid lightning, and such appalling peals of thunder that the earth seemed to tremble under me. Two trees were torn into splinters within a few rods of my lodge."

The largest turkey Meshach Browning ever killed weighed twenty-six pounds, after it was cleaned. In 1797 he killed the largest panther of his career. The beast measured "eleven feet three inches from the end of his nose to the tip of his tail. I took from this fellow sixteen and a half pounds of rendered tallow. It is somewhat softer than mutton tallow, but by mixing it with one-fourth of its weight of bees wax, it makes good candles."

"When hearing a turkey gobble close to me," Browning wrote, "I spoke a few words in the turkey language. In a minute he came to see, as he thought, a new sweetheart; but the crack of my gun convinced him of his error."

"The bear," he wrote, "is a bold, undaunted beast, though not apt to pick quarrels with other animals; but if any others trespass on its rights, it then becomes furious and vindictive. I love and admire the bear, because it desires to insult neither man nor beast, nor will it suffer any to insult it." Browning trapped the bruin as frequently, almost, as he hunted it. "To entice the bears," he recorded, "I used to roast the leg of a deer, and while the meat was roasting, rub honey over it, so that it would smell strong of the latter. Then I would cut off pieces, tie them under my moccasins, walk through the grounds the bears frequented, and return to the trap; when every bear which smelled my tracks would follow the trail to the trap, and generally get caught."

"The panther," he wrote, "although possessed of great strength, perhaps fully equal to that of the bear, is a most dastardly coward; and will suffer itself to be driven into a tree by a half grown dog, when one snap of its teeth, or a single blow from its paw, would forever silence the dog. The panther is a great sneak."

Browning considered the wolf, "beyond all other animals, the most cunning." It is "next in strength and size, but far more cunning and mischievous then the panther," he noted. "It is seldom seen during day-light, but in the night it is mischievous, as well as impudent.... A premium of eight dollars was paid for his head by the county, and this sum [I] set apart for Mary to buy wares for her dresser."

Browning occasionally hunted deer at night on Deep Creek. "I would take the canoe up the creek in the evening," he wrote, "and be ready to drift down as the deer entered the water; all the time setting unobserved under the shade of the bank, though I could in that position see to shoot by the light of the candle." One night he "started down the stream after deer, discovering along the route otter, muskrats, ducks, and even hundreds of trout, as they jumped out of the water." He subsequently "waded into the water, hip and thigh, with a piece of venison for bait [and] just as fast as I could bait my hook, and let it into the water, I pulled out the largest kind of trout. I gathered up what I had caught and counted forty-seven."

The Grantsville historian Jacob Brown referred to Meshach Browning as "a farmer by occupation, but a hunter from taste, or rather passion." His contemporary Richard Fairall of

Accident noted that he "was among the first settlers here, and is one of Nature's noblest works."

"He lived to an extreme old age," commented the critic Rebecca Harding in a review of his autobiography, "and told the history of his life shortly, before he died [in autumn, 1859], in the rude, marrowy pioneer's vernacular. It fills a certain gap in American literature, being not only a picture in detail of the savage youth through which every one of the states has passed in turn, but of a man of the woods, simple and honest as Esau, in whom the senses and the hunting instinct were as keen and strong as in a sleuth-hound."

"As I lingered over his thrilling descriptions of the wilder portions of the deep, frightful and illimitable forest through which he hunted," suggested Colonel William Kilgour, the "Silver-Tongued Orator of Montgomery County," in 1902 "I could not but feel that vast, unbroken and indescribable solitudes ... magnificent sunsets bathing in flood of light the ragged cliffs of the innumerable chains and spurs of mountains; the gloomy grandeur of the deep shadows creeping down the mountainside, the music of the streams as they went dashing down the dark and almost inpenetrable ravines ... the mighty roar of the winds ... the low murmurs of sinking blasts."

"The short and simple annals of the poor were never better told," contended F. P. Blair, who wrote the original introduction to the Browning book in 1859, "nor [were] the difficulties which beset them in struggling into civilization in the midst of a wilderness." Neither were they ever "more graphically portrayed," he suggested.

Garrett County pioneer hunters, like the Indians before them, took to the woods through both necessity and choice. As early as 1783 they established temporary works at John Friend's cave near Sang Run for the purpose of manufacturing gunpowder from salt peter. Augustine Friend, brother of John, was among the earliest of the white highland Garrett hunters. The traveling German, Eric Bollman, breakfasted at Augustine's cabin near Swallow Falls in 1796 on his journey west over the old Warrior Indian Path and later described his host, "If ever Adam existed," he wrote in German, "he must have looked like this Teen Friend. I never saw such an illustration of perfect manhood, large, strong and brawny; every limb in magnificent proportion, energy in every movement and strength in every muscle, his appearance was the expression of manly independence, contentment and intelligence. His conversation satisfied the expectations which it awakened. With gray beard, 60 years old, 40 of which he had spent in the mountains, and of an observing mind, he could not find it difficult to agreeably entertain people who visited for information. He is a hunter by profession. I cannot abstain from believing that the manly effort which must be put forth in the hunt, the boldness which it requires, the keen observation which it encourages, the dexterity and activity which are necessary to its success, act together more forcibly for the development of the physical and mental strength than any other occupation."

The writer F. G. Skinner visited John McHenry and William Campbell at Buffalo Marsh thirty-seven years later and found the old hunter, then about ninety-five years of age, still enjoying good health. "Augustine Friend," he wrote, "is one of the most extraordinary men I ever beheld—a small bright little fellow made up apparently of skin, muscle and bone with an eye like a hawk. For big game such as bear, deer and wolves, he was still the most successful hunter in all that district. He was a great favorite with Campbell and they were on familiar terms and hunted much in company."

Other early nineteenth century Garrett County hunters of note included John and Henry Sines, Holmes Wiley, "Lightfoot" John Durst, and Christian Garlitz. "Garlitz in his nature and character [like the other hunters] was strong, decided, emphatic and industrious," recorded Jacob Brown of Grantsville. "In hunting he had no superior in this or Allegany County, unless it was Meshach Browning. Old 'Christly' carried his rifle and manipulated his traps for forty seasons, and only gave them up when infirmity and waning of his favorite game compelled him. Deer, bears, panthers, and wolves were his staples, and he hardly ever condescended to anything smaller. Sometimes he would take a hand in reducing the number of such 'varmints' as wild cats, catamounts, foxes and coons. He killed a great many deer in his time, but only enough for his table and such as he could conveniently sell. He never would slay this beautiful animal wantonly, or out of season. But he was the untiring foe of the bear, panther, and the wolf—the latter he hated the worst. (Like Meshach Browning) Christly had a story or anecdote for any place, time or situation, nearly always of his own experience. No one dared exceed him."

Buffalo, elk, panthers, bears, wolves, catamounts—all were the quarry of early glade country hunters; nearly all disappeared from the highland hills by 1850. The Friend brothers shot a buffalo at the mouth of Sang Run in the late 1700s. One of the sons of William Ashby shot two of the last four buffalo ever seen in the county a few years later on a hill southeast of present-day Crellin. Thousands of bison had grazed in herds in the highland glades in the seventeenth century; by the nineteenth century none remained.

Christopher Gist shot an elk at Little Meadows in 1751. In the early 1800s Gabriel Friend shot one along the Youghiogheny River near present-day Friendsville. William Wiles killed seven in one day in the upper Youghiogheny Glades. Christian Garlitz later shot one near the headwaters of Savage River. "This was the last of the race in this country," recorded Jacob Brown, "but their immense antlers in early times were frequently found."

"The country abounds in panthers," wrote Meshach Browning of the 1791 Deep Creek Glades. By 1850 nearly all were dead. "Bears are not so numerous now in the glades as when forty years ago old Steen Friend killed three in one day," noted William Campbell in 1834. "In fact I have seen but two in the five years that I have been living here."

Trout and rattlesnakes were also greatly depleted in number by early nineteenth century Garrett settlers. "The Alleganies have been famous for trout, and there are great numbers there at this time," observed Meshach Browning in 1859, but "they have been much reduced by residents from other states, who with seines catch them in great quantities, and leave on the ground all that are considered too small for use." The poisonous rattlesnakes were even less fortunate.

They "are now greatly diminished in numbers, as they are always destroyed when seen," Browning observed in writing his book. "They are now comparatively rarely seen, except in a few localities difficult of access, or near their dens."

The wild game of early Garrett lured increasing numbers of sportsmen from the cities to the highlands in the early 1800s. Often the city hunters stayed at local farm homes. "Everybody, in all the country round, was acquainted with everybody else," reflected the Rev. D. A. Friend in 1920, "and if a stranger came into the neighborhood he was entertained free by the people and soon formed an acquaintance with all the folks in the place." Meshach Browning concurred. "The people in the country west of Cumberland were exceedingly generous," he wrote, "and particularly so to strangers traveling through their territory. If there was danger apprehended of a stranger losing his way, a hunter would pilot him five, six, or even ten miles, until he was out of danger of being lost and then would not receive any compensation for his services."

So many sportsmen visited the Youghiogheny Glades in the early nineteenth century that Isaac McCarty added extra rooms to his house for their accommodation. "We can come here at any time," suggested William Campbell, "and get a wild turkey with nearly as much certainty as we could a tame one in a barnyard."

While hunters came to the highlands in the early 1800s to kill the wild game of the forest, other persons from the eastern valleys came to graze domestic animals on the wide open ranges of Garrett glade grass. These were the herders. Eric Bollman noted as early as 1796 that "many hundred head of cattle are driven yearly from the South Branch and entrusted to the care of the people who live here."

"There were then hundreds, if not thousands, of acres of grass growing where there is now nothing but bushes, and a rough and very inferior kind of grass, which serves very well for early pasture, but is of very little worth for hay," observed Meshach Browning over half a century later. "Men of other States, but first those of Virginia, becoming acquainted with our glades were so much delighted with these unbounded pasture-lands that they prevailed on some of the settlers to herd large quantities of cattle in them, for which they paid from fifty to seventy-five cents per head. This soon being discovered by Pennsylvanians, they followed the example of Virginia; and from April to September they crowded the glades with hundreds and thousands of cattle, eating, tramping, and running over every place in the glade country."

The herders "were at all times in the glades," Browning recalled, "calling and whooping at the cattle, besides shooting at the deer and other game, until the [wild] animals became alarmed, and all the best of those that were not suckling fawns abandoned the glades and hid on the mountains.... After the lapse of a few years, the same plan of herding (as had prevailed before) was again put in operation, with more ruinious consequences than before; and it resulted in the almost entire destruction of all the grass and game in the country, and the loss of many [local] cattle, which have been driven off with the foreign stock. Nobody was benefited by the operation but the owners of the herded cattle, and a great injury has been done to the settlers in the glade country."

Local herders included William Williams Ashby, Jonathan Wilson, John Arnold, Daniel McHenry, John Lynn, Israel Thompson, Peter Gortner, and John M. Davis. The destructive results of their vocation so disgusted the pioneer Charles Friend that he abandoned his highland hunting grounds and moved west to Missouri. Other settlers remained and retaliated.

The "cruel practice was carried on until the neighboring settlers became so much annoyed at it that they petitioned the legislature to pass some law or laws, for their relief," noted Meshach Browning, "but, unhappily, no law was ever enacted which could prevent the practice, and the people, seeing themselves still imposed on, and the laws made for their benefit and relief entirely disregarded, rose, and went to the glades in the night, and there attacked and shot numbers of the cattle; and no doubt they would have shot the herders also if they attempted to rescue their stocks."

The herders uttered defensive threats and warnings. "I wonder what old man Calmes would think if he missed one of his slaves," suggested William Williams Ashby to the neighbor of a man who had instructed his servants to stampede herds grazing near his farm, "if he missed one of his slaves, and, upon going to hunt for him, found the slave all swelled up and lying in the grass." One day soon afterward Ashby found a threatening notice nailed to a tree: *Indian War on Arnold, Ashby and Wilson.* The partners discovered over a hundred of their herd dead of gunshot near Herrington Creek a few days later and subsequently abandoned their grazing project. Meshach Browning recorded that, "This, in a great measure, put a stop for some years to the herding of foreign cattle, but not until the game was seriously threatened."

The pioneer farmers, hunters, and herders of western Allegany County transformed the highland plateau from a wild, open region of unbroken forests and glades to a land dotted with plowed fields and crisscrossed with split-rail fences. A land of elks, panthers, and bears became a land of grain, cattle, and sheep. The hunters thinned the game; the cattlemen opened the ranges; the farmers fenced the fields. In the end, the farmers won. They endured, they worked, they sweated, they prevailed. Garrett became a patchwork land of small agrarian communities.

As the communities of Garrett grew, the pioneer settlers established churches and schools for the transference of their culture and the social retention of their values and norms. "Schools and churches were the centers around which the social life of the community revolved," according to Ross C. Durst, local historian. The same log buildings usually housed both secular and religious gatherings; the functions of church and state were seldom distinguished in matters of education. Both were private in terms of funding; state subsidization was unknown, unheard of, unexpected, unsolicited.

The earliest ministers of later Garrett County were circuit riders. "In those early days," recorded Jacob Brown, "there was much of what might be called circulating services. Ministers would go among remote members and there hold home services. Houses would always be filled and the worship profitable." The Rev. D. A. Friend recalled that "on Sundays the people thought nothing of riding, or walking four or five miles to church, or to meetings as it was termed. The most beautiful part of it was that everybody in those days went to church." "Worship," noted Jacob Brown, "was held in private houses, and even in barns, especially [among] the Dunkards and Amish persuasions."

John Taylor, a Southern Baptist farmer of the South Branch of the Potomac River in Virginia, was the first of the glade country traveling missionary preachers. "Through these glades by different pass ways I had to go to pass from the eastern waters to the west," he wrote of his summertime circuit riding experience in the 1770s, "and the distance from one settlement to another [was so extensive] that a hard days travel would not accomplish it, so that camping out often attended the traveler. . . . We made the lonesome forest ring with the praises of God, as if there was not an Indian in the world."

A contemporary described Taylor as "strong of body and bold as a lion. He was very effective as a preacher though very plain in his style. No man knew better than he how to reprove, rebuke, and exhort, and when he used the rod of correction all were made to tremble. He was always willing to preach, was always cheerful; he was judicious and zealous."

John Taylor visited the Sandy Creek Glades in 1772 and helped organize the Baptist Meeting House there on a path between the Youghiogheny and Cheat rivers just west of the Maryland-Virginia state line. The Sandy Creek Church, doubling as a school and a religious hall, was the first Baptist church organized west of the Appalachian Continental Divide and the first church building of any denomination ever built to serve residents of later Garrett County. Persons of all religious persuasions were welcomed at Sandy Creek.

John Stauch of the Green Glades, "born of poor but pious parents," served his community as a horseback nondenominational circuit rider for five years beginning in 1788. His circuit often took him as far as twenty-five miles from his home, and he conducted services almost daily for weeks at a time, sometimes preaching two or three times a day. From twenty to thirty persons usually accompanied him from settlement to settlement, and not uncommonly they listened attentively to the same sermon delivered several times. Stauch left the Glades following the death of his wife in 1793. (He is remembered today as the founder of Aurora, West Virginia.)

Itinerant circuit-riding Catholic priests at Blooming Rose in the early 1800s included James Redmond of Cumberland, Edward D. Fenwick of Ohio, and Thomas Heyden of Pennsylvania. During the visits of Father Fenwick to the community, a few remaining Indians were instructed and baptized, and the mission at one time in the 1820s included as many as fifteen Indian communicants. According to the Rev. Thomas J. Stanton, historian of Catholicism in western Maryland, "The Indian converts of Blooming Rose were not of the most hope-inspiring class. Tradition says that when they went to church they were nearly always late and, as a rule, they fell asleep during [Latin] Mass." Father Thomas Heyden began visiting Blooming Rose in 1823, preaching nearly every evening from the steps of a local farmhouse while his audience made themselves comfortable on the grass, demonstrating their appreciation of the young priest's eloquence by frequent shouts of uproarious applause. In 1825 Father Charles C. Pise, assistant at the Baltimore Cathedral, came to Blooming Rose for several months, and the community began considering the construction of a local Catholic church.

Garrett County's first organized church was founded by local Baptists just north of Blooming Rose at Frazee's Ridge around 1773. In the 1780s a log building was erected at Mount Zion east of Backbone Mountain near Elk Lick Creek for use both as a local church and school. The Lutheran George Reinhart organized the Union Church at his home near later Oakland as "The First Church of Jesus Christ in the Youghiogheny Glades" in 1784. In 1820 local German Lutheran and Dutch Reformed Congregation members built a church of hewn logs on Reinhart's property at Sunnyside, naming the structure "Susan's Church" in honor of Reinhart's wife Susanna. The church was dedicated by the area circuit rider, C. F. Heyer, in 1821, and was used as both a school and church meeting-house until 1868, when the cabin of Peter Gortner across the meadow at Sunnyside was first put into use for these services.

Methodist circuit riders were invited to preach in the Friend settlement on the Youghiogheny as early as 1790. Local Methodists met in the home of Joseph Friend at Friend's Choice until Wesley's Chapel was built on Blooming Rose Ridge around 1858. Saint Mary's Roman Catholic Church was erected at Blooming Rose in 1827. Its priest, the Reverend Father Henry Meyers, was Garrett County's first resident priest. "He rode on horseback to the farm houses and became well acquainted with all his far and near neighbors," recorded the church historian Thomas J. Stanton; "he succeeded in adding many converts to his congregation." Among them were Mary McMullen and Meshach Browning.

The Catholic Church at Blooming Rose closed around 1850 due to the movement of many of its members to Johnstown, now Hoyes, just east of Sang Run. The original Johnstown Catholic Church was built in 1853. (This log structure was replaced with a frame building in 1890.) Johnstown Methodists organized an active Sunday school and church in 1855. Sang Run Methodists erected a meetinghouse a few miles to the west two years earlier.

A Lutheran congregation was organized at Accident around 1880. The original log meetinghouse there was replaced in 1869 by the "Little Brown Church," which housed the English Trinity Congregation until a red brick structure, constructed of local fire clay, was built in 1895 near the center of town. The congregation then became the Accident Evangelical Lutheran English Congregation, and their church later became known as Saint Paul's.

German Lutherans in the Cove, near Accident, also formed a congregation around 1800, initially meeting in a rough log building built by congregation members. Germans at Accident built the first Zion Evangelical Lutheran Church there in 1851. The first meetinghouse of the Church of the Brethren near Accident was built on a small lot just southeast of town, along Little Bear Creek, seven years later. The Brethren at

Accident had organized in 1846, initially holding their services under the leadership of itinerant ministers in local homes and barns. The services of all denominations at Accident were originally held in German. Even after 1900 the German Lutherans used the German language once every fourth Sunday until the advent of World War II.

Methodist circuit riders in northern present-day Garrett County in the 1780s included Francis Asbury, Robert Ayres, and John Smith. Even earlier Amish-Mennonite families north of the Braddock Road had met for the Sabbath in homes and barns, conducting their services in German, singing without instrumental accompaniment. In 1793 the Methodist Reverend Thomas Scott, of Cumberland, lodged and preached a sermon at Tomlinson's Inn at Little Meadows, noting that "a class had been previously formed in that neighborhood."

The carpenter Samuel Brown built the first hewn-log church in Old Grantsville for the use of local Methodist Episcopals in 1816. The structure was originally intended for use as a hotel, but was soon converted for use in religious functions. "It was primitive in all its features," recorded Jacob Brown, son of the architect, "with an ancient pulpit high up in the air, about the size of a sugar hogshead, and of course with an opening barely sufficient for entrance and amply high to hide the whole of the domini except his intellectual parts. There was also a gallery where the more ungodly would gather, and where there was usually more whispering and giggling than worship." The Braddock Road log church served Grantsville area Methodists until 1840, when the people of the neighborhood replaced it with a large log house, intended for use by all denominations, on a lane leading north to Salisbury, Pennsylvania. The new meetinghouse was also used as a local neighborhood school. "Even earlier," noted Jacob Brown, "young folks would come far and near [to the original Grantsville M.E. Church on the Braddock Road for educational purposes]. It was almost essentially a day school in its character; spelling books [were] far more common than the New Testament."

A "powerful revival took place [in the new Grantsville

meetinghouse] in 1846," according to Jacob Brown. The minister for the occasion was the Reverend Robert Laughlin, "a strong, earnest and untiring man from the hills of Virginia. The fire he kindled spread to a small reformed element that had been forming for a few years before. It was agreed on all hands that a new and comfortable church edifice should at once be erected. At first the idea was in favor of a Union church, for the joint use of the Methodist and German Reformed, but as matters progressed and were discussed, dissensions arose, and ultimately it was agreed, and wisely so, that each of the rapidly growing congregations should build a church, and so they did, under a friendly rivalry which should be first to have a place for worship." Both new Grantsville churches were built in the year 1847—one Methodist, the other the Grantsville Charge of Saint John's Evangelical Reformed Church. "The race was about an even one," noted Jacob Brown, "and the two buildings [were] about alike in structure." Grantsville Lutherans, organized during the 1840s, used the Reformed Church building for their services until 1858, when they built their own meetinghouse on a nearby property donated by Adam Shultz.

Grantsville area Amish-Mennonite and Brethren meanwhile continued to hold services under the direction of visiting circuit riders. Benedict Miller, ordained as minister in 1809, served local Amish-Mennonite settlers from 1813 until his death years later. Jeremiah Beegly and Jacob Pysell rode horseback from Bear Creek at Accident once a month to serve local Brethren, who had organized south of Grantsville around 1840.

In 1845 the Reverend Charles L. Brenner took permanent charge of the Mount Savage Ignatius Catholic Church and established a mission at Grantsville. Two years later Catholics began to hold regular services once every three months at a home near Keysers Ridge, a few miles west of Grantsville. The Ridgely family, south of Grantsville, had meanwhile been holding mass in their own home since about 1820. Area Catholics often traveled as far as Cumberland to attend church between local services.

John McHenry built a community nondenominational

church on Locust Tree Bottom near Buffalo Marsh in 1822 with money provided by his uncle, Dr. James McHenry. Early settlers at Bittinger organized a Lutheran congregation as early as the mid-1840s. Early in the 1850s Peter Lohr erected a building for the Bittinger Lutheran congregation on his own property about a quarter mile east of the crossroads. The building was replaced by a frame structure erected in 1874 by Christian Brenneman, a young local carpenter and sawmill operator. The new Evangelical Lutheran Church at the forks featured one front door for men, another for women and small children, and a waist-high wall separating the interior of the building into two different sections for the segregation of the sexes.

In 1828 George Loar opened his home for the first Methodist meetings of the Youghiogheny Glades, conducted under the leadership of settler Isaac McCarty. The following year McCarty organized Garrett County's first Sunday School at the Loar home. "The Yough Glades Sabbath School Auxiliary to the Sunday School Union of the Methodist Episcopal Church," and began a twenty-year superintendency of the school. The Yough Glades Methodists built a log church building on McCarty's farm in 1831. This structure served the congregation for twenty years. In 1852 it was replaced with a new structure in the recently surveyed town of Oakland.

Saint Peter's Roman Catholic Church was also erected in Oakland in 1852. The town's first Lutheran Church and parsonage were built in 1860. In 1868 the railroad magnate John W. Garrett erected the stone Garrett Memorial Church in Oakland in memory of his brother, Henry S. Garrett. Oakland Presbyterians organized the same year, and subsequently held services in the Garrett Church until 1938. Oakland Episcopalians also organized in 1869, holding their first services in the Garrett church, moving to their own local meetinghouse in 1874.

The prominent Oakland merchant John M. Davis was also an early Oakland Methodist preacher. "I began to preach March 13, 1862," he recalled at the age of eighty after the turn of the century. "On that occasion delivered an address to young people. Subject, 'Religion'. For 41 years, without change, I was superintendent of the Oakland Sunday School. I attended quite a number of funerals, visited the sick, baptized children, etc., extending over a large territory in the country, not only among Methodist families, but other denominations and outsiders represented within a distance of 10 or 15 miles. I never allowed my friends to use the title [of D.D., bestowed on me in 1902 by Taylor University], in addressing me though while a businessman I did not object to the title of 'Rev.' when people desired to use it."

In 1828 John Templeman deeded a parcel of land near the mouth of Savage River "for the use of a Meeting House, School House, and a grave yard." The Union Meeting House of later Bloomington was "intended to be free for all denominations of Christians to preach in. It is further understood," the original deed specified, "that the Meeting House is to be used as a School House under the direction of the Trustees. When this building is used as a School House should any mischief be done to it or the furniture by the scholars it shall be the duty of the Preacher to report such offenses to the parents or guardians and the Trustees shall make them pay the damage."

Mass was first said at Bloomington in 1849 by a Father O'Connor, a visiting priest. Local Catholics converted an old warehouse into a church the following year, naming the structure Father Slattery's Cathedral in honor of a local priest from Frostburg. In 1857 a Catholic church was built across the Potomac in Westernport, and the Bloomington church was eventually abandoned.

The Methodists at Bloomington built an area meetinghouse in 1857. An earlier Methodist congregation had built a church on Savage Mountain about five miles north of Bloomington in 1832. Eight years later Methodists erected a church-school near later Kitzmiller. A white nondenominational church was built in Ryan's Glade in 1871.

Pioneer Garrett County settlers were Presbyterian, Methodist, Brethren, Amish-Mennonite, Lutheran, Episcopalian, and Catholic in religion. They organized churches for the retention of their religious beliefs and values. They organized schools for the transference of secular knowledge and norms.

"In early times," recorded the Grantsville historian Jacob Brown, "there were no school houses at all, as such. Schools, as they were, were held in empty dwellings or out-houses. In one case, I remember a horse stable, after a little refitting, was thus utilized. School houses were mere log pens with furniture in keeping."

"The early Garrett County schoolhouse," noted Brown, "was poorly ventilated, lighted, and heated. The seats were pine slabs with flat side up, with heavy pins in the ends to keep them up. The writing desks were rough pine boards, generally fastened to the wall. Hardly ever a chair or seat [was provided] for the master, other than the end of a bench not occupied by the scholars. The reliable rod was always in view. It was believed to be as necessary for the teacher as the sword for the military officer."

The curriculum of early Garrett County schools was simplistic in the extreme. "The U. S. Spelling book, Pike's arithmetic, a slate, and a New Testament for the 'reader' were about the contents of the scholar's satchel," Brown observed. " 'To read, write and cipher to the rule of three' in Pike's Arithmetic, was the desideratum" for boys. Girls were generally discouraged in the study of mathematics. The pioneer Leo J. Beachy recalled that his mother "was never taught arithmetic, because during those days it was thought unnecessary for a girl to learn to cipher. In fact, when her grandmother, with whom she stayed, found out that the teacher had started to give my mother some instruction in arithmetic, she stopped it. It has always seemed to me a sad vexation that she could not add and carry, subtract, multiply and divide."

Early Garrett County education was a private endeavor. Parents wishing to educate their children provided their own buildings, engaged their own instructors. Churches often took the initiative in educational matters, teaching Bible reading in Sunday schools. The Oakland Methodist Sunday school of 1854, for example, offered classes in the alphabet, reading, spelling, and the Testament. Old and young alike attended its sessions.

Though the Maryland General Assembly established a free

school fund in 1814 through a tax on state banks, most of the money collected was devoted to other projects, invested in non-educational enterprises, or simply squandered. When the General Assembly authorized a local option county system of education in 1826 with provisions for the public support of schools, Allegany County voters (including those of later Garrett County) rejected the plan by an overwhelming vote of 1,031 to 249. An 1837 state "Act for the promotion of education in Allegany County" was similarly rejected by county commissioners. A General Assembly effort to establish free schools in Allegany County two years later was also flatly voted down.

As late as 1865 the president of the Board of Commissioners of Public Schools in Allegany County (of which Garrett was then still a part) raised serious questions concerning the quality of local education. "Supervision is supposed to be exercised by the local directors," he reported, "but they are often illiterate men who pay little attention to the schools. Little money is spent on schoolhouses; they are poorly built and poorly furnished. Teachers are often very ignorant. The general intelligence of the people of the county is at an extremely low ebb. A large portion can neither read nor write. We have, literally, not one schoolhouse in the county. In some schools I have been made sick in ten minutes after entering them."

Only five years earlier the Maryland General Assembly has passed "an Act to establish a uniform system of public schools in Allegany County," providing for a Board of Commissioners of Public Schools to consolidate control of public education throughout the county under the direction of a single secretary-treasurer and three appointed directors in each school district. The Allegany County commissioners, however, had refused both to levy local taxes for the support of such a system and to release appropriated state funds to the new school board until they were compelled to do so by order of the state court of appeals. Then, in 1865, the General Assembly established a central state department of education and provided for increased public support of all local schools. The pioneer log schoolhouses of later Garrett

County were subsequently gradually replaced by new one-room frame structures, teachers' salaries were increased, and some progress was made in introducing a uniform system of educational opportunity throughout the state. The county remained the unit of local administration, however, and each school continued to be served by a local board of trustees. Present-day Garrett County's first schoolhouse was established at Blooming Rose in 1793 under the direction of teacher Robinson Savage. The Mars Hill School near later Grantsville opened before the turn of the century, as did a school near later Selbysport, "where switches were plentiful," according to an early student. A school at Susan's Church near Sunnyside opened in the early nineteenth century under the direction of Ann Thayer, daughter of Stephen Thayer, the New England emigrant. Other Garrett County schools were established early in the century at Crabtree Bottom, Accident, Buffalo Marsh, Little Meadows, Grantsville, and Clifton. Pupils attended as many as five schoolhouses erected near Little Crossings by 1831: Tomlinson's, Grantsville, Little Youghiogheny, Custer's, and the German Settlement School. A second educational district that year included schools at Ryan's Glade, Henry Lower's, P. H. Bray's, and the Sanging Ground. A third district was composed of schools at Selbysport, Hazlet's Mill, Blooming Rose Ridge, Asher's Glade, Jonathan Frantz's, and Abraham Schockley's. In all, western Allegany County children were being educated in a total of fifteen different schools by 1831. Private Catholic education began in the county in 1870 in a school built by Father O'Sullivan in Oakland. In 1872, when Garrett County was first recognized as a political entity, separate and distinct from Allegany, the county had fifty-seven schools, almost three thousand pupils and seventy-six teachers.

Glimpses of the characters of early western Allegany County teachers are found in the reminiscences of Jacob Brown on early Grantsville area instructors. He described Benjamin Payton as a man of "not much learning but of good intentions." James Mimma was "a quiet mannerly Irishman [who] could wield the old quill pen with great nicety and precision." John Wiley was likewise "a gentleman by nature," while a Mr. Lackey was "young and tall, full of dash, fond of society." A teacher known as Professor Pell, by way of contrast, was "a bachelor in declining years," nervous, temperamental, mysterious—an opium addict. David McCarty recalled an early teacher in the Youghiogheny Glades simply as "a terror," while John McHenry described Master John Yaldwin of Buffalo Marsh, a solitary and eccentric Englishman, as an "incessant talker." "His head runs on experiments and new inventions," McHenry wrote a relative; "I have insured him a place in our Lazy Club at Cumberland." Most early Garrett County teachers, such as Master Yaldwin, boarded with the parents of their students. Some received as much as two dollars per term for each pupil they taught as extra remuneration.

The terms of early Garrett County schools were short in duration, usually lasting only about three months. Boys were needed at home for spring planting and autumn harvest; girls were needed for domestic household chores. Families desiring quality education for their children sometimes sent the siblings away to school. Isaac McCarty of the Yough Glades, for example, sent his two oldest children to attend school with relatives at Keyser and Romney, a daughter to Morgantown, a younger son to Clarksburg Academy and Hiram College in Ohio, and two younger daughters to private boarding schools in Washington, Pennsylvania. Most pioneer youngsters, though, either received a basic education at local schools and churches or else simply remained illiterate.

Roadways reflect the advance of civilizations. "In early times," noted Meshach Browning, "there being but few roads [in present-day Garrett County] suitable for wagons, and only narrow paths leading from one settlement to another. Packhorses were the only mode of conveying goods from one place to another." As settlers began to establish homesteads in western Maryland in the early 1800s, packhorse paths, once Indian trails and buffalo traces, were gradually widened and smoothed for the passage of wagons.

The Old Morgantown Road, extending southwest from the Bear Camp on the Braddock trail to Virginia by way of

Blooming Rose and later Selbysport, was deemed a public road by the Maryland General Assembly as early as 1800. In 1823 it was extended north from the Bear Camp to the new Cumberland Road recently built along Braddock's Trail. At the junction of the two routes John Simkins and Maryland Governor Thomas Johnson laid out West Union Towne, but the village never grew.

William Wilton Ashby laid out the Ashby Road from the Bray settlement by the Potomac across Backbone Mountain to the Youghiogheny Glades prior to 1790. In 1800 the General Assembly authorized the construction of the Blooming Rose Road along a "path that leads from Richard Hall's House to the Meeting House on Sandy Creek." The roadway was to be opened as a public highway at the expense of local petitioners.

The Allegany County Levy Court ordered the opening of a road from Selbysport east to Swanton in 1807. The new trail served local settlers for many years as an outlet to markets at Westernport and Cumberland. A covered bridge over the Youghiogheny River at Selbysport was already in use at the time. A new covered bridge was erected there in 1869.

Sanging Ground settlers petitioned the commissioners of Allegany County to open a public road from the farm of William W. Hoye to the Virginia line at Pine Swamp in 1828. Corbin West surveyed the road two years later. In 1863 the Allegany County Board of Commissioners advertised for bids to construct a second wooden bridge over the Yough at the Sanging Ground to replace the original which had been destroyed by flooding.

Early Garrett County roads were rough, stony paths cut through forest and glade for the passage of wagons and horses. Grass and brush grew wild between their ruts. Rainwater swept away the top soil and left deep trails between their banks. The early roadways connected settlements and provided channels of communication with the outside world. Three major roadways built across the Garrett mountains in the early nineteenth century connected the eastern seaboard with the developing trans-Appalachian frontier. These were the Virginia-Maryland Interstate Road, the Northwestern

Turnpike and the Cumberland Road. The history of these three roads reflects a saga of the American experience—the settlement of the Mississippi Valley, the old American West.

"Nothing stopped the white man who must go west," wrote the Garrett County historian Walter W. Price in 1958. "He paid his toll of scalps, inexpressible physical agony, the blessings of death, and always his kind come from salt waters to the foot of the Alleghenies and crawled upward toward the challenge and the promise and, sometimes, the rewards of the land beyond this seemingly endless chain of up-thrust rock and murmuring forest. The Gists, Cresaps, Fraziers, and McCulloughs ignored the risk of sudden death and found their way into the Indian country."

The King's Proclamation of 1763 forbidding settlement west of the Appalachians did not stop these rough and ready early pioneers. The brutal rebellion of the western Indians under Chief Pontiac following the French and Indian War did not stop them. Not even the threat of death decreed in 1768 by the Pennsylvania legislature for those refusing to return to white territory east of the 1763 Proclamation line stopped them. From the waters of the east they came; to the valleys of the west they went. Nothing, nobody stopped them.

The Appalachian frontier bulged first with settlers at its center—in the western portions of Maryland, Virginia, and Pennsylvania. As early as 1763 Fort Pitt, at the Forks of the Ohio, was surrounded by several hundred houses, and a thin chain of outpost settlements bordered the entire length of the upper Monongahela River. Within six years nearly five thousand families lived on the Pennsylvania frontier; by 1771 the population there had doubled. "All this spring and summer," noted the Pennsylvania fur trader George Croghan at the time, "the roads have been lined with wagons moving to the Ohio." The Pittsburgh Post Office was established in 1794 with mails arriving once every two weeks from Philadelphia. The state of Ohio was first recognized by act of Congress in 1803. Nothing, nobody stopped the white man who must go west.

The first trans-Appalachian white settlers squatted with arrogance, ignorance, and no small degree of self-righteousness on the forbidden lands of the native American Indian. Then, in 1768, the middle colonies negotiated two treaties with the western tribes which opened the Ohio Valley to settlement east and south of the great river as far as the mouth of the Kanawha. The six Iroquois Nations that year sold "2,400,000 acres of land at the back of Virginia" to the English Crown for ten thousand pounds through the Treaty of Fort Stanwix. The Treaty of Hard Labour negotiated with the Cherokees around the same time opened western lands even farther to the south. Land speculators saw their moment, dreamed of wealth and glory, and seized the initiative in the development of the Old West to the Mississippi. The American course of empire pursued the western star. Nothing stopped the white man who must go west.

"Before the cramped pioneers lay tempting highways," recorded the American frontier historian Ray Allen Billington in 1949. "From Pennsylvania, Maryland, and Virginia they could follow the crude traces—Braddock's Road or Forbes' Road—cut by Britain's armies to the Forks of the Ohio. From western Virginia and Maryland they could make their way along the valleys of the Cheat or Youghiogheny Rivers to that same spot. Further south lay one of nature's grandest passage-ways, Cumberland Gap, which offered easy passage from back-country Virginia and North Carolina into the hilly uplands of Kentucky. [The] combination of land-starved frontiersman and easy transportation routes explains why the Appalachian frontier bulged first in the center."

The 1768 treaties of Fort Stanwix and Hard Labour sent streams of land-hungry settlers west by the score. Both Pennsylvania and Virginia claimed land in the Ohio region and sold territory there freely to speculators and homesteaders. Farther south, in eastern Tennessee, Captain Evan Shelby, the prominent Maryland frontiersman and founder of Selbysport (Garrett County's first established town), induced numerous pioneers to settle as early as 1769 near his store at Shelby's Station. Daniel Boone meanwhile kindled pioneer interest in the hills and forests of Kentucky. Nothing, nobody stopped the white man who must go west.

Some of the migrants of the late eighteenth and early nineteenth centuries, such as the family of Garrett County's William and Wilton Ashby, traveled no further west than the crest of the Alleghenies. Most reached their destinations. Some died along the way. One of the victims of the great westward movement was John Prentice Allen, a young boy buried at the site of Braddock's sixth camp along the Nemacolin Trail in present-day Garrett County in 1796. "At the house of one Mr. Tumblestone [Jesse Tomlinson] the child was taken in a fit," explained the boy's father in a later letter to relatives in Connecticut, from whence the migrants had come. "Polly [the boy's mother] said she was afraid the child would die [but] Mr. Tumblestone spoke in a very lite manner and says with a smile it will save you the trouble of carrying it any farther." The child died the next day at the house of John Simkins. "Polly was obliged to go rite off as soon as his eyes was closed for the waggoners would not stop," the father wrote. "Two of the men that was with me were joiners and had their tools with them. They stayed with me and made the coffin. Mr. Simkins, the man of the house, sent his negroes out and dug the grave whare he had buried several strangers that dyed acrossing the mountain. His family all followed the corps to the grave black and white and appeared much affected." Nothing stopped the white man who must go west. Nothing, nobody stopped the white man who must go west.

Among the most prominent of the early western speculators was George Washington, whose interest in the area had first been kindled by the activities of the Ohio Company of Virginia in the mid-eighteenth century. When the Virginia regiment of 1754 was first organized for the defense of the Ohio Forks against the intruding French from the north, Governor Dinwiddie had issued a proclamation promising two hundred thousand acres of Ohio Valley land as a reward for the services of volunteers. At the conclusion of the war, in 1763, despite the king's settlement proclamation, the newly organized Mississippi Company, with Washington serving as principal promoter, purchased many of the small bounty grants from former soldiers at a fraction of their value and petitioned the Crown for enough land at the junction of the

Ohio and Mississippi rivers to satisfy the warrants. Five years later the Treaty of Fort Stanwix with the Iroquois and the Treaty of Hard Labour with the Cherokee opened the Ohio Valley to settlement east and south of the river as far as the mouth of the Great Kanawha. At a subsequent meeting of Virginia regiment veterans held in Fredericksburg late in the summer of 1770, the assembled land claimants authorized their former colonel to travel west to review the lands they had been promised in 1754. Washington's expenses were to be shared by all. He departed from Mount Vernon on October 5.

Seven days later he recorded that "we left Killam's [on George's Creek near later Frostburg] early in the morning, breakfasted at the Little Meadows [Joseph Tomlinson's Inn] 10 miles off, and lodged at the Great Crossings 20 miles further, which we found a tolerable good day's work. The country we traveled over today (present-day Garrett County) was very mountainous and stony, with but little good land, and that lying in spots." Washington traversed today's Garrett County by horseback over the old Braddock Road in a single October day. With seven assistants and an escort of Indians he canoed down the Ohio River from Fort Pitt in November and marked a corner of the reserved soldiers' lands at the river's mouth. He killed five buffalo, then returned by land, following the Braddock Road eastward from western Pennsylvania. On November 26 his party "reached Killam's [on George's Creek near later Frostburg] where we met several families going over the mountains to live. The snow upon Allegany Mountains was near knee deep."

In 1772 Virginia officials allotted Washington four Ohio Valley tracts of land totaling over twenty thousand acres for his services in the French and Indian War. Fifteen thousand acres rested on the former colonel's own claims; five thousand rested on claims purchased by him from other regiment veterans. Washington himself later noted that he had obtained "the cream of the country."

As early as 1759 the former colonel had recommended that the Virginia House of Burgesses consider the subject of a highway connection between the waters of the east and those of Ohio Valley west. Two years after receiving his extensive 1772 land allotments he again made such a recommendation, introducing and moving the adoption of a legislative bill empowering individuals to subscribe toward the construction of a trans-Appalachian route at their own expense. The advent of the Revolutionary War precluded follow-through on such an endeavor, though, and it was not until 1784 that Washington, now former commander in chief of the victorious colonial armies, was again enabled to pursue his interests in Ohio development.

Washington resigned his command at Annapolis on December 20, 1783. In autumn of 1784 he again traveled west to inspect his Ohio properties and to investigate the possibilities of linking, by road or canal, the eastern waters of the Potomac with the western waters of the Ohio. "Having found it indispensably necessary to visit my landed property west of the Appalachian Mountains," he recorded, "I set out on my journey," departing from Mount Vernon on September 1. Five days later he arrived at the town of Bath (now Berkeley Springs, West Virginia), and remained two full days because of steady rainfall. At Bath he met a man who advised that the distance between the Potomac and a branch of the westward-flowing Youghiogheny was "but about 6 miles" by way of McCullough's Path—a rude packhorse trail, once a buffalo trace, which traversed the southernmost portion of present-day Garrett County.

The Washington party passed Fort Cumberland on September 10, dined at Evan Gwynn's Tavern near Allegany Grove, and followed the old Braddock Road to Tomlinson's Tavern at Little Meadows, where it lodged for the night. The next morning the travelers reached the Casselman River. "The road is not bad," recorded Washington; "this is a pretty considerable water and, as it is said to have no fall in it, may, I conceive, be improved into a valuable navigation." They ate breakfast at Joseph Mountain's Inn on the eastern slope of Negro Mountain, and then continued west to the Youghiogheny and the Great Meadows of Pennsylvania. "In passing over the Mountains," Washington noted, "I met a number of persons and pack horses going in with Ginseng, and for salt and other articles at the Markets below."

On his return trip to Mount Vernon the former general decided to abandon the Braddock Road and to journey to the North Branch of the Potomac by way of the Sandy Creek Glades and McCullough's Packhorse Path, as he had been advised in the town of Bath. His nephew, Bushrod Washington, accompanied him; his servants and the remainder of the party continued eastward with baggage and supplies on the old British army route.

The two Washingtons arrived at the Youghiogheny Glades on September 25 and camped that night near Swallow Falls in a heavy downpour of rain "with no other shelter or cover than my cloak." The next morning they "started at the dawning of day, and, passing along a small path much enclosed with weeds and bushes, loaded with water from the overnights rain and the showers which were continually falling, we had an uncomfortable travel to one Charles Friends [near present-day Oakland] where we could get nothing for our horses, and only boiled corn for ourselves. In this distance, excepting two or three places which abounded in stone, and no advantage taken of the hills [which were not large] we found the ground would admit an exceedingly good Wagon Road with a little causeying."

"Part of these glades is the property of Governor [Thomas] Johnson of Maryland who has settled two or three families of Palatines upon them," noted Washington of the Youghiogheny region. "These glades have a pretty appearance, resembling cultivated lands and improved Meadows at a distance; with woods here and there interspersed. Some of them are rich, with black and lively soil; others are of a stiffer, and colder Nature; all of them feel, very early, the effect of frost; the growth of them is a grass, not much unlike what is called fancy grass without the variegated colors of it; much intermixed in places with fern and other weeds, as also with alder and other Shrubs. The Land between these glades is chiefly white oak, on a dry stony soil. In places there are Walnut and Crab tree bottoms, which are very rich. The glades are not so level as one would imagine—in general they rise from the small water courses which run through all of them to the Ridges which separate one from another—but they are highly beneficial to the circumjacent Country from whence the Cattle are driven to pasture in the Spring and recalled at Autumn."

Washington dried his clothes and rested for a time at the home of Charles Friend, member of present-day Garrett County's first permanent white resident family. The two men enjoyed an extensive conversation. "The little Youghiogheny from Braddocks Road to the Falls below the Turkey Foot," recorded the president-to-be, "may, in the opinion of Friend, who is a great Hunter, having lived in that Country and followed no other occupation for nine years, be made navigable—and this . . . would open a very important door to the trade of that Country. . . . He is also of the opinion that a very good road may be had from the Dunkers bottom to the No[rth] Branch of Potomac, at or near where McCulloughs path crosses it [between present-day Gorman and Steyer]."

From Charles Friend's cabin, Washington traveled eastward through the Pleasant Valley Glades by Archer's Spring, which had been named after an early settler, and proceeded across Backbone Mountain to Ryan's Glade where he met the pioneer settler Joseph Logsdon. Logsdon agreed "precisely with Charles Friends respecting the Nature of the Road between the North Branch and the Dunker's bottom," but insisted "that Friends ought to be left two miles to the Westward." "Here it may be well to observe," Washington carefully noted, "that however knowing these people are, their accts. are to be received with great caution . . . as private views are as prevalent in this, as any other Country; and are particularly exemplified in the article of Roads; which [where they have been marked] seem calculated more to promote individual interest, than the public good."

Washington arrived home at Mount Vernon on October 4. "I was disappointed in one of the objects which induced me to undertake this journey," he recorded, "namely to examine the situation quality and advantages of the land which I hold upon the Ohio and Great Kanawha, and to take measures for rescuing them from the hands of Land Jobbers and speculators [who] had enclosed them within other surveys and were offering them for sale at Philadelphia and in Europe."

The former general made other salient observations on his experiences in the West. "No well informed mind need be told," he concluded, "that the flanks and rear of the United Territory are possessed by other powers, and formidable ones too—nor how necessary it is to apply the cement of interest to bind all parts of it together, by one indissoluble bond—particularly the middle states with the country immediately back of them.... The Western Settlers—from my observation—stand as it were on a pivot—the touch of a feather would almost incline them any way.... A combination of circumstances [however] makes[s] the present conjunction more favorable than any other to fix the trade of the Western Country to our Markets.... The way is plain, and the expense, comparatively speaking deserves not a thought, so great would be the prize. The Western Inhabitants would do their part towards accomplishing it, weak as they are now, they would, I am persuaded meet us half way rather than be driven into the arms of or be in any ways dependent upon, foreigners, [the French at the mouth of the Mississippi] the consequence of which would be a separation, or a war. The way is to open a wide door and make a smooth way for the produce of that Country to pass to our markets, before the trade may get into another channel. No route is so convenient as that which offers itself through Youghiogheny or Cheat River—the certain consequence therefore of an attempt to restrain the extension of the Navigation of these Rivers ... would be a separation of the Western Settlers from the old and more interior government; towards which there is not wanting a disposition at this moment in the former."

Already Washington had noted that "From the Mouth of Savage River the State of Maryland [as I was informed] were opening a Road to their western boundary which was to be met by another which the Inhabitants of Monongahela County [in Virginia] were extending to the same place from the Dunkar Bottom [on the Cheat] through the glades of Yohiogany." The reference was to the Maryland-Virginia Interstate Road ... the first major wagon trail to be constructed across the mountains through state funds and interstate cooperation. In November 1784, the Maryland General Assembly resolved that "three-thousand-three-hundred-and-thirty-three-and-one-third dollars be appropriated to defray one half of the expense of examining, surveying, cutting, clearing, improving, and keeping in repair, a proposed road from the waters of Potomack river to the river Cheat, and, if necessary, to the Monongahela." The Virginia legislature soon passed a like resolve. The road was constructed in 1786. Nothing stopped the white man who must go west.

The Virginia commissioner for the construction of the new interstate road was Joseph Nevill of Hampshire County; the Maryland commissioner was Francis Deakins, the prominent Georgetown engineer and 1787 surveyor of western Maryland Revolutionary War military lots. Deakins visited George Washington at Alexandria in May 1785, for consultation preparatory to his return to the Appalachian Mountains the following year. In June 1786, Joseph Nevill, the Virginia commissioner, reported to his state governor that "Colo. Francis Deakings and myself has been out a viewing and laying off the Road over the Allegania mountain, to be cut by this state and the state of Maryland, and is now preparing to open the same." The route the two men chose ran west from Winchester, Virginia, to the mouth of the Savage at the Potomac near Bloomington. It crossed the mountains of present-day Garrett County along the trail of the old Glades Indian Path, which had formerly been a buffalo trace, ascending the slopes of Backbone Mountain at Castle Hill, then crossing the Youghiogheny Glades by way of Captain George Calmes's residence at Deer Park and Charles Friend's cabin on the Little Yough. From the Maryland-Virginia border it descended the mountain slopes to Dunkard Bottom on the Cheat and continued west to Morgantown and Clarksburg.

Construction on the roadway began in August 1786. Day labor was employed in Maryland for the building; the state provided camps and supplies for the workers. In May 1789, Joseph Nevill filed a complaint and a report with his governor. "I have opened them a very good Road through many Mountains," he wrote, "the distance of seventy miles for which I received nothing, or next to nothing." The road itself fulfilled George Washington's 1783 dreams of a connective wagon link between the waters of the east and those of the west, between "old" America and frontier America. In present-day Garrett County it provided a major outlet for the farm products of the Youghiogheny Glades and the Bloomington area to the markets of the eastern establishment.

The interstate road was first repaired in 1795. The following year the traveling German Eric Bollman commented that "The road is not in bad condition and could be made most excellent. This will, without doubt, be accomplished just as soon as the country is sufficiently inhabited, since there is no nearer way to reach the western waters."

A chain of log inns and taverns was established along the route of the road in the late eighteenth and early nineteenth centuries for the service and comfort of travelers and migrants. The easternmost interstate road inn in present-day Garrett County was built at Frog Hollow near the mouth of Savage River. Extra horses were available at Frog Hollow for years to aid freight wagons up the nearby slopes. Other early Garrett County rest stops and taverns along the route included Brien Gainor's Inn east of Backbone Mountain, the Castle Hill Inn (first operated by James Stackpole at the summit of Backbone Mountain), John Haye's Place (later Henry Ingman's Inn) at the intersection of the route with the Glades Road from Selbysport, and William Armstrong's Tavern on the Little Yough near later Oakland. (Contemporary Maryland State routes 135 and 39 follow the basic path of the old Maryland-Virginia Interstate Road.)

A second major Southern Garrett County east-west roadway (the Northwestern Turnpike) was constructed south of the interstate road along the route of present-day U.S. Route 50, the old northwestern Indian Trail and buffalo trace, under the supervision of the eminent French engineer Claude Crozet, chief engineer of the state of Virginia, in the late 1830s. The turnpike ran west through later Garrett County from Gorman on the North Branch of the Potomac through Red House and the western Maryland border into Virginia.

Construction began in 1834 and was completed by 1840. The road was paid for and maintained by tolls.

A series of taverns and inns erected in the early nineteenth century accommodated early turnpike travelers as well as interstate road passengers between the borders of present-day Garrett County. The Alexander Smith House near Gorman was converted into the Winston Tavern by E. Tower, of Washington, D.C., shortly after 1839. The Peter Shirer family, early Oakland tinners, operated a drover's pasture and inn from a frame house sided with red planks at present-day Red House in the 1850s. The Reinhart Tavern at Sunnyside, in use as early as 1790, continued to accommodate turnpike travelers and drovers as late as 1892.

"I have been informed that the [inn] proprietors seldom took in less than one-hundred dollars a day," recorded Mae Yost of Oakland in 1892, "and that, too, when two meals and a night's lodging were only fifty cents." Early traffic on the turnpike—mail coaches, freight wagons, horseback riders, drovers, travelers on foot—was heavy. "It was not unusual," noted Yost, "for three thousand horses and one hundred thousand head of cattle to pass over the road in a single year to the eastern markets." Even hogs, turkeys, sheep, and geese were frequently driven along the roadway. So were slaves. "A man named Samuel Brady used to buy negroes in the river counties of Virginia," recorded Yost, "and drive them over the Pike, chained two and two, and kept them moving at a lively gait by a blacksnake whip. One poor creature was so distressed at having been taken away from her baby that she committed suicide on the Pike."

Mae Yost traveled the route of the old pike by foot in the summer of 1892. "The roadway [today]," she wrote, "is fringed with a riot of feathery ferns up to the wheel tracks; and crystal springs gush out from the rocks, and run alongside, and across dimpling and gurgling, till lost in a leafy tangle far below. Great rocks and crumbling trees lie clad in robes no loom of the Orient can rival; velvety mosses, dainty lichens, delicate tracery of vine and leaf covers the cool moist earth where the sun never reaches. . . . Eight times I have traveled the picturesque old Pike from Druid Hill [on Backbone Mountain east of Table Rock] to Grafton, and though the coaches [are now] gone, the old stage houses [are] crumbling into ruins, and the grass [is] growing thickly where thousands of hurrying feet once stirred up the dust... I never cease to drink in with enraptured eyes the glorious panorama or to marvel at the magnitude of the undertaking which had carried to a successful completion the building of the Northwestern Turnpike so many years ago."

Nothing stopped the white man who must go west. As early as 1758 the Maryland General Assembly authorized a six-man committee (whose membership included Colonel Thomas Cresap of Oldtown) to research the feasibility of constructing a new wagon road through western Maryland between Fort Frederick and Fort Cumberland. The committee filed its report with the legislature at the end of the year (1758): "Your committee have made an inquiry into the situation of the present wagon-road from Fort Frederick to Fort Cumberland and are of the opinion that the distance by that road from one fort to the other is at least eighty miles, and find that the wagons which go from one fort to the other are obliged to pass the river Potomack twice, and that for one-third of the year they can't pass without boats to get them over the water. Your committee have also made an inquiry into the condition of the ground where a road may be made most conveniently to go altogether on the north side of the Potomack, which will not exceed the distance of sixty-two miles, at the expense of 250 pounds current money. Your committee are of the opinion that a road through Maryland will contribute much to lessen the expense of carrying provision and warlike stores from Fort Frederick to Fort Cumberland, and will induce many people to travel and carry on a trade in and through the province, to and from the back country."

The Fort Frederick-Fort Cumberland Road was built in 1759. It connected interior Maryland with the eastern terminus of the Braddock Road across the mountains. The old military road itself was used only by infrequent scouting parties of whites and marauding bands of Indians passing to and fro between the Potomac and Monongahela rivers over the mountains of present-day Garrett County throughout the French and Indian war—the Great War for the Empire. "During the war of the Revolution," wrote the Reverend Thomas Scott, a Cumberland Methodist preacher of the 1790s, "less danger was to be apprehended from the Indians in traveling the Braddock Road than on either of the others over the Allegheny Mountains; and the consequence resulting from the greater security to travelers was that an almost daily communication was kept up between the settlements in the Redstone country and those east of the mountains." The Grantsville historian Jacob Brown noted in 1896 that "After the organization of the general government, in 1789, the tide from the East to the West, mainly over this way, increased steadily, so much that the road became worn out, and utterly inadequate to the public necessities." The Maryland legislature subsequently passed laws for the improvement and straightening of the Braddock Trail as early as 1795. They passed acts of a similar nature again in 1798 and 1802.

Early white travelers of the Braddock Road leaving written records of their journeys through present-day Garrett County included the Reverend David Jones of Freehold, New Jersey, an eighteenth century missionary to the Ohio Indians; William Brown, a migrant to Kentucky from Hanover, Virginia; Samuel Allen, the Ohio Valley emigrant from Connecticut whose young son was buried in 1796 near the home of John Simkins at the site of Braddock's sixth camp; the Garrett County pioneer hunter, Meshach Browning; and Gerald T. Hopkins, a Quaker who traveled west from Baltimore to Ohio in 1804. All found the road over which they passed and the surrounding countryside worthy of note.

The Reverend David Jones, 1772: "This day [May 25] we began to ascend that mountain from others distinguished by name Allegini. This mountain is truely worth notice, great part of which abounds with excellent timber; in general either oak, chestnut or white pine, variegated according to the nature of the soil. That part of it called Savage Mountain is beautifully covered with stately white pines. . . . In passing this mountain we cross many crystal streams, the principal are called the Little and Great Crossings. It is said to be sixty miles across [the Alleghenies] from Fort Cumberland to Redstone. Thro the whole as you travel, you may lodge every night in some kind of houses; but the entertainment is a little rough, for such as are but strangers to the new country. In this an amendment may be expected, for a number of frugal and civil people are preparing good accommodations, both for man and horse."

William Brown, 1790: "Soon after you pass Gwyns Tavern in Maryland you enter upon the Alleghany Mo. and then you have a great deal of bad road, many ridges of Mo.—the Winding Ridge—Savage, Negro, etc. and Laurel Hill which is the last. . . . Just before you get to the Little Shades of Death [a few miles east of present-day Grantsville] there is a tract of the tallest pines I ever saw. The Shades of Death are dreary looking valleys, growing up with tall cypress and other trees and has a dark gloomy appearance. Tumblestones, or the Little Meadows, is a fine plantation with beautiful meadow ground. Crossing of Yoh, is a pretty good ford. There is some very bad road about here."

Meshach Browning, 1790: "My mother determined to leave Frederick County, and go out to the back woods. Having our property all in the wagon, off went the horses, with whip cracking, negro cursing and swearing, until we were in the main road to Frederick. We went on in good order until we reached Sideling Hill, where the road was very rough and rocky: by and by we arrived at a very sideling place, with a considerable precipice on our left. The wheels struck a rock on the other side, and away went wagon, horses, and all down the hill, rolling and smashing barrels of rum, hogsheads of sugar, sacks of salt, boxes of dry-goods, all tumbling through one another, smashing the bed of the wagon, and spilling rum, molasses, sugar, and all. All was bustle and alarm, until at length I was found under some straw and rubbish, stunned breathless, mangled, and black with suffocation. The wagon was broken to pieces, the left hind-wheel smashed, and entirely useless. By the time we made a substitute for the broken wheel, night had come on us; a large fire was made, and my mother took her place by the root of a tree, with [son] Joshua by her side, who was about twelve years old, and myself in her arms; she has often told me that she never closed her eyes until daylight appeared next morning. After breakfast, everything made ready, the whip cracked again, and off we started, Joshua walking and my mother carrying me on her back. We proceeded on our journey slowly, reached our destination, and found ourselves in Oldtown. We remained here two or three weeks, until my wounds and bruises were well, or nearly so, when we went to my grandfather's on the headwaters of the Flintstone and remained during that fall and winter."

Meshach Browning, 1791: "I was awakened a long time before daylight; all was ready for a move, with three horses loaded, and the young man soon had the cattle ready to follow the horses. I was put on one horse, my aunt on another, and uncle drove the third; aunt in the lead. On we went, without noise, over the mountains towards Cumberland; and, as the sun began to show its beautiful reflection on the high top of the Dan Mountain, westward of the town, we arrived in sight of the valley in which the town was situated. Here was a new scene to me entirely. The whole valley was covered with a dense fog; nothing was to be seen but the high tops of the western mountains, with here and there stripes of sunlight; whilst all around was in uproar, with cows bellowing, calves bleating, dogs barking, cocks crowing, and, in short, all sorts of noises. By the time the sun had driven away all the misty clouds, the town was in plain view; and I think that there were not more than twenty or thirty houses, and they mostly cabins, surrounded by large corn-fields, containing heavy crops of corn.

"After breakfast we resumed our march for the new country before us; and, on we went; and in the evening we found ourselves at the Little Crossings; here we halted for the night; the horses and cows were taken to pasture, for few houses of entertainment in those times kept oats or grain of any kind for feeding purposes, in summer, but depended altogether on grass. Supper being ready, we partook with others of a welcome meal, made up of buckwheat cakes, fresh fine butter, delicious honey-combs, venison steaks, as also some fine jerk, and sweet milk, of which we all took a good share. We had our bedding with us, which we laid down on the floor, and prepared for resting our tired limbs. Soon we were down and sound asleep. The next morning, by the time I could see to walk, I was called up to fetch the cows, while my uncle saddled the horses, and got ready for breakfast. All this being done, and breakfast over, we bid good-bye to Little Crossings, and took the road again for the Blooming Rose. We traveled without halting, save to water our beasts, until late in the afternoon, when we arrived at the residence of my uncle's father."

Samuel Allen, 1796: "The men all walked the hole of the way. I walked the hole distance it being allmost three hundred miles and we found the rode to be pretty good until we came to the mountains [where] we found the roads to be verry bad. We left the city of Allexandria on the Potomac the 30th day of June and arrived at Morgantown on the Monongahely the 18th day of July."

Gerald T. Hopkins, 1804: "Feb. 29 Traveled 30 miles upon the Alle. Mts. and at night loged at Smith's Ordinary. Near this part of the Mts. our road led us thru the most beautiful and lofty forest of spruce and pine I ever saw. This forest is called 'The Shades.' The trees are generally from 108 to 180 ft. in height, many of them without a limb for 100 ft. with a body not more than 12 inches in diameter at the surface of the earth. . . . Over the greater part of our journey we found snow 2 ft. in depth. A tolerable tract is, however, beaten for us by a description of peddlers, who pass by the name of 'packers.' These people carry on a considerable trade between the Red Stone settlements and Winchester, in Va. It is not unusual to meet a packer having with him half a dozen loaded horses, loaded with merchandise."

Nothing stopped the white man who must go west. By 1802 nearly sixty thousand homesteaders lived in the fertile Ohio Valley. They petitioned Congress for statehood that year, and with the aid of President Thomas Jefferson and sympathetic congressmen, an enabling act was passed in April. The act stipulated that 5 percent of the proceeds from the sale of public Ohio lands be set aside for the construction of roads to and through the area. Ohio's constitutional convention of 1803 modified the 5 percent plan by insisting that no less than three-fifths of the land funds be expended on roads within the new state to be constructed under the jurisdiction of the local legislature, and that only 2 percent of the funds be available for the construction of federal roads to and through Ohio under the jurisdiction of the Federal Government. Congress accepted the recommendation.

Late in 1805 Senator Uriah Tracy of Connecticut reported to his fellow lawmakers that "the road committee have thought it expedient to recommend the laying out and making a road from Cumberland, on the northern bank of the Potomac and within the State of Maryland, to the river Ohio at the most convenient place between a point on the easterly bank of said river, opposite to Steubenville and the mouth of Grace Creek which empties into said river Ohio, a little below Wheeling in Virginia." The Senate passed the Cumberland-Ohio Road Bill on December 27, 1805; the House passed it on March 24, 1806. Congressional debate on the federally funded internal improvement issue was both heated and lively. The South was generally antagonistic because it feared a western highway would drain its native population and sectionally unite the agrarian West with the commercial North. Already the States' Rights constitutional issue which would eventually lead to the great civil strife of mid-century was beginning to emerge as a southern rallying point. Virginia was antagonistic because Richmond was not included in the proposed route. Pennsylvania was antagonistic because Philadelphia was bypassed and the road would pass through only a small portion of its domain. New Hampshire, Connecticut, Maryland, Delaware, Georgia, Kentucky, and Ohio supported the measure with every vote they cast.

Late in 1806 Thomas Jefferson, a zealous advocate of internal improvements and westward expansion—"Manifest Destiny"—appointed Joseph Kerr, of Ohio, and Thomas Moore and Eli Williams, of Maryland, commissioners to lay out the newly authorized road. The commissioners employed Josias Thompson, "a surveyor of professional merit," to chart the route of the highway westward from Cumberland.

"The Cumberland road," recorded Jacob Brown of Grantsville in 1896, commenced on the west side of Will's Creek, crossing Will's mountain at Sandy gap, following the general route of Braddock, first on one side and then on the other, rarely on the identical line." It crossed Savage Mountain in later Garrett County a little south of Cranberry Swamp, traversed the Shades of Death and cut through Little Meadows, bypassed Old Grantsville (which, according to Jacob Brown, soon fell as a consequence into "inocuous desuetude"), ascended the successive ranges of Negro Mountain and Keyser's Ridge, then passed just north of a valley known as Devil's Half Acre into the state of Pennsylvania and toward Uniontown. (The route today follows the basic outline of U.S. Route 40.)

"Technically," wrote Jacob Brown, the new highway "was called the 'Cumberland Road' but popularly it was known as the National Road, because it was the Nation's enterprise." The National Road was the first public highway built across the Appalachian Mountains at federal expense. Superintendent of construction was David Shriver, Jr., a young Cumberland engineer fired with ambition and keen initiative. On May 8, 1811, eight years after the admission of Ohio into the federal union of states, Shriver announced the award of the road's first construction contracts. Work began almost immediately at Cumberland. "The manner of construction," noted Jacob Brown, "was first to clear and grade the bed and then to closely overlay it with strong flat rocks, and upon this face, or foundation, was placed a covering of coarsely broken stone, and earth, and as thus completed was considered a very fine road." All work was done by man and horse power. Some oxen were used. Most laborers were of Irish nationality.

The road workers first cleared a right-of-way strip sixty-six feet wide by cutting trees, burning brush, removing natural impediments, and grubbing roots. They then leveled a roadbed thirty feet in width by pick and shovel. They cut hills and filled hollows. They trimmed slopes and dug water ditches on both sides of the roadbed. They built bridges of stones and wood. Then they filled the prepared bed. They broke base stones by hammer into seven-inch diameter rocks; they shattered top stones small enough to pass through three inch rings. "Slowly," recorded road historian Philip D. Jordan in 1948, "the hope of the West inched forward, mile by mile and section by section until by the end of December 1813, two years after the initial contracts were let, Shriver was able to report the completion of the first ten miles."

The Cumberland Road was completed to Little Meadows early in 1815. Two years earlier contractors had built an eighty-foot, single-span stone-arch bridge over the Casselman River at Little Crossings, just east of Grantsville. The arch of the bridge was twenty-six feet wide and three feet thick. The bridge itself was the largest stone arch structure ever built in the United States at the time of its construction. The night before the public celebration of its opening; David Shriver, the lead road superintendent, quietly ordered the removal of the bridge's key supporting timbers while he himself stood under the arch, proclaiming that death in the event of failure would be preferable to a ruined reputation. The bridge stood.

"The Bridge over the Little Crossings of Little Youghegany River is possitively a superb Bridge," noted an 1816 traveler. It carried traffic (first horse-drawn wagons and coaches, then automobiles) for 120 years. In 1953 it was closed to all vehicular traffic due to deterioration of its side walls and approaches. Two years later Delegate Harry C. Edwards, of Grantsville, helped obtain state funds for its restoration. In 1956 the State Road Commission purchased land surrounding the bridge as a public park. The State Department of Forests and Parks began development of the park the following year. The Casselman River Bridge still stands today just north of Interstate Route 48 as a monument to the laborers and craftsmen who built the first National Road across the mountains in the early nineteenth century.

David Shriver reported the completion of twenty-eight miles of the National Road west of Cumberland in December 1816. The entire Maryland section of the road (through present-day Garrett County) was completed the same year. By that time the bridge over the Youghiogheny River in Pennsylvania was already under construction. "The National

Turnpike from Fort Cumberland to this place," reported a Wheeling editor in 1818, "is in a considerable state of forwardness, and promises fair to be one of the best and most permanent roads in the United States. The advantage of this road to the nation at large begins now to be acknowledged, even by those who scoffed at it a few months back. They perceive that, as soon as the road is finished, a complete change will take place in the carrying trade between the Atlantic and the Western Waters." A contemporary Pennsylvania farmer considered the road "good enough for an emperor to travel." The cost of the highway from Cumberland to Uniontown totaled nearly ten thousand dollars per mile. The road was completed to the banks of the Ohio River in 1818. Thirty-two years later it reached its terminus at Vandalia, Illinois.

The Grantsville historian Jacob Brown contended that the National Road, "in its grandest days, from about 1834 to say 1845, was the finest road in America, and in all probability in the world, considering its length, reaching from Baltimore to or near St. Louis. None other in this country ever had such travel and traffic. The number of wagons, coaches, animals, and all other conceivable modes of travel over it daily when it was in its finest condition was fabulous. In the busy season there was a perfect throng all day long and at night the many taverns would be overflowed with motley and jolly crowds. These were flush times indeed, money plenty, everybody employed and happy. We all thought the freight and people over the pike was amazing, and so it was at that time."

"The wagons were so numerous that the leaders of one team had their noses in the trough at the end of the wagon ahead," recorded western Maryland historian J. Thomas Scharf in 1882. "Besides the coaches and wagons, there were gentlemen traveling singly in the saddle, with all the accoutrements of the journey stuffed into their saddle-bags, and there were enormous droves of sheep and herds of cattle, which at times blocked the way for miles and elicited from travelers expressions of disgust often more 'striking than classic.' "

The Grantsville historian Ross C. Durst agreed in 1956 that "a constant stream of traffic flowed along this great Appian

Way. Some traveled by coach, some by wagon, and some on horseback. Large droves of cattle, sheep and hogs moved slowly along to the accompaniment of loud and raucous shouts of the drovers. A short distance on either side of the highway one plunged into the primeval forest where all was peace and quiet. Settlers cabins were few and far between."

Jacob Brown found that "the greatest volume of travel on the National road was for the years between 1842 and 1852. In the traveling season it was no extraordinary thing to see 100 people sent west from here in coaches per day. Stage owners made money and grew rich."

"There were sometimes sixteen gayly-painted coaches each way a day," recorded Thomas Scharf; "the cattle and sheep were never out of sight; the canvas-covered wagons were drawn by six or twelve horses, with bows of bells over their collars; the families of statesmen and merchants went by in private vehicles; and, while most of the travelers were unostentatious, a few had splendid equipages and employed outriders."

"There were a great many people in those days who made wagoning a regular business," noted Jacob Brown, "and in the busy season quite a number of small teams, called Sharp-Shooters, would turn in for a few trips. These latter were held in great contempt by the old regulars, who would hardly take a glass of common whiskey with them. Some of these old teamsters when home were pretty decent men, but when upon the road they lived according to their code, which was a rough one. They always carried their own bed in a roll like a bundle of carpet. The bar-room floor was their sleeping place, which was often packed with them like cobble stones in a street, and woe to the person who happened to invade their lair."

Even Indians occasionally traveled the road. "Once," recorded Brown, "one came to our home drunk on a cold winter evening for shelter. A good mother could not turn even a savage away. He was given a place behind an old-time wood stove with two stalwart sons on the opposite side as a guard."

Many of the most prominent men of the nation also passed

over the National Road in the early 1800s on their way to and from the seat of government in Washington, D.C. Four western presidents traveled the road. President Andrew Jackson traveled the road in 1829 from his home at the Hermitage at Nashville, Tennessee. President-elect William Henry Harrison dined at Alexander McCurdy's Little Crossings Hotel on an 1841 journey east to Washington. Jacob Brown described the old Indian fighter's arrival: "On a very cold frosty afternoon in February, several coaches drove up to the hotel for dinner, with unusual vim and style. . . . We saw descending from the coach an aged, but distinguished looking man of slow, feeble step with complexion and hair bleached into whiteness, deeply wrapped in macinaw blankets." Brown was a schoolboy at the time. "The President-elect's appearance," he wrote, "was awe inspiring to a youth."

Four years later President-elect James K. Polk stopped at Little Meadows and remained at the Stone House Inn long enough on his journey to Washington to address a neighborhood crowd. Then, in 1849, President-elect Zachary Taylor crossed the mountains in a snowstorm. "The road was a perfect glare of ice," recorded J. Thomas Scharf, of Cumberland, "and everything above ground was literally plated with sleeted frost. The scenery was beautiful; to native mountaineers too common to be of much interest, but to a Southerner like Gen. Taylor, who had never seen the like, it was a phenomenon. In going down a spur of Meadow Mountain, the presidential coach, with the others, danced and waltzed on the polished road, first on one side and then on the other, with every sign of an immediate capsize, but the coaches were manned with the most expert of the whole corps of drivers. The iron gray head of the General could with frequency be seen outside of his window, not to see after anybody's safety, but to look upon what seemed to him an artic panorama. After a ride of many miles the last long slope was passed and everything was safe. At twilight the Narrows were reached, two miles west of Cumberland, one of the boldest and most sublime views on the Atlantic Slope. Gen. Taylor assumed authority and ordered a halt, and out he got in the storm and snow and looked at the giddy heights on either side of Will's Creek, until he had taken in the grandeur of the scenery. He had beheld nothing like it before, even in his campaigns in Northern Mexico. The president-elect was tendered a reception on his arrival at Cumberland, and the next morning he and his party left on the cars for Washington."

Stagecoaches began to appear on the National Road almost as soon as its easternmost portions were completed. The Maryland historian J. Thomas Scharf has distinguished four distinct types of coaches used on the road at different periods of pike development: "The first was built at Cumberland by Adam Russell, and carried sixteen passengers; and when this was found too cumbrous, a lighter vehicle, almost egg-shaped, and built at Trenton, New Jersey, was adopted. The latter was succeeded by the Troy coach, built at Troy, New York, carrying nine passengers inside and two outside, which was finally superseded by the familiar Concord, constructed at Concord, New Hampshire." "The Concord, like the Troy coach," noted Grantsville's Jacob Brown, "was very strong and durable, neatly upholstered inside, with three cross-wise seats, accommodating nine passengers inside and one or two outside."

James Reeside of Cumberland brought the first Troy coach to western Maryland from Philadelphia in the winter of 1829. Having won the vehicle in a presidential election wager the prior year, he intended that the new president-elect, Andrew Jackson, should be the first to ride the coach from Cumberland to Washington. Jackson, however, politely refused. "He would be under no obligations to anyone," suggested Jacob Brown. "So his shabby two-horse carriage not only took him to the seat of government, but back to the Hermitage, eight years thereafter. However, Old Hickory unbent so far as to permit a portion of his family to christen the virgin coach which had been won on his own election."

Early nineteenth century coach lines on the National Road included the National Road Stage Company, the Good Intent Stage Company, the June Bug Line, Landlord's Line, and the Pilot Line. Coaches were popularly known as "turtle-backs" and "shake-guts." The first stage line between Baltimore and the Ohio River was organized in four relays. Stages in the 1820s left Baltimore and Washington at 2:00 a.m. on Sundays, Tuesdays, and Thursdays, and arrived at Wheeling within seventy-eight hours. Special stages departed on Mondays, Wednesdays, Fridays, and Saturdays. Travelers paid seventeen dollars to journey by stage from Baltimore to Wheeling in 1825; they paid only four dollars to journey from Cumberland to Uniontown. Coach lines introduced a system of running stages both day and night over the Cumberland Road around 1827, reducing the Baltimore-Wheeling travel time to fifty-two hours. A Philadelphia newspaper columnist noted that year that one "could leave Philadelphia with a hot johnny cake in his pocket and reach Pittsburgh before it would grow cold."

Thomas Scharf recorded in 1882 that "there were rival lines of coaches, and the competition led to overdriving and many accidents. The rival lines brought rival taverns into existence, and as two opposition coaches drove into a town for supper, they pulled up before separate houses."

Jacob Brown concurred, "Stage wars were common in those days," he wrote. "Passengers were sometimes carried for nothing, and mealed besides. When the competition was quite spirited, riding was almost free. However," he noted, "these sports never lasted long."

Mail stages in 1825 departed from Cumberland westward at 4:00 p.m. on Mondays, Wednesdays, and Fridays. As early as 1817 the fourteen-year-old Joseph Strong of Cumberland was employed to carry the mail from that city to Uniontown, a distance of sixty-five miles. "The leather mail bag, with its meager contents was carried by the plucky boy on horseback," recalled Jacob Brown. "No stage coaches operated at that time, but they appeared soon thereafter. In this way Strong became acquainted with all the early hotel keepers along the now historic highway." Only two post offices existed at the time between Cumberland and Uniontown—one at Little Meadows; one at Smithfield, Pennsylvania.

The early nineteenth century stage drivers "were a jolly set of men," wrote Jacob Brown, "proud of their situation, some of them of more importance in their own estimation than the

Congressman or Cabinet minister riding in the coach below them. They were in some respects, at least, picked men, and their places much sought after; politics no test; religion not expected; a reasonable amount of profanity and a sprinkle of 'Perry grove' no bar to employment; they were expected to be reliable, and to possess a good share of knowledge in horse anatomy, to use the long whip gracefully, but not too much."

"The drivers were all provided with a horn," recorded Thomas Scharf, "(which they blew on arriving at or departing from a station), and were armed with whatever weapons they chose to carry. In the traveling season, it was not extraordinary for one hundred people to be sent west per day from Cumberland in their coaches."

"Coach riding," wrote Brown, "was a very pleasant mode of traveling during the summer season over the mountains, but the very reverse in the winter. Just think of a stage load of men and women in the mountains, with two or three feet of snow, thermometer many degrees below zero, without a particle of fire nearer than the next changing place."

"The ordinary speed," Brown suggested, "was about six or seven miles an hour, but in an emergency ten have been made." "Ten miles an hour," agreed Thomas Scharf, "including delays, was not an unusual degree of speed in the days of stage coaches."

The road the early lines traveled was often fraught with hidden danger and thieves. "Robberies were numerous and of easy accomplishment," wrote Brown; the National Road was the scene of many crimes, "from the lowest to the highest degree." In 1834 highwaymen ambushed Samuel Luman, a mail carrier and driver of a four-horse coach, near the Shades of Death east of Grantsville. "It was just at the eastern end, ascending a hill where this bold effort to rob was made," recorded Brown. "The great highway at this dreary spot had been barricaded with logs as a means of obstructing the coach while the rifling was to be done. The horses were seized by the bridles whilst other ruffians were to over-power the driver and take possession of the mail bags. But Luman was young and powerful, as well as brave. He had no weapon of defense except his long whip, which in the hands of an expert, could be used with powerful effect. The lash was plied with great rapidity and energy upon the unknown faces of the robbers, as well as upon the backs of the steeds. The horses became frantic from fear and punishment, and broke away from their restraint, and in a minute horses, coach and driver had leaped the breastwork to safety."

The tavern business flourished even more along the National (Cumberland) Road in the early nineteenth century than it did along the Virginia-Maryland Interstate Road and the Northwestern Turnpike to the south due to the northern route's heavier volume of traffic. "Stagecoach changing places or relays," noted Brown, "where fresh horses were employed in the place of the tired ones, were usually ten or twelve miles apart." Hotels and inns could be found almost every mile along the trail by mid-century. "These early accommodations," Brown wrote, "were in most cases plain buildings of logs or frame work, with annexes from time to time, as circumstances would authorize; however, there were some brick and stone edifices among them, notably at Grantsville and Little Meadows. The chambers in these buildings were neither large or numerous, with but little furnishings, always a good clean bed. The table usually extended from one end of the room to the other. All the edibles were placed upon the table, which was generally so crowded as to not leave room enough for a napkin, but there were none in those days. The guests were summoned to their meals by the ring of a bell which would electrify all concerned, and who would respond in a manner according to their breeding and education. In busy seasons even these numerous inns were insufficient to comfortably accommodate the immense travel on the road. Many a way-farer had to submit to pretty hard lodging; but always there was plenty to eat."

J. Thomas Scharf: "Those who have participated in the traffic over that renowned thorough-fare are loath to admit that there were ever before such landlords, such taverns, such dinners, such whiskey, such bustle, or such endless cavalcades of coaches and wagons as could be seen between Wheeling and Frederick in the palmy days of the old National 'pike'.

The gilded and glittering sign of the road's many taverns swung out from a pole or staff, and a moss-grown trough overflowed and trickled melodiously before the porch. The floors of the inn interiors were sanded, and the beams in the ceiling were uncovered. An hour before the coach was due the landlord was to be found in a little alcove of the tap-room transferring his liquors from demijohns to bottles, setting his glasses in single file, and bidding his servants make haste with supper. The villagers appeared at their doors; for the arrival of the coach, although a very familiar event, acquired a fresh interest from day to day."

Taste-tempting meals could generally be had in the early pike taverns for as little as twenty-five cents. "Mountain provisions were plenty, cheap and the very best," noted Brown. "The mutton cannot be equaled by any other climate, and in those days venison and other game meat, such as wild turkey, pheasant, etc., were abundant, and easily obtained, with brook trout at about the price of beefstake." An 1830 writer for the *Baltimore Gazette* agreed. The mountain "venison and its mutton, its butter and its potatoes have long been known and appreciated," he reported. "Its vegetables ... there are no such carrots elsewhere. Delicious meats ... pheasants and wild turkeys ... the little streams are well supplied with trout." The National Road hotels were "an excellent market at all times for the local producers of grain, meat, and dairy products," recorded Jacob Brown. "There were never a happier people than those who lived on and along this road."

Whiskey was also cheap and abundant in the early pike taverns. "In the front part of the hotel was always found the *bar-room*," recalled Brown, "which formed a lobby for the guests and the public generally. The bottles were numerous and sometimes grotesque in shape, but the varieties of the liquors not so manifold; the taste generally much the same. Sometimes a little cheap brandy and gin would be found in a secret part of the lock-up. Common whiskey cost from 18 to 25 cents per gallon, and was doled out at 3 and 5 cents per drink. It was mostly made of corn, and generally hard stuff, and had many hard names, such as rotgut. It was drunk freely and almost by everybody."

The operation of early pike taverns and inns was generally a family affair. "Old National Road hotel keepers were a very influential class of people," noted Brown, "because they were great consumers and afforded a market for nearly the whole produce of the neighboring country. Nearly every person had something to do with the hotel keepers; indeed they were both deferred to and feared, especially in the more early times. The landlady, as the proprietor's wife was styled, if clever in her ways was an important and helpful factor about the establishment. She certainly could do much to cause the stranger to feel he had a temporary home when away from his own." Children helped with the maintenance of the stables, the preparation of foods, and the cleaning of linens and floors.

Jacob Brown distinguished several types of hotels along the old pike: "The hotel business, like all others, had its grades and specialties," he wrote. "Those who were fortunate enough to secure the patronage of the great stage lines were the upper crust and did not care for other customers except the more genteel kind. Then there were the wagon stands pretty much monopolized by the men who drove the great Connestoga Wagons with their six powerful horses. As a class they were pretty rough, some very much so. Some of their lodgers were well-to-do farmers; a good deal more civil at home than abroad. Most of their frequenters were terribly profane and boisterous, and could almost annihilate each other with threats and gesticulations. Then there were the drovers' taverns, preempted by the cowboys and pigpelters, who were generally noisy and loud-mouthed, but manageable as they were in the most boys."

Three taverns served travelers of the old Braddock Road through later Garrett County prior to the construction of the National Road in the early 1800s. Joseph Tomlinson established the log Red House Inn on his Good Will tract of Little Meadows in the 1760s. Aaron Parker settled at the sixth camp of Braddock's 1754 army prior to 1774 at a place known to early hunters as "the Bear Camp" and shortly afterward opened "The Hotell." John Simkins bought the Parker settlement in 1786 and operated the Bear Camp Inn until 1817, when the new Cumberland Road passed one mile north of his establishment, ruining the local business. Daniel Gorman bought the Mount Nebo tract south of Little Meadows in the late eighteenth century and cut a Braddock Road bypass through the woods to his Nebo House. For a while the Nebo House prospered; Tomlinson's nearby business suffered. Then Tomlinson barricaded the Gorman bypass by felling trees on a portion of his own property in the woods which the Gorman Road traversed. Business at the Red House Inn again flourished; Gorman abandoned his enterprise and moved west.

Then the National Road came to the mountains and the hotel business boomed. Almost a full score of inns and taverns were established along the road's right-of-way in the mountain glade country of present-day Garrett County by mid-century. Meshach Frost built Highland Hall at Mount Pleasant (present-day Frostburg) in 1812. By 1832 his establishment had been enlarged for the accommodation of as many as three hundred guests. Thomas Beall also operated an early tavern at later-day Frostburg—the Franklin House, headquarters of the Good Intent Stage line. Highland Hall served as headquarters of the Stockton Line.

The Widow Ward operated the Sand Spring Tavern wagon stand at the foot of Big Savage Mountain, a mile west of Frostburg, as early as 1836. Chaney's Wagon Stand Inn stood nearby on the mountain's eastern slope. Thomas Beall opened a tavern across the ridge at the foot of Little Savage around 1830. Thomas Johnson, who succeeded Beall in the operation of the establishment, "was a noted character," according to pike historian T. B. Searight. "He was a good fiddler and dancer. He owned a negro named Dennis who was also a good dancer. Night after night in the cheerful bar room Dennis performed the 'double shuffle,' responsive to lively music furnished by his old master."

John Reckner kept a log and frame wagon tavern shaded by large pine trees at the eastern approach to the Shades of Death as early as 1830. He operated the business until his death. Jacob Brown noted that "His was a wagon stand mainly, yet he kept it orderly, though he had occasionally to be a little disorderly in doing so." Sons of Maryland's first governor, Thomas Johnson, Joshua and Thomas J. Johnson, operated the Brunley Inn on the north side of the road at Piney Grove between the Shades of Death and Little Meadows early in the century. Other innkeepers near Piney Grove included Isaac Beall and M. D. Cade.

The National and Braddock roads coincided at Little Meadows, the site of Joseph Tomlinson's Red House Inn, the oldest on the road. In 1816 Tomlinson's son, Jesse, erected the Stone House Inn still used today as a farm house in the natural meadow glades. The house was built four stories high, primarily by slave labor. Local fieldstones were used to build its massive walls, two feet thick. Fireplaces warmed ten of the house's eighteen rooms. The younger Tomlinson met his future wife at the Stone House when the young lady's family paused there on a westward journey to "Old Kentuck" early in the century. Jacob Brown: "The young lady never got any further west than Little Meadows."

The Stone House was operated by a succession of managers after 1817—men with the surnames Sides, Endsley, Thistle, Stoddard, Huddleson, Fairall, Cross, Mahaney, Garlitz, Layman, and McGraw. "The Tomlinson Inn was the center of the social and political life of the county until the coming of the B&O Railroad through Oakland," suggested Grantsville's Marion Viola Broadwater in 1956. As early as 1896 Jacob Brown contended that the inn was "one of the most beautiful and charming places in all the Alleganies. When Huddleson kept the hotel, it was quite a resort for the invalid as well as the pleasure-seeker; but when the railroads spanned the Alleganies on either side, its gay seasons were ended. The invalid came from afar for the cure of ailments by the delightful atmosphere, scenery and water, and the well for the enjoyment of the same elements in nature, that ailments might not come to them."

The family of Eileen Dudley lived in the Stone House in 1973. "Stone House," Ms. Dudley wrote, "was a center of politics and society during the years that stage coach traffic was heavy on the National Road. At one time it was not only an inn and a tavern, but also a post-office and a country store. Stone House was also used as a voting place during the elections, and once a trial for a chancery suit was held there. The house even served at one time as an exclusive school for some children of the area. Because it was sociable and cheerful, local people used the tavern as a gathering place. A good innkeeper always kept a comfortable fire going and his whiskey was cheap, usually 3¢ a glass. Racks of small clay pipes with long stems were kept for guests. As each smoker finished his pipe, he broke off a small piece and discarded it. Under the ground floor at Stone House we have found pieces of broken stems and the discarded bowls of clay pipes, one of them beautifully carved to resemble a woman's head. My family and I are reminded in small sudden ways of people who were once here at Stone House. They left modest traces of themselves for us to happily discover a century later: a button from the coat of a Confederate soldier, a small bottle upon which is imprinted 'Husband's Calcined Magnesia,' a little boy's clay marbles, the broken halves of plates hidden under the floor, a tiny china doll's head with the tint on the cheeks still fresh and pink. We were profoundly moved and strangely quiet when we discovered a solitary tombstone near a huge boulder in the south meadow. We brushed away the earth and leaves from the crudely carved surface to read, 'In memory of Patty Newman who departed this life March 26 A.D. 1815, aged 25 years?' "

William Wooden operated an inn and a small store at Smooth Valley west of Little Meadows until his death in 1834. His widow subsequently continued the business for a time, then turned it over to her son-in-law, Peter Yeast. A tavern established near the Little Crossings Bridge by Alexander Carlisle around 1836 was operated at different times by John and Samuel McCurdy, David Johnson, Elisha Brown, Jacob Conrad, and David Mahaney.

Two taverns were built at Grantsville in the 1830s, three in the 1840s. Samuel Gillus kept a wagon stand at the town's east end as early as 1833. Adam Shultz erected a large brick structure nearby the following decade. His son, Perry, continued operation of the business until 1852. (Part of the Shultz building is presently incorporated in the Grantsville Elementary School.) Soloman Starner opened the Starner House in 1842 and managed the inn until his death ten years later, when he was succeeded by his son Archibald. The Starner House became known as the Farmer's Hotel in the 1840s, when it was converted to a major cattle drover's stop with a large outdoor corral. Today, the Casselman, it is recognized as Garrett County's oldest hotel and restaurant in continuous operation. Henry Fuller built the National House (also currently open to the public) in 1843 on the site of a demolished tavern erected by John Lehman—the Lehman House—in 1836. Subsequent owner and operator of the National Hotel was John Slicer.

Thomas Thistle kept a tavern as early as 1836 at the eastern foot of Negro Mountain, two miles west of Grantsville, at a place where the National Road crossed the old Braddock Trail. William DeHaven operated the Thistle Tavern in 1844 and later turned it over to Levi Dean. The Haldeman Tavern on the eastern slope of Negro Mountain was originally managed by the widow of John Haldeman, who later married Daniel Smouse. Dennis Hoblitzell presided at a stone tavern on the crest of Negro Mountain beginning in 1836. The Hoblitzell Tavern was later operated by William Sheetz. "William had experience on the 'Stage box,' " recorded Jacob Brown, "as well as that of teamster on the National Road. He drifted into hotel keeping when in mature life. Kept an inn on Negro Mountain, where it is fearfully bleak and cold in winter, but most charming in the summer season on account of its pure and bracing atmosphere, and its magnificent and far-reaching view to the east and south. Here Sheetz played the roll of 'tavern-keeper' for many years. It was the drovers' retreat. How the 'cow boys' and 'pig pelters' would pelt their halting animals to reach this favorite resort; and well they might, for they were always well cared for and fed of the best. The house had a good run of customers; was orderly and in good repute."

The drover Jesse J. Peirsol recalled the Sheetz Tavern in a letter dated 1892: "I have stayed over night with William

Sheets on Nigger Mountain when there would be thirty six-horse teams in the wagon yard, one hundred Kentucky mules in an adjacent lot, one thousand hogs in other enclosures, and as many fat cattle from Illinois in adjoining fields. The music made by this large number of hogs in eating corn on a frosty night I will never forget. After supper and attention to the teams the waggoners would gather in the bar room and listen to music on the violin furnished by one of their fellows, have a 'Virginia Hoe-Down,' sing songs, tell anecdotes and hear the esperience of drivers and drovers from all points on the road. When it was over they would unroll their beds, lay them down on the floor before the bar room fire, side by side, and sleep, with their feet facing the fireplace, as soundly as under the parental roof."

James Stoddard opened the Stoddard Tavern on the eastern slope of Keyser's Ridge, the highest point in the mountains along the National Road—nearly three thousand feet above sea level—around 1820. Truman Fairall built a tavern on the ridge in 1840 but abandoned the enterprise when he moved to Iowa thirteen years later. John Woods also kept a tavern at Keyser's Ridge for several years. Daniel Fear operated a wagon stand about two miles west of the ridge early in the century. James Reynolds managed a tavern at "West Union Towne" near the junction of the old Morgantown Road with the National Road until 1843, when he sold out to Daniel Fear. The National Road crossed the Maryland-Pennsylvania state line just northwest of the Reynolds' enterprise.

Nothing stopped the white man who must go west. They came slowly at first, these pioneer settlers from the Atlantic seaboard who abandoned their homes and pressed over the mountains to the broad Ohio and Mississippi valleys; then they came in ever-increasing numbers until by mid-century they flooded the Appalachian highways in one continuous stream. They took two steps forward, one step backward, two steps forward until they reached their destination, and, sometimes, their hopes and dreams.

One caustic wag remarked early in the nineteenth century that the National Road fell into disrepair even quicker than it could be built. In a sense he was right—never at any time was the road a smooth highway all the way from Cumberland west to Vandalia. It demanded constant attention, constant maintenance.

"Notwithstanding the large sums of money appropriated for and expended on the old National Road," noted Jacob Brown in 1896, "the year 1830 found it in a worn out and almost useless condition. Travel and traffic on it had increased heavily. Little of it was left except the rough stone bed."

"Generally speaking the surface is entirely destroyed or sunk under the foundation, leaving the large stone on top," observed Uniontown's Lucius W. Stockton in 1826. "In one place the foundation itself has been carried away by the breaking up of the winter, which, with heavy rains, left a broken link in the road impossible to be crossed even by horsemen. On the Eastern side of the Great Savage Mountain there cannot be found a handful of earth on the road for some distance, it being washed out by the filling up of culverts or drains, carrying with it all the same stone on the surface. In fact, it is *distressing* to a traveler to see this great work in its present condition."

The army engineer J. K. F. Mansfield reported in 1832 finding the road "in shocking condition, and every rod of it will require great repair; some of it is almost impassable." Congress subsequently passed several substantial appropriations that year for the road's improvement. "In pursuance of that arrangement," one of the contemporary Cumberland papers reported, "Samuel Slicer illuminated his large and splendid hotel, which patriotic example was followed by James Black. In addition to the illumination, Mr. Bunting [our famous 'old Red'], agent of L. W. Stockton, ordered out a coach, drawn by four large gray stallions, driven by George Shuck. The stage was beautifully illuminated, which presented to the generous citizens of this place a novelty calculated to impress upon the minds of all who witnessed it the great benefits they anticipated by having the road repaired. There were also seated upon the top of the vehicle several gentlemen who played on various instruments, which contributed very much to the amusement of the citizens and gave zest to everything that inspired delight or created feelings of patriotism. They started from the front of Mr. Slicer's hotel, and as they moved on slowly the band played 'Hail Columbia,' 'Freemason's March,' 'Bonaparte Crossing the Rhine,' 'Washington's March' together with a new tune composed by Mr. Mobley, of this place, and named by the gentlemen on the stage, 'The Lady We Love Best,' and many others, as they passed through the principal streets of the town. On their return they played 'Home, Sweet Home' to the admiration of all who heard it."

Appropriations for road improvements delighted settlers and businessmen living along the highway's right-of-way. Congress authorized two major improvements in 1834: alteration of the route immediately west of Cumberland to avoid the long pull up Will's Hill and the macadam procedure of replacing the road's original surface. The macadam procedure (named after the distinguished contemporary Scotch road builder John L. McAdam) involved the breaking up of stones to small sizes for a hard, packed top surface of small rocks and gravel, "which shall unite," in the words of McAdam himself, "by its own angles so as to form a solid, hard surface." "Limestone was quarried wherever it could be obtained," recorded Jacob Brown, "and in some instances was drawn as much as ten miles by teams of four and six horses, and strung along the way on each side, then reduced by sledge hammers to the size of about three or four pounds, and after that broken down to an egg size by small round hammers in the hands of the laborers in a sitting position—very hard and tedious work." The resurfacing was completed in stages until at least nine inches of crushed stone covered the roadbed.

Appropriations for National Road improvements delighted settlers and businessmen living along the route's right-of-way, but irritated and antagonized Southerners who had long been opposed to federally funded and sectional internal improvements. Representative T. R. Mitchell, of South Carolina, called the road "a perfect quagmire" in 1829, "a speaking proof of the feebleness, extravagance, and incompetency of the National Government . . . only benefiting, at the expense of the people, the superintendent and the workmen employed on it." Mitchell typified the Southern view with his pointed observation that "while millions and tens of millions have been projected to be laid out in improvements north of the Potomac, thousands, beggarly thousands, have been with difficulty obtained for the fertile plains of the South. These works are classified, not according to the necessities of the people, but according to their number. Pennsylvania! You contain more than a million of people; you must be first served. Ohio! You are increasing every day in wealth and population; that entitles you to precedence. Are not all the states, in the eye of the Constitution, Sovereign, of equal dignity, and on a perfect footing of equality?" (It was an ill wind which blew north to the pike from the heart of the South—even as early as 1829.)

The fate of Uncle Sam's highway was influenced by each change of presidential administration in Washington. In 1822 James Monroe, of Virginia, vetoed a bill providing for road improvement and maintenance, contending that "this power of sectional improvement can be granted only by an amendment to the Constitution and in the mode prescribed by it." Monroe's successor, John Quincy Adams, of Massachusetts, was a strong advocate of internal improvements, and thereby delighted Westerners while alienating Southerners. John Tyler, of Virginia, reversed the channels of affection by comparing the federal patronage which had funded the road with an "old, wrinkled hag, corrupted and corrupting." Tyler apparently agreed with the views of Senator Nathaniel Macon, of North Carolina. "I know it is a very pleasant thing to travel over a fine road for nothing," Macon had commented to his Congressional colleagues in 1828. "But I should like it better had it cost the Government nothing; but been made by the enterprise of the states."

Then in 1828 the popular Andrew Jackson, of Tennessee, was elected to the White House. The following year he delivered his first annual address to Congress. "Every member of the Union, in peace and in war," he argued, "will be benefited by the improvement of inland navigation and the construction of highways in the several states. Let us, then, endeavor to attain this benefit in a mode which will be satisfactory to all. That hitherto adopted has by many of our fellow-citizens been deprecated as an infraction of the Constitution, while by others it has been viewed as inexpedient. All feel that it has been employed at the expense of harmony in the legislative councils."

Old Hickory's words signaled a significant change in administration outlook. A few months later the new president emphasized the alteration by vetoing subscription by the federal government in stock providing for improvement of the Maysville Turnpike, formerly Ebenezer Zane's Trace, leading southwest from the National Road at Wheeling to Maysville, Kentucky. Jackson agreed with his predecessor Monroe that "if it be the wish of the people that the construction of roads and canals should be conducted by the Federal Government, it is not only highly expedient, but indispensably necessary, that a previous amendment of the Constitution, delegating the necessary power and defining and restricting its exercise with reference to the sovereignty of the States, should be made."

"The Cumberland Road should be an instructive admonition of the consequences of acting without this right," the president suggested. "Year after year contests are witnessed, growing out of efforts to obtain the necessary appropriations for completing and repairing this useful work. Whilst one Congress may claim and exercise the power, a succeeding one may deny it; and this fluctuation of opinion must be unavoidably fatal to any scheme which from its extent would promote the interests and elevate the character of the country."

The Maysville veto whetted the desire of Southerners to fully halt further federal appropriations for sectional improvements. Those appropriations which subsequently did pass Congress were usually insufficient to either extend the National Road or keep it in good repair. "Westerners," noted pike historian Philip D. Jordan in 1948, "who had fought for years in defense of the highway, decided to retreat rather than surrender. If the road must be given up, then the relinquishment should take place gradually."

Ohio led the way. On February 4, 1831, the Buckeye legislature passed an act providing for the preservation and repair of the National Road in Ohio through state funding. Congress approved the act. Debate in the Senate was mild. Everyone agreed, for once, with an Ohio spokesman, who contended that the road soon would become useless if provisions were not made for its care. Everyone agreed, for once, with Ohio Senator Jacob Burnet's opinion that "as the road had been constructed by Congress, at a great expense, it was unreasonable to rely on them for yearly appropriations of money from the national treasury, to keep it in a state of preservation; that the road, being once completed, ought to sustain itself without imposing a further burden on the national treasury." Everyone agreed for once—almost everyone. The vote of approval stood twenty-nine to seven in the Senate and eighty-nine to sixty in the House. The act became law on March 2, 1831.

Similar acts for Pennsylvania and Maryland were approved on July 3, 1832, though both states refused to accept jurisdiction over their portions of the road until the central government had them repaired and erected tollgates. The federal maintenance was completed by 1835, and the two states finally accepted custody of the road that year. The great Cumberland Road, costing the federal government a total of nearly seven million dollars, was national no longer.

Nothing stopped the white man who must go west. He first came to the highland glades of later Garrett County searching for a passageway to the west in 1750. He built a crude trace across the mountains in 1752. He fought an international war for western sovereignty from 1753 to 1763.

In 1784 the white man voted interstate funding for the construction of a wagon road across the eastern continental divide at Backbone Mountain from Winchester to Clarksburg, Virginia, the Maryland-Virginia Interstate Highway. In 1806 he provided federal funding for the construction of a national highway west from Cumberland through the Ohio Country, the Cumberland Road. In 1834 he authorized the construction of an interstate turnpike west through Maryland and Virginia from the North Branch of the Potomac, the Northwestern Turnpike.

Nothing stopped the white man who must go west. The roads he built across the mountains of present-day Garrett County in the early nineteenth century reflect the advances of an entire civilization in its pursuit of the western star. The roads he simultaneously built within the highland glades reflect his success in taming one small portion of the western wilderness. Pulitzer prize-winning historian Bernard DeVoto: "Westward the course of empire takes its way."

Garrett County historian Walter W. Price: "Nothing stopped the white man who must go west."

Nothing, nobody stopped the white man who must go west.

Garrett County pioneer settlers were farmers, hunters, and herdsmen. They established their homes in the woods, cut the trees, farmed the land. They supplemented the products of the soil on their tables with the wild game of the forest. They built sawmills and gristmills and pastured large herds of cattle in the open glades. Eventually the glades were fenced, the wild game was thinned, and the farms thrived. Communities were established; schools and churches were built. Towns became centers of trade and social intercourse. The frontier was tamed. Roadways were cut through glade and forest. The red man was pushed ever toward the horizon. The westward course of American empire took its way.

"Too many people!" wrote Daniel Boone when he opened the Wilderness Road west through Cumberland Gap into Kentucky in 1794. "Too crowded! Too crowded! I want more elbow room."

A half century later John L. O'Sullivan, editor of *U.S. Magazine and Democratic Revue,* espoused for the first time the divine right or "manifest destiny" of the people of the United States to occupy and govern the land of the entire North American continent. "The far-reaching, the boundless future will be the era of American greatness," he wrote. "In its magnificent domain of space and time, the nation of many nations is destined to manifest to mankind the excellence of divine principles; to establish on earth the noblest temple ever dedicated." O'Sullivan's "manifest destiny" depicted the thoughts of millions behind the great nineteenth century era of American expansion and western settlement.

General "Mad" Anthony Wayne defeated the Ohio Valley Indians at the Battle of Fallen Timbers in 1794, opening the trans-Appalachian West to white settlement as far as the Mississippi River. Three new states joined the Union the same decade: Vermont (1791), Kentucky (1792), and Tennessee (1796).

Ohio entered the Union as the seventeenth state in 1803. The same year President Thomas Jefferson doubled the size of the nation in the largest real estate deal of United States history by purchasing over 800,000 square miles of the Louisiana Territory from Napoleon's France for $15 million. The Lewis and Clark expedition explored over 8,000 miles of western wilderness along the Mississippi and Columbia rivers, as far west as the Pacific Ocean, over the next three years. The state of Louisiana entered the Union in 1812.

Between 1810 and 1830, when the first covered conestoga wagons reached the foot of the Rocky Mountains, over two million Americans left the eastern establishment for the west. After Louisiana, six new states joined the Union during these two decades: Indiana (1816), Mississippi (1817), Illinois (1818), Alabama (1819), Maine (1820), and Missouri (1821).

"These lands are ours," asserted the Shawnee chief, Tecumseh, of the trans-Appalachian West in 1810. "No one has a right to remove us, because we are the 1st owners. The Great Spirit above has appointed this place for us, on which to light our fires, and we will remain." The following year President-to-be William Henry Harrison shattered the western Indian forces united under Tecumseh and his brother Tenskwatawa, the Prophet, at the Battle of Tippecanoe in Indiana. Three years later General Andrew Jackson defeated the Alabama Creeks in the Battle of Horse Shoe Bend and the natives subsequently migrated west.

President James Monroe in 1817 informed Congress of exchanges made with the red man for extensive land tracts in the states of Ohio, Indiana, Michigan, North Carolina,

Georgia, and Tennessee. Then, in 1830, President Andrew Jackson signed the Indian Removal Act, requiring all eastern Indians to resettle west of the Mississippi. "Rightly considered," the president wrote, "the policy of the general Government toward the red man is not only liberal but generous."

Two years later the Sac Chief Black Hawk recrossed the Mississippi River to plant corn in his tribe's former fields in Illinois. The white settlers there panicked, killing a Sac holding a truce flag, igniting the Black Hawk War of 1832. The bloodshed ended in August with the massacre of the entire tribe by the Illinois militia, which slaughtered old men, women, and children with reckless abandon, despite truce flags and pleas for mercy.

The flood of white settlers crossed the Mississippi and continued unabated its movement west after 1830. Six new states joined the Union by mid-century: Arkansas (1836), Michigan (1837), Florida (1845), Texas (1845), Iowa (1846), and Wisconsin (1848). The first white wagon train arrived in California in 1841. Within nine years a total of over two million white Americans had settled west of the Mississippi. California joined the Union as its thirty-first state in 1850. The American empire of states then stretched across the entire North American Continent and linked two major oceans. The Indians fought back for a time, then retired to reservations.

In 1893 the American historian Frederick Jackson Turner first read his essay "The Significance of the Frontier in American History" before the American Historical Association in Chicago and immediately became the object of great historical acclaim and no small degree of intellectual controversy. "Stand at Cumberland Gap," he wrote, "and watch the procession of civilization marching single file—the buffalo following the trail to the salt springs, the Indian, the fur-trader and hunter, the cattle-raiser, the pioneer farmer—and the frontier has passed by. The exploitation of the beasts took the hunter and trader to the west, the exploitation of the grasses took the rancher west, and the exploitation of the virgin soil of the river valleys and prairies attracted the farmer. The buffalo trail became the Indian trail, and this became the trader's 'trace'; the trails widened into roads, and the roads into turnpikes, and these in turn were transformed into railroads."

"Steadily the frontier of settlement advanced and carried with it individualism, democracy, and nationalism, and powerfully affected the East and the Old World," Turner suggested. "In the crucible of the frontier the immigrants were Americanized, liberated, and fused into a mixed race, English is neither nationality nor characteristics. The growth of nationalism and the evolution of American political institutions were dependent upon the advance of the frontier.

"The works of travelers along each frontier from colonial days onward describe certain common traits," asserted Turner, "and these traits have, while softening down, still persisted as survivals in the place of their origin, even when a higher social organization succeeded. The result is that to the frontier the American intellect owes its striking characteristics. That coarseness and strength combined with acuteness and inquistiveness; that practical, inventive turn of mind, quick to find expedients; that masterful grasp of material things, lacking in the artistic but powerful to effect great ends; that restless, nervous energy; that dominant individualism, working for good and for evil, and with all that buoyancy and exuberance which comes with freedom; these are traits of the frontier, or traits called out elsewhere because of the existence of the frontier.

"From the beginning of the settlement of America," Turner wrote, "the frontier regions have exercised a steady influence toward democracy. Simplicity and economy in government, the right of revolution, the freedom of the individual, the belief that those who win the vacant lands are entitled to shape their own government in their own way; these are all parts of the platform of political principles to which the frontiersman gave his adhesion, and they are all elements eminently characteristic of the western democracy into which he was born.

"The frontier produces antipathy to control, and particularly to any direct control. The frontier individualism has from the beginning promoted democracy."

The Garrett County settlement experience merely reflected in isolated detail the century-long westward movement of American men and women from the Atlantic to the Pacific.

Garrett County pioneer settlers worked hard, sweated much. They endured; they survived; they prevailed. They also entertained themselves in rare hours of leisure. They filled the vacant moments of their lives with music and society. They fought in two major international wars.

"Settlers were few and far apart," recorded Garrett County historian Charles E. Hoye in 1930, "but children were many. William Hoye reared seventeen." Isolated by forests and mountains, early present-day Garrett County families lived miles from their nearest neighbors. Families grew up as close-knit and homogeneous groups; they entertained themselves. Occasionally they met with distant neighbors for social and religious functions. More often than not, though, they lived lonely lives far from the comforts and luxuries of civilized society. "Several little farms appear among the bleak, barren hills," wrote a 1797 traveler of the old Braddock Road. "I have rode through the Negro Mountains, through the Shades of Death, through the Savage Mountains, and many other desparate mountains in this part of Maryland, but I have seen nothing half so savage and desparate as many of the people. Some of them appear but in slight degree like the human race."

Garrett County pioneer families were large—families of ten were not uncommon. The Reverend John Taylor recalled in 1823 that Ephraim Frazee of Sandy Creek Glades "had numerous offspring of children and grandchildren. One day I asked him how many children he had and he replied nineteen, and my remarking that it was a goodly number but he considered it only moderate, for his father raised twenty-nine, nineteen by his first wife and ten by a second." A typical Garrett County pioneer family was that of George and Lydia Matthews of Selbysport. The couple raised thirteen children early in the nineteenth century on their four-hundred-acre Joseph in Egypt farm on the west banks of the Youghiogheny. Three children died at the early ages of one, six, and seventeen. Mortality rates, like birth rates, were both high and accepted as such.

Rather than send their children to school, Garrett County pioneers sometimes apprenticed their minor siblings to tradesmen to learn occupations. The practice of apprenticeship was especially common in the case of orphans. In 1818 John Simkins and William W. Hoye, Allegany County justices of the peace, apprenticed Jesse Rutan, orphan, aged nineteen, to David Hoffman, saddle and harness maker, until age twenty. In 1813 Simkins apprenticed Juliana Jackson, aged two, with the mother's consent, to John Fike for a period of fourteen years, specifying that the child "be taught to read and write, to card, spin and sew." At the conclusion of the girl's apprenticeship Fike was to "give her a new suit of clothes and a new spinning wheel." In 1803 Elie Simkins apprenticed himself, with the consent of his parents, to James Scott for a period of three years "to learn the art of merchandise." Jesse Tomlinson took the illegitimate free children of the Negro Hannah till age twenty-one in 1802 "to learn the arts and mystery of farming."

Early Garrett County pioneer families often either amused themselves during their rare hours of leisure and frequent days of isolation, or else they enjoyed the finer comforts of social life not at all. The daughters of George Matthews often spent evenings at a time singing songs together from the high Blooming Rose bluff above Friendsville. Meshach Browning recalled in 1859 that "a cold winter in the 1830's confined my pleasures entirely to my home circle, comprising my wife and children; and several of the latter . . . were passionately fond of music and dancing. Myself and wife being no less fond of seeing our children enjoying a dance, the young people would often collect at my house, and there spend an evening in merriment; and at other times they would join a dancing party at different places in the neighborhood." When the boys of John Friend journeyed upriver along the Yough to the cabin of Augustine Friend in the late 1700s following an arctic blizzard which had prohibited travel for two long weeks, they found their uncle and his companions snowbound but dancing and singing in their snug log shelter. Teen's family not only had endured the blizzard, they had triumphed over it.

"Fiddleing in those times was an occupation, in the winter season especially," noted Jacob Brown of Grantsville, "and the musicians were usually quite well compensated. Joseph DeWitt, Sr., of the Flatwoods . . . would occasionally make his appearance in his fringed hunting shirt and deer skin moccasins, thus presenting quite a picturesque figure, as well as excellent ballroom music. Tommy Drane, of the same section, would occasionally furnish music. There was another queer old fiddler, Aaron Ramsey—a tri-mixture of negro, indian and caucasion. He could produce noise as well as music but he often filled the bill."

"Those early fiddlers were gents with pliant supple wrists and nimble fingers, acquired by much practice," noted Dennis T. Rasche in 1961. Nearly all played by ear. Fiddling was a talent handed down from father to son to grandson. Locally developed tunes of the early nineteenth century included "Fox and Hounds," "Shady Dell," and "Cheat River." Musical favorites included folk music—fast and rollicking—jigs, reels, and hornpipes. The background sound of baying hounds formed the introduction to "Fox and Hounds" developed by descendants of Meshach Browning around mid-century. The baying gradually increased in tempo during the course of the tune until a final hurried and feverish ending in which the fox was musically brought to earth.

An 1834 visitor to Cherry Tree Meadows succinctly described one old-time Garrett County fiddler, Lish Stallings, as "a bachelor who had no special home of his own, but lived at free quarters at every house and cabin in the mountains for fifty miles around. He played the fiddle, and no apple butter boiling, quilting, or other frolic could go on without him. He was the most popular man in the county and could have fiddled himself into office had he not preferred his freedom. We took it for granted he would stay all night, but no, he was to play the fiddle at a wedding on the Youghiogheny, full ten miles away, and he strode forth as buoyantly as if it were not more than as many yards." Other old-time Garrett County fiddlers included William Drane, Jere Bittner (who walked for years six miles every Saturday night from his farm to Friendsville to play for local dances), Alfred Hinebaugh, Lloyd and Lucius Baker, and the black Mr. Progue, of Altamont.

Inns, taverns, and blacksmith shops were popular gathering places for early Garrett County social activities. So were churches and schools. D. A. Friend recalled in 1920 that "the people had singing schools, and spelling bees, and taffy pullings and the like. In this manner they were continually mingling together, and what one knew of any importance soon became the common property of all." Social events centering around church and school included special Christmas and Easter programs, summer picnics and socials, autumn and winter revivals, sing-ins, cake walks, intellectual debates, and covered-dish suppers. Harvest festivals were common, especially around butchering time. Boys finding red ears of corn at huskings were usually allowed to kiss the girls of their choice. Churches and schools occasionally raised funds by auctioning packed lunches to the highest bidders. Buyers were encouraged to enjoy not only the contents of the lunch boxes but also the company of the cooks. Courting was by horse and buggy in summer, by sleigh in winter.

Nearly everyone in the early history of Garrett's development looked forward to the Christmas season as a special time of festivity and leisure. "Presents in those days were common," noted Jacob Brown, "but plain and simple as well as in point. Persons often challenged each other for a xmas gift, and the one who spoke first was entitled, and generally received it, be it ever so small. Sometimes it would be a treat at a tavern bar if one should be convenient."

The Christmas gift giver in those days was known by several names—"Kriskinkle," "Beltznickle," or simply "the Christmas Woman." "The annual visitor," wrote Brown, "would make his appearance some hours after dark, thoroughly disguised, especially the face, which would sometimes be covered with a hideously ugly phiz. He or she would be equipped with an ample sack about the shoulders filled with cakes, nuts, and fruits, and a long hazel switch which was supposed to have some kind of charm in it as well as a sting. One hand would scatter the goodies upon the floor, and then the scramble would begin by the delighted children, and the other hand would ply the switch upon the backs of the excited youngsters."

"But the main features of the holiday festivities," Brown recorded, "were sleighing and balls at the many hotels along the National Road. Deep snows then covered the ground during all the winter months, and the sleighing upon the old pikes was superb and enjoyed to the utmost. Most of the young men could sport a sleigh and horse. Some times great convoys of them would move together. Balls were very frequent and numerously attended by well behaved and well dressed young ladies and men. Cumberlanders often patronized mountain balls."

Slaves anticipated the Christmas season as much as did their white owners. "There was no class of people who so much enjoyed the holiday season as the colored folks," Brown suggested. "To them Christmas never came often or speedily enough. The anxiety for its approach was almost unbearable. When it did come, their enjoyments were a source of real pleasure to the whites to see the negroes in the ecstacies of their amusements, which usually lasted a week or more." One slave owner, Jesse Tomlinson, customarily allowed his servants to enjoy a period of Christmas leisure as long as a special festival back log lasted in the flames of his fireplace. One winter Tomlinson's favorite servant, Ephraim, soaked the Christmas log for weeks in advance in a goose pond. The festivities that year at Little Meadows lasted nearly a month. (Tomlinson freed Ephraim Carter in 1839.)

Secular and political divertisements complemented those of religious and agricultural origin in early nineteenth century Garrett County. A large group gathered at the home of John Simkins along the Braddock Road in 1792 to celebrate Independence Day with a special dinner and fifteen toasts. Several hundred persons, "including seventy-five women," met at the home of George Rinehart at Sunnyside in 1834 to celebrate the nation's birthday with "thirteen 'regular' toasts" and "thirty 'volunteer' toasts." "At the break of day two guns were fired," reported the *Maryland Advocate*. "At noon a procession formed, led by a small band, and marched to the place of dining, when Meshach Browning, Esq., was unanimously appointed President of the day, and Ralph T. Thayer, Vice President. The Declaration of Independence was read by Dr. Lewis Klipstine followed by an oration by R. F. Furguson. The company then sat down to a dinner that, for sumptuousness, variety, and taste was scarcely ever equalled; the choicest vegetables of that healthy climate, venison and trout were plentyful and served up in a manner that showed the host regarded his guests."

"In those times," recorded Meshach Browning, "politics were but little understood; and all the voters in the glade country were Federalists, except one. We always held an election on the first Monday in November; when would be seen a goodly array of hunting-shirts and moccasins, and almost every man with a big knife in his belt. A foreigner would have supposed that the voters were really some military party going to oppose a threatened invasion; and if a quarrel occurred, they would take off perhaps both coat and shirt, and fight until one or the other acknowledged that he had as much of a beating as he was willing to receive. Then their friends, if they did not get into a scrape among themselves, would take the combatants to the nearest water, and wash off the blood. If no serious injury was done, which was seldom the case, that would, in nine fights out of ten, be the last of the quarrel."

The Jackson party of the Glades District met at the Sunnyside home of George Rinehart in 1834 to adopt resolutions and select delegates for the Allegany County convention. Jacob Brown recalled the political campaign of 1840 as "the most excited and interesting in the history of politics. Large mass-meetings were common all over the country, with able speakers who made speaking a daily occupation. 1840 was the beginning of log cabins, balls, hard cider, coon, fox skins, etc. One of these log cabins passed over the National Road from Uniontown, Penn., to Baltimore on an immense wagon. It was complete in every respect, even down to the wooden latch and leather string hanging outside. The log cabin represented General W. H. Harrison's first home at Northbend, Ohio, in contrast with the magnificent residence of his opponent [Martin Van Buren]." National Road historian T. B. Searight noted that the Uniontown log cabin boys "had with them, on wheels, a regular log cabin, well stored with refreshments of every kind, and the very best; and every mile of their long journey resounded with lusty shouts for 'Typecanoe and Tyler, too.'"

"The Democracy was not so prolific in emblems [as were the Whigs]," recorded Brown of the 1840 campaign, "but they shouted very loudly to the laboring men, 'two dollars per day and roasted beef.' As a faint representation of this promise I once saw a stuffed ox hide in a procession with a good Democrat astride of it, with a wooden carving knife in hand."

In 1844 a Little Crossings delegation of Whigs attended a large rally in Cumberland in a wagon "drawn by 16 horses, with a bed as large as a gondola car. The whole getup was elaborately decorated with everything calculated to lend beauty and attraction. Little Crossings took the cake that day easily."

"Glee clubs," noted Brown, "were very popular in those days. They followed up the meetings and enlivened them with campaign songs which would interlude the speeches. There were great orators: Chas. Ogle, of Somerset, Penn., literally spoke himself to death." In an early campaign for Congress, Maryland governor-to-be Francis Thomas addressed a large outdoor crowd at Grantsville to defend his tarnished political reputation. "I have been told of the villainous remarks of my opponent," he ad-libbed, "and apparently some of you have believed him. I say to you, that if this kind of prejudice keeps up, the day will come when your Congressman will have to be born in the dark of the moon, cradled in a sugar trough and baptized in stump water." Thomas won the campaign.

The settlement period of Garrett County history was interrupted by two major international wars, the War of 1812 with England and the Mexican-American War of 1846. Both conflicts were locally controversial; both involved local volunteers. Forty-nine Garrett Countians served the armed forces of their country in 1812; six served in 1849.

A Canada-hungry "manifest destiny" dominated Congress, declared war on Great Britain on June 18, 1812. Upon learning of the declaration, Meshach Browning immediately "went home and prepared two pairs of new, strong buckskin moccasins. Mary made me a new knapsack, into which she stowed my clothes; and . . . In the morning I bade her and the children farewell, took the road for Cumberland, and arrived there the second day." Before Browning's departure, Colonel John Lynn, of Buffalo Marsh, had advised him to "do all you can to prevent the war; but if it comes, do all you can to bring it to an honorable and speedy close." "Have you turned fool," friends demanded of the hunter in Cumberland; "to go and fight against the only people who dare to resist the greatest tyrant [Napoleon] with which the earth was ever cursed? Go home, and attend to your own business; and let those who declared the war fight the battles of their own making." Browning followed the advice.

Once back in the mountains, though, the hunter received the commission of sergeant at the head of a local company of militia headquartered at Selbysport. "When the major came to make the draft for eighteen privates and one sergeant," Browning later recalled, "tickets were prepared, and disinterested persons selected to conduct the drawing. This, being but a small job, was soon over." Browning accepted his appointment. Robinson Savage also accepted an appointment as sergeant.

When the two commanders met at Selbysport to muster in their company a few days later, an opposition party endeavored to raise a second group. "These formed two lines," Brown recalled, "on both sides of a tail-race belonging to Hoffman's mill, about twenty on each side, determined to attack and beat me as I should pass the bridge. Many passes were made at me, but the cowards would run as soon as they struck. Let me turn my face which way I would, it met somebody's fist. I let them beat away; but once in a while I would get a chance at one who would be exposed, and give him a good send. This happened about the middle of November, and I was not able to carry firewood till the first of May following." Both personality and politics were involved in the termination of Browning's brief military career. Other Garrett Countians served longer but suffered less in the War of 1812.

Congress declared war on Mexico on May 13, 1846, after expansionist President James K. Polk informed the legislative body that Mexico had "invaded our territory and shed American blood on American soil." Over six months later Polk asserted that "the war will continue to be prosecuted with vigor as the best means of securing peace." The war raged until February 2, 1848.

At least six Garrett Countians served the American forces in the Mexican War: Samuel McCurdy, Henry Garlitz, George W. Gould, James Paul, David Strong, and Samuel Fouch. McCurdy, a young Grantsville merchant, and Samuel McCleary, a National Road coach driver, each joined the American forces under Captain Samuel H. Walker's company of rangers in order to "win the heart of one who yet kept it as her own," according to Jacob Brown. "So off went the twin sons to far-away Mexico to engage in a war each believed unnecessary; the two gallant young Americans were for their country 'right or wrong.' They sought the post of honor and danger, not one of ease and safety." McCleary was killed along with Walker at the battle of Huamantla; McCurdy survived and aided General Winfield Scott in the 1847 invasion of Mexico City.

Triumphant and in Mexico City, McCurdy sent a diamond ring to his Grantsville girl friend, a young lady named Charity. "Upon the young soldier's return home," recorded Jacob Brown, "ovations came from hosts of friends, among them was 'Chat,' but nearer than that she would not come." Charity returned the ring.

Years later, in 1891, Jacob Brown wrote of the frustrated love affair for a local newspaper. The article was soon reprinted under the title "Romances in Real Life" in Cincinnati and throughout the South. Sam McCurdy first read the story while a resident at the National Soldiers' Home at Hampton, Virginia; he quickly dashed off a few lines to the author.

"Your article . . . has given me a notoriety that will last at least as long as I live," the old Grantsville soldier wrote. "I am receiving letters from old maids, widows and old Mexican soldiers from all parts of the country . . . and to tell you the truth, from the way they write I believe if I wished to marry I could have a wife in less than week; but 'Chat' the purest and best of women, rules my ancient heart. I am and have been for this great country of ours, right or wrong."

Over two thousand Americans lost their lives in the War of 1812; more than thirteen thousand died in the war with Mexico. The American course of empire took its way.

Mountain Lake—Boathouse and Icehouse. This lake, created when the town was founded in the early 1880s, enlarged in 1894, provided boating as a popular recreation for this resort. The boathouse in the foreground included a dock. The large building in background is the icehouse built in 1894 with a capacity of twenty-five hundred tons. Ice cut from the lake was stored here. A railroad siding served for loading carload shipments on the B&O R.R. (See *Glades Star*, vol. 2, pp. 278, 289; vol. 4, p. 17.) Photo from Garrett County Historical Society collection

Mountain Lake Park Amphitheater. The Bashford Amphitheater was dedicated in 1900 and had a seating capacity of five thousand. It was the second largest such building in the United States. The large facility was needed for great crowds attending Chautauqua programs in August. Important people who appeared in the amphitheater included: William Howard Taft, William Jennings Bryan, Mark Twain and Billy Sunday. The building was used as needed also for large community gatherings. It continued in use until 1939 and then due to its deteriorating condition was razed in 1944. (See *Glades Star*, vol. 2, pp. 270-80; vol. 3, p. 544.) Photo courtesy Joseph H. Welch

Sugar Maple Camp. New England? No, this is a Garrett County scene. In several such camps in sugar maple groves, the owners collect sap in the spring and boil it down for syrup in commercial quantities. Some also make maple sugar. Photo courtesy Robert J. Ruckert

C&O R.R. Station, Friendsville, 1891. Construction on the C&O (Confluence and Oakland) from Confluence, Pennsylvania, to Friendsville was completed in 1890. It was abandoned in 1942 when the waters of the newly constructed Youghiogheny Dam flooded much of the roadbed. The appearance of the station changed very little from 1891 until it was dismantled in 1942. Photo courtesy Mrs. Selma Neil

Fuller-Baker Log House. The only log tavern remaining between Cumberland and Wheeling on the Old National Road (Route 40), is one mile west of Grantsville. Built about 1815, it is now owned by the Council of the Alleghenies which plans authentic restoration. The old house is about one hundred yards from General Braddock's Fifth Camp and near the historic Braddock Road and primitive Nemacolin Indian Trail. Photo courtesy Robert J. Ruckert

The Braddock Road. This scene on the historic Braddock Road is near the summit of Big Savage Mountain not far from Saint John's Rock in Garrett County. Robert J. Ruckert of Oakland, author of "The Braddock Military Road," photographed his wife, Adeline, here during their mapping of the route through the county. He quotes from source material in the Journal of Captain Robert Orme, aide-de-camp to Major General Edward Braddock describing the British army's ascent of the mountain: "June 15, 1755. On the morning of June 15 the line began to move from this place at 5 of the clock ... it was found necessary to make one-half of the men ground their arms and assist the carriages while the others remain advantageously posted ... We this day did pass the Alligany Mountain which is a rocky ascent ... in passing we demolished three wagons and shattered several others."

Oakland Railroad Station. The world's oldest railroad station on a mountaintop was established in 1851 at Oakland, Maryland. Built by the B&O Railroad in 1884 to replace a frame structure, this fine example of station architecture of its period is now a national landmark. The present building served for more than ninety years as a passenger and freight shipping facility. Only a small room there now shelters occasional Amtrak passengers. The Chessie System owns the station and uses it for a rail section maintenance headquarters. Photo courtesy Robert J. Ruckert

Compton Schoolhouse. This is the last log structure used as a school in Garrett County after 1872 and stands beside the New Germany Road south of Route 40. A deed for this property was made on October 28, 1863, by Elizabeth and David Compton to the Allegany County School Commissioners, but birth records show that Armanda Compton was born in this building in 1872 after the area became part of Garrett County. From glass plate negative courtesy Mrs. Maxine Broadwater

Garrett Cottage. This was the summer home of John W. Garrett, president of the B&O R.R., and located on the grounds of the Deer Park Hotel. It was built in 1881 and burned on December 25, 1939. Mr. Garrett died here on September 26, 1884, at 5:25 a.m. Photo courtesy Mrs. Robert B. Garrett

Stone House Inn. Still standing as a private home beside U.S. Route 40 east of Grantsville, the inn was built on the National or Cumberland Road at "Little Meadows" by Jesse Tomlinson about 1818. He was an influential landowner, slaveholder, and served in the state legislature. This inn replaced the log "Red House Inn" which stood about a hundred yards away beside the Old Braddock Road and was built before the Revolution by Joseph Tomlinson. Photo courtesy Robert J. Ruckert

The Pennington Cottage. Located in the Deer Park Hotel grounds, this building was erected in 1881 and designed also by Josias Pennington, a member of the Baltimore firm, Baldwin and Pennington, Architects. The "Cottage," three stories high with fourteen rooms, was one of many cottages that graced the hotel grounds; some were smaller, and many much larger. All but five have been destroyed, either by fire or torn down, as well as the hotel, which was demolished. The cottage is now owned by Mr. and Mrs. Joe V. Faulkner and furnished with much of its original furniture.

Friend's graveyard.

The fenced graveyard.

Grave of Gabriel Friend.

Grave of John Friend, Sr.

The Friend Cemetery. The old Friend Cemetery just off Route 48 in Friendsville contains the remains of John Friend and his son, Gabriel, who were the first permanent white settlers in Garrett County. The pictures clockwise from the upper left are: (a) The roadside marker, (b) The cemetery, (c) Gabriel Friend's grave marker and (d) John Friend's grave marker. Courtesy Raymond O. McCullough

Deer Park Hotel. This hotel, built by the Baltimore and Ohio Railroad Company, opened for business July 4, 1873. It paved the way for the development of this area as a resort. The hotel was an immediate success and two wings were added in 1887. It became a gathering place for well-known people in business and government. Among the noted guests were Presidents Grant, Cleveland, and Harrison. The hotel continued in operation until 1929. During the Second World War it was razed. (See the *Glades Star,* vol. 1, p. 334; vol. 2, p. 122.) Photo courtesy Mrs. Robert J. Ruckert

The Drane House. Probably the oldest house once used as a residence is still standing on the farm of Albert Richter at Accident in Garrett County. James Drane was a Revolutionary War veteran and came from Prince Georges County to live in this house. Photo courtesy Albert Richter

Drane Grave. The grave of Lieutenant James Drane in Zion Lutheran Cemetery north of the Drane House at Accident has been suitably identified with this Revolutionary War veteran marker by the Daughters of the American Revolution. Photo courtesy Mrs. Charles Strauss

The Oakland Hotel. The success of the Deer Park Hotel prompted the Baltimore and Ohio Railroad to build a similar hotel at Oakland in 1875. It was located some distance south of the railroad across the Little Youghiogheny River opposite the station. The milk collecting station is now approximately on this site. This hotel did not successfully compete with the Deer Park Hotel, resulting in its being closed around 1907. It was razed in 1911. (See *Glades Star,* vol. 1, p. 331; vol. 2, p. 177; *Oakland Centennial History,* p. 51.) Photo courtesy of Garrett County Historical Society

The Glades Hotel. This was one of the early hotels probably built after the railroad came through Oakland in 1851. It was a dining stop for passenger trains before they had dining cars. This hotel was located close to the railroad on the south side. The present station is on the north side.

The first Glades Hotel burned in 1874 and was immediately replaced by a new one on the same side and fronting on the railroad.

The Glades had many famous persons as guests which included Jefferson Davis (Confederate president); Lieutenant William McKinley (later United States president); William F. "Buffalo Bill" Cody; General Lew Wallace, author of *Ben Hur*; General Benjamin F. Kelley (Union two-horse general); and David Belasco of theater fame.

The Glades Hotel was also a central meeting place for local affairs and meetings leading to the creation of Garrett County. The first session of the new county's court was held there. (See the *Glades Star,* vol. 2, pp. 179, 180, 181; vol. 3, p. 282; *Tableland Trails,* vol. 1, no. 2, p. 40.) Photo courtesy of Garrett County Historical Society

Early Auto. This International Harvester automobile was numbered 17 and believed the seventeenth one made by the firm. The scene is at Accident, Maryland, and William Miller, owner, sits behind the wheel. Fred Miller is beside him. Miss Rose Miller, of Accident, is seated in the rear and beside her is the Rev. Paul Miller of Fort Wayne, Indiana. Photo courtesy of George and Carl Miller

Stanley Steamer. This was one of the first automobiles in Garrett County. The auto was owned by Colonel George Truesdell who operated the Altamont Spring Farm and Altamont Spring Water Company. His chauffeur, Jacob, sits behind the rightside steering wheel. Source and date of photo is not known. It is from the collection of Paul T. Calderwood of Deer Park.

Bear Creek Iron Furnace. This furnace at the Bear Creek Iron Works was located along Bear Creek about a mile from Friendsville. It represents the first incorporated business in what is now Garrett County from its date of incorporation in 1828 as the Allegany Iron Company, Inc. The name later changed to the Youghiogheny Iron Company. Employing about one hundred men, this company produced pig iron for about ten years.

The activity of the ironworks stimulated the growth of Friendsville where a post office established as "Friends" in 1830 was changed to Friendsville in 1832. In the photo from left to right is Harry Black and Jim Butler. The photo was taken about 1898 and given to the Garrett County Historical Society by Mr. and Mrs. Harry Black in 1950. (See also the *Glades Star*, vol. 2, p. 1.)

Bandstand. This is probably the only community bandstand still existing in the county. It is at Deer Park and marks an era when most communities had a band composed of local citizens. Photo by Paul T. Calderwood

Mountain Lake Hotel. The central section of this hotel was built in 1882 by J. M. Jarboe of Oakland. During the next fifteen years its guest facilities were doubled. This hotel was the center of many important social functions and for sixty years after its enlargement provided fine accommodations and delectable cuisine for its guests. The last operators of this summer place were Mrs. June Dunnington Grimes and Mrs. Lillian Davis. It closed in the early 1960s and the furnishings were sold at public auction in 1966. The building was razed in 1968. The site is now privately owned and may be used for a residence. Photo courtesy Garrett County Museum

Courthouse. The second Garrett County Court House seen here had its cornerstone laid October 15, 1907, in a ceremony by the Masonic Lodge of Oakland. The building fronts on Third Street.

The first courthouse for Garrett County was built on the hill northeast of the present one between Fourth and Fifth streets on Green. It opened for September term of circuit court in 1877. The structure is now part of the board of education offices.

The present courthouse is undergoing extensive changes. The front lawn has been excavated and will be replaced with new jail quarters and other county facilities. An open plaza will surmount the new front structure. A new extension to the rear will be integrated with the main building after the stone jail and the sheriff's residence have been razed. The cost estimate is $4 million and to be a grant of federal funds. Photo by W. A. Gonder, Oakland

Loch Lynn Heights Hotel. This imposing structure stood "across the tracks" from the town of Mountain Lake Park. It was built to offer worldly pleasures to its guests and this was somewhat frowned upon by early officials of its sister town. Built around 1893-94, the facility was operated for many years by Mrs. L. C. B. List, of Wheeling, West Virginia. It was destroyed by fire in the World War I period. A large frame structure stands near the hotel site and was called the Casino. It provided recreational features. This property is owned by W. Blair Simmons. Mr. and Mrs. Simmons resided in the Casino building for a few years. They now live in a modern residence near it. Photo courtesy Garrett County Museum

III

DESTINY

> We have constructed a fate, an *Atropos,* that never turns aside. (Let that be the name of your engine.)
>
> Henry David Thoreau

"If it were possible that I should be here twenty years longer," suggested the pioneer highland hunter Meshach Browning in 1859, "perhaps I would then be as much astonished at Allegany County's progress as I would have been thirty years ago, if at that time a man had stated in my neighborhood that an engine would be constructed to transport as great a burden as fifty or an hundred horses could draw on wagons. Every man would either have pronounced such a person entirely crazy, or else would have thought he was trifling with their good understanding."

The Baltimore and Ohio Railroad Company laid the first steel tracks of the iron horse across the Allegheny highlands of western Maryland in 1851. Within two decades a new county was formed west of Allegany: Garrett. The new county was named after the nineteenth century railroad magnate John W. Garrett, president of the Baltimore and Ohio. Garrett County was the daughter of Allegany County, the granddaughter of Washington County, the great-granddaughter of Frederick County, the great-great-granddaughter of Prince Georges County. Today Garrett is Maryland's youngest county, Maryland's westernmost county, Maryland's least densely populated county, Maryland's second largest county.

The railroad brought timber and coal capitalists to western Maryland. (They stripped the forests and pillaged the earth.) It provided new markets for local farmers. It lured soldiers to the highlands during the Civil War. It brought the wealthy and the sophisticated of the eastern cities to the mountaintop for summer seasons of leisure and recreation. It gave birth to a dozen new towns. It sealed the fate of western Maryland for fifty years.

"We have constructed a fate, an *Atropos,* that never turns aside," wrote the philosopher-naturalist Henry David Thoreau of the railroad at Walden Pond near Concord, Massachusetts, in 1845. "(Let that be the name of your engine.) Men are advertised that at a certain hour and minute these bolts will be shot toward particular points of the compass and we live the steadier for it. We are all educated thus to be sons of Tell. For through unfrequented woods or the confines of towns, where once only the hunter penetrated by day, in the darkest night dart these bright saloons without the knowledge of their inhabitants; this moment stopping at some brilliant station-house in town or city, where a social crowd is gathered, the next in the Dismal Swamp, scaring the owl and fox. I am, as it were, related to society by this link. I am refreshed and expanded when the freight train rattles past me, and I smell the stores . . . reminding me of foreign ports, of coral reefs, and Indian oceans, and tropical climes, and the extent of the globe."

"So is your pastoral life whirled past and away," Thoreau observed. "All the Indian huckleberry hills are stripped, all the cranberry meadows are raked into the city. The startings and arrivals of the cars are now the epochs in the village day. They go and come with such regularity and precision, and their whistle can be heard so far, that the farmers set their clocks by them, and thus one well-conducted institution regulates a whole country. Have not men improved somewhat in punctuality since the railroad was invented? When I hear the iron horse make the hills echo with his snort-like thunder, shaking the earth with his feet, and breathing fire and smoke from his nostrils . . . it seems as if the earth had got a race now worthy to inhabit it. If all were as it seems, and men made the elements their servants for noble ends!"

Jacob Brown, Grantsville (1888): "This is an age of railroads."

J. M. Davis, Oakland (1906): "Instead of the heavy road wagon and the stage coach, we have the iron horse, with his heart of fire and terrific roar as he rushes ... over our hills and valleys with the velocity of the wind."

Frederick Jackson Turner, Chicago (1893): "The buffalo trail became the Indian trail, and this became the trader's 'trace'; the trails widened into roads, and the roads into turnpikes, and these in turn were transformed into railroads."

Henry David Thoreau, Walden Pond (1845): "What's the railroad to me? / I never go to see / Where it ends, / It fills a few hollows / And makes banks for the swallows, / It sets the sand a-blowing, / And the blackberries a-growing. I will not have my eyes put out and my ears spoiled by its smoke and steam and hissing."

Thoreau called the railroad a "traveling demigod," a "cloud-compeller." The late nineteenth century was the great era of American railroad expansion. In western Maryland the railroad gave birth to a new county and destined the building of the first railway station on top of any mountain in the world at Oakland. It also made the sand blow and the blackberries grow. It filled a few hollows and made banks for the swallows.

The Appalachian Mountain chain stood as an immense barrier of upthrust earth and rock between the commercial establishments of the East and the expanding frontier resources of the West in nineteenth century United States as American men and women sought the fulfillment of manifest destiny and pursued the hope and the promise and the dream of the western star. "Let us bind the republic together with a perfect system of roads and canals," exhorted the expansionist Senator John C. Calhoun in 1816. "Let us conquer space."

The construction of the National Road across the Alleghenies early in the century was one solution to the expansionist's dilemma. The construction of canals was a second. The construction of railroads was a third.

As early as 1755 Maryland's governor, Edmund Sharpe, and Sir John St. Claire of the Royal British Army descended the Potomac River in a small boat from Fort Cumberland to

Alexandria to study the feasibility of transporting goods and supplies between the two points by raft and boat. St. Claire believed the project to be entirely practicable. Fourteen years later the Virginia House of Burgesses authorized George Washington and Richard Henry Lee "to bring in an important bill for clearing the Potomac and to make it navigable from the great falls of the river, a little above Alexandria, to Ft. Cumberland." Though little came of this effort, Washington again introduced bills of a similar nature in the Virginia legislature in 1770, 1772, and 1774. Then the advent of the Revolutionary War precluded, for a time, further work on the canal-clearing project.

Finally, in 1784, a group of Virginia and Maryland businessmen organized the Potomac Canal Company; they selected Washington as their president. "My opinion coincides perfectly with yours," the former general wrote his friend Thomas Jefferson at the time, "regarding the practicality of an easy and short communication between waters of the Ohio and Potomac, of the advantage of that communication, the preference it has over all others." They dreamed great dreams, these early would-be canal builders, but their plans come to naught; politics and interstate rivalries, not mountains, were the chief obstacles lying in the path of their success.

Then, in 1821, the states of Maryland and Virginia accepted the report of a specially appointed canal commission which recommended the construction of a waterway along the Potomac from Georgetown to Cumberland. Two years later the Potomac Company surrendered its charter and construction rights to the recently organized Chesapeake and Ohio Canal Company, financed primarily by the states of Maryland and Virginia, with congressional approval. The new company was authorized to build a canal from Georgetown to either Cumberland or the mouth of Savage River, thence across the Allegheny Mountains to either the Ohio or one of its tributaries.

"The first scientific view of this ground [for the route of the proposed canal over the mountains] was made by the late Thos. Moore in September, 1820," reported Maryland's

General R. G. Harper from the McHenry Glades in 1823. A second highland survey was completed in 1822 by a specially appointed Maryland-Virginia Commission. A third was conducted by a party of Maryland engineers under the leadership of James Shriver in 1823. The Shriver party began its examinations on Deep Creek near Hooppole Ridge, then proceeded northwest. "It is stated that after the usual thaws in the spring of the year, and melting of heavy snows which commonly fall in this quarter," Shriver noted, "an inundation is produced, which covering the flat lands for many miles along Deep Creek, produces a lake of considerable extent." William Hoye suggested that the area of land which would be submerged in the region by the proposed mountaintop storage lake for the canal's locks would cover three thousand acres. After examining the terrain of the area, the Shriver party favored a forty-one-mile canal route across the mountains from Savage River to the mouth of Bear Creek on the Youghiogheny at Friendsville by way of Crabtree Run through Little Backbone Mountain to Deep Creek and Buffalo Marsh Run. It estimated that the rise from Savage River to the base mark of the proposed Deep Creek storage lake would be just over fourteen hundred feet.

The following year Secretary of War John C. Calhoun, accompanied by John Hoye, James Shriver, John McHenry, and others, inspected the proposed canal route across the mountains, and accepted, in general, the conclusions and proposals of the Shriver party. "We all went to McHenry's where we met with a kind reception, and that sort of Highland welcome which does the heart good," reported an accompanying correspondent for the *Maryland Advocate* of Cumberland. "We were highly delighted with the appearance of Deep Creek, and sincerely gratified to find there was so much more water in the remarkable stream than the most sanguine among us had anticipated. This was a scene for contemplation—a spot well calculated to fill the mind with sublime ideas, with thoughts too big for utterance—a place where the imagination might rove at large and call the past, the present, and the future, up to view.

"But a few years ago, a white man's footsteps had never

trodden these paths, but the wild beast held sole dominion over this territory. Even now, bears, panthers and wolves, are yet the inhabitants of these precincts; even now, for miles and miles, a cabin, a cottage is not to be seen, and a human face rarely; even now, within three days travel of Washington, the seat of government of many millions of freemen, the charming country remains a desert, continues unnoticed and unknown. Thousands and ten thousands, on the right and on the left, pass it by; they have never heard that there is such a beautiful country in existence. Maryland, yes, even Maryland herself—intelligent, enterprising Maryland does not know her own Allegany. She has, from ignorance of her worth, treated her youngest child with neglect; but the darling girl has grown up, fair in form and face, notwithstanding, and, whilst rosy health beams on her cheek, love laughs in her keen dark eye, and she will soon be more adored and caressed, and more sincerely beloved, than some of her elder sisters.

"But who can unveil the future, when this spot, the most important in the New World shall become the resort of nations! When cities shall spring up as if by magic; when these extensive plains shall be filled with a busy population; when flocks and herds shall adorn every hill and every glade; when the lamb shall walk safely in the wolf's path, and there shall be nothing to hurt or destroy in all these mountains. And thou, Deep Creek, that now moves along unseen, unknown, shall become famous, as the stream of Washington; for thou shalt mingle thy waters with Potomac, and pass the shades of Mount Vernon, where he who first formed the grand design of uniting the waters of the west and the east ... now rests in peace; thou shalt flow from the summit level, and find a sea on every side; and in the Western course, before thy waters meet the ocean, thou shalt pass by the spot where Jackson saved his country and gained an immortal name.

"And where were we at this impressive moment? In the center of the United States and yet amidst woods and wilds, where few, very few, had ever before been. We came to the place where the everlasting doors of the East and the West were to be unbarred, and thrown open, where the last deed was to be done, and the last act which is to render the union of these States permanent, lasting and secure forever, was to be performed. It was, indeed, an interesting moment, a highly interesting place. We poured out a libation and drank to the great work."

They toasted a vision, a dream, not a reality nor either a coming fact.

Secretary Calhoun submitted a report of his highland observations and surveys, along with a report of his engineers, to President James Monroe on February 12, 1825. Two days later Monroe transmitted the reports to Congress with his own opinion on the proposed canal: "I contemplate results of incalculable advantage to our Union, because I see in them the most satisfactory proof that certain impediments, which had a tendency to embarrass the intercourse between some of its most important sections, may be removed without serious difficulties."

Work on the Chesapeake and Ohio Canal began on July 4, 1828, at Georgetown. President John Quincy Adams turned the first spade of dirt. The canal was opened for traffic as soon as each section was completed: from Georgetown to Seneca in 1831, to Harper's Ferry in 1833, to Hancock in 1839, to Cumberland in 1850. Here, at Cumberland, the canal met its final terminus. The faster and more economical Baltimore and Ohio Railroad, which had reached the Queen City eight years before the C&O Canal, had made the canal obsolete. After spending $22 million to build 184 miles of waterway, complete with seventy-four lift locks, eleven stone aqueducts, seven dams, a single three-thousand-foot tunnel, and hundreds of culverts and drains, the managers of the Chesapeake and Ohio Canal Company decided to halt all further major construction.

Though the canal itself never did generate any great measure of financial success, it did provide for many years a dependable and leisurely means of transporting coal, flour, grain, and lumber from Maryland's western counties to the Washington markets. A major flood in 1889 left the C&O Canal in a state of ruin, but it was soon rebuilt and used until 1924, when flooding, again, seriously damaged its locks and channels. The National Park Service of the Department of the Interior bought the canal and its property in 1938, and restored its lower twenty-two miles by 1942. In 1961, only a few hours before President John Kennedy's inauguration, President Dwight D. Eisenhower declared the canal a national monument to the dreamers and the promoters of America's nineteenth-century canal age. Congress declared the Chesapeake and Ohio a national historical park on January 8, 1972, and provided funds for its complete restoration for the enjoyment and leisure pleasure of bikers, hikers, picnickers, and horseback riders. The canal's terminus remains at Cumberland.

While President John Quincy Adams was turning the first spade of dirt for the construction of the Chesapeake and Ohio Canal at Georgetown on July 4, 1818, Charles Carroll of Carrollton, the then sole surviving signer of the Declaration of Independence, was simultaneously turning a few spades of sod forty miles away in Baltimore before five thousand spectators in the opening ceremony of the construction of the Baltimore and Ohio Railroad. "I consider this among the most important acts of my life," the ninety-one-year-old Carroll noted at the time, "second only to my signing the Declaration of Independence, if second even to that."

The orator of the day in Baltimore was the merchant John B. Morris. "It is but a few years since the introduction of steamboats effected powerful changes," Morris observed. "Of a similar and equally important effect will be the Baltimore and Ohio Railroad. While the one will have stemmed the current of the Mississippi, the other will have surmounted and reduced the height of the Alleghenies."

Construction on the Baltimore and Ohio Railroad and the Chesapeake and Ohio Canal began on the same day. The iron horse beat the canal barge to the mountains by eight years. The barge stopped at Cumberland; the train raced on to the banks of the Ohio. A county in the highlands of western Maryland was named after one of the railroad's presidents, John W. Garrett.

The Maryland State Legislature formally sanctioned the incorporation of the Baltimore and Ohio under president

Philip E. Thomas, a former Maryland commissioner of the Chesapeake and Ohio Canal, with a capital stock of $5 million, on February 28, 1827, the same year the first railroad of United States history was built at Quincy, Massachusetts. Only a few weeks earlier twenty-five leading Baltimore businessmen had met at the home of banker George Brown "to take under consideration the best means of restoring to the city of Baltimore that portion of the western trade which has recently been diverted from it by the introduction of steam navigation and by other causes." Within days a specially appointed committee had recommended "that immediate application be made to the legislature of Maryland for an act incorporating a joint stock company to be styled 'The Baltimore and Ohio Railway Company,' and clothing such company with all the powers necessary to the construction of a railroad, with two or more sets of rails, from the city of Baltimore to the Ohio River." Thus, noted Edward Hungerford, the 1928 historian of the B&O, "The United States immediately entered upon an era of railroad mania, with Baltimore leading, that was not to subside until the great panic of 1837."

With a population of nearly eighty thousand, 1827, Baltimore was the third largest city of the nation. The National Road, which officially terminated at Cumberland, but practically ended (or began) at Baltimore, had been a chief factor in its development as a major market city and world seaport. The promoters of the Baltimore and Ohio desired above all else to retain through their project the business and purchasing power of a rapidly expanding West.

The first construction contracts for the Baltimore and Ohio Railway line west to Ellicott's Mills were awarded by October 1, 1828. The following summer the Englishman Horatio Allen operated the first steam locomotive in United States history on a rudely built track at Honesdale, Pennsylvania. "The Baltimore and Ohio Railroad [that year] had run its tracks down to Ellicott's Mills, thirteen miles," recalled the New York merchant and businessman Peter Cooper in 1882, "and had laid 'snakehead' rails as they called them, strap rails you know, and had put on horses. Then they began to talk about the English experiments with locomotives. But there was a short turn of 150 feet radius around Point of Rocks and the news came from England that George Stephenson, locomotive builder, said that no locomotive could draw a train on any curve shorter than a 900-foot radius. The horse cars didn't pay and the directors had a bad fit of the blues. I had naturally a knack at contriving and I told the directors that I believed I could knock together a locomotive that would get the train around Point of Rocks.

"So I came back to New York and got a little bit of an engine, about one horse-power, and carried it back to Baltimore. I had an iron foundry and some manual skill in working in it. But I couldn't find any iron pipes. The fact is that there were none for sale in this country. So I took two muskets and broke off the wood part, and used the barrels for tubing to the boiler. . . . I went into a coachmaker's shop and made this locomotive, which I called the Tom Thumb because it was so insignificant. I meant to show two things: first, that short turns could be made; and, secondly, that I would get a rotary motion without the use of a crank.

"I got steam up one Saturday night; the president of the [B&O] road and two or three gentlemen were standing by, and we got on the track and went out two or three miles. All were delighted."

The highest speed ever attained by Peter Cooper's Tom Thumb was eighteen miles per hour. It was defeated in an 1830 race by a grey horse.

The Baltimore and Ohio Railroad opened to the public the first division of its line from Pratt Street at Mount Clare to the Carrollton Viaduct on January 7, 1830. This was the first public use of any railroad service in the nation; horses and mules pulled the 120 passengers of the line's initial voyage in four excursion cars.

The following January the line offered a prize in the *Baltimore American* of "four thousand dollars for the most approved engine, which shall be delivered for trial upon the road on or before the 1st of June, 1831." The winner of the contest was Phineas Davis, a York, Pennsylvania, watchmaker, for his three-and-one-half-ton York, a small locomotive which averaged in speed from twenty to thirty miles per hour. "We learn," the *Baltimore American* reported in July, "that the transportation of passengers upon the Baltimore and Ohio Railroad will hereafter be by locomotive steam engines."

Double tracking of the Baltimore and Ohio line was extended to a point twenty-five miles west of Baltimore by November 1831. Two months later a single track was completed to Frederick, sixty-one miles west of the road's Baltimore terminus. The first regular train of the line rolled into Frederick on December 1 to a tremendous local reception. The Stockton and Stokes Stage line announced that month that it would henceforth deposit the passengers from the west and the National Road at Frederick to complete their journeys to Baltimore by rail.

Five small locomotives comprised the rail line's total motive power at the time the Baltimore and Ohio reached Harper's Ferry in the fall of 1834. From here it crossed the Potomac River into Virginia, and reached Hancock by June 1, 1842. "The results which have been realized in the few months since the railroad has been in operation to Hancock have been of the most gratifying character," the *Cumberland Civilian* reported in August. "The travel to and from the West has been doubled, having been attracted to this route by the superior advantages of comfort and expedition which it presents over others; and there can be no doubt that when the road is open to Cumberland so that the trip between Baltimore and Wheeling and Pittsburgh can be made easily in twenty-four hours, or probably less, the question of the course of travel between the East and the West will be settled definitely and permanently in favor of this Great Central Route. There is no other that can come into competition with it in any one of the prominent particulars of expedition, comfort or economy, and it must therefore *command* the travel between the Atlantic States and the vast valley of the Mississippi." "I suppose you know the Railroad is finished as far as Hancock," Martha McHenry wrote her friend Susan Drane in Missouri from Buffalo Marsh in June.

"They leave Baltimore at seven in the morning and arrive at Cumberland at nine in the evening."

"No other event has ever transpired in the history of the place which created so much pleasurable excitement," recorded Will H. Lowdermilk in his 1878 *History of Cumberland* on the arrival of the first B&O train in that town on November 1, 1842. "Business was entirely suspended, and men, women and children gathered about the terminus of the road to witness the arrival of the trains. From the mountain top, and valleys, throughout the adjoining country, the people came in crowds, and the town was in a fervor of excitement for many days."

On December 5, exactly one month after the official Cumberland opening ceremony, a special locomotive from Washington rushed a copy of President John Tyler's annual congressional message one hundred and seventy miles west to waiting trans-Appalachian coaches at Cumberland in five hours and fifty minutes. "Civilization," noted Edward Hungerford, the 1928 historian of the B&O "with a ladder-like wand of wood and steel that looked like a link of railroad track was waving her hand."

"The opening of the road proved the inauguration of a new era in the history of the town," contended Cumberland's Lowdermilk. "Hotels were erected for the accommodation of travelers, and large ware houses, along the railroad track, for the storing of goods which were to be transshipped from cars to wagons for the West, and from wagons to cars for the East. The facilities this furnished for rapid transportation induced many persons to make the journey across the mountains, and the stage companies were compelled to build new coaches and to erect large stables. Every morning and evening upon the arrival of the cars long lines of stages drew up in front of the hotels. In a little while after the completion of the railroad to Cumberland, the National Road became a thoroughfare, such as the country has never before or since seen. Those were 'good old times,' and the 'pike boys' still living look back to them with many a sigh of regret." Cumberland remained the western terminal of the Baltimore and Ohio for a full decade, until 1852.

The first surveys to locate the route of the B&O in the Allegheny highlands of present-day Garrett County west of Cumberland were conducted in 1836 under the supervision of Benjamin H. Latrobe, the railroad's chief engineer and son of the architect of the White House when that structure was rebuilt after being burned by the British in the War of 1812. Latrobe surveyed two possible routes and considered a third. The northern proposed route ran from Cumberland up Wills Creek through a tunnel at Sand Patch, then along the Casselman River to Turkeyfoot and points west. The southern alternative, "one of much beauty and interest, especially that which lies west of the Little Backbone, where are found those elevated natural meadows, so well known under the name of the Glades," the southern alternative passed from Cumberland through Westernport where it crossed the Savage River, then ascended the Great Backbone Mountain to Crabtree Creek and the summit of Little Backbone at Hinche's Spring, from whence it passed through a proposed eighty-foot cut into the Glades and followed Green Glades Run and Deep Creek to the Youghiogheny just above Swallow Falls and continued west into Virginia. The third, intermediate route, first surveyed in 1824 for the proposed Chesapeake and Ohio Canal, ran up Buffalo Marsh Run from the mouth of Cherry Creek by "the residence of John McHenry, Esq. near Yaldwin's farm" to Bear Creek and the "Youghiogheny Iron Works," from whence it passed downriver through Selbysport and Turkeyfoot into Pennsylvania. None of the three proposed 1836 routes was ultimately followed.

Instead, Latrobe returned to the mountains in July of 1847 with three groups of engineers to select a final route across the eastern continental divide. The path he chose followed the basic route of the Maryland-Virginia Interstate Road. It crossed the Potomac from Virginia at Westernport, then followed Savage River and Crabtree Creek uphill to the summit of Little Backbone Mountain, from whence it descended to the glades and followed the Little Youghiogheny to the Big Youghiogheny and once again crossed the state line into Virginia. Before the end of the year Latrobe had surveyed in detail sixty-five miles of the extension west of

Cumberland. The road was then ready for contract. Latrobe set a railroad construction precedent on the seventeen-mile eastern slope of the Great Backbone Mountain by following a path which ascended 116 feet to the mile, a ruling grade of 2.2 percent. Years later, when transcontinental railroads were built for the first time over the Rockies in the Far West, Congress specified that the builders not exceed the 116-feet-to-the-mile ascension precedent set by Benjamin Latrobe on the slopes of the Great Backbone of Western Maryland.

"Before (the advent of the railroad) there was neither village nor town in the southern part of Garrett County," suggested a 1956 Baltimore and Ohio public relations brochure, "but in the footsteps of the Iron Horse came the development of the timber and coal resources. Farms were cleared, towns and villages appeared, in fact the whole area atop the mountains began to grow." B&O engineers and construction gangs began to arrive in the highland glades as early as 1849. By the autumn of 1851 five thousand men and twelve hundred horses were working on the roadbed in the mountains between the Potomac and Cheat Rivers. They graded by pick and shovel, drilled by hand, moved earth and stone on horse-drawn carts, and blasted with explosive powder. Their construction camps dotted the mountains and glades. Israel Thompson provided beef from his herds; Isaac McCarty provided office space in his home. They built a single track only. A new generation of Baltimore merchants, men such as Johns Hopkins and Robert Garrett, provided financial support for the costly extension.

The mountain laborers of the Baltimore and Ohio were chiefly Irish immigrants, "Corkonians" from southern Ireland and "Fardowners" from the north. Occasionally the two groups got into scraps and brawls. "Supply of labor on the line has been abundant, and disturbances among the workmen have not been numerous or serious," noted Latrobe in 1849, "altho the party feuds among the greater part of the foreign laborers render the maintenance of peace among them insecure . . . [were] it practical to enforce the prohibition of the use of ardent spirits upon or near the line, the chief cause of all the broils which happen would be removed." Thomas J. Brandt, of Oakland, recalled in 1900 that at Kennedy's Grog Shop on the northwest corner of present-day Second and Oak streets "I witnessed a free street fight in which about 25 Irish laborers of the railroad who had been sampling Kennedy's whiskey became too enthusiastic. They swarmed out of the building into the street and the fun began. There were no friends nor foes as far as I could distinguish. Everybody tried to hit somebody else with something. There were numerous bloody noses and faces." Some of the Irish laborers of 1851—William Canty, John Carney, Michael Flaherty, Martin Pendergast—remained and settled in the highlands for life.

The Baltimore and Ohio Railroad gave birth to a string of new towns in the southern part of present-day Garrett County. "I certify that I have at the request of William Combs and P. Hamill laid off a town of thirty-nine lots near the mouth of Savage River at the Potomac in Allegeny County, Maryland, called 'Bloomington,' " reported the local James D. Armstrong on June 17, 1849. The stone railroad bridge built across the North Branch of the Potomac at Bloomington in 1851 is still in use.

Francis Thomas and Jacob Markell deeded the 1787 Revolutionary War military lot No. 36 in the valley of Crabtree Creek to the B&O Railroad Company on October 10, 1849, specifying that the company establish a depot, switch, and siding there to accommodate local rail trade and travel. The station was later named Frankville in honor of the former governor of Maryland, Francis E. Thomas, who lived in the vicinity until 1876, when he was struck and killed by a helper engine while walking along the mountain tracks near his home.

The town of Swanton, which grew up along the tracks of the railroad near Backbone Mountain a few miles west of Frankville, in ensuing years was named after Thomas Swann, president of the road from 1849 until 1853.

The town of Altamont at the summit of Little Backbone Mountain (2,628 feet above sea level—the highest point on the entire B&O line) sprang up after 1851 on both sides of the B&O tracks as a shipping point of local farm produce, livestock, and lumber. A railroad station established at Altamont in 1851 served passengers of B&O accommodation trains until the twentieth century. A wye track established on the north side of the tracks there in 1851 was also used for years to turn helper engines around. ("Helpers" were employed at Altamont throughout the late nineteenth century to assist trains up the long seventeen-mile grade east of the village, up the Deer Park grade west of the town.) Altamont of 1851 also featured a water reservoir to replenish the engine tanks of B&O steam locomotives; later it boasted a telegraph tower for the regulation of local train traffic. (The early "AM Tower" operators at Altamont communicated by Morse Code; today they speak directly with train crews over two-way radio systems.)

(A local resident shot an Irish laborer of the B&O in the head at Altamont in 1851 in a fight over stolen horses. The victim was buried in an unmarked grave near the place he fell.)

"The village in the Youghiogheny Glades west of Backbone Mountain that began to take form with the coming of the Iron Horse to the glade country in 1851," noted Robert B. Garrett, local historian, great-grandson of Meshach Browning, no direct relation to John W. Garrett, "was given the name 'Deer Park.' " By the gay nineties Deer Park was renowned as an exclusive railroad resort town for the elite of the eastern American cities. Not more than three or four houses were located at Deer Park in 1851 when the railroad was built through the valley.

James A. Armstrong platted sixty-four town lots five miles west of Deer Park along the banks of the Little Youghiogheny on October 10, 1849, "at the request" of Edward McCarty, son of the pioneer, Isaac McCarty. The elder McCarty deeded half the new town lots to the B&O Railroad, specifying that both parties sell their lands without price increases as the proposed town grew. Railroad officials suggested that the town be named McCartysville, but Isaac modestly declined the honor. His daughter Ingaba then suggested the name Oakland, and the name stuck. In 1854 the Yough Glades postal address officially became Oakland. The original Oakland railroad station, built in 1851, was the first rail depot ever erected on top of any mountain in the world.

From Oakland the path of the steel rails proceeded west across the Big Youghiogheny River to the Cheat River in the state of Virginia (now West Virginia).

The first iron horse came snorting, choking, and chugging up the seventeen-mile grade eastern slopes of Backbone Mountain and into the highland glades of western Maryland in the fall of 1851. Destiny.

John R. Thompson, editor of the *Southern Literary Messenger,* 1859 Baltimore and Ohio mountain passenger: "For the first two hundred miles of its course the road seems to be a scientific chase after the headwaters of the Potomac River.... This engineering chase grows most exciting in the narrow and torturous ravine where the Potomac has dwindled into the Savage River, and where the road is carried off for more than fourteen miles up a continuous grade of 116 feet to the mile. The lonely grandeur of the scene at this point is indescribable. The dark masses of the forest on the mountain side; the lofty firs and chestnuts in the deep valley seeking vainly to lift their topmost branches to the level of the road, the intense blue of the sky as contrasted with sombre tints of surrounding objects; the rivulet far below, seen only in fearful glimpses now and then through the dense foliage. All these make up a picture of desolate magnificence which only the highest art could transfer to canvas.

"The sense of perfect security which is felt by the traveler, even in the giddy ascent of the Allegheny along Savage River, was heightened in our case by a furious storm, which burst upon us about two-thirds of the way up from Piedmont to Altamont. We were seated on the fender or 'cow-catcher,' watching the majestic marshalling of the thunder clouds over the mountain tops, and enjoying to the full the excitement of the moment, when suddenly the wind blew a terrible gust, filling the air with dust and dry leaves, and threatening to carry us individually over the precipice. The train was stopped and we sought shelter in the comfortable car, which then moved on through the driving floods that continued to descend for half an hour, forming cataracts on every side of us. But the rain ran off harmlessly from the solid track and our engine bid defiance to the tempest, which hurled huge branches of trees into the angry abyss beneath. The triumph of science over nature was complete; and as the sinking sun threw a glow over the glades, where the clouds had parted, I think my companions caught some inspirations of the 'Poetry of the Railway.' "

Rebecca Harding, writer for *Harper's New Monthly Magazine*, 1880 Baltimore and Ohio mountain passenger: "The woods in this division of the Alleghanies are so vast and engrossing as to be oppressive. It is not peak nor valley whose influence you feel, but a nightmare of trees stretching from horizon to horizon. When you have jogged through them past the first skyline, new horizons open of interminable hills shouldering hills, lifting to the skys the same monotonous growth. The trains rushed, without any warning, into a wilderness so savage that even the phlegmatic American traveler was startled out of his ordinary composure. The track stretched like a thread along the edge of a stupendous gorge; opposite, a range of peaks stuck straight up into the cloudy sky. The effect of vastness and impregnable solitude was sudden and electric."

J. G. Pangborn, author of *Picturesque B. and O.*, 1883 Baltimore and Ohio mountain passenger: "At Piedmont commences the seventeen-mile grade, as railroad men call it, and it is one stretch of grandeur that is, perhaps, without an equal. The locomotive at once gives evidence of the increased strain to which it is subjected, and its hoarse breathings are echoed in the recesses of the distant mountains. The Potomac, dwindling into comparative insignificance, loses itself at last in the hidden springs of its source. The goodbye to the familiar thread of water is uttered with regret, but for this the fury of the Savage River, which plunges onward between the gorges of the peak from which it derives its name, abundantly compensates. Deeper now and more sonorous the engine growls as it grasps the steel in its steep ascent. There is a turn in the mountain-side, and the steam-choked motor is allowed a few moments' respite. Meanwhile, the eye of the traveler is delighted with what would seem to be an infinity of space were its width not limited by the walls of the gorge, upon the rugged edges of which are to be found growing in scant soil the spruce and the pine. Struggling waters trickle down the crumbling sandstone, and vegetation of a sparse description hangs over on the verge of despair.

"Here is nature in her glory; here she reigns in majesty undisputed, her power untrammeled, and her sway absolute. Progressing by slow strides the engine is once more within the confines of mountain solemnity, and there is no other evidence of human existence than the seared rocks, the crossties, and the steel over which the way is made. The ascent continues, and the aptly-named station Altamont comes into view, and the snorting and long-suppressed efforts of the steam to escape from the great iron-bound boiler cease. The mountains are now below, for the train has reached the summit and the eye roams at will over the billowy masses. The elevation is now nearly three thousand feet above the tide-water, and the atmospheric change is very perceptible. The lungs, stirred to unwonted activity by the exhilarating draught, expand to new action, and one stands more erect, feeling that there is much in life, and that he is infinitely better prepared to enjoy it when every physical power is so invigorated.

"The lay of the glade country is of the meadow order, with undulating surface and billowy eminences. A three-mile jaunt westward from Altamont and Deer Park comes into view, its location upon the brow of a long, sloping promontory striking the observer at first sight as singularly picturesque."

Ele Bowen, author of *Rambles in the Path of the Steam Horse,* 1855 mountain passenger of the B&O: "The verdure of the glades is peculiarly bright and fresh, and the streams watering them are of singular clearness and purity, and abound in splendid trout, which nowhere else attain the flavor peculiar to it in the mountain brooks. Oats, rye, hay and potatoes are the principal crops; but the main business is grazing, there being scarcely a limit to the extent of the pasturage."

Anonymous 1857 mountain passenger of the B&O: "The

meadows are plentifully interspersed with forest groves in all their native wildness, and divided by ridges, which break them up into a series of unfenced fields, over which the herds rove almost as wild as the buffalo on our western plains. This region is famed throughout Virginia and Maryland for its excellent butter no less than its superior mutton, abundant venison and other game and innumerable trout streams. The air is highly rarefied, and very cool and bracing throughout the summer months."

Brantz Mayer, writer for *Harper's Magazine,* 1857 mountain passenger of the B&O: "There are few routes of travel in America, and none probably by rail, worthier of attention than the region between the slopes of the western gladeland at the mountain exit at Kingwood [Tunnel]. It presents splendid bits of forest scenery. There is everywhere the same ragged gloom, the same overarching hemlocks and firs, the same torrent roar, foaming over rocky beds, the same fringing of thick-leaved laurel, the same oozy plashes of morass, rank with dark vegetation, the same black mountain face, the same absence of people and forms, the same sense of absolute solitude. In these central solitudes everything seems to be the property of wilderness, a wilderness incapable of yielding to any mastery but that of an engineer; and it may fairly become a matter of national pride that scientific men were found in our country bold enough to venture on grades by which any mountain may be passed. They who desire to understand the power of science in conquering nature by steam and iron, must climb and cross the Alleghenies between Piedmont and Kingwood."

Tracking on the Baltimore and Ohio Railroad was completed to Fairmont, Virginia, on June 22, 1852. On Christmas Eve of that year the last rail was laid, the last spike was driven at Roseby's Rock in present-day West Virginia to connect the levee of the Ohio River at Wheeling with the city of Baltimore, 379 miles to the east. The first excursion train entered Wheeling from Baltimore on January 1, 1853. Five hundred Baltimoreans traveled eighteen hours to the road's western terminus that year for a grand celebration of speeches, dinners, toasts, and music. The iron horse had at last conquered the heights of the Alleghenies.

In 1857 the nation celebrated the opening of a through rail line from Baltimore to Saint Louis. "Before the railroads to the West were built," noted the writer Brantz Mayer in *Harper's Magazine* that year, "the tide of travel found its way [west] by the great turnpike, known as the 'National Road'.... The completion of the northwest Virginia [now West Virginia] arm of the Baltimore and Ohio Railroad, from Grafton on the main line, to Parkersburg on the Ohio—and the Marietta and Cincinnati Railroad, from a point near Parkersburg to Cincinnati, formed the very shortest line between that city and the seaboard and the city of St. Louis. This fact, as well as the high character and the importance of the several roads constituting the route, has caused it to be known as the 'American Central Line,' a title used by Governor Salmon P. Chase, of Ohio, Mayor Thomas Swann of Baltimore, and others, in their speeches made upon the great opening celebrations of 1857."

Among the distinguished guests of the railroads at the grand Cincinnati celebrations of 1857 was the noted historian George Bancroft. "The Baltimore and Ohio is unequaled in the difficulties which it has surmounted," Bancroft declared at the time. "When we came to the foot of the Alleghenies, on the east [at the seventeen-mile Backbone Mountain grade], we saw the steepness of the dividing ridge, that seemed impassable. But a railroad is a work of art. Michelangelo used to say that all forms of beauty lie hidden beneath the surface of the marble quarry, waiting only for the hand of the sculptor to call them into being. The eye of Benjamin Latrobe saw at a glance the capacity of the mountain, and scoffing at the threatening ravines and precipices, and lofty summit, gave himself no rest until commerce had carried its safe and easy pathway in triumph over the mountain top, and proved to the world that there are no difficulties which true enterprise cannot surmount; that nature herself is in league with genius.

"Tomorrow and the days after we extend our course to the further west; we celebrate the opening of the direct communication between Baltimore, Cincinnati and St. Louis. The occasion is due of national interest; the system of roads bind indissolubly the East and West. The triad of cities which are the fortresses of the Union are now but one in commerce and culture; in the arts of life and the enjoyments of society; in enterprise and love of country. How would Washington, who, when he last came to the West, crossed the mountain by fatigued marches—how would he have exulted could he have but seen his great cherished idea of an international highway carried out with a perfection and convenience which surpassed the powers of his century to imagine?

"How young America is fulfilling the destiny which her fathers manifestly designed for her; she more and more subdues nature and gives freedom to men. Under her influence the world will be united in peace and commerce, and liberty be owned as the birthright of every nation of the earth."

On May 10, 1869, only eighteen years after the first rail locomotive chugged up the hills of western Maryland, the tracks of the Union Pacific Railroad, beginning near Omaha, Nebraska, and the tracks of the Central Pacific Railroad, terminating at Sacramento, California, met and were joined by a golden spike at a point called Promontory in the Promontory Mountains of Utah, north of Great Salt Lake. "THE LAST NAIL IS LAID," an excited telegrapher flashed across the wires to points east and west. "THE LAST SPIKE IS DRIVEN . . . THE PACIFIC RAILROAD IS COMPLETED!" A single strand of steel and wood at last united the waters of the Atlantic with those of the Pacific. Destiny.

"My humble prayer is now, and shall ever be," wrote Garrett County's pioneer hunter Meshach Browning in 1858, "that Divine Providence will at all times so guide the councils of our nation, that all the laws may tend to the preservation of our peaceful habits and fair fame, and to the perpetuation of our equal rights and liberties . . . till this country arrives at its highest glory and renown, and is fully competent to enforce every just demand it may have on every other nation and people." On October 17 of the following year the night conductor of the eastbound Baltimore and Ohio express from Wheeling flashed a prophetic message across the telegraph wires from Monocacy, Maryland, to the railroad's master of transportation in Baltimore. "Express train bound east under my charge was stopped this morning at Harpers Ferry by armed abolitionists," the conductor wired. "They have possession of the bridge and of the arms and armory of the United States. They are headed by a man who calls himself Anderson [John Brown of Osawatomie, Kansas] and number about 150 strong. They say they have come to free the slaves, and intend to do it at all hazards. It has been suggested that you had better notify the Secretary of War at once."

The Civil War came to present-day Garrett County on the steel rails of the Baltimore and Ohio Railroad. The road's 1928 historian, Edward Hungerford, noted that "the sun was brightly shining in Maryland that autumn of 1859 as the first annual report of the road's new president, John W. Garrett, came rolling off the presses . . . when suddenly there flashed from under the finger of the telegraph operator at Monocacy the message which was to reverberate around all creation and send millions of men into the mightiest conflict the world had ever known."

Alexander H. Stephens, vice-president of the Confederacy, observed in later years that "the real crisis [of the war] was passed in those early months, after the fall of Fort Sumter, in April, 1861, when the South was waiting for Maryland to act, and Lincoln prevented that state from seceding, largely because of the fact that the overwhelming influence exerted by the Baltimore and Ohio was exerted in favor of Washington." The railroad's historian, Edward Hungerford, agreed. "From Baltimore to Harpers Ferry and Martinsburg," he recorded, "at least the majority of the rank and file of the road were aroused Southern sympathizers. At the outbreak of the conflict, no small proportion of them left their tasks, crossed the Potomac and enlisted in the army of the Confederacy. Nevertheless, by sheer will power and force of energy, to say nothing of increasing wit and tact, Garrett not only held his road and himself loyal to the Union, but kept both of greatest service to it."

At the outbreak of hostilities in 1861, a deputation of influential Baltimoreans suspecting the railroad's president of being sympathetic to the southern cause (Garrett's own brother Henry was once arrested in Baltimore after a vehement outburst in favor of the Confederacy) called on President Lincoln to advise John Garrett's removal from the head of the strategic Baltimore and Ohio line. Lincoln refused to consider their advice. "Throughout the four years of the war," Robert B. Garrett of Deer Park, no direct relation to John, noted in 1970, "Mr. Garrett was either at his Baltimore office receiving reports from all along the line and issuing orders for movements of trains or repairs to bridges, track and rolling stock, or else out along the road endeavoring to maintain and improve the morale of his faithful employees."

"Mr. Garrett personally saw or communicated with Secretary of War, Edward M. Stanton daily till the end of the war," recorded the biographer Frank A. Flower, "using his railroad and his energies and information in aid of suppressing the Rebellion. As he knew almost everybody in the South, possessed enormous resources, and was fully trusted by Stanton, his services were of great value." An 1863 observer later recalled encountering Garrett in a corridor of the Treasury Building in Washington during the war with the then Secretary of Treasury, Salmon P. Chase. "Arm in arm," he recalled, "these two eminent men walked slowly along, Mr. Garrett talking in a low tone, and the great financier of the war, the man who has been known ever since as the 'Father of the greenbacks,' and later as the great Chief Justice of the Supreme Court, listening intently to what was said. These were nerve-racking days in Washington, and although Mr. Garrett was still a young man, his face had a tired, worried look, showing that he felt the awful strain caused by the great task imposed upon him. These two great figures of the history of the war, walked slowly down the steps of the Treasury, and crossed over to the White House." Lincoln himself later recognized Garrett as being "the right arm of the Federal Government in the aid he rendered the authorities in preventing the Confederates from seizing Washington and securing its retention as the Capital of the Loyal States."

"Very soon after the outbreak of war it became clear that the Baltimore and Ohio was to be by far the most important railroad in the country, coveted alike by North and South," noted Robert B. Garrett in 1970. Western Maryland historian J. Thomas Scharf recorded in 1882 that "the road ran through the theatre of the principal military operations of the war. For four years contending armies swept across it, and frequently miles of track were torn up and valuable engines and rolling-stock destroyed. And even with the road thus constantly threatened or crippled, Mr. Garrett was frequently called upon by the national authorities for assistance in moving troops at critical periods. His energy seemed unbounded, and it was soon demonstrated that he possessed a will and nerve of iron." President Lincoln and his advisors posted nearly twenty-four thousand federal soldiers along the Baltimore and Ohio line between Parkersburg and the Monocacy River during the course of the war. They stationed thousands more at points farther west.

"The old Baltimore and Ohio Railroad got it at every turn," recalled Major Sidney F. Shaw, superintendent of construction of all federal defenses along the line during the war, in 1898. "How many times it was torn up no man can tell, but several times during the period it was ripped from stem to stern. It appeared to be great sport to tear up the track of this railroad, pile the ties in heaps, fire them, place the rails across the fire, leave them there till they were red hot, then take them out and tie them around trees, like neckties, so that they had to be cut off or it was necessary to cut the trees down to secure the iron. What is now known as '17 mile grade' [on Backbone Mountain] near Piedmont, was a favorite place with the Confederates, who could conceive of no finer sport that to turn a car or engine loose on the grade and let it come dashing down the mountain wrecking anything with which it might come in contact."

To defend the Baltimore and Ohio line, the federal government early in the war erected blockhouses all along its route from Monocacy to the Ohio River and erected forts at Harpers Ferry, Winchester, Cumberland, New Creek (present-day Keyser), and Piedmont. At Oakland they built an earth and stone mound fifteen feet high above the tracks for the protection of the wooden bridge across the Youghiogheny. On the top of the mound they dug trenches around a small log shelter and installed rifle pits. "The importance of keeping this great highway open as a means of communication between the West and the Army of the Potomac," noted a writer for the road's *Book of the Royal Blue* in 1898, "compelled the National Government to guard it with watchful care, and tens of thousands of the 'Boys in Blue' bivouacked and did sentry duty along its line."

The Civil War, "the War Between the States," "the War of the Rebellion," "the War of the Secession," "the War for Southern Independence," was the first modern war, the first total war. It claimed more American casualties—nearly one million men were either killed or wounded in its battles—than did any other war in history. It divided family against family, friend against friend, brother against brother. It threatened the severance of an entire nation. It introduced new and deadlier weapons to warfare, new battle strategies, new techniques, new sources of manpower. Its guns aimed at the heart of a nation, not merely at its armies; its bullets destroyed souls and ideologies, not mere soldiers.

Its causes were many and diverse: economic rivalries, sectional jealousies, the growing pains of rapid national expansion, flaming and fire-baiting rhetoric. But its chief causes were differing opinions over the institution of slavery and the extension of slavery into new territories.

The first abolition society in the nation was organized as early as 1775 at Philadelphia, Pennsylvania. In 1811 Josiah Quincy, of Massachusetts, argued before the House of Representatives that the proposed purchase of the Louisiana Territory from France would be the ultimate dissolution of the nation. When the territory of Missouri, carved from the middle of the Louisiana Purchase, applied for statehood in 1818, eleven states favored the recognition of slavery there, eleven states opposed it. The dilemma was resolved by the Missouri Compromise of 1820 when Maine also applied for statehood, slavery was allowed in Missouri, outlawed in Maine. The slave-antislave balance was maintained; the solution was a temporary expedient at best.

The black Denmark Vesey led an ill-fated slave insurrection in Charleston, South Carolina, in 1822. On January 1,

1831, William Lloyd Garrison published the first issue of his militant abolitionist newspaper, the *Liberator,* in Boston, asserting that "I do not wish to think, or speak, or write with moderation. I will not equivocate; I will not excuse; I will not retreat a single inch; AND I WILL BE HEARD." That August a black preacher in Virginia, Nat Turner, led a violent slave insurrection in South Hampton in which fifty-four whites were killed. "I heard a loud noise in the heavens," Turner later confessed, after at least one hundred blacks were killed in retaliation, "and the Spirit instantly appeared to me and said the Serpent was loosened, and Christ had laid down the yoke He had borne for the sins of men, and that I should take it on and fight against the Serpent, for the time was fast approaching when the first should be last and the last should be first." Turner himself, along with twenty other conspirators, was hanged.

John C. Calhoun became the first vice-president in United States history to resign from office on December 28, 1832, after being elected senator from South Carolina, doing so in order to more effectively champion the institution of slavery and the ideology of States' Rights. "I hold that in the present state of civilization," Calhoun later exhorted, "where two races of different origin, and distinguished by color, and other physical differences, as well as intellectual, are brought together, the relation now existing in the slaveholding states between the two is, instead of an evil, a good—a positive good." In 1840 the House of Representatives, bowing to Southern pressure, passed a resolution refusing to accept further petitions concerning abolition. In 1843 John Quincy Adams, returning to Congress after a term as president, rose to the floor of the House of Representatives and declared that "If slavery must go by blood and war, let war come."

In 1848 third-party advocates organized the Free Soil party to urge the prohibition of slavery in new territories. Two years later Congress passed the Compromise of 1850, which provided that California be admitted to the Union as a free state; that new territorial governments be formed without restrictions pertaining to slavery; that the slave trade—but not slavery itself—be abolished in the District of Columbia, and that a new and more effective fugitive slave law be passed. The Compromise of 1850, like the Missouri Compromise of 1820, proved to be little more than a brief and uneasy truce, a parlay.

In 1854 Senator Stephen A. Douglas of Illinois pushed through Congress the Kansas-Nebraska Act which established two new western territories, voided the Compromise of 1850, and proposed to settle the slavery question by popular sovereignty. The North blazed with fury at this latest demonstration of the power of the Southern slavocracy. The Whig party split asunder; the Republican party was born. (Southern Whigs became Democrats.)

Hundreds of supporters and opponents of slavery clashed in armed conflict in "Bleeding Kansas" after 1854. On the floor of the Senate in Washington, Preston Brooks, a member of the House from South Carolina, approached Charles Sumner, of Massachusetts, and beat the senator with a cane until he lay unconscious on the floor. Sumner left his office for four years; Brooks resigned under pressure and congressional censure, then returned to Washington after an almost unanimous vote of support by his constituency.

In 1857 the Supreme Court itself ruled that Congress could not legally exclude slavery from the new western territories in the celebrated and famous Dred Scott decision. The abolitionist Frederick Douglass declared that "This very attempt to blot out forever the hopes of an enslaved people may be one necessary link in the chain of events preparatory to the complete overthrow of the whole slave system."

On October 16, 1859, the antislavery fanatic from bleeding Kansas, John Brown, at the head of eighteen followers, descended on the town of Harpers Ferry and captured the Federal Arsenal there for guns and ammunition he needed for a planned slave insurrection. The next day he was captured and subdued by citizens and local militia companies, reinforced by a detachment of United States Marines. On December 2 he was hanged for treason against the state of Virginia. "John Brown's body lies a-mouldering in the grave; His soul goes marching on."

Abraham Lincoln described the country as "a house

divided . . . half slave and half free" in 1860. On December 20, 1860, the state of South Carolina seceded from the Union. Mississippi, Florida, Alabama, Georgia, and Louisiana followed South Carolina's lead in January 1861. Texas seceded in March 1861. Virginia, Arkansas, North Carolina, and Tennessee all withdrew within a matter of months. (Despite extreme Southern pressure, Maryland remained with the Union.)

Confederate forces opened fire on Fort Sumter in the harbor of Charleston, South Carolina, on April 12, 1861. The Federal defenders of the garrison surrendered two days later. The Civil War, the first modern war, the first total war, had become a living reality.

The highland settlers of the nineteenth century brought their slaves as well as their families to the mountaintop. "Little Crossings," noted Jacob Brown, "contained more colored people, mostly slaves, than any other district in old Allegany county, except Cumberland. The institution did not fail to impress its peculiar features upon the community. The tint of slave aristocracy was plainly seen and felt. But the slave owners were mostly kind, hospitable and sociable. The colored people happy and contented."

"The old bee makes de honeycomb," the slaves of present-day Garrett County used to sing as they plowed their masters' fields—"The young bee makes de honey; / Colored folks plant de cotton an' corn, / An' de white folks gits de money."

Charles E. Hoye recorded in 1942 that "on holidays the Hoye children often went to the Hoye slave cabin at Sang Run to hear the negroes of the neighborhood play and sing and to see them dance. The place was out of sight and hearing of the white folks' houses and on special occasions, when the McHenry, Drane, Brooks, Lynn, and Ridgely negroes gathered there, joy was unconfined: The valley rang with music and laughter."

The issue of slavery was as much an issue of contention in the mountains of western Maryland as it was elsewhere in the border states. "The first political meeting that was ever held in Oakland that I can recall," noted Thomas J. Brandt in

1900, "was held in a ten pin alley located a little way north of Kennedy's grog shop. It was during the Buchanan and Fremont campaign of 1856. Dan Vorhees was the orator. He defended slavery and said 'the tropical sun of the South would broil the brain out of a white man if he tried to do labor there.' The audience was seated on the sides of the alley or stood up as they chose. Mr. Duval led the cheering by stamping his cane on the floor of the temporary rostrum."

The historian of Catholicism in western Maryland, the Rev. Thomas J. Stanton, recalled in 1900 that Rev. B. S. Piot "was long remembered at Blooming Rose for his opposition to slavery." (Father Piot was also remembered for buying and decapitating the ducks of Buffalo Run after he became annoyed at their quacking during services.)

Most of the early slaves of present-day Garrett County lived in small shacks and cabins separate from their masters' homes. Many were freed by their owners when their dependency became a liability, rather than a financial asset, due to the short growing season of the high elevations. When George B. Newman of Grantsville deeded four of his fifteen slaves, along with a sizable part of his farm to a son in 1823, he specified that the Negroes be required to serve their new master only until they reached twenty-one years of age, "at which time I direct that they shall be set free." Isaac McCarty of the Youghiogheny Glades, freed all of his slaves before the Civil War. Along with freedom, he gave Bill, the oldest servant, a set of clothing, a horse and saddle, and one hundred dollars. (Bill settled nearby.) He donated a house and town lot in Oakland after mid-century to blind Fanny, whom he freed, along with her two daughters, Harriet and Rachel. (The three survived through the income generated by Harriet's subsequent laundry business.) He rewarded his overseer, John Davis, with freedom after his farm was cleared and cultivated. Davis remained on the McCarty farm as a paid laborer for seven years, then met Phoebe Galloway, a Ryan's Glade slave of Philip Bray, and offered to "buy" the girl for sixty dollars. Bray gave the young lady away, the couple married and moved to Ryan's Glade, bought land, cleared a farm, and raised a large family. During the Civil War the Davis family invited F. A. and Walter Thayer, of Oakland, to their home for dinner. John stood modestly by the table to ask the blessing, but refused to eat along with his white guests. When Isaac McCarty moved to Iowa in 1855, he granted freedom to the remainder of his slaves.

John McHenry of Buffalo Marsh freed his many slaves early in the century, but the former servants remained with him for years as paid laborers. One of the McHenry servants was a young woman named Susan, who was saving money to free her husband, James Dorsey, who belonged to William Waller Hoye of Crab Tree Bottom, McHenry's nearest neighbor, when the Lincoln Emancipation Proclamation was issued in 1862. One of the Dorsey sons served in the Union army; Jim and Susan lived near Buffalo Marsh all their lives; they are buried in the abandoned McHenry graveyard.

Jesse Tomlinson of Little Meadows granted his slaves freedom one year before his death, in 1839. Philip H. Bray of Kitzmiller likewise freed his servants—Bill, Phoebe, Jane, Louisa, Nancy, Isaac, Lewis, and Emel Galloway—by will in 1844. The Galloways subsequently lived for many years on a small farm south of "Brayton" near Wolf Den Run. All highland slaves attained freedom through the Emancipation Proclamation.

Stephen Willis Friend of Sang Run operated a station of the underground railroad for fugitive slaves escaping from the South prior to the Civil War. Among others whom he helped attain freedom was Nancy, a slave belonging to his neighbor, William Hoye. (By 1850 an estimated twenty thousand blacks had escaped to the North by way of the secret, illegal "railroad.")

In the early 1840s Mortimore D. Cade, a Red Ridge hotelkeeper on the National Road, suffered a fractured skull while participating in a futile attempt to capture three runaway slaves near the Stone House at Little Meadows. A young constable suffered a "fearful" cut in the face from a corn cutter in the same encounter. "The negroes won this battle," noted Jacob Brown, "and very likely their freedom."

William Thomas and Jesse Ashby also fought with three runaway slaves near Crellin in the 1850s. They captured one of the three; William argued for his release but his brothers overruled him for a six-hundred-dollar reward.

A few years before the Civil War broke out, a "gentleman of elegant appearance and dress," a mulatto, appeared at the Stone House Hotel at Little Meadows and asked for the address of George Newman, a local farmer. The gentleman's first name was Jerome. In the 1830s he had run away from the highlands as a slave. George Newman had been his former master. According to Jacob Brown, Jerome "invited his old former quasi master to accompany him to his hotel and spend the remainder of the day together. A fine dinner of the catering of the late Lemuel Cross was partaken of. Before Newman took leave of his confidant, the former slave put fifty dollars in gold in Newman's hand, and told him that that was to compensate him for his interest in 'run-away Jerome.' Jerome simply said, at his home in the distant, he was free, white, prosperous and respected as any man in the community."

After the Civil War the former highland slaves drifted north and south, east and west. "Strange to say," reported Jacob Brown in 1888, "there is now scarcely a dozen colored people in the county."

The Civil War pitted family against family, brother against brother. Western Maryland was then a border territory; most of her sons served the Northern cause, some joined the Confederacy. Richard T. Browning served the Federal forces; Edward R. Browning, his cousin, served the Rebels. William Harrison Hoye went north; William D. and Samuel Hoye went south. Jonathan Hinebaugh joined the Confederates; his sons—John, Sebastian, and Alfred—joined the Federal army. Peter and W. Wallace Chisholm fought with the boys in gray; John H. and Alexander Chisholm fought with the boys in blue. Eleven highland Harveys served the Northern cause; one, John L., served the Confederacy. And so it went.

D. A. Friend recalled in 1920 that "my older brother, and nearly all the young men of the neighborhood were in the army." A total of twenty-three highland Friends served the Army of the Republic. D. A. Friend, then only sixteen years old, left home secretly with Andrew Dollins against the wishes of their parents to enlist with the Federal forces at the Altamont recruiting station.

Seven highland Savages, eight Sines, and four Upholds served with the Union army during the Civil War. Four Masons served the South. Samuel A. Dean, of Grantsville, was twice rejected by Federal recruiters as being too young to serve before he was finally allowed to join his father and older brother in the field. The Presbyterian minister, Rev. John Phillips, of Red House, substituted as schoolmaster and pastor at Susan's Church in Sunnyside during the war, while the regular teacher and minister, Rev. John H. Cupp, worked as chaplain with the Union army. Daniel Turner, a teacher at Mount Zion, worked as a Confederate commissioner in Europe during the war's last years. (He returned to Garrett County only once—for a brief visit in 1883.)

Francis Thomas, the one-time governor of Maryland, emerged from his self-imposed seclusion at New Germany at the outbreak of Civil War hostilities to raise a northern regiment of three thousand men. By October 1862, Allegany County had already furnished over fourteen hundred volunteers for the North. Present-day Garrett County, by war's end, was the home of a total of 728 Civil War veterans of both the United States and the Confederacy.

The Civil War came to present-day Garrett County on the steel rails of the Baltimore and Ohio Railroad.

On June 8, 1861, only two months after the fall of Fort Sumter, the B&O Railroad transported the troops of the Eleventh Indiana Volunteers, under the command of Adjutant General Lew Wallace, over the eastern continental divide at Backbone Mountain to Cumberland, Maryland, for the defense of the eastern terminus of the National Road and the railroad from Baltimore. "When Wallace's Eleventh occupied the town" noted pike historian Philip D. Jordan in 1948, "Cumberland was confused and divided in its loyalties. Parlors were battlefields with demure ladies suddenly becoming violent partisans. . . . Traffic on the Baltimore and Ohio Railroad was interrupted. The normal trade routes between Virginia and Maryland were cut. From Washington, not too far away on the Potomac, came wild rumors that increased, instead of diminishing, Cumberland's unrest. When Wallace's soldiers entered town, merchants slept at their counters afraid to go home lest raiding parties pilfer shelves. Down from the hills came grime-crusted miners, laying aside pick and shovel to mill about and spread war gossip. Railroad shops closed down. Saloons and taverns were thronged with talkative men, whose tongues wagged faster with every drink. A slave uprising, the threat of arson, the fear of robbery, all these were turned over in conversation until the population lost the sense to think clearly."

Wallace soon alleviated Cumberland's apprehensions with a "grandiloquent" proclamation assuring local citizens that the Hoosiers would not interfere with their daily lives. He then moved the bulk of his men southwest by train to secure the B&O Railroad bridge at nearby New Creek, near Romney, Virginia. The troops disembarked at the river, then marched by foot to the Confederate town of Romney with Wallace in the lead, "thinking by my example to stimulate the weary and faint of heart."

"This is what I beheld," Wallace later recalled of the column's arrival in town, "The road ran down to a wooden bridge over the South Branch of the Potomac; beyond the bridge it coursed sinuously up a long hill to the town on the summit. On the side of the hill, facing us and probably a mile away, stretched a line of men carefully ordered, their arms glittering in the sunlight. In the center two field pieces were conspicuous, as doubtless it was intended they should be."

The war was still very young when Lew Wallace and the Eleventh Indiana Volunteers entered Romney, Virginia, on July 13, 1861. They took the town and secured the B&O bridge at New Creek with only a single casualty. An enemy bullet severed a sergeant's suspender buckle. After returning to Cumberland, Wallace reported to superiors that his Romney action had "brought home to the insolent 'chivalry' a wholesome respect for Northern prowess." *Lew Wallace and the Eleventh Indiana Volunteers brought the Civil War to western Maryland for the first time.*

Wallace's actions at Romney may or may not have brought home to western Virginia Confederates "a wholesome respect for Northern prowess," as Wallace himself claimed, but it did not silence for long the marauding of mountain Confederate guerrillas intent on interrupting the lines of Northern transportation between the East and West. In fact, the Confederacy sought to hold the western Virginia mountains intact from the outset of the conflict. Romney itself was to change hands at least fifty-six times during the course of the war years.

First in command of the Southern troops in western Virginia at the war's outset—they numbered about forty-five hundred—was General Robert S. Garnett, positioned with a large force at Laurel Hill Pass near Elkins in late June 1861. In opposition to the mountain Confederates were twelve to fifteen thousand well-armed Union soldiers under the command of General George B. McClellan, supplemented by two Federal columns stationed on the Ohio River, one at Parkersburg, one at Wheeling, under the command of Colonel (later Major General) Benjamin F. Kelley.

On May 27, 1861, Colonel Kelley moved the two Ohio River columns east for the protection of the Baltimore and Ohio Railroad line between Grafton, Virginia, and Cumberland, Maryland. He encountered some minor opposition at Philippi on June 3, sustained a bullet wound in the lung, took Grafton after a brief battle, and then proceeded east with his men to Cumberland and promotion. Meanwhile, General McClellan maneuvered his troops into position in the mountains to overpower the Rebel foe piecemeal, planning to take each of the several opposition forces one at a time.

Federal troops under General William S. Rosecrans overwhelmed thirteen hundred Confederates at Rich Mountain, a few miles southwest of Elkins, on July 11, taking by right of war sixty-three prisoners, seventy-five horses, thirty wagons, and two hundred tents. The Southern General Garnett, with forty-five hundred men, was still positioned at nearby Laurel Hill Pass. Hearing of the Rich Mountain reverse, he realized that his small army was hopelessly overmatched and decided to retreat. Heavy rains slowed both the Confederate retreat to the Shenandoah Valley of Virginia and the Union pursuit. When the Confederates encountered Union fire at Corrick's

Ford on the Cheat River on July 13, Garnett himself with only ten riflemen remained at the river bank to hold off the Federal vanguard and give his men time to prepare for rearguard action. Garnett was shot and killed along with several of his riflemen. General Henry R. Jackson assumed command and continued the retreat. Only one route lay open to the defeated Rebels—the old Northwestern Turnpike through western Maryland. (McClellan with strong forces could block other escape routes.)

Rather than choosing immediately to follow the Confederates after the skirmish at Cheat River, the Union generals in charge, Norris and Steedman, decided to remain at Corrick's Ford a full day to rest and bury the dead. The Confederates continued their retreat without pause, hoping against hope to outdistance the Federal troops they knew would arrive soon by way of the railroad, a little to the north of their only remaining escape route.

Several hours before dawn on July 14 a number of eastbound train cars stopped at Oakland and discharged passengers in the quiet of starlight. The men who remained at the tracks when the trains sped on wore uniforms of blue and carried a banner of Union infantry, the Sixteenth Ohio, commanded by a Colonel Irvine. Three other companies present composed a regiment led by a Major Walcott. The force quickly fell into marching formation and proceeded at a fast pace toward the Northwestern Turnpike at West Union (present-day Aurora), Virginia, fourteen miles to the southwest. Their objective? To intercept the retreating Confederate forces of General Henry R. Jackson.

When his column arrived at West Union early in the morning, Colonel Irvine learned that the fleeting Confederates had left Red House, four miles to the east, at 5:00 a.m. after a brief rest. Irvine at once ordered his troops eastward in pursuit. A few miles beyond Red House he encountered a network of fallen trees on the road. Here several companies of fresh troops, having arrived recently from Oakland, caught up with his forces. The Federals gave up the chase.

The Rebels turned south at Mount Storm and continued their retreat. They left behind a partially completed fortification above a covered bridge on the Northwestern Turnpike over the North Branch of the Potomac.

Confederate forces had begun construction of Fort Pendleton, named after landowner Philip Pendleton (near present-day Gorman), in June 1861. The Northern route of early July caused them to leave their structure without firing a shot. In August the Fourth Ohio Volunteer Infantry began further work on the fortification, and completed the project by mid-September. They cut timber between the hilltop fort and the river below; they dug trenches and built earthworks for nearly a mile down the hill and over its eastern slopes. They occupied the structure from August 1861, until January 15, 1862.

During this time they fired not a single shot of defense. General B. F. Kelley, the Union area commander in Cumberland, recorded that the troops of Fort Pendleton were prone to neglect picket duty, avoid blockading roads, and preferred fishing to military service. They entertained themselves with dancing in the nearby Presbyterian church. Kelley once warned the post commander, Captain Joseph M. Godwin, that he would be dismissed from the service of his country if he failed to discipline his men. Godwin failed. His men ripped the weatherboarding from the nearby church for firewood, leaving the structure open to rain and snow, but he was not dismissed. The half-dozen men who died of illness while the Fourth Ohio occupied Fort Pendleton were all buried in the Presbyterian church graveyard. Strategically, the structure was an almost total waste of time and money during the period it was garrisoned.

While Union troops were rebuilding Fort Pendleton above the banks of the North Branch of the Potomac in early autumn 1861. Dr. J. Lee McComas of Oakland, appointed army surgeon early in the war, was busy organizing post hospitals for the Federal wounded and sick at Oakland and New Creek. President Jefferson Davis of the Confederacy had been a patient of Dr. McComas in Oakland in 1859. Early in 1861 Mr. Davis commissioned a mutual friend to offer the doctor a place of honor and dignity in his own personal entourage. McComas refused to accept the honor, volunteering, instead, to join the service ranks of the Union. He managed the Oakland and New Creek stations till the end of the war. During this time several score of wounded were brought to the Oakland vicinity for health care. Some of these were quartered in Saint Paul's Methodist Church; others were placed in boardinghouses and private homes. McComas used the frameboard, one-room Penn School (on Fourth Street) as his operating room and hospital throughout the war.

In a 1909 interview Dr. McComas gave the following account of treating his noted patient:

"In that summer of 1859 I had a noted man for a patient, Jefferson Davis, United States Senator from Mississippi, and later on President of the Confederate States. He was in bad shape physically, and was accompanied by Mrs. Davis and three children. A doctor came with them from Washington, and I could see Mrs. Davis' look of suspicion and distrust as the doctor (who had to leave at once) committed the Senator to the hands of a youthful and semmingly inexperienced country physician. However, I was lucky enough to effect a complete cure for my patient. When he asked me for his bill and I told him $30, I still recollect that he was not at all pleased and asked me if that wasn't a steep charge for a country doctor. My answer was that it was much less than a city M.D. would have assessed and that no city man could have done more than I did—that is, cured him. This put Senator Davis in a good humor and he paid me three ten-dollar gold pieces, which I have yet."

Meanwhile, to the east, hospitals and medical stations were established at Cumberland and Clarysville. "Both towns," recorded National Road historian Philip D. Jordan, "became receiving stations for the sick and wounded. Medical officers cantered from Wheeling to inspect the meager facilities hurriedly afforded soldiers needing surgery. Ambulances crept over the pike from Frostburg and up from Virginia to discharge their pathetic loads at barns and stores hastily transformed into wards."

"Straw is scattered all over the floor," noted one contemporary Cumberland doctor, "upon which are placed three rolls of filthy bed-sacks, with no other bedding." Jordan elaborated: "No sheets or coverlets protected the wounded and they had no pillows. Bedpans and chamber pots, overflowing with excrement, stood in rooms. Stairs were crowded with slop buckets. Fifty yards away stood a privy. Only a shed built over two trenches, "the Cumberland Institution," was filled with dirty clothing cut from the men. Blood-soaked and nauseous, the place was unbearable." "I do not hesitate to say," noted one contemporary doctor accustomed to reviewing all types of makeshift, wartime army hospitals, "that such a condition of affairs does not exist in any other hospital in the civilized world."

Abraham Lincoln issued his first call for troops on April 15, 1861, two days after Confederate troops attacked Fort Sumter. On April 19 he proclaimed a blockade of the South. On May 21 the Confederates chose Richmond, Virginia, as their capital. Exactly one month later Northern troops retreated in disorder after suffering nearly three thousand casualties at the first Battle of Bull Run at Manassas, Virginia, only a few miles southwest of Washington, D.C. The North realized for the first time the seriousness of the war ahead, and no longer anticipated an easy and early victory.

Northern troops captured Fort Henry on the Tennessee River and Fort Donelson on the Cumberland River in February 1862. On March 9 the ironclad ships Monitor *and* Merrimac *battled to a draw near the southern end of Chesapeake Bay. Both the North and the South suffered heavy losses at the Battle of Shiloh at Pittsburg Landing, Tennessee, on April 6-7, but the North triumphed. The Confederacy began to draft soldiers on April 16.*

On April 29, a Union fleet captured New Orleans. Union troops occupied Yorktown, Virginia, on May 4, and began advancing toward Richmond. Northern forces occupied Corinth, Mississippi, on May 30. Memphis fell to Union troops on June 6. Confederate forces under Lee saved Richmond in the Seven Day's Battle the last week of June. During the last week of August, Lee and Jackson led Southern troops to victory in the Second Battle of Bull Run.

"In September, 1862, I found myself at the Glades Hotel, at Oakland, on the line of the Baltimore and Ohio Railroad, and in that part of Allegany County, Maryland, which is now known as Garrett County," recorded mountaintop visitor Dr. John W. Palmer, of Baltimore, in 1891. "Early on the 16th there was a roar of guns in the air, and we knew that a great battle was begun." *The Battle of Antietam, near Sharpsburg, Maryland, one of the bloodiest of the war, September 17, 1862, claimed twelve thousand Northern casualties and eleven thousand of the South. It also repelled the northern most Confederate advance made to that point in the hostilities and gave Lincoln a long-awaited major victory. Lincoln subsequently issued a preliminary Emancipation Proclamation on September 22.* Meanwhile, back at the Glades Hotel in Oakland, Dr. John Palmer, of Baltimore, scrawled the lines to a poem he later titled "Stonewall Jackson's Way":

> Come, stack arms, men! Pile on the rails,
> Stir up the campfire bright;
> No growling if the canteen fails,
> We'll make a roaring night.
>
> Here Shenandoah brawls along,
> There burly Blue Ridge echoes strong,
> To swell the Brigade's rousing song
> Of "Stonewall Jackson's Way."
>
> What matter if our shoes are worn?
> What matter if our feet are torn?
> "Quick step! We're with 'im before morn!"
> That's "Stonewall Jackson's Way."
>
> Ah, wife, sew on, pray on, hope on;
> Thy life shall not be all forlorn;
> The foe had better ne'er be born
> That gets in "Stonewall's Way."

(General "Stonewall" Thomas J. Jackson, famous for his Shenandoah Valley Campaign of spring, 1862, was shot by one of his own men, mistaking him for the enemy on the night of May 2, 1863, near Chancellorsville, Virginia. "He has lost his left arm," Robert E. Lee remarked after surgery, "but I have lost my right arm." Jackson died May 10.)

President Lincoln visited the Army of the Potomac at Antietam on October 3, 1862. He traveled to the battlefield on a special train provided by the Baltimore and Ohio Railroad. John W. Garrett accompanied the president. The Union army photographer Mathew B. Brady photographed the president of the United States and the president of the Baltimore and Ohio Railroad, along with General George B. McClellan on the war-ravaged battlefield in front of the general's tent.

Southern forces repelled a Northern invasion of Kentucky on October 8, 1862. On December 13 they dealt a crushing blow to Union forces at Fredericksburg, Virginia. The last major battle of the year began on December 31 at Murfreesboro, Tennessee. Union troops forced the Confederates into retreat there on January 2, 1863.

On December 31, 1862, President Lincoln signed a statehood bill for West Virginia. "We do not wish to be connected any longer with the miserable one-idea Negro policy that has cursed us all the days of our lives so far," a Wheeling editor had written earlier. "That policy is always arrogant, selfish, and absorbing. It hangs upon the steps of progress and hobbles both its feet. We have had enough of it. . . . We want in a few years to become a free state."

The new state of West Virginia began to function as an independent political entity on June 20, 1863, after adopting a constitution providing for the gradual abolition of slavery. Crowds met at Wheeling for the celebration. "Red-white-and-blue bunting fell in graceful folds over front porches," recorded historian Philip D. Jordan. "Brass bands paraded in a frenzy of martial music. Spick and span the Fourth and Fifth Regiments of West Virginia swung into place before the McClure House. Thirty-five little girls, representing each state in the Union including those in rebellion, smoothed their pleats and giggled.

"A clergyman stepped forward and bowed his head. 'Grant us, we pray thee, Almighty God, that this state born amidst tears, and blood, and fire, and desolation, may long be preserved, and from its little beginning, may grow to be a might and power that shall make those who come after us look upon it with joy and gladness and pride of heart.' Governor Arthur Boreman took the oath, and a new state was organized." *Western Maryland had a new neighbor.*

President Lincoln formally issued the Emancipation Proclamation on January 1, 1863. Several western Maryland blacks subsequently joined the Northern troops. *The North passed its first draft law on March 3.* When the brother-in-law of Elk Lick Run's Tom Paugh was drafted into the Northern ranks a few weeks later, Tom, a noted story teller, accompanied the young man to Cumberland to testify that the draftee was too nearsighted to serve, claiming that while hunting one day, Jim, the draftee, had shot six times at a squirrel in a hickory tree only to find upon close inspection that he merely had been aiming at a knat in his own "eyewinker." The ruse failed.

The Civil War came to present-day Garrett County on the iron rails of the Baltimore and Ohio Railroad. In early spring, 1863, Robert E. Lee ordered a northern expedition into the hills of western Maryland and West Virginia to destroy the strategic railroad bridges of Tray Run Gorge on Cheat River, and those at Oakland and Rowlesburg. Secondary objectives of the proposed raid included the capture of men, cattle, and horses, and, in the event of a subsequent successful Northern campaign, political recognition of the Confederacy by Britain and France and defection of the state of Maryland.

Confederate leaders in western Virginia assembled to plan the raid near Harrisonburg in late May. Major General Samuel Jones, commanding a force of forty-five hundred men, chaired the meeting. Also present were Brigadier General John D. Imboden, Brigadier General William E. Jones, Colonel Asher V. Harman, Major Ridgely Brown, and Captain John H. McNeill (whose Partisan Rangers included several recruits from the hills of western Maryland). After considerable discussion, the commanders decided upon a plan of action. Proceeding northwest from the Shenandoah Valley— the Great Valley of Virginia west of the Blue Ridge—General Imboden was to advance through Randolph County to Grafton and destroy as much of the railroad there as possible.

General W. E. Jones, Colonel Harman, Major Brown, and Captain McNeill were to advance northward from the Valley through Hardy County to Oakland, Maryland; then they were to proceed west on the Northwestern Turnpike to a rendezvous with Imboden near Grafton. The raid was to last a full month. The Confederates were ready for their mission in early April.

The "Great Raid" began on April 20, when General Imboden abandoned the Great Valley with a force of three thousand men. The next day General W. E. Jones abandoned camp at Lacy Spring, a few miles northeast of Harrisonburg, and moved with thirteen hundred men northwest to Moorefield. Heavy rains had raised the waters of the South Branch of the Potomac at that point, necessitating a twenty-five mile detour southwest by way of Petersburg. Jones ordered his infantry and artillery back south before crossing the river, and advanced with cavalry only toward Oakland. At Greenland Gap, north of Petersburg, the Confederates met and overpowered a small contingency of boys in blue, then pushed once again northward.

"We reached the top of Alleghany on April 25," recorded Colonel Lomax of the Eleventh Virginia Cavalry, "where Captains McDonald and Dangerfield were detached with their companies." The McDonald-Dangerfield detachment of the Eleventh Virginia crossed the North Branch of the Potomac into Maryland at Kitzmiller, then proceeded along the Baltimore and Ohio tracks toward Altamont. They cut telegraph wires at Wilson's Station, fifteen miles west of Piedmont.

General Jones's main force crossed the North Branch at Gorman early in the morning of April 26, then burned the Northwestern Turnpike bridge which crossed the river at that point. At Gorman, Jones dispatched Colonel Harman, Major Brown, and Captain McNeill northwest through Ryan's Glade toward Oakland with the Twelfth Virginia, Brown's Maryland Battalion, and the Partisan Rangers; Jones himself proceeded west on the old Pike toward Aurora and Cranberry Summit (present-day Terra Alta).

At the home of former Garrett County slave John "Black Jack" Davis near the White Church, the Ryan's Glade detachment paused to demand food and water for themselves and their horses. The Davis daughters fed the men breakfast; the sons tended the animals. (Davis himself, forewarned of the Confederates' approach, had hidden his own horses in the woods earlier in the day.) After breakfast a Confederate officer ordered one of the Davis sons to ride along with the troops to Oakland to point out the way. John panicked at first, then begged the Rebels not to take his son south to slavery. The soldiers teased the old Negro for a time, then departed, leaving the family intact and free.

Years afterward, Rachel Olive Harvey of the Glades told her children how she, her sister Huldah, and their neighbor Florence Fitzwater, upon receiving word of the Glade detachment's approach, had hurriedly snatched up their new red calico dresses and followed her father, Nathaniel B. Harvey, to the woods, where the family's livestock had been concealed. Isaac Thompson likewise recorded in the 1940s that his grandmother, Katie Thompson, had received word of the Rebel approach through the Glades in time to bury the family stash of three thousand dollars in gold (which the Thompsons had saved for a farm payment) in the garden before the cavalry arrived. Since her husband had been away at the time, Mrs. Thompson herself had also concealed the family horses and livestock under cliff rocks in a nearby wooded ravine.

The Ryan's Glade detachment of Jones' Cavalry—Harman's Twelfth Virginia Cavalry, Brown's Maryland Battalion, McNeill's Partisan Rangers—divided into several groups to approach Oakland by different routes. One group paused near Table Rock at the Frazee farm, where they requisitioned a roan mare. Another sacked the home of the Swartzentruber family at Red House, where they ordered the women of the home to bake griddle cakes for hours until the family's flour supply was exhausted. A third stopped at the Peter Gortner residence in Sunnyside to demand livestock. Mr. Gortner gave them an old mare and a colt. (He later recovered his best animals from their hiding place in the woods.)

Meanwhile, the McDonald-Dangerfield detachment had reached Altamont. The Altamont raiders searched the barn of

Mrs. Elizabeth Friend, then took one of her horses from a neighboring pasture. Mrs. Friend's son, Elijah Hoye, witnessed about twenty-five of the raiders ride past his mother's farm.

"As we were descending the mountain near Altamont," recorded Lieutenant John Blue of the Eleventh Virginia Cavalry, "we heard a train approaching from the direction of New Creek. Capt. McDonald halted us in the woods a short distance below the station. The train stopped at the station and all hands went into the grog shop nearby, I suppose to take something. We rode briskly forward and captured the train before it got away. There were eight or ten cars, all empty except two which were loaded with oats. It was now about the middle of the day. We fed our horses all they would eat, each now carried a two bushel sack and put into it as much oats as he could carry conveniently, and the Captain then asked if there was anyone in the company who knew enough about an engine to back the train a short distance down the road and then open the valve and let the train run over the bank a little way above the station. At the same time he sent men to tear up the rails, so as to let the train run off. Dr. John Dailey, a member of our company, said that he could back the train, but he got the wrong notion and the train moved forward instead of backward. The doctor jerked the valve open and jumped off. The rail had not yet been removed, and the train rolled on at a rate of speed I will venture to say never was equaled before or since. We could see the train for a long distance as it rolled onward toward Oakland, through a comparatively level grade. The farther it got the faster it seemed to run until at length it appeared to just sail through the air."

The Confederates rode into Oakland, Maryland, at 11:00 a.m., Sunday, April 26, 1863. The Union garrison stationed in the town at the time, Company O of the Sixth West Virginia Infantry, locally referred to as the "Groundhog Company," was not popular at the time among the residents due to its lack of vigilance and patriotic spirit. It was even less popular after the Confederates arrived in town that April Sunday morning. Cornelius Johnson, the company picket, stationed at the eastern edge of the village, fired the single shot of the day, a warning shot, then took to his heels across a field toward the cover of woods before being captured.

The Confederate raid that Sunday morning in Oakland was a complete surprise to everyone: To the picket, to the citizens, to Company O. "Get off my property, Sir!" shouted Alexander MacInnes, an 1858 Scottish immigrant (grandfather of the late Dr. William W. Grant of Oakland), when the troops rode across his lawn just east of town. "I am a British subject, and I will appeal to her Majesty, the Queen!" Then he addressed the commanding officer: "Sir, you appear to be a gentleman. I am amazed at you being engaged in a guerrilla warfare trying to destroy an established government." The officer merely replied politely that he was tired; MacInnes relented and invited him to tea. Together they drank tea and ate scotch cakes, then the troops rode on, assuring their host that his property would remain undisturbed.

At the Little Yough a soldier ordered Peter Helbig, the town baker, to halt and raise his hands, but Helbig, instead of complying with the order, threw a handful of gravel into the trooper's face and ran to the bakeshop by his house where he hid in an oven.

When the Confederates rode into Oakland the Federals all either were attending church, relaxing, or out in the fields hunting groundhogs. Solomon Sines, one of the bridge guards, later reported that he and a companion were off duty when they saw Rebels ride up—unable to reach their muskets, they hastily "went fishing" on the Youghiogheny to avoid capture. Colonel Asher Harman later reported that "I reached Oakland at 11:00 A.M.; surprised and captured a company of 57 men, with two commissioned officers, and paroled them. Destroyed a railroad bridge east of town and the railroad and turnpike bridges over the Youghiogheny River; also a train of cars at Cranberry Summit. I captured the guard (at Cranberry Summit—fifteen men) and paroled them with 20 citizens."

Once secure in the town of Oakland, the Confederates seized forage for their animals, took food for themselves from hotels and stores, ate dinner in private homes, and rested for a time. Though many citizens hurriedly hid their money and valuables, most private residences remained unmolested. Few housewives refused to serve the well-mannered Rebels food; they were reimbursed for their hospitality with Confederate bills.

Before sitting down to eat at the home of Peter Baker, one Confederate officer unsheathed his saber and laid it on a table. An outside noise startled him. He hurriedly jumped up and seized his weapon, leaving a nine-inch scratch on his host's table top. Running to a window, he saw at once the source of the noise he had heard: Outside a small stalled train, still wheezing and choking, hung precariously with its front drive wheels spinning impotently in the air over the edge of the burned railroad trestle (Bridge 88). The train was a present to the Confederates in Oakland from the Eleventh Virginia McDonald-Dangerfield detachment at Altamont. "When we reached Oakland about sundown," recorded Lieutenant John Blue, "we found the train still standing at the edge of the bridge . . . the steam having been exhausted on an upgrade. The engine on reaching the abutment dropped its front wheels over it and the train stopped."

A small party of the April 29 raiders pushed as far north in western Maryland as Deep Creek. They commandeered two horses from Samuel Specht's sawmill on Cherry Creek, two from Patrick Hamill, and three from the John L. Browning farm. Two of the Confederate party remained all night at the Browning home. The next morning, while they were eating breakfast, Browning's daughter, Maria Louise, slipped quietly from the house, mounted Baldy, her white-faced mare, and rode the animal to a field on Roman Nose Mountain, where the two remained safely hidden until evening.

"From Oakland I moved west to Kingwood and Morgantown, which places I took without opposition," reported Colonel Harman after the raid. The Confederates left Oakland Sunday evening. From the North Branch of the Potomac at Gorman, General Jones earlier had marched west over the Northwestern Turnpike with his main force to Cheat River, arriving there around 2:00 p.m., Sunday, April 26. He captured the pickets at the Cheat River and hastily tore up the floor planking before moving on. Meanwhile, troops of the

Sixth, Seventh, and Eleventh Virginia Cavalry attacked the nearby town of Rowlesburg, but were repelled by its three hundred defenders. General Jones decided to abandon the attempt to capture the town, and, after a few hours of night marching, established camp.

The next morning, moving on to Evansville, Jones's troops secured corn for their horses and meat rations for themselves. Late in the evening a courier brought news that the Confederate Lieutenant C. H. Vandiver and a party of eight men had captured the small town of Independence, defended by a guard of twenty Union regulars. A force was dispatched at once to Independence, and the double-span Baltimore and Ohio bridge near the town was destroyed. The entire command then crossed the railroad at nightfall, proceeded north, and established camp around midnight. Colonel Harman arrived at daybreak, "bringing the first tidings of his and McDonald's success at Oakland and Altamont."

On April 28 the entire Jones command marched northwest to Morgantown, arriving there around noon. The army rested until dark, then marched southwest to Fairmont, camping in the woods from 9:00 p.m. until 1:00 a.m. At Fairmont the Confederates attacked from both sides of the river; two hundred and sixty Federal soldiers soon surrendered. A trainload of Union artillery and infantry from nearby Grafton, arriving as the Fairmont prisoners' arms were being stacked, failed to recover the railroad bridge. The Confederates completely destroyed the triple-span iron Fairmont bridge over the West Fork of the Monongahela; it tumbled into the river soon after dark.

The army of the South left their wounded at Fairmont, then marched further southwest toward Clarksburg. Learning that the town was defended by a strong Federal garrison, they captured Bridgeport, five miles to its east. The next day, confiscating horses and cattle on their way, they arrived at Philippi. On May 2, they joined General Imboden at Buckhannon. Then Imboden marched southwest, while Jones and his cavalry proceeded northwest toward Parkersburg.

Jones's troops captured Cairo and destroyed three bridges, wrecked the oil plant at Oilton, then rejoined Imboden's command at Summersville. From Summersville the Confederates marched by leisurely stages homeward to the Valley of Virginia.

General Jones summarized the results of his raid near Harrisonburg, Virginia, on May 26, 1863: "In thirty days," he reported, "we marched nearly 700 miles; we killed from 25 to 30 of the enemy; wounded probably three times as many; captured nearly 700 prisoners, 2 trains of cars; burned 16 railroad bridges and one tunnel; 150,000 barrels of oil, many engines and a large number of boats, tanks, and barrels; bringing home with us about 1,000 cattle and probably 1,200 horses. Our entire loss was ten killed and 42 wounded; the missing not exceeding fifteen."

General Robert E. Lee endorsed the Jones report a few weeks later. "The expedition under General Jones," he noted, "appears to have been conducted with commendable skill and vigor, and was productive of bountiful results. The injury inflicted on the enemy was serious and we will doubtless be induced to keep troops to guard the railroad who might be otherwise employed against us. General Jones displayed sagacity and boldness in his plans, and was well supported by the courage and fortitude of his officers and men."

The Baltimore and Ohio Railroad brought the Civil War to western Maryland.

Once again in early 1863 the Union General Benjamin F. Kelley, commanding the Federal Department of West Virginia, in charge of the protection of the B&O from Harpers Ferry to Grafton, established headquarters in the Maryland Allegany County seat of Cumberland. "His wagon trains, high-wheeled, canvas-covered, choked the streets," recorded historian Philip D. Jordan. "Cavalry officers, bright in dark blue and contrasting yellow stripes, urged spirited mounts up the slopes of the Alleghenies to picnic with enthusiastic young ladies. The piano tinkled after dark in homes that opened their doors to Kelley's braided staff. No loud music sprang from Cumberland's Southern sympathizers. They came and went secretly."

Then, suddenly, in June, after Jones's raid through western Maryland, Kelley evacuated Cumberland to concentrate his forces at New Creek, leaving Cumberland unprotected. Colonel G. W. Imboden soon afterward surrounded the town with his 350-man Confederate cavalry and called for surrender, agreeing to respect private property. Terms of surrender were drawn up and signed, and Imboden invaded Cumberland with his forces and two pieces of artillery. Merchants did a thriving business, selling hats, clothing, and boots, receiving their pay in Confederate bills. The Rebels cut the telegraph wires, rested a few hours, ate, and then rode away.

Southern troops under Robert E. Lee and Stonewall Jackson defeated the Federals under General "Fighting Joe" Hooker in the Battle of Chancellorsville in Virginia on May 4, 1863. Troops under Ulysses S. Grant defeated the Confederates of Mississippi on May 19 and began to besiege Vicksburg. On July 3, the Battle of Gettysburg in south-central Pennsylvania ended in a resounding Southern defeat, marking a final turning point in the long war. (The guns of Gettysburg, like those of earlier Antietam, were heard as far west as the continental divide of western Maryland.) *Vicksburg fell to Northern troops the following day. On July 8, Northern forces occupied Port Hudson, Louisiana. Then, on September 20, Southern troops under General Braxton Bragg won the Battle of Chickamauga in Tennessee, savagely defeating the Northern forces of General William Rosecrans, the 1861 hero of western Virginia's Rich Mountain, who lost seventeen thousand men in the Chickamauga conflict.*

Rosecrans retreated to Chattanooga after his Chickamauga loss. Within two months his troops were reinforced by twenty thousand regulars fresh from the North; the reinforcements were transported by rail from Washington, D.C., over the eastern continental divide along the Baltimore and Ohio line in western Maryland. The entire movement was completed within eleven days under the leadership of John W. Garrett. "The circumstances," noted Colonel L. B. Parsons, the Northern army's chief of river and rail transportation, "render it not insidious that I should especially refer to the management of the Baltimore and Ohio Railroad, whose indomitable will, energy, and superior ability have been so often and conspicuously manifested."

Ulysses S. Grant and George H. Thomas replaced Rosecrans at Chattanooga in early November. On November 25, they dealt the Southerners there a staggering blow and took the town, from whence they marched into Georgia and Atlanta to split the eastern Confederacy in two. The Battle of Chattanooga ended the major military campaigns for the year.

Meanwhile, in western Maryland, General B. F. Kelley, the "Two Horse General," star of the 1861 "Philippi Races," in charge of defense of the B&O from Grafton to Harpers Ferry, bought the six-hundred-acre Swan Meadows tract in the Cherry Creek Glades near Gortner for the rehabilitation of broken-down army horses. The animals were removed from battlefields and transported to Oakland by train, then herded the four miles to Swan Meadows. Those which survived the walk had a "better than even change of recovery." Many died.

Fort Pendleton, overlooking the Potomac at Gorman, was regarrisoned for a time in late 1863 as a consequence of Jones's destructive May raid through western Maryland. Northern troops also began patrolling the Northwestern Turnpike on a regular basis that year.

The German town of Accident in early 1863 was pillaged by two Union deserters posing as Confederates. "It was during sheep-shearing time that news reached us one evening that rebel raiders had invaded Accident and were after plunder," recalled M. P. Lichty of the Cove in 1900. "When we got to town we left our horses at Mr. Menhorn's Smith-shop, and then went over to Boyer Brothers store. Sure enough, here were two bold looking men in rebel uniform, and apparently armed to the teeth, keeping the Boyers busy tying up bundles of goods. By evening time we had made up a company of ten men, armed with rifles, shotguns and a few old single-barrel pistols.

"Down in Bear Creek hollow, just across the bridge, on the right hand side of the road under a clump of spruce trees, with the tall laurel in the background, there we took our stand to guard the road and capture the raiders should they happen along." In the darkness and fog of night the ten surprised a lone footman walking north; in no uncertain tones they ordered the man to halt. " 'Och, mein Gott! Mein Gott!' " the traveler cried, according to Lichty. " 'Shoot me not—Shoot me not, for I am only poor John Deitrick.' " The Bear Creek ten lowered their guns, then learned from Deitrick that the raiders earlier had left town to join their supposed regiment a few miles to the south. All agreed to wait until morning before beginning pursuit.

"Early the next morning we hastened to Accident," recorded Lichty, "and soon learned that another party of gentlemen were after the raiders. The Glotfelty boys of the Glades, and their neighbors, routed them early at the Truman West farm, giving them a hot chase and a close shave for their lives." Captain West, the previous night, had hidden the clothes and personal property of the raiders, so that the two were forced to "flee minus these essentials." One of the raiders escaped to the woods. The other, after robbing an old Negro at the McHenry farm at Buffalo Marsh, was apprehended the next morning by the Glotfelty posse a little north of the National Road and transported to the Cumberland jail. "On our return home, following the capture," recalled Lichty, "we discharged our guns near Bear Creek. There was a mighty roar and thunder down through the glen. Soon every house in the neighborhood had a light shining."

Only later did the Bear Creek ten learn that the two Accident raiders actually had been deserters from the Fifty-fourth Pennsylvania Volunteers. (The raider retained in the Cumberland jail escaped when the Confederate Colonel G. W. Imboden captured the town in June.)

Confederate raiders seeking to interrupt traffic on the Baltimore and Ohio Railroad penetrated present-day Garrett County a second time in May 1864. Sixty-one strong, they left Old Fields, in Hardy County, Virginia, soon after dark, May 3, under the leadership of Captain John Hanson McNeill. They traveled all night; the next day they took cover in the dense woods between Patterson's Creek and Mill Run. That night they rode through Doll's Gap on Knobley Mountain;

then they followed a narrow path to the top of the Alleghenies at the Northwestern Turnpike. They crossed the pike and followed the Elk Garden Road to its intersection with a road leading to Piedmont and Bloomington. They arrived in Bloomington at daybreak, May 6.

Soon after they occupied the town, a trainload of horses rumbled down the mountain from the west. Though Captain McNeill ordered the train stopped; its engineer threw open the throttle. The train escaped. A second train soon arrived from the west. This train the raiders did succeed in stopping. They ordered its engineer to detach its engine to transport three raiders to nearby Piedmont to demand surrender. Captain McNeill himself rode to Piedmont with the main body of his troops, leaving only eleven Confederates behind to guard Bloomington.

The raiders at Bloomington cut telegraph wires and guarded the Potomac bridge. They stopped two freight trains loaded with foodstuffs and distributed the captured goods to local citizens. Soon they could see smoke rising from Piedmont. Then a resident warned them that the next train from the west would be loaded with Federal soldiers fresh from Oakland.

"Although I did not believe this report," later recorded Captain John T. Peerce, "I dismounted the men and scattered them along the road. I soon heard the signal for down brakes, followed shortly after by the cry from my men, 'loaded with soldiers.' I had full view of the train. I could see there were two full cars of soldiers, and that they were fully armed and equipped; their guns sitting diagonally across the windows.

"I knew that McNeill's only chance lay in my charging that train and capturing those soldiers before they could be informed as to our numbers. In a twinkle of an eye, I was upon them. I passed around the rear of the train to get to the platform. I first met Samuel Gill, the conductor, who at my request pointed to the Captain in command, standing at the rear end of the car. I dashed my horse upon the platform, and with my pistol at his breast, demanded his surrender. I ordered him to bring his men out, to which someone added, 'leave your guns inside,' and the order was immediately obeyed."

One of the raiders rushed to the platform while the Federals were disembarking and shouted to an imaginary command to send up Companies F and G. Captain Peerce simultaneously dispatched a messenger to Captain McNeill in Piedmont to inform him that a hundred prisoners had been taken and to request immediate reinforcement. Peerce then rode along the windows of the train's rear car, assuring the passengers within that his men had been gentlemen before becoming soldiers, informing them that no lady need feel the slightest alarm. Five Confederates soon escorted the hundred Union captives to the Virginia side of the Potomac, where they were met shortly afterward by the troops of McNeill.

McNeill's rangers burned the trains at Bloomington and paroled the prisoners, then began wrecking the railroad bridge across the Potomac. Before they had completed their task, though, a trainload of Union soldiers arrived from New Creek and opened fire. The Federals stampeded; the Confederates retreated. Several citizens of Hampshire Hill in Piedmont, including a young woman and three children, were killed in the ensuing battle. McNeill's troops, however, escaped to the Valley of Virginia without a single casualty. The scars of their lightning raid still remain on the Bloomington bridge. (The bridge itself, though, escaped destruction.) The Civil War came to present-day Garrett County on the rails of the Baltimore and Ohio Railroad.

On May 12, 1864, Captain P. A. Chisholm and D. M. Mason of Oakland, Confederate privates, fell prisoners to the Union army. "The Confederates who were imprisoned in Fort Delaware," Mason later recalled, "ate rats and were glad to get them. I have seen the poor hungry creatures along the walls with clubs waiting for a rat to appear, and oftentimes I have seen a man who was lucky enough to capture one have to fight to keep it. I got a box from home now and then, but I got hungry enough to eat rats between times, and did. Many of the prisoners suffered from scurvy and died on account of the prison fare. I have no doubt that those who were in prison down South suffered more than we did, because the people who were not in prison were compelled to live on short rations." Chisholm and Mason were released on June 20, 1865, after being held in captivity for more than a year. Their prison experience reflected the experience of thousands of Civil War prisoners of both the North and the South.

Confederates under Gen. Richard Taylor defeated the Federals on April 9, 1864, at the Battle of Pleasant Hill in Louisiana. Robert E. Lee prevented Ulysses S. Grant from turning the Confederate flank in northern Virginia in the Battle of the Wilderness in early May. The antagonists clashed again at Spotsylvania a week later, and again neither side won a victory. On June 3, Grant made a third attempt to smash Lee, this time at Cold Harbor, a few miles north of the Confederate capital. He lost six thousand men in one hour of battle, and failed. In a month of fighting he lost nearly fifty-five thousand men. Then, on June 20, he laid siege to Petersburg, a major railroad center south of Richmond. The siege lasted for nine months.

On July 12 the Confederate General Jubal A. Early attacked the outskirts of Washington and pelted bullets at President Lincoln himself. In August Admiral David G. Farragut completely blockaded the harbor of Mobile, Alabama. (Farragut: "Damn the torpedoes! Full speed ahead!") General William T. Sherman occupied the city of Atlanta on September 2, and began preparing for his march to the sea. General George H. Thomas won one of the most smashing victories of the war against the Confederates in the Battle of Nashville on December 16. Sherman's troops occupied Savannah, Georgia, on December 21. The North was closing in. The South was beginning to fall.

The town of Cumberland in 1865 was guarded by more than seven thousand Federal troops. Pickets patrolled the roads leading into the town; the National Road especially was heavily patrolled. In the pre-dawn hours of February 21, thirty-seven Confederates, led by Lt. Jesse McNeill, son of John Hanson McNeill, crept into the town and captured its leading generals, Benjamin F. Kelley and George Crook.

McNeill's rangers included ten later Garrett Countians:

Charles Daily, W. Wallace Chisholm, Edward R. Browning, Samuel Hoye, William D. Hoye, James W. Mason, Henry W. Ridder, John L. Harvey, William H. Poole, and John Baptist Fay. "Lt. McNeill consulted me as to the feasibility of getting into Cumberland and capturing Generals Kelley and Crook," Fay later recorded. "He referred to suggestions I had made to his father during his lifetime, to capture General Kelley, and informed me of his desire to capture both generals if on examination it was found to be practicable. Cumberland was my native place. I had on several occasions entered it with ease, once remaining a week, and on my giving McNeill every assurance that his design could be successfully executed it was determined to make the attempt. I was commissioned to proceed at once to Cumberland and its vicinity and prepare the way for our entry by learning the number and position of the picket posts, the exact locations of the sleeping apartments of the generals, and any other information deemed necessary. With me went L. S. Hallar, a teen-age lad from Missouri."

Fay completed his mission successfully. McNeill and his thirty-seven men traveled north from Virginia at night, February 21, and forded the icy waters of the Potomac at Brady's Mill a few hours before dawn. A thin blanket of snow muffled their movements. A few miles outside of Cumberland a picket discharged his pistol before being subdued. A second sentinel was captured without noise. The Confederates entered town an hour and a half before dawn.

They divided into two squads of ten men each and rode casually up Baltimore Street whistling Yankee tunes and exchanging banter with the Federal guards on duty. Their gray coats were indistinct in the early morning light.

General Kelley blinked awake in his quarters at the Windsor Hotel to find ten Confederates in his room and a pistol at his chest. He dared not resist.

General Crook was sleeping in the Revere House that morning. He, too, chose the course of least resistance when he woke to find a carbine at his head.

The Confederates escorted the two generals down Baltimore Street in a quiet and dignified manner. They carried a

Union military flag. At Wills Creek they confiscated several horses from the town livery, including Philippi, Kelley's favorite charger, so named in memory of the 1861 battle at Philippi, western Virginia. They captured a dozen guards near the Chesapeake and Ohio Canal, then galloped along the towpath until they were halted by pickets a mile outside of town. The pickets stood aside when told that their generals were seeking to intercept a party of Rebel raiders reported ranging in the neighborhood.

The Confederates and their captives were five miles from town when they heard a boom of cannon to their rear. They spurred their horses to quicker flight. By nightfall the enemy was far behind. Within twenty-four hours they rode ninety miles. Crook remained silent, but Kelley talked frequently and freely with his captors. Both expected the war to end within months.

Confederate soldiers escorted the two Union generals all the way to Richmond. At the Confederate capital, Robert E. Lee ordered their release, providing them with safe conduct back to the Federal lines, apologizing for the actions of his men, explaining that he did not condone such extreme guerrilla warfare. Crook and Kelley both returned to Cumberland.

Ulysses S. Grant seized the railroads supplying Richmond in early April 1865. The Confederates evacuated Petersburg and their capital. Robert E. Lee requested terms of surrender. He accepted Grant's terms Sunday, April 9, at Appomattox Court House. General Albert S. Johnston surrendered to General William T. Sherman on April 26 near Durham, North Carolina. Jefferson Davis fled southward, but was captured in Georgia. General Richard Taylor surrendered the Confederate forces of Alabama and Mississippi on May 4. General Edmund Kirby Smith surrendered the last Rebel forces still in the field on May 26 at Shreveport, Louisiana. The Civil War—the Great War Between the States, the War of the Southern Secession, the War of the Rebellion, the War for Southern Independence—the first modern war, the first total war, ended not with a bang but with a whimper. It destroyed the institution of black slavery and preserved the Union at a cost of $15 billion and 600,000 lives. It left a legacy of hate and *bitterness which still emerges today, over a hundred years later. The North whipped the South.*

The Union veteran John McKenzie returned home to Grantsville after the Civil War "broken down in health," according to Jacob Brown. Once a shinglemaker, he became an incurable invalid. "The shaving knife brought the support to the humble dwelling in the pinery," wrote Brown, "and when the once stalwart soldier had to lay it down from disabillities incurred in the army the wife took it up. A few years of such labor broke her down. Then the elder daughter (there were no sons) learned the art, and for several years supported the family with her cunning hands. But she in time got married and left home, and then it was the fair girl of the woods (her thirteen-year-old sister, Helen) who took up the bread-winning knife." The Civil War changed people's lives.

Confederate boys returning to the highlands were denied voting rights until court decisions reinstated the franchise privilege to former Rebels late in 1865.

General Benjamin F. Kelley returned to Swan Meadows in 1865 and remained there until his death. One of his captors, John B. Fay, settled in nearby Oakland.

General George Crook began building a retirement home on a hill—Crook Crest—west of Oakland after the war, but died in Chicago in 1890 before its completion. William McKinley, of Ohio, and "Buffalo Bill" Cody served as his pallbearers in Oakland. Oakland's Crook Post No. 35 of the Grand Army of the Republic, whose membership included at least sixty-three highland Civil War veterans at the time of its organization, was named in the old general's honor.

The Civil War destroyed the institution of slavery in America (an institution as old as Jamestown itself), preserved the federal union of states, expanded the powers of the Federal Government, and put sharp spurs to the nation's early industrial development. It also changed people's lives.

"In a little while after the completion of the Baltimore and Ohio Railroad to Cumberland (in 1842)," noted Will H. Lowdermilk of that city in 1879, "the National Road became a throughfare, such as the county had never before or since seen."

Ten years later the railroad crossed the mountains. "A wail went up along the National Road when the cruel railroad innovation came," observed Jacob Brown of Grantsville. "Ruin and starvation were in plain view of inexperienced and narrow minds. The Baltimore and Ohio Railroad reached the Ohio and made a grass plot of the pike."

Travel on the National Road decreased rapidly after the iron horse first chugged across Backbone Mountain. Innkeepers converted taverns into farmhouses. Scheduled stagecoaches ceased running the road in 1853. The last coaches disappeared around 1870. The teamster business dwindled. The pony express died. Towns settled down to a long period of anticlimactic complacency.

The old pike's condition became so bad "that it was eventually shunned and flanked as much as possible," recorded Brown. "The people became very tired, and even clamorous about paying toll on an impassable road. So two years ago (in 1878) tolls and superintendent were abolished, and the road turned over to Allegany and Garrett Counties by an act of the legislature."

"To prevent excessive erosion," recalled Ross C. Durst of Grantsville in 1967, "a series of 'breakers' or 'Thank-you-marms' were built at intervals to divert the water diagonally across the road. When a vehicle was driven across these ridges, it created a swaying motion which created the illusion that the occupants were bowing and nodding. Hence, the name of 'Thank-you-marm.' "

On August 4, 1894, Charles Brown of Grantsville called the attention of *Republican* (the county weekly) readers to the fact that the deteriorating condition of the old National Road necessitated the power of four horses merely to pull a ton of hay from Grantsville to Frostburg.

"We hear no more of the clanging hoof, /And the stage coach, rattling by; /For the steam king rules the traveled world, /And the old pike's left to die."

Northern present-day Garrett County began to decline in significance as a center of trade and social intercourse after the B&O reached the mountaintop in 1851; southern present-day Garrett County began to boom.

A post office established at the mouth of Savage River in 1852 under the name of Llangollen, a local mining company incorporated in 1849, became the center of a bustling coal and market town. In 1854 the Llangollen Mining Company employed William Owens to survey and plat an additional 168 lots around the town's 39 original tracts. A General Assembly act of that year constituted the town of Llangollen "a body politic and corporate," and provided a governmental framework for the town's political system. An act of 1855 restored the original name of Bloomington to the area. Though acts of 1868 and 1878 authorized further incorporation of the town, locals remained adamant in their opposition to the measures.

A small-town post office delivered mail to residents of Frankville, a few miles northwest of Bloomington, from 1852 until 1871. The Baltimore and Ohio Railroad was the lifeline of the town. The families of a number of Irish railroad workers lived there until the end of the century. (Only nine families live at Frankville today; its only street remains unpaved.)

The Summitville Post Office, renamed Altamont in 1869, opened in 1852 under J. H. Wilson. The town grew quickly after the iron horse conquered Backbone Mountain. Within a decade its new buildings housed a railroad depot, two general stores, a boardinghouse, a saloon (with a nearby croquet court, two shoe shops, a lumberyard office, a school, a livery stable, a blacksmith shop), and a gunsmith shop. Altamont, like Llangollen before it, blossomed.

The Deer Park Post Office was established on August 13, 1864, under Emil Droege. Two years later directors of the Baltimore and Ohio authorized the building of a second-class railroad station there. (William Reinhart served as first station agent.) Already the town boasted a few dwellings and a nearby distillery operated by the German immigrant John Albert Droege.

Tableland historian Felix G. Robinson (1967): "About three thousand feet west from where the first railroad train crossed the first mountain in the world, a man built a home in a spacious grove of oaks beside an extensive glade where once the deer and the buffalo roamed. He named the place Deer Park. His name was Henry Gassaway Davis."

Henry G. Davis lived at Deer Park intermittently from 1867 until 1892. He is often credited as being the founder of the town. Penniless as a boy, he climbed the railroad management ladder in Virginia from brakeman in 1842 to division superintendent in 1858. With his brothers he moved into the mercantile, lumber, coal, and banking businesses. During the Civil War, H. G. Davis and Company made substantial profits in the West Virginia lumbering industry. Davis became a land speculator. "Unfortunately," noted Felix Robinson, "we have very little to report on Mr. Davis's concern for the reforestration of the Great Wilderness where his sawmills had reduced it to barrenness. The numerous towns that sprung up around the mills, and were for a time prosperous, have known but the increase of economic insecurity. It was the state, not big business, that sent about the task of reforestation. In order to do this the state bought up most of this cut-over land, perhaps as much as a million or more acres. It is a good illustration of private enterprise exploiting raw resources and by this fruitless method cancelling its own individual freedom." Henry Gassaway Davis himself grew rich.

After the Civil War he served as a West Virginia delegate, a state senator, and a United States senator (from West Virginia) in Washington. He moved to Deer Park in 1867. His twenty-five years in Deer Park, noted Robinson, was the town's "most brilliant period." Davis included Daniel Webster, Henry Clay, John C. Calhoun, and Sam Houston among his friends. At Deer Park he managed a large farm, raising sheep and cattle. He spent his winters in Washington.

Henry Gassaway Davis operated a large lumberyard at Deer Park and built connecting tramroad links from the village to his timber holdings at the Thayer-Browning settlement (at present-day Deep Creek Lake), Red Run and Swallow Falls, Tolliver Run and Muddy Creek, and Greenwood. He built a large sawmill at Deep Creek near the Youghiogheny. Teams of mules pulled his cut timber to his large lumberyard at Deer Park, where his business enterprises provided employment for many of the town's residents. From Deer Park Davis shipped his lumber to points east and west on the B&O. Colonel E. C. Tillson, from Maine, served as his agent; Tillson was later elected town mayor. Davis built a substantial general store at Deer Park and employed numerous local people. He moved to Elkins, West Virginia, in 1892, helped found Davis and Elkins College, and campaigned unsuccessfully for the office of vice-president of the United States in 1904.

The Davis activities at Deer Park after the arrival of the iron horse greatly spurred the development of the valley town. A number of the town's young men, including Harry Thrasher, Dan Hinebaugh, Jim Hardesty, Earl George, Mason Smith, Otto Droege, Charles A. Garrett, John Jankey, and George W. Riley worked for years as firemen on the B&O. All of these later became engineers.

In 1860 John W. Garrett, president of the Baltimore and Ohio, noted in a report to his board of directors that "the salubrious climate and beautiful country among the highlands of Western Maryland have elicited much attention . . . but the absence of adequate hotel accommodations has materially checked the tendency to seek these Glades for summer homes. Arrangements are being made for additional hotels; and a large population from the South, East and West will probably hereafter select this singularly picturesque and attractive region for summer resort. A considerable increase of local traffic may be anticipated from this source." Eight years later the Baltimore and Ohio purchased a portion of the 1774 Peace and Plenty tract just west of Deer Park for the construction of a magnificent summer resort hotel. The bustling and prestigious vacation accommodations gave the growing town an added and unique dimension.

If Bloomington, Frankville, Altamont, and Deer Park blossomed when the B&O came to town, Oakland boomed. "The first house erected was the railroad depot," recorded western Maryland historian J. Thomas Scharf. "The second building put up was a store-house and residence by Daniel R. Brant. The third building was a store-house and residence by J. L. Townshend."

In 1860 Daniel Brant added 101 lots carved from the Wilderness Shall Smile tract to Isaac McCarty's original sixty-four 1849 town lots. Streets were surveyed and platted: Water, Oak, and Alder streets running east and west; First, Second, Third, Fourth and Fifth streets running north and south. "Brant's Addition to Oakland" included all lots north of First Street, extending east and west from Green to Church streets. Allegany County election District No. 15, Oakland, was recognized by act of the General Assembly the same year.

At mid-century only two or three houses stood in Oakland. Within a decade twenty-five dwellings, two churches, two stores, a livery stable, a gristmill, a tannery, a blacksmith shop, and a hotel were added to the town. The population sprang from less than 10 to more than 150 inhabitants.

"Oakland was the principal trading point for a large area of country," recalled J. M. Davis in 1906 of the town in the 1860s. "Its market radius reached from St. George, Tucker County, West Virginia, to the National Road, on the borders of Pennsylvania. All kinds of produce was brought to this market to be exchanged for goods. Venison, poultry, butter, furs, ginseng, etc., were brought a long distance in wagons. These articles were considered legal tender in payment of bills or exchange for goods. The trading was kept up all day, and frequently more than half the night. Those who came in the evening with their loaded wagons were anxious to start for home early in the morning."

Oakland was incorporated by act of the Maryland General Assembly on March 10, 1862. A third survey, adding thirty-seven new lots to the town, was made November 10, 1865, extending Second Street north and opening Liberty Street west to Wilson. A fourth survey in 1866 on the Stewart's Delight tract extended Second, Third, and Fourth streets further north and added forty-five more lots to the town. Thomas Wilson's 1867 addition provided sixty-one additional lots, and extended Liberty, Center, and Pennington streets west from Wilson. A second Wilson addition, completed in 1869, added forty-one more lots to the growing town.

As Oakland grew, ordinances were passed for the retention of civil social order. A two-dollar fine was ordered in 1873 for persons throwing balls on the streets. An 1875 ruling made it unlawful to damage any lamppost, awning, spout, door, window, railing, bridge, fence, ornament, or tree. In 1877 horses were prohibited from running at large through the town. In 1879 it became illegal for "horned or black cattle" to roam loose at night. An 1881 ordinance prohibited the owners of cows from having bells on the animals between the hours of 8:00 p.m. and 7:00 a.m. in order "to insure more peaceful repose." The Oakland town lockup was used almost exclusively by drunks as a place to sober up.

A score of businesses was established in Oakland during the first quarter-century of the town's growth: C. E. Berry and Company, general merchants, Hughes' Drug Store and General Merchandise, J. T. Ward and Sons' Cabinet Shop, J. B. Brandt Meat Market, Whetzel's Blacksmith Shop, P. A. Matthew's General Store, John Michael's Tavern, Lloyd Baker's Tin Shop, Black Harriet's Laundry. Thomas J. Brandt, 1900: "Black Harriet's residence was on the north side of what is now Third Street, and some ten yards north of the corner. She was the washwoman of the town. On Saturday evenings she might be seen all togged up in a bright-colored gown, and a wide ribbon around her kinky hair, going over to the hotel to collect her bills. She supported an aged and blind mother, her own boy and herself on the proceeds of her washing." King's Tavern; "Yankee" Miller's Notion Store; Probst's General Store; D. R. Brandt's General Store; "Coon" Michael's General Store; Spedden's Store; Kennedy's Grog Shop; Merrill's Meat Market; Daniel Chisholm's Drug Store; Kepner's Cobbler Shop; Tom Martin's Livery; Jonathan Hinebaugh's General Store; Tom Little's Store; John Helbig's Tannery; Margaret Crystal's Dress Shop; Davis, Bishop and Townshend's General Store; Peter Shirer's Tin Shop (established in 1866; still operated today by Shirer descendants); George Legge's General Store; Colardeau's Woolen Mill (Dr. St. Felix Colardeau, born in Paris, France, was elected Oakland's first burgess or mayor in 1862; Offutt's General Store; Owen Hart's Dry Goods Store; and "Cheap John" Michael's Toy and Candy Shop. Whereas Bloomington, Frankville, Altamont, and Deer Park blossomed when the B&O came to town, Oakland boomed. Over five hundred persons lived there by 1870.

"Western Maryland in 1858 would have been the delight of Theodore Roosevelt," contended Dr. J. Lee McComas in 1909. "All about Oakland were wild, wooded tracts, through which deer, bear, panthers, and wildcats roamed. Venison retailed at four cents a pound, and many a fat pheasant and woodcock have I bought for ten cents, the seller thinking in his secret heart that he had cheated me."

"The little village of Oakland," noted a westward traveler of the B&O in 1857, "nestled in the center of the Glades, promises to become, within a few years, a favorite summer resort for those who seek healthful recreation and pure air. A modest but comfortable hotel is located here, which has already made quite a reputation among the enterprising sportsmen and healthseeking travelers." John Davis recalled in 1906 that "the Glades Hotel was, then in its palmy days, and hundreds of summer visitors from distant cities spent the summer in that historic place."

Brantz Mayer, founder of the Maryland Historical Society, accompanied by the well-known sympathetic American historian George Bancroft, visited Oakland in June 1856. "Nature, of itself, is not sufficiently attractive for artificial society," Mayer noted of his visit for *Harper's Magazine*. "Yet I do not despair of seeing the day when the Maryland Glades, the headwaters of the Potomac, Youghiogheny and Cheat, and the romantic cascades of the neighboring Blackwater will be crowded with health hunters. A little village is already growing up at Oakland . . . as a sort of nestling place for folks who are willing to be satisfied by being cool, quiet, and natural during summer. For several years many of our Maryland and Virginia sportsmen have been fishing the streams here, beating up the deer, pheasant and wild turkey; driving over the fine upland roads; drinking the pure water; sleeping soundly every night of July and August; and getting back to their work in the fall, as hearty as the 'bucks' they made war on in the mountains."

Oakland's first resort hotel, the Glades Hotel, was built in the early 1850s by Rowan White and a man named Burton, south of the railroad tracks, opposite the B&O Station. John Daily took over operation of the Glades Hotel in 1858 from Perry Lyle. Other early Oakland hotels included the John Thayer Tavern, S. L. Boyer's Central Hotel, Scott Shirer's Oak Street Hotel, S. M. Miller's Commercial Hotel (later known as the William James Hotel), the George Bosley House, the Smithman Hotel, the Manhattan Hotel, the Davis House, and the Browning House.

"We slept at Oakland," recorded Brantz Mayer of his 1856 visit. "The mists hung low over those highlands long after sunrise, and the air was so bracing that we found overcoats necessary in June as we bowled across the great Youghiogheny on a single arch of timber and iron, and passed the picturesque Falls of Snowy Creek where the railroad quits the prairie, and strikes a glen through which the stream brawls in foam, contrasting bravely with the hemlock and laurel that line the pass."

Oakland grew like a wild flower after the iron horse passed through town in 1851. In 1872, when Garrett County was first organized, it was selected as the county seat.

John W. Garrett was elected president of the Baltimore and Ohio Railroad Company on November 17, 1858. *Work* was his middle name.

Western Maryland historian J. Thomas Scharf described the new rail president in 1882 as a man "of large, commanding frame. His face is full, with large forehead, heavy eyebrows, and a trim mouth. It is a face full of keen intelligence, the listener's attitude natural to it; full also of benevolence and appreciative human kindliness."

The 1928 Baltimore and Ohio historian Edward Hungerford depicted Garrett as a man "of vast powers and abilities. Of huge size, he usually dominated the men round-about him, both physically and mentally. He possessed all the great qualities of leadership. He had, when he needed it, real charm. He could, upon occasion, be as tactful and as diplomatic as he was, upon other occasions, brusque and commanding. Seemingly, he could bend as easily as he could remain firm; and he was the personification of firmness itself."

Garrett remained the road's president until his death at Deer Park in 1884, holding the office for a period of more than twenty-five years.

When he entered the office as president in 1858 the line was in trouble. Competition was stiff; a general financial crisis had decreased the number of rail customers nationwide. The B&O itself had just completed a series of connecting routes to its main stem, the Marietta and Cincinnati, the Northwestern Virginia, the Central Ohio, and the Ohio and Mississippi, with no initial return to cover expansion expenses. Creditors were knocking loudly at the president's door when John W. Garrett assumed office.

On October 1, 1860, Garrett submitted his first annual report to his board of directors. "The careful cultivation of the local trade begins to effect favorable results," he informed them. "The charges upon way traffic have been arranged at rates materially under the average tariffs of other roads and we have the satisfaction of witnessing a marked development of business, population and prosperity in the sections of Maryland and Virginia traversed by the road and its branches." In 1860 the B&O profit-loss tide began to turn.

John Garrett devoted the Civil War years to the maintenance and rebuilding of his road, not to further expansion. Despite considerable opposition, he reorganized the road's board structure to give private financial interests in the line a majority control over those of city and state connection.

When the war ended, Garrett pushed his road north, south, east, and west. "The Baltimore and Ohio, vastly expanded during the decade of the 'fifties, was none the less, just now entering upon its period of real expansion," noted road historian Edward Hungerford. "Garrett was going to make Baltimore, nearly two hundred miles distant from the open sea, a great ocean port; a world port, if you please." John Garrett tried; John Garrett succeeded. He first extended his railroad from its original Wheeling terminus to Columbus, building two bridges over the Ohio River in 1871. His trains reached Pittsburgh from Cumberland for the first time the same year. In November 1874, B&O trains arrived for the first time in Chicago.

John W. Garrett completed branches of his railroad north to Newark, Ohio, and Lake Erie in 1869. In the early 1880s he began to push rails toward Philadelphia and New York.

Garrett survived good road times and bad. He worked tirelessly throughout the Civil War. He was shot at while sitting in his Baltimore library during a railroad strike of the "black seventies." The bullet lodged in a book he was holding.

As early as 1860 he had advocated the building of resort hotels along the B&O mountain route. The Grafton Hotel in Grafton, Virginia, "not to be surpassed upon any line of railroad in this or any other country composed of the Gothic and Corinthian style of architecture ... gorgeously furnished ... large and commodious ... a first-class station where a good, well-prepared meal can be enjoyed ... the acme of comfort ... one of *the* institutions of the country," according to an 1857 *Cincinnati Enquirer* correspondent, was built in 1856, two years before Garrett became the road's president. The main building of the Deer Park Hotel was built under his management in 1872; opened July 4, 1873. He also built the four-story Queen City Hotel in Cumberland in 1872 and the Oakland Hotel, near Washington Spring, in 1876.

Five of later Garrett County's ten 1862 post offices were opened after John W. Garrett's railroad made the mountaintop boom: Bloomington, Frankville, Swanton, Summitville, and Oakland. The other 1862 post offices included Accident, Friendsville, Grantsville, Johnstown, Hoyes and Selbysport.

John W. Garrett died September 26, 1884, at his Deer Park cottage, aged sixty-four. "The directors of the Baltimore and Ohio, as well as many other institutions with which he had been more or less directly connected, passed resolutions upon his death," noted Edward Hungerford. "For twenty-six years he had ruled the road as its president; with an iron hand. Until it became known colloquially as 'Garrett's road,' just as the Pennsylvania of those days was known as 'Tom Scott's road,' and the New York Central as 'Vanderbilt's.' That was, indeed the era of personal railroading. Of doubt and disaster in rail transport giving way to soundness and large profits; of men reaching for the smaller and the weaker roads and gathering them into their larger combinations; not so much with thought for the public weal as for the aggrandizement of their own properties. It was the era that immediately preceded the coming of strict regulation; both state and federal. It was the era of fine pickings. Of sharp business. In all of it, the Baltimore and Ohio forged still further forward.

"Garrett had found the B&O a penniless, politics-stricken line, still lingering on the east bank of the Ohio, and he had made from it a mighty railroad system, reaching from the shores of the Delaware to those of the Mississippi and the Great Lakes."

Recipients of Garrett philanthropy in the 1860s and 1870s included the Peabody Institute Art Gallery, the Baltimore Druid Hill Park, the Baltimore Boys' Home and Young Men's Christian Association, the Mount Clare Reading Room, and the Oakland Stone Church. John Garrett built the Garrett Memorial Stone Church at Oakland on the corner of Liberty and Second streets in 1868 of Cheat River rock as a memorial to his brother, Henry, who had died in 1867. Noted a later church member: "It appears to have been Mr. Garrett's intention to provide community church for the people of Oakland, more especially for congregations not having regular places of worship." The high-arched structure housed Episcopalians until about 1869, then Presbyterians until 1938, then once again Episcopalians. Garrett heirs placed the Oakland Stone Church under the administration of a local board of religious trustees in 1885.

When he died early that September morning in 1884 an elaborate train draped in black and bearing a front metal plate marked *At Rest* was organized at Deer Park to carry his body to Camden Station in Baltimore. More than ten thousand Baltimoreans attended his Sunday funeral services at Greenmount Cemetery.

John W. Garrett: his middle name—*Work*.

Fourteen years after John W. Garrett was elected president of the Baltimore and Ohio Railroad, a new county in western Maryland was formed from the western section of Allegany County and named in the railroad president's honor. Garrett is the youngest county of Maryland: She is also the youngest county of the entire bordering tri-state area. What follows is a three-year chronology of Garrett County's organization and early development:

1870. Western Allegany population by district: Accident, 1,006; Altamont, 1,133; Grantsville, 1,786; Oakland, 1,396; Ryan's Glade, 854; Sang Run, 673; Selbysport, 1,419. Total, 8,267 (76 black).

Jacob Brown: "About the year 1870 the movement for the formation of a new county began to take an active turn under the zealous leadership of Judge P. Hamill and Colonel J. M. Schley, with a number of active supporters, mostly of the territory of the proposed county." Among the most outspoken advocates for the formation of a new county west of Allegany in 1870 are Israel Thompson of Oakland, Allegany County commissioner; William A. Brydon of Bloomington, superintendent of Virginia's Hampshire Coal Mines; Richard T. Browning of Sang Run, grandson of hunter Meshach Browning and Allegany County tax collector; Rev. J. M. Davis of Oakland, businessman and speculator; and "Squire" William Hinebaugh of Accident, tanner and justice of the peace. Brown: "These men were met by a vigorous opposition . . . as is usual in such movements."

1871. Advocates for Allegany County division advance as public reasons for the proposed county the extensive distance of extreme western Maryland from the existing county seat in Cumberland, a desire for greater western Maryland and local representation in the state General Assembly, and anticipation of greater returns and more appropriate expenditures for local tax revenues under a new county system of public allocations. They present petitions to the General Assembly for county division. They suggest two possible names for the proposed county: Glade and Garrett. The grounds of the Oakland Glades Hotel are converted into a public park in the summer of 1871. Grass is sown, trees are planted, a decorative arbor is built, and a footbridge is constructed across nearby Wilson Creek.

Baltimore and Ohio railroad bridges over the Ohio River open for train traffic in June 1871. The first Garrett trains enter Pittsburgh in July.

In August of 1871 E. S. Zevely of Oakland begins

publication of Maryland's first newspaper west of Cumberland under the banner the *Glade Star*. Though the *Star*, published at Oakland, survives for only fifty-two weekly issues, finally terminating in July of 1872 under the banner of the *Garrett Star*, it serves as an instrumental media form in stirring up considerable public sentiment in favor of the formation of a new Maryland county.

Zevely early selects "Work for the New County" as his publication slogan. He editorially notes, issue after issue, that the required Maryland constitutional requisites for the formation of new counties—a population of at least ten thousand persons and a land area of at least four hundred square miles—are easily satisfied in his proposals for western Maryland. He suggests that the recent formation of Wicomico County on Maryland's eastern shore has disturbed the political equilibrium of the state by giving that section the unfair advantage of an additional senator and delegate in the state legislature; he recommends that the political balance can be restored only by the formation of a new western county. He points out that the residents of the proposed new western county currently pay $28 thousand per year in taxes under the existing Allegany County levy, but receive less than $19 thousand per year in appropriations. He notes that Allegany County is physically a hundred miles in length, and contends that such a size creates inconveniences in the transaction of county business. And he reviews the extraordinary resources of his proposed new county, the potential agricultural capability of the glades farmland, the potential coal and timber production of the mountains. E. S. Zevely, 1871: "Work for the New County."

1872. E. S. Zevely, January 6: "The *Glade Star* is free, independent, and untrammeled in politics, and expects to continue so." The *Cumberland News,* January 22: "Only Oakland, [proposed] new county seat, will benefit [if the new western Maryland county proposal passes]. It is like jumping from the frying pan into the fire, and we think the mountaineers had better stay in the pan." The *Cumberland News,* January 29: "The *Glade Star* says they have a man in Oakland who is willing to enter into bonds to erect all necessary, good and sufficient county buildings for $3,000. Go on, Mr. Star; we are willing that you should have your $3,000 county seat, new county, and your own taxes. The *News* will not oppose your efforts." Zevely publishes his last issue of the *Glade Star* on July 13, noting at the time that "All who have paid for the *Star* are so far clever people, and have evidenced some progressive spirit, deserve PRAISE,—those who have not done so . . . are a mean set of contemptibles, behind the age, enemies to progress, enemies to their own households,—enemies to their country,—who will sink into ingnominious graves and be forgotten."

Pursuant to western Maryland petitions of the preceding two years, the state General Assembly in early April 1872, approved an act providing for a public vote to determine popular support in the area of the proposed new county. Governor William Pinkney Whyte approved the enabling act, which established the polling day as November 4, and determined the boundary line between the proposed county and Allegany as a straight line running from the summit of Savage Mountain to the mouth of Savage River on the Potomac.

In the summer of 1872 John Garrett's Baltimore and Ohio Railroad Company completed construction of its four-story Queen City Hotel in Cumberland and began construction of the main building of its proposed four-story Swiss resort hotel in Deer Park. "This day has been an auspicious day for Deer Park," succinctly notes the *Cumberland News* on July 4, "as ground was broken there for the new hotel to be erected by the B&O Railroad Company."

In the summer and early fall of 1872 a vigorous campaign was conducted in western Maryland for the formation of a new county and the location of its seat of government. On July 4, while ground was being broken in Deer Park for a new railroad resort, a public barbecue and mass meeting was held in Oakland on the shady west bank of the Little Youghiogheny in advocacy of the new county. Five hundred persons attended the event for speeches, dinner, dancing, fireworks, and an evening ball at the Glades Hotel. Richard T. Browning, grandson of the hunter Meshach, suggested that Oakland be considered for the county seat and advocated the name

Garrett for the new county. Colonel James M. Schley addressed the crowd: "About the name of the new county. Other names have been suggested, but I give you a reason for calling it *Garrett* and no good reasons have been advanced for other names. When in Baltimore I met Mr. Garrett and he told me to say to the citizens of this section that he appreciated the great compliment of the new county being named for him. That he would take it into his care and keeping. That he held himself in readiness to do anything he could for its prosperity. He would make Oakland a first class station, erect new and commodious buildings here and do everything in his power to assist the new county and seat." Not a single voice at Oakland was raised in opposition to the new county proposal.

Grantsville and McHenry also held mass meetings and barbecues pertaining to county formation and selection of county seat in the summer of 1872. "The McHenry barbecue," according to one observer, "is remembered chiefly because of the Duvall-Browning fight, in which Absalom Duvall, a server at the feast, was beaten up." Nearly two thousand persons attended the Grantsville mass meeting held October 31, in a large wagon factory on main street. State Senator William R. Getty was chief advocate for the selection of Grantsville as county seat. Other Grantsville speakers on October 31 included Jacob Brown, H. W. Hoffman, Thomas I. McKaig, and George L. Layman. Layman opposed county division but suggested that if division became a reality, Grantsville should be selected government seat of the new political entity. Five communities were considered in 1872 as possibilities for the seat of the proposed county's government: Oakland, Grantsville, McHenry, Accident, and Deer Park. "Am much surprised to hear," Judge Patrick Hamill wrote John Garrett on September 15, "that Deer Park has determined to contend for the county seat. This, if persisted in, will certainly locate the county seat at Grantsville or Accident in the Northern part or section of the proposed New County and away from the Rail Road, and this will be so much to our disappointment." Both Accident and Deer Park withdrew from county seat consideration prior to the November vote.

On November 4, 1872, residents of western Maryland cast their votes on the new county proposition. Results: 1,297 in favor of the creation of a new county west of Allegany to be named Garrett, 405 in opposition. Majority in favor: 892. Results pertaining to county seat location: Oakland, 653; Grantsville, 590; McHenry, 461. Oakland carried the vote with a plurality of 63 ballots. "The new county of Garrett has carried," the *Baltimore Sun* reported November 7, 1872. "The chances are in favor of Oakland as the county seat."

Jubilant Garrett Countians held a new county ratification celebration November 7, 1872, at the Oakland Glades Hotel. They offered victory speeches, conducted a torchlight procession, shotguns and pistols, and lit bonfires. "It was a grand time," later recalls one participant, "a happy time, a glorious time."

On December 4, 1872, Maryland Governor William Pinkney Whyte proclaimed that the extreme western triangle of the state "has become and is now constituted as a new county to be called 'Garrett County.' " He also declared that "the inhabitants thereof shall henceforth have and enjoy all such rights and privileges as are held and enjoyed by the inhabitants of the other counties of this state."

1976. Garrett County—the daughter of Allegany County, the granddaughter of Washington County, the great-granddaughter of Frederick County, the great-great-granddaughter of Prince Georges County—is Maryland's youngest county, Maryland's most mountainous and least-densely populated county, Maryland's westernmost county, Maryland's second largest county. Garrett is a coal county, a timber county, an agricultural county, a resort county. Garrett County is also a very green, very clean county. Her inhabitants today, as in previous years, live a little closer to the stars, a little nearer the earth, than do the residents of any other section of the state.

Garrett County comprises a land area of 668 square miles.

The county's northern boundary was established in 1767 by English surveyors Charles Mason and Jeremiah Dixon, whose famous Mason-Dixon Line also serves as the dividing line between Maryland and Pennsylvania. The western boundary of Garrett County—the boundary line, also separating Maryland from western West Virginia—was first surveyed in 1787 by Colonel Francis Deakins. The Deakins line, long a matter of contention between officials of the two bordering states, ran due north of the 1746 Fairfax Stone, the marker planted near the headsprings of the North Branch of the Potomac by officials of the King of England to designate the northwestern corner of the Virginia-Fairfax estate. The United States Supreme Court in 1910 confirmed the Deakins meridian line as the true western border of the state of Maryland, thereby ending the one-and-a-half-century boundary dispute between the two bordering states. The southeastern boundary of present-day Garrett County follows, as it has since the Mayo-Winslow surveys of 1736, the course of the Potomac's North Branch from a point a few miles north of the Fairfax Stone northeast to Bloomington. The Potomac separates southwestern Maryland from northeastern West Virginia. Garrett County is thus almost surrounded by the states of West Virginia and Pennsylvania. Only with the western portion of Allegany County is she connected with the state of Maryland.

The boundary line separating the two westernmost Maryland counties was first surveyed in late 1872 following the division of Allegany County. The surveyor was Daniel Chisholm, official surveyor of Allegany County. Chisholm's line, however, failed to comply with the provisions of the Garrett enabling act of April 1872, which stipulated that the summit ridge of Big Savage Mountain at its intersection with the Mason-Dixon Line be the boundary line's northern terminal point. Chisholm chose the summit of the more westerly Little Savage, rather than Big Savage Mountain, as his northern terminal survey point, thus depriving Garrett County of over four thousand acres of valuable timber and coal land, land which rightfully belonged to Garrett, not Allegany County, under state law. The blunder was corrected following a disputed 1878 joint Allegany-Garrett resurvey through a state General Assembly Act of 1889, which provided for the "definite establishment and location" of the county dividing line. Dr. L. A. Bauer of the State Geological Survey supervised the new survey authorized by the assembly, and completed his work in July 1898. The Bauer line, ever since recognized as the true dividing line separating Garrett from Allegany County, runs in a southwesterly direction from the summit of Big Savage Mountain at its intersection with the Mason-Dixon Line to the mouth of Savage River at the Potomac.

The four border lines of Garrett County—each major matters of dispute at different times in county history—are now firmly and undisputedly etched on maps of central Appalachia.

Two conventions of interested Garrett County citizens met in late 1872 to nominate candidates to fill the positions of the various county government offices provided for and authorized by state law. The first nominating convention, meeting December 14 at the Oakland Glades Hotel, was generally deemed a failure when the Grantsville delegation withdrew from the hall as a gesture of its dissatisfaction with the ensuing ticket. A second convention, held at Accident on December 21, was more successful. Except for the single position of state's attorney, county voters endorsed the full ticket nominated by the Accident convention in a special election held January 7, 1873. They selected the following as Garrett County's first public officers: commissioners—William Casteel, H. M. Frazee, and A. Borig; state's attorney—Gilmor S. Hamill; orphans' court judges—William Harvey, D. H. Friend, and Joseph DeWitt; clerk of the court—William H. Tower; register of wills—William L. Rawlings; sheriff—William Coddington; surveyor—Alexander Mason.

Garrett County voters selected their first representatives for the state assembly in the regular statewide election of 1874. They elected Richard J. West and E. H. Glotfelty as delegates; they elected William R. Getty as state senator.

Judges of western Maryland's Circuit Court appointed Andrew Arendt, W. A. Brydon, and G. W. Delawder to Garrett County's first board of school commissioners in early 1873. In June the board elected Aza Matthews the county's first school secretary-examiner. Matthews assumed supervision of the county's fifty-seven existing schools, seventy-six teachers, and twenty-nine hundred pupils in early September.

On March 10, 1874, the state legislature officially declared Oakland Garrett County's seat of government. Disgruntled northern Garrett residents subsequently spearheaded a movement to form a new northern county with Grantsville as its seat. Two public meetings held in Grantsville in 1875 to advance the movement failed to gain the support of the state legislature, however, and the movement died as suddenly as it had risen. The sectional feelings of jealousy which it sparked, though, remain—even today.

The first sessions of the circuit court in Garrett County, as well as the first board meetings of the county commissioners, were held in the Oakland Glades Hotel. Subsequent sessions and meetings were held in store houses and school buildings in lieu of an appropriate Oakland courthouse for the transaction of county business, due to the jealous opposition of northern county residents and those who frowned upon the requisite expenditures on fiscal principle. Finally, on October 14, 1876, the circuit court, responding to the petitions of numerous local citizens, issued a writ of mandamus compelling Garrett's commissioners to authorize the construction of a county courthouse and jail. The two structures were erected on Green Street in November 1877.

The present county courthouse and jail were built in 1907-1908. Judge Andrew Hunter Boyd, of the Fourth Maryland Judicial Circuit, spoke at the cornerstone ceremony, October 15, 1970. "When you separated from Allegany County," he suggested, "your county was sparsely settled, and being remote from educational centers the young men and women had but few advantages for the development of their minds. But now schoolhouses are within easy reach of most of them, and any observant person can see that many are taking advantage of their opportunities."

The judge then addressed himself more immediately to the matter at hand. "I trust that while you can still speak of this building as your 'new Court House,' " he announced, "your County will have so progressed in its educational, moral and spiritual interests that the residents of the lowlands of this State will look up to the highlands of Garrett, to find a people who have made it one of the most prosperous, intelligent, law-abiding and religious counties of the State.

"If such hope be realized, then the money of the taxpayers of this County expended upon this building will be returned many fold, and this will in reality be a 'Temple of Justice,' wherein the rich and poor, the high and the low, will stand on an equality, and can be assured that their rights will be preserved and their wrongs redressed, as impartially and abundantly as is possible to be done by human tribunals."

Garrett County was formed from the western triangular section of Allegany County, Maryland, in 1872, seven years after the completion of the War Between the States, twenty-one years after tracks of the Baltimore and Ohio Railroad were laid across the eastern continental divide of western Maryland.

The United States in 1872 was still an expanding nation, an industrializing nation, a growing nation. The second half of the nineteenth century in America witnessed an immense extension of the railroad industry, an unprecedented boom in industrial capitalism, a wild and exciting period of urbanization. The growth of the nation during this period necessitated the exploitation of more and more raw resources for manufacturing and energy and construction. It produced a new middle class of professionals and entrepreneurs. It encouraged new investments and promoted new technologies and new developments in transportation and communication. The late nineteenth century in America was an age of industrialization, an age of diversification, an age of centralization, an age of booming capitalism.

The age promoted three new industries in western Maryland which have been central to Garrett County's economy ever since—lumbering, mining, and resort recreation. The railroad, the B&O of 1851, as well as subsequent western Maryland rail construction and expansion, played a prominent, if not an essential, role in the growth and development of all three industries.

"When the B. and O. Railroad was built across the mountains it was primarily concerned with reaching markets farther west," noted Ross C. Durst of Grantsville in 1970. "Yet, in cutting across the lower end of the Savage River Valley, its effects were felt throughout the valley. None of the larger lumber operations would have been possible without it."

Timbering in western Maryland before the construction of the Baltimore and Ohio Railroad across the mountains in 1851 was a small-scale, family-oriented industry chiefly concerned with providing building materials for local markets. The B&O of 1851 considerably altered the industry's status quo. By providing new and distant potential markets for local lumber products, it lured large-scale timber capitalists to the wooded hills of western Maryland for the first time. These capitalists built new towns, erected large sawmills, laid new rails into the woods, and provided work for hundreds of men. They plundered and stripped the land, then left, their hip pockets bulging. Behind them, in western Maryland, they left the legacy of their work—acres of scarred hillside, dozens of abandoned buildings and mills, a few scattered ghost towns.

Western Maryland lumbering in the late nineteenth century followed the paths of rail lines and the courses of rivers. Prior to the construction of railroads in the northern and extreme southern sections of Garrett County, the timber industry centered at points along the Baltimore and Ohio line. The *Cumberland Daily News* reported as early as 1872 that "Henry Gassaway Davis and Brothers have 75 men employed in construction of a boom on the Potomac River above Piedmont, West Virginia, and in making excavations for a reservoir in which to float logs as they come down the River. . . . A large sawmill is to be erected on the Maryland side of the river near Bloomington. The bed of the Potomac for 50 miles is to be cleared and obstructions to logs removed." Piedmont and Bloomington were natural shipping points for lumber products in 1872. Both towns boasted B&O rail depots.

Bloomington, located at the mouth of Savage River on the Potomac, was Garrett County's second largest town in 1872, and the site of the county's easternmost rail station. It was also the first center of extensive logging operations in the county. The first major lumber company to establish headquarters in the area, the Lochiel, employed scores of men for nearly two decades in cutting white pine timber along the Savage River for lumber production at its mill just northwest of Bloomington. The company closed in 1886.

The largest lumber operation in the Savage River valley, which depended on the B&O Railroad for marketing and transportation, was organized in the spring of 1900 under the name DuBois and Bond Brothers Lumber Corporation, a company headed by five residents of western Pennsylvania. DuBois and Bond bought ten thousand acres of Savage River timberland that year from a Philadelphia land speculator. The next year the company laid over six miles of standard-gauge railroad along the valley from a junction with the B&O—Bond Junction—about four miles west of Bloomington. It later extended branches of the Savage River Railroad along Monroe Run, Big Run, and numerous other streams feeding into the Savage. About five miles north of Bond Junction the corporation erected a company town for its employees. Bond, as the new town was named, featured company offices, a general store, a boarding house, a church, a school, a post office, and about forty modest dwelling houses.

DuBois and Bond built its sawmill near the mouths of Monroe and Big Run on the Savage. The company also erected four large dining rooms and bunk buildings to accommodate its logging crews in the woods. It produced lumber for about ten years, then sold all its holdings in 1910 to other interests. The town of Bond died slowly through ensuing decades.

Bloomington was but one of six lumber-shipping areas along the Baltimore and Ohio Railroad in Garrett County that gave rise to the county's expanding timber industry in the late nineteenth century. The other B&O shipping points included Swanton, Deer Park, Oakland, Hutton, and Skipnish.

Beginning in the 1870s, a private narrow-gauge railroad transported logs from the Swanton area just west of Backbone Mountain to the B&O depot in that town for nearly two decades. Lumbering in Deer Park between the 1860s and the 1890s was conducted under the management of Henry Gassaway Davis, whose tramroads extended north to several sawmills along Deep Creek. Peter Martin began operating a sawmill on the Little Yough near Oakland around 1879.

In 1881 W. A. Luraw bought the William Ashby sawmill at Sunshine, later known as Crellin, and erected a shingle mill nearby. A few years later he sold the operation to John A. Connell. In 1891 Connell transferred the property to the Preston Lumber and Coal Company, a corporation headed by a group of Pennsylvania capitalists under the leadership of Rolland P. Crellin. The Preston Company simultaneously bought some thirty thousand acres of nearby timberland, began construction of a major new Crellin sawmill, and laid a standard-gauge railroad from the town to the B&O depot at Hutton. The Preston sawmill began operation in 1892.

The Preston Lumber and Coal Company managed the Crellin area lumber industry until 1905, when it sold all its holdings to officials of the Kendall Lumber Company of Pennsylvania. During its thirteen years of operation the Preston Company processed and shipped over two hundred and fifty million board feet of lumber, plus numerous carloads of mine props, bark and pulpwood. The town of Crellin flourished under its management. Its timber rails penetrated deep into the woods of West Virginia along Laurel Run and south along the Youghiogheny to Breedlove.

The Kendall Lumber Company continued the rail expansion to the woods from Crellin, begun by the Preston Company, for nearly twenty years. In Crellin it built new company homes, new stores and offices. In Tucker County, West Virginia, it built the sixteen houses and large store comprising the lumber town of Shaffer. During the height of its operations it ran seven steam locomotives at once. Eventually one branch of its railroad approached to within a few miles' distance of the town of Saint George, West Virginia. Another branch terminated only six miles from Parsons.

The Kendall Lumber Company sawed its last log at Crellin on November 13, 1925. In the twenty years of its operation it had produced over three hundred fifty million board feet of lumber, sixty-two million feet of lath, two million feet of slats, three million props, and hundreds of carloads of squares, wood cords, palings, pit ties, railroad ties, locust poles, telephone poles, bark and pulpwood. It had regularly employed from 275 to 750 men annually. After the sawmill at Crellin closed in 1925, many of the town's residents sought lumber jobs elsewhere or else remained in the vicinity to mine coal.

(Though the Hutton junction of the B&O served as a major shipping point for the timber products of Crellin for years throughout the late nineteenth century, the town of Hutton itself depended only indirectly on the timber business for survival. Named in honor of the Hutton family of New York in 1851, the village grew only slowly until 1893, when the Enterprise Tanning Company established a large tannery there. The tannery thrived for thirty-two years, employing as many as fifty men at a time, obtaining bids from Chicago meat packing plants, extracting tannin for its curing process from local oak and hemlock bark.)

Around 1880, John W. Garrett authorized the private construction of a narrow-gauge logging railroad from a B&O junction point about two miles east of Hutton, at Skipnish, northward along the Youghiogheny River to Swallow Falls. Garrett himself owned extensive tracts of timberland along the Skipnish Road, as the rail line came to be called. Near the head of Tolliver Run he operated a sawmill until the early 1890s, by which time all the large timber of the area had been cut. The small village which had grown up around the sawmill during its years of productivity soon decayed and disappeared after the termination of logging in the area in the late 1890s.

The Baltimore and Ohio Railroad, with shipping points at Bloomington, Bond Junction, Swanton, Deer Park, Oakland, Skipnish, and Hutton, was the initial lifeline of the timber and lumber business in southern Garrett County throughout the late nineteenth and early twentieth centuries. At least five notable southern Garrett County lumber producing areas—Vindex, Kitzmiller, Wallman, Steyer, and Wilson—depended on a second major railroad for transportation of their products to eastern markets during later years. (So did a number of nearby West Virginia timber towns, including those of Dobbin, Henry, and Dill.) The railroad they relied upon was the original Potomac and Piedmont Railroad, incorporated under Henry Gassaway Davis in 1866 for development of the timber and coal resources of the Potomac Valley. The road extended, by 1880, southwest from Cumberland to Westernport. In 1881 it was reorganized into the West Virginia Central and Pittsburgh Railway. Its line was extended that year southwest to Shaw, West Virginia. The following year it reached Minesville. In 1883 it entered Gormania; in 1884, Davis. Parsons and Elk Garden branches were completed in 1888. In 1906 the Western Maryland Railway Company bought the West Virginia Central and Pittsburgh. The road's Kempton branch was completed in 1914.

Around 1860 a man named George W. Wilson settled just south of the North Branch of the Potomac, in present-day West Virginia, about four miles southwest of Gorman, Maryland. In the latter part of the decade he began producing barrel staves in the area, transporting his product by team and wagon to the B&O depot in Oakland for shipment to eastern and western markets. In 1882, when the West Virginia Central and Pittsburgh Railway entered Wilson, as the area came to be called, George Wilson erected a large circular sawmill near his home on the Maryland side of the Potomac. His sons succeeded their father in management of the Wilson Lumber Company until around 1900, when the local timber stand (including about twenty-five hundred acres in Garrett County along the forks of Sand Run and along the slope of Backbone Mountain) was finally exhausted. The Wilson Lumber Company then moved its theater of operations southwest to the Fairfax Stone area and deeper into the hills of West Virginia.

Lumbering at Dobbin, West Virginia, less than two miles southwest of Wilson, began around 1889, when the Pennsylvania timber capitalist J. L. Rumbarger erected a large band sawmill there on the flats between the Western Maryland Railway and the Potomac River. Rumbarger earlier had bought nearly three thousand acres of nearby Garrett County timberland along Big Laurel Run. He also owned extensive tracts in West Virginia. Dobbin grew to a town of some three hundred residents under Rumbarger's management.

In 1898 Rumbarger sold his Maryland holdings near Dobbin to the Davis Coal and Coke Company; in 1901 he sold his actual Dobbin holdings to the Parsons Pulp and Paper Company of West Virginia. Dobbin thrived until the advent of World War I, under the management of the Parsons Company. The town itself was extended to the Maryland side of the river. When the local timber resources were exhausted, though, Dobbin died.

Large-scale lumbering began in the Kitzmiller area in the spring of 1894 when the York, Pennsylvania, farm implement manufacturing firm of Hench, Dromgold and Shull bought extensive timber rights in the vicinity and established a mill and company store at nearby Dill (later known as Potomac Manor) in the state of West Virginia. For five years the York company cut the virgin timber of Garrett County's Wolf Den Run and Lost Land Run, manufactured plow beams, handles, and chair stocks at Dill, and shipped their products northeast on the West Virginia Central and Pittsburgh Railroad.

Lumbering at Wallman, located on the Potomac about four miles northwest of Gorman, also relied on the West Virginia Central and Pittsburgh Railroad for market transportation. Wallman itself, a company town built in the early 1900s, was the western terminal of a private narrow-gauge railroad extending into West Virginia timberlands east of the Potomac. Morrison, Gross and Company was the last operator of the Wallman Mill, which closed in the early 1930s. The town today is a ghost town.

Lumbering at Steyer, Maryland, less than two miles west of Wallman, began under the direction of a Mr. Miller early in the twentieth century and extended along the timberlands of Garrett County's Steyer Run. Lumbering at Henry, West Virginia, about a mile southwest of Dobbin, also began early in the century. It, too, relied on the transportation capabilities of the Western Maryland Railway, and also extended into the western Maryland hills northwest of the Potomac. (Lumbering at Henry ended in 1934.)

Lumbering at Vindex in Garrett County, just north of

Kitzmiller, lasted for only a year (1924) under the Three Fork Lumber Company along Three Fork Run. (Vindex itself thrived chiefly through the production of coal.)

Late nineteenth century timbering in southern Garrett County depended upon the construction of the Baltimore and Ohio Railroad and Western Maryland Railway; late nineteenth century timbering in northern Garrett County depended upon the construction of two railroads built south from Pennsylvania along the Youghiogheny and Casselman River valleys. The first of these railroads was the Confluence and Oakland; the second, the Jennings' Brothers Railroad. Both were built chiefly for the exploitation of Garrett timber resources.

Construction of the Confluence and Oakland Railroad began at the Confluence junction of the Pittsburgh division of the Baltimore and Ohio Railroad in Pennsylvania on April 1, 1889. The chief promoter of the new road was the Yough Manor Land Company, which owned large tracts of virgin timber throughout the Youghiogheny Valley. On January 1, 1890, after the road reached Friendsville, its directors leased all its property to the Baltimore and Ohio Company for a period of 999 years. The following year the road was extended south to its final terminus at Yough Manor, later known as Kendall, a small but growing lumber town located a few miles south of Friendsville.

Lumbering in Selbysport, Friendsville, and Kendall thrived as never before after the Confluence and Oakland opened to traffic. Residents of Friendsville were so jubilant at the prospects of economic growth when the railroad reached that point in 1889 that they staged a grand celebration for its opening. More than one thousand persons attended the affair; they barbecued an ox, drank hundreds of toasts, gave speeches, danced and fiddled, and conducted footraces, greased pig catching contests, and crosstie making contests. The railroad promised to give new life to the old town, and it soon fulfilled its promise.

The first major lumber company to establish headquarters at Friendsville was that of Clark and McCullough, later known as the Bear Creek Lumber Company, headed by J. W.

McCullough, of Friendsville, and H. E. Clark, of Lock Haven, Pennsylvania. Clark and McCullough established their mill in 1894 near the mouth of Little Bear Creek. A few years later they sold substantial interests in their operation to the Meadow Mountain Lumber Company, headed by Walter S. Taylor, who owned over five thousand acres of prime timberland on Negro and Meadow mountains. In 1898 Taylor authorized the construction of a second major Friendsville lumber mill.

The Meadow Mountain Lumber Company constructed over twenty-five miles of thirty-six-inch narrow-gauge rail lines through the timberlands of Big Bear Creek to Negro and Meadow mountains early in the twentieth century. One branch of its road terminated near Swanton; another, in the swamplands bordering Cherry Creek. The company employed hundreds of men in its timber operations, constructing a bunk house and living facilities for them along its tracks between Negro and Meadow mountains. Nearby it built a large steam-powered sawmill capable of producing from twenty to thirty thousand board feet of lumber per day. For nearly six years the company's four locomotives pulled approximately one and a half million feet of logs per year from the woods to Friendsville for shipment north on the Confluence and Oakland. Then, in 1904, it removed its track from the mountains to Engle's Mill on Bear Creek and sold its interests to the Johnstown Planing Mill Company. The Johnstown company continued operation of the business for only about four years. At the same time, another Friendsville-based timber company, the Lock Haven Lumber Company, exploited the timber resources of Little Bear Creek at a point near Accident. Like the companies before it, the Lock Haven built a tramroad from its mill near Friendsville to the woods on the hills.

The lumber town which grew up at the southern terminal of the Confluence and Oakland Railroad on the banks of the Youghiogheny a few miles south of Friendsville at the turn of the twentieth century was originally called Manor Land after the Yough Manor Land Lumber Company, but later became known as Kendall and sometimes as Krug. The town served as headquarters for two local lumber companies, A. Knabb and

Company (organized under Henry Krug), manufacturers of staves and oil and whiskey barrels, and the Kendall Lumber Company of Pittsburgh. The Knabb company built a large barrel factory at Manor Land in 1898; the Kendall company simultaneously built a large sawmill in the area. Both companies laid narrow-gauge railroad tracks into the surrounding woods. One rail line, running southwest along the Youghiogheny River, connected with the Skipnish Railroad in the Tolliver Run area. The other line crossed the Youghiogheny and ran westward toward West Virginia. Numerous branch lines connected with both major routes.

In 1972 Mrs. J. P. Scales, of Albany, Georgia, recalled the town of Kendall as it existed in 1908. "It was quite a thriving town," she recalled, "on the banks of the Yough river. There was a school and church, a company store with post office in back, a large boarding house and some smaller ones." Today, Kendall, like Wallman, is a ghost town of empty foundations and deserted elevated rail grades, accessible only by foot. The Confluence and Oakland Railroad, like its terminal depot, has also disappeared. Traffic on the road was finally discontinued in 1942.

A second major northern Garrett County lumbering railroad was constructed by the Pennsylvania timber capitalists Cord H. and Worth B. Jennings, through the Casselman River Valley in 1898. The Jennings Brothers' Railroad, also known as the Casselman River Railroad, began at the Worth, Pennsylvania, interchange of the Pittsburgh division of the Baltimore and Ohio and ran south through Grantsville to the lumber town of Jennings, where the Jennings brothers owned extensive timber tracts and established a large band sawmill in 1900. The Jennings Railroad served local timber capitalists, including the Garrett Lumber Company and the firm of Ballot and Billmeyer for seventeen years. All along its length petty timber capitalists constructed branch lines into the virgin forest of the Casselman Valley. Today only traces of these roads remain.

Other major turn-of-the-century northeastern Garrett County lumber enterprises included mills operated by Charles Durst, C. J. Otto, and Philip McAndrews in New Germany;

one operated by George T. Brew in the Shades of Death; and an extensive timber enterprise conducted by the Juniata Lumber Company on Big Savage Mountain.

Garrett County timber company employees in the late nineteenth century were commonly referred to as *wood hicks*. Wood hicks worked from sunrise till sunset six days a week. Often they lived in bunkhouses provided by their employers. They cut and trimmed trees, erected log slides down mountain slopes, drove horse teams, constructed splash dams along river beds for transportation of logs to mills, drove locomotives, constructed railbeds. They endured freezing cold, sweltering heat, bunkhouse life, ticks. Often they were rovers; sometimes they were family men. They were rugged and tough. On Saturday nights they raised hell in town. On weekdays they razed the forests. They transformed the Garrett earth in the relatively short period of a few decades from a virgin forestland into a land of stumps and farms. Only a few acres of Garrett primeval forest (near Swallow Falls) escaped the blow of their axes, the rasp of their saws.

"This whole neighborhood was once densely covered with white pine and spruce," recorded Jacob Brown of the Avilton vicinity in 1888, "but it has in years past been cut and made into lumber in various forms." Brown wrote similarly of the Shades of Death. "Nothing now remains of its former gloom and dread," he noted, "except the thousands of stumps of a once-dense piece of forest." And so it went.

The railroad brought large-scale timber and coal operators to the hills of Western Maryland for the first time in the late nineteenth century. The poor conservation practices of the time led to considerable governmental regulation of these two industries and present practices continue to be under close scrutiny.

Though the Garrett pioneer settler, Philip Hare, opened extreme western Maryland's first coal mine as early as 1792 on his Coal and Timber tract about two miles north of Little Meadows for the service of blacksmith shops along the Braddock Road, large-scale commercial mining in Garrett County proved unprofitable until the rail innovation of the late nineteenth century provided coal capitalists for the first time with easy transportation facilities to distant markets.

The first commercial mines in Garrett County opened at points along the route of the Baltimore and Ohio Railroad in Bloomington, Crellin, and Oakland. Later mines opened at points along new rail tracks laid through valleys rich in coal and timber. By the early decades of the twentieth century, coal capitalists were operating at points throughout the northern Potomac Valley (serviced by the Western Maryland Railway), the Youghiogheny Valley (serviced by the Confluence and Oakland Railroad), the Casselman River Valley (serviced by the Jennings Brothers' Railroad).

The western Maryland coal promoters of the late nineteenth and early twentieth centuries constructed numerous company-owned towns throughout Garrett valleys rich in coal, and opened scores of mines in the county's mountains. Coal was the great necessity of the industrializing era, and the western Maryland coalfield was among the most accessible to the eastern markets. A few decades of exploitation soon exhausted the most convenient seams, however, and the Great Depression of the 1930s virtually ended coal mining in the area for years. When coal operators first abandoned the hills of western Maryland in the 1930s, and then again during the national post-World War II coal slump, they left behind a legacy of numerous ghost towns, as well as some huge gob piles and empty, ravished holes in the ground.

The first major Garrett mines were opened along the route of the Baltimore and Ohio Railroad. The Llangollen Mining Company began digging the fuel from mountains near Bloomington in 1876. The Offutt Mining Company opened a seam four miles west of Oakland the same year.

Two new mines opened near Bloomington in 1878: the North Branch Mine, owned by the North Branch Coal Company, and the Empire Mine, owned by the Piedmont Coal and Iron Company. The Oakland Coke and Coal Company built six coke ovens near Oakland in 1888. By 1897 two mines were operating near Crellin—the Guthrie Mine, owned by Leroy Guthrie, and Arnold Run No. 1, owned by the Preston Lumber and Coal Company. Coal production at

Crellin gradually increased as timber production there fell early in the twentieth century, until by 1925 seventy-five families lived in the town in company-owned houses.

Bloomington, Oakland, and Crellin were early centers of coal production and shipment in Garrett County; all three depended on the transportation capabilities of the Baltimore and Ohio Railroad for economic growth based on the rising coal industry of an industrializing era.

Garrett County's second major southern rail line—the Potomac and Piedmont of the 1870s, the West Virginia Central and Pittsburgh of the 1880s, the Western Maryland of the early 1900s—Garrett County's second major nineteenth century southern rail line also spurred early development of Garrett coal resources. Mining at Kitzmiller began on a commercial basis in 1898 with the opening of the North American Mine under management of the Blaine Coal Company. Within a year the North American Mine was producing approximately one hundred tons of coal each day. In 1903 the Weston-Dodson Company of Bethlehem, Pennsylvania, opened a second mine at Kitzmiller under the name of Garrett County Coal Company. A third Kitzmiller mine, the Pee Wee Mine, opened in 1907 under the management of John W. Davis. The Hamill Coal and Coke Company opened a fourth mine the following year.

Kitzmiller was but one of eight Garrett County coal towns located along the upper Potomac which entirely depended, by the early decades of the twentieth century, upon the Western Maryland and Railway from Cumberland for economic survival.

Mining at Louise, a few miles north of Kitzmiller, began under the direction of the Pee Wee Coal Company very early in the century, but the town was abandoned shortly after the more productive nearby Vindex mine of the Three Fork Coal Company opened under the management of Dan Beckman in 1906. The town of Vindex on Three Fork Run, serviced by the Chaffee extension of the Western Maryland, produced coal until 1950. A company-owned town, it boasted five hundred residents by 1920, today it is a ghost town. Mining companies operating at Vindex early in the century included the Chaffee Coal Company, the A. B. Creighton Coal Company, and the Johnstown Coal and Coke Company.

Five coal towns grew up south of Kitzmiller in the Garrett County Potomac Valley during the early twentieth century—Shallmar, Dodson, Wallman, Gorman, and Kempton. Dodson, Wallman, and Kempton, like Louise and Vindex, are now ghost towns. Shallmar and Gorman are now small residential communities. All five towns once thrived on the production of coal; Kempton, in 1920, boasted seven hundred residents. Those coal towns of the upper Potomac which survived the Depression of the 1930s were fatally damaged by the post-World War II coal slump, and none now thrive.

Early twentieth century mining in northern Garrett County followed the routes of the Confluence and Oakland Railroad through the Youghiogheny River Valley and the Jennings Brothers' Railroad through the Casselman Valley.

The Confluence and Oakland served mining operations in the Lower Yough Basin from 1890 until 1942. The first major operator in the area was the Penn-Garrett Coal Mining Company, organized in 1906.

The first major coal mining company operating in the Casselman basin, serviced by the Jennings Brothers' Railroad of 1898, was the Meadow Mountain Coal and Coke Company, which opened a mine near Bittinger in 1902. In 1918 the Casselman railroad was reorganized under the Northern Maryland and Tidewater Company, which sold the rail property to William A. Mogart and the Casselman Valley Railroad Company in 1923. Mogart, president of the new rail company, also headed the Mogart Coal Mining Corporation, a company which opened three Jennings-area mines the same year Mogart assumed control of the Casselman Railroad. Mogart also bought the town of Jennings in 1923, and provided it for the first time with a major coal-oriented economy. In 1928 he sold his rail holdings to the Casselman River Railroad Company, which transported Bittinger-Jennings coal north to Pennsylvania until 1959, when it finally terminated Casselman Valley rail traffic. In 1976, Jennings, in the words of one of its own residents, is a "small town with few opportunities and a future of the same." Jennings, a lumber town, a coal town, dies slowly—fades away.

Late nineteenth, early twentieth century coal miners, like the wood hicks before them, lived rugged, bleak, dangerous, hard-working lives, and resided, more often than not, in frame houses owned by their companies. They bought necessary commodities in company-owned stores and used company-issued scrip currency. They depended socially and economically on the success of their companies, and when their companies suffered, they suffered.

When the miners' companies succumbed they suffered. George A. Fizer, writing of twentieth century upper Potomac coal-born ghost towns, noted in 1974 that "most of these . . . towns can (now) be identified . . . by ruins of old buildings amid the brush, cement foundations of former bridges, other (empty) structures, stationary engines, and remains of coal tipples. The real tombstones, however, are the large gob piles, partially hidden by tangled brush and scrub trees on the hillsides, that mark the coal mines that once gave life to so many of these old towns."

Crellin, Kitzmiller, Louise, Vindex, Shallmar, Dodson, Wallman, Gorman, Kempton, Jennings—all once thrived on the production and shipment of coal. During their peak years nearly all boasted town bands and baseball teams, churches, schools, and stores. Nearly all have now expired.

Mining techniques progressed rapidly throughout the twentieth century. Early in the century nearly all Garrett coal was mined and loaded by pick and shovel. Child labor was common. Horses and mules were used to pull heavy cars from mines to tipples. Only railroads were employed for major transportation.

Today, with the current threat of renewed energy crises, the coal industry in western Maryland is experiencing a resurgence. The company-owned towns are gone. The horses and mules are gone and the secondary rail lines of the early decades of the century are gone. Coal today is strip-mined and deep-mined with heavy machinery. It is transported by truck from mine to tipple. Miners live in private homes. Land restoration following strip mining is required by law.

The Baltimore and Ohio Railroad, coupled with the subsequent western Maryland rail innovations of the late nineteenth century, lured large-scale timber and coal capitalists for the first time to the hills of Garrett County. They stripped the land and exploited the earth. The late nineteenth century rail innovations also lured resort financiers to the mountains. They erected commodious hotels, opened parks, speculated in land sales, and introduced western Maryland to the growing leisure-time resort industry of the Gilded Age. They provided Garrett County with a major new summertime economy, one which still grows despite periods of recurrent adversity, one which still exercises a major influence in the overall county economy—resort recreation.

The development of large-scale resort recreation in Garrett County depended upon the quick, economical transportation facilities from city to mountaintop initially provided by the Baltimore and Ohio Railroad. As early as 1857 Virginia Lyles, daughter of Perry Lyles, owner of Oakland's first resort hotel, the Glades Hotel, noted that the "[rail] cars taking meals here makes it necessary for constant and never flagging exertion. . . . Twice we thought we had received both Housekeeper and Cook but both times were disappointed. Every thing has been done, but on account of the bleak climate free servants object to living in Oakland and being so near the boundary, slaves cannot be had."

The Glades Hotel nevertheless prospered. Among other early guests of note at the hotel was the widow of Francis Scott Key and her daughter, Mrs. Charles Howard, daughter-in-law of General John Eager Howard. (General Howard was a lieutenant of the Revolutionary War, a general in the War of 1812, a Maryland congressman, governor, and senator.) The Keys and Howards first visited Oakland in 1857; their children and grandchildren established a home on Alder Street and visited the highlands year after year throughout the late nineteenth century. The vacation tradition prompted Frances Key Howard, late in the century, to note that "a very deep love for Oakland and Garrett County is born into and inherited by all the descendants of Francis Scott Key."

Jefferson Davis, later to receive notoriety as president of

the Confederate States of America, resided at the Oakland Glades Hotel for a few weeks during the summer of 1859 while serving as United States senator from Mississippi. "One Sunday when [Joseph Sharp] was to preach [at the Oakland M. E. Church]," recalled the local Thomas J. Brandt in 1900 of the celebrity's initial appearance in town, "Mr. John Dailey [who had acquired the Glades Hotel from Perry Lyles in 1858] and a slim, pale-faced man took opposite seats [in the church] to the one I occupied. The stranger attracted my attention more than the sermon. He wore fine clothes, expensive jewelry, and even had a gold toothpick which he used once during the sermon. Mr. Sharp, who never did preach long sermons, was more brief than usual. [The pastor later related] how embarrassed he [had been] in trying to tell such a man as Jefferson Davis anything he did not already know."

Jefferson Davis was accompanied in his 1859 visit to Oakland by his family and a good friend, Montgomery Blair, chief advocate of the rights of slaveholders in the 1857 Supreme Court Dred Scott Case. Two years after vacationing in Garrett County, Davis was elevated to the office of president of the Confederate States. He never returned to the highlands of western Maryland.

The Glades Hotel in Oakland was the first mountaintop resort hotel in the world served by a railroad. It was the original headquarters of the political organization that created Garrett County, the county's first major resort hotel and the site of its first court sessions—the Glades Hotel, built in the early 1850s, was destroyed by fire in 1874. Proprietor John Dailey rebuilt the structure the same year on a new location south of Railroad Street near Wilson Creek. The new three-story Glades featured fifty guest rooms, spacious parlors, a large lobby and dining and ballroom, and a broad veranda extending across the entire facade of the building. Later nineteenth century guests of the hotel included William McKinley, "Buffalo Bill" Cody, and Lew Wallace, author of *Ben-Hur,* the novel based on the life of Christ. Wallace worked on *Ben-Hur* while relaxing on the veranda of the Glades. The hotel itself prospered under the direction of

John Dailey, whose operating slogan was simple: "Give people something good to eat and plenty of it."

The Glades Hotel in Oakland, across the railroad tracks from the B&O station, was Garrett County's chief resort hotel until the 1870s. The Baltimore and Ohio built two new resort retreats on the mountaintop glades that decade, two retreats which elevated Garrett County in the eyes of vacationers from Baltimore and Washington and Cincinnati as no previous enterprises had done. The new resorts were the Oakland Hotel and the Deer Park Hotel. Both enterprises were financed exclusively by the Baltimore and Ohio Railroad; both were exclusive railroad resorts.

B&O president John W. Garrett had advocated the construction of new highland resort hotels in western Maryland as early as 1860, noting that a "considerable increase of local [rail] traffic may be anticipated from this source." Twelve years later—on July 4, 1872—he authorized immediate construction work on the main building of a four-story Swiss Alpine retreat on the three hundred-acre B&O portion of the 1774 Peace and Plenty land tract bordering the town of Deer Park just west of the eastern continental divide of Backbone Mountain. The building work lasted a full year. The exterior of the Deer Park Hotel was constructed of native white pine; the roof was made of slate of contrasting colors. The entire structure was surmounted by a decorative cupola for observation of the surrounding countryside. The Deer Park Hotel formally opened for guests on July 4, 1873, with 104 bedrooms.

Construction work on the grounds surrounding the Deer Park Hotel continued through 1887. Grounds improvements included a golf course, stable and carriage house, laundry building, servants' quarters, icehouse, chapel, recreational building for billiards and bowling, and a large glass-covered bath house containing two swimming pools as well as Turkish and Russian baths. Deer Park resident Henry Gassaway Davis constructed five large summer cottages nearby in the 1870s; the B&O Company constructed another five.

In 1882 the company added two large wings to the main building of the Deer Park Hotel, doubling the structure's guest capacity. The cottages opened for guests on June 1 of each year; the hotel opened June 24. Most rooms in both cottages and hotel featured large fireplaces for cool summer nights.

The Deer Park Hotel of 1873 was such an immediate success that John W. Garrett authorized the construction of a second major Garrett County railroad resort along the tracks of the B&O in 1875—the Oakland Hotel. The Oakland resort, three stories high with long porches and spacious parlors, opened in the summer of 1876 at the foot of Totten Hill across the B&O tracks from the Oakland railroad station. Washington Springs, visited by George Washington in 1784, bubbled nearby. The Oakland Hotel featured a large ballroom, accommodations for over a hundred guests, and a large park of maple, oak, and pine.

The B&O mountaintop resorts at Deer Park and Oakland accommodated Garrett County visitors for about a half century. Civil War generals William Tecumseh Sherman and Ulysses S. Grant vacationed at Deer Park one summer late in the 1870s. Grant returned to the Oakland-Deer Park mountaintop glades with his wife in 1883. The same year Alexander Graham Bell relaxed for a few weeks at the Oakland Hotel and directed the installation of Garrett County's first telephone service, supervising the erection of a line between the two mountaintop B&O resorts. After the line was strung and the final connections made, the manager of the Oakland Hotel spoke with the manager of the Deer Park Hotel, some five miles distant, in Garrett County's first telephone conversation. "How many guests have you today?" asked the Oakland manager of his Deer Park colleague. The reply? "Seventy-six."

President Grover Cleveland honeymooned at the Number 2 cottage of the Deer Park Hotel with his bride, the former Frances Folsom, in early June 1886. Deer Park resident H. G. Davis noted in his May 22 journal entry that year that the president "sent for me through Colonel Lamont, his private secretary; told me he is to be married early in June, and asked me to arrange so he can go to Deer Park with bride and spend a week. The marriage and place they go is known to very few."

The Clevelands were married June 2 in the White House in Washington; that night they traveled in the private railcar of B&O president Robert Garrett (son of John W.) to the Deer Park retreat. They arrived at the securely guarded Number 2 cottage early in the morning, June 3. Almost immediately piles of telegrams and letters of congratulation began to pour into Deer Park from around the world. Henceforth the retreat would be known as the Spa of Presidents.

H. G. Davis noted the president's stay at Deer Park in his journal entries of June 1886. On Saturday, June 5, he recorded, "President and Mrs. Cleveland went to Bantz at Deep Creek to fish, we caught a fine lot of trout." On Sunday "President and Mrs. Cleveland, Colonel Lamont and Mrs. Lamont, Mrs. Davis and I went to Oakland to church [at the Stone Garrett Memorial Church]." Later the same day "President and Mrs. Cleveland, Colonel Lamont and Mrs. Lamont dine with us at 7 o'clock." On Monday "President and Colonel Lamont, took my mountain wagon to Leeland's place on Deep Creek. Got about fifty trout." On Tuesday, June 8, "President and Mrs. Cleveland, Colonel Lamont, Mrs. Davis, Kate and I drive to [Deer Park] Boiling Spring. At one o'clock President and party left on special train for Washington. President said he had had a very pleasant visit and might return during the summer."

Before leaving Deer Park, Grover Cleveland chatted informally with the local villagers and entertained reporters' questions. He spoke well of the western Maryland mountaintop retreat. "Both myself and Mrs. Cleveland are more than pleased with our visit to Deer Park," he noted. "Of course we expected to have a good time, but so far the pleasure of the visit has far exceeded our most sanguine expectations. . . . I came here to find rest and I am getting it. I never slept better and the air and temperature are simply delicious. . . . I could not have found a more suitable retreat had I searched the United States."

American Roman Catholic Archbishop James Gibbons, renowned as an international diplomat, was vacationing at Deer

Park later in the summer of 1886 when he received notification that Pope Leo XIII had elevated him to the office of cardinal. Gibbons was only the second American in history to receive such an honor; his reception at Deer Park was unequaled in the resort's history.

In August 1887, General and Mrs. Benjamin Harrison spent two weeks of leisure at Deer Park with the H. G. Davis family. The Harrisons returned to the mountaintop two years later, after the general had been elected president of the United States. On this occasion they lived at the hotel's Spencer Cottage. The Davis family entertained the nation's first family with a large dinner party of eighteen guests, August 31, 1889.

The renowned banker and philanthropist, W. W. Corcoran, vacationed at Deer Park in 1892. Four years later William McKinley stopped at the resort during a national tour as part of his presidential campaign. A number of United States senators also visited the resort late in the century for recreation and relaxation. Deer Park boomed as a presidential and political retreat. The late nineteenth century, the Gilded Age—those were the "glory days" of Deer Park, according to village resident Charles A. Jones.

They were also the glory days of Oakland. Rebecca Harding, writing for *Harper's New Monthly Magazine* in 1880, spoke of the Garrett County seat as a "drowsy little village, ramparted about with wooded heights." She spoke of numerous hotels, fashionable Negro waiters, and "women with dresses fresh from New York ... promenading the weedy street past the station."

Six westbound trains, six eastbound B&O trains stopped daily at Oakland in the 1880s. "People coming by train could hire 'rigs' by the day or hour," recorded the local Dennis T. Rasche in 1955. "Saddle horses were available too for any who would want them." Liveries prospered; the tourism business boomed.

S. M. Miller opened the Commercial House Hotel on Second Street in Oakland in the last quarter of the nineteenth century; S. L. Boyer opened the Central Hotel on the corner of Second and Alder streets; John Swann opened The

Rest on the corner of Alder and Seventh; John T. Browning reopened the Browning House (first established by Richard T. Browning in the seventies). In 1895 Percy Proctor, of Cincinnati's Procter and Gamble Corporation, built Surmount, a large private Oakland home later opened as a boardinghouse. A Dr. King of Washington, D.C., built the Monte Vista summer resort just south of Oakland prior to 1897. Around 1901 Joseph M. Conneway capitalized on the Oakland tourist business by building the twenty-one room Conneway restaurant and retreat on the southern slope of Backbone Mountain. (Joseph Lincoln, a first cousin of Abraham Lincoln, lived his last years and died in the Conneway House.)

The Baltimore and Ohio's *Book of the Royal Blue* depicted Oakland in 1899 as "a little city with a regular population of 1,500 people . . . a thriving little town. It contains many beautiful homes and is most picturesque. There are innumerable lovely private cottages in the neighborhood of Oakland owned by residents of distant cities, notably: Cincinnati, Baltimore and Washington. These cottages are occupied every summer, and their owners claim the climate is the most beautiful to be found."

On February 16, 1899, the *Mountain Democrat* of Oakland, commenting on the area's expanding tourist business, noted that "it certainly does look strange to see lights in the windows of the Oakland Hotel at this time in the year. This is the first time in the history of the hotel that it has not been dark through the entire winter."

The late nineteenth century "glory days" of Oakland and Deer Park lasted for approximately half a century. They became memories with the development of the automobile in the early twentieth century, though, and finally ended with the Great Depression of the 1930s. But they were glory days indeed for the leisure class railroad set of the late nineteenth century. Rebecca Harding, writing for *Harper's New Monthly Magazine* in 1880, noted that the seven-year-old Deer Park Hotel was at that time already fast becoming "a favorite mountain resort for fashionable people from Baltimore, Cumberland and Wheeling." She described the hotel and its surroundings in an article entitled "By-Paths in the Mountains." "Deer Park," she wrote, "is a hotel perched on a lofty plateau . . . surrounded by a few picturesque cottages. . . . The far-off peaks [are] hooded in clouds, and rivers of gray mist [sweep] through the valleys. . . . Inside [are] found brilliantly lighted rooms, a corps of white-cravatted negro servants, elegantly dressed women, pianos, art, needlework, and gossip."

Glory days, memories. Western Maryland historian J. Thomas Scharf wrote in 1882 that the Deer Park Hotel "is situated on the slope of one of the prettiest valleys on the summit of the mountain, and faces to the southeast, having a background of heavy timber. The valley sloped down to a beautiful meadow, through which the railroad runs. The opposite slope has been cleared of all undergrowth, leaving only stately oaks scattered here and there to the distant summit, where earth and sky seem to meet, and about which the clouds often gather and expand themselves in those sudden summer storms—always grand and beautiful as seen from the hotel—which preserve the continual freshness and verdure of the hills and valleys. Nearly all the land in the neighborhood has been cleared of timber, but the woods in the rear of the hotel is carefully preserved by the railroad company, and is one of the special attractions of the spot. . . . Flocks of sheep and herds of cattle add pastoral beauty to the scene."

Glory days, memories. J. G. Pangborn, *Picturesque B. and O.*, 1883: "[Deer Park-Oakland] is less than twenty-four hours' ride [from] Chicago or St. Louis; and leaving Cincinnati in the evening, breakfast is taken on top of the Alleghenies. So, too, from New York and Philadelphia, as it is only a single night's ride from either of these cities, and from Baltimore and Washington but the matter of eight or nine hours. . . . The [B. & O.] company has expanded money with almost prodigal hand on these two resorts, improvements and additions having been completed which have doubled their capacity and met every requirement. . . . So popular are these houses that heretofore only those who came at the commencement of the season were certain of entertainment, and it was not an infrequent occurrence, prior to the enlargement, to decline the reception of more guests that the house contained. The reputation of the culinary department is such that heads of families who can spend only Sundays with their families at the resorts look forward to their brief visit with as keen anticipations of the good things for the inner man as of those for the outer man.... Every room at both resorts is carpeted and provided with furniture of the most substantial character, in designs pleasing to the eye and meeting all the requirements of practical use....

"Patrons may take their choice of location," noted Pangborn. "Should one desire to be out upon the open mountain, with an unobstructed view of many miles' extent, and with more country rambles than he can ever make in a stay of reasonable length, he may stop at Deer Park. On the other hand, if it pleases him best to be quartered where noble old trees cast over him their protecting shade; if he loves to sit where his eyes can roam down through clustering foliage, affording here and there glimpses of clear and sparkling streams, alighting presently upon the snug and peaceful village of stores and churches and cozy homes, then he will go to Oakland. Perchance he may prefer a variety, spending a portion of his time at the one place and a portion at the other. In such a case the wish need be no more than father to the accomplishment. A fine road connects the two resorts, affording a taste of mountain driving and valley speeding, with the only regret that it is not double the distance. During the season it is almost a boulevard, presenting as it does all the animated appearance of a fashionable drive. Many of the guests having their own equipages make daily trips backward and forward. Others not so provided are afforded ample privileges to enjoy their liking for a splendid drive, as the livery facilities are all that the most exacting could wish for.... In so wide and varied an extent of country as the Glades one may find new delights every day of the season....

"The character of the guests at Oakland and Deer Park has since the opening of the resorts been strictly of the highest order. The old aristocratic families of Baltimore, Washington and Philadelphia have for many seasons spent the summer in the Glades of the Alleghenies, and of late years western people have become attached to the locality, and not a few of the best-known families regularly make the season at Deer Park or else at Oakland. The result is that the social aspect at either of those places corresponds with that which is found at only a few of the summer resorts, and the friendships established during the season very often last for life. . . .

"An important characteristic of the Glades," noted Pangborn, "is the first-class facility for hunting, game being abundant in the vicinity. It is no uncommon thing to meet, in the office or halls of either Deer Park or Oakland, gentlemen attired in flannel shirts, closely-belted blouses and high-top boots, their ruddy complexions and springy step denoting recuperated powers and perfect health. . . . The fishing is on a par with the hunting, the strings of trout sent back being not infrequently of such dimensions as to warrant the introduction of the delicacy upon the hotel bill of fare."

Oakland, Deer Park—glory days, memories. The management itself of the Deer Park Hotel in 1897 boasted of the resort's "delightful atmosphere during both day and night, pure water, smooth winding roads . . . cricket grounds, ball grounds, golf links, tennis courts, and the most picturesque scenery in the Allegheny range." The Baltimore and Ohio's 1899 *Book of the Royal Blue* billed the retreat succinctly as "the most beautiful resort in the Alleginies," and boasted that "were Deer Park desirable for no other reason, it would be for its most delightful air and water. Nature supplements what men supplied by such surroundings as would render existence in a log cabin a delight. The absolute purity of the air is like invisible champagne to the lungs; it brings roses to the cheek of the invalid, strength and health to the weak and over-worked brain and body. . . . The hotel is supplied with every conceivable modern appliance for the convenience of its guests. In fact, there is nothing omitted which is necessary to the taste of the most fastidious person, notwithstanding its isolation on top of a mountain. It is a city in itself, provided with its own gas and electric plants and water system. . . . The famous 'Boiling Spring,' which supplies water to Deer Park, is a short distance from the hotel. . . . Vehicles of all kinds can be furnished, from a dog cart to a tally-ho, and good horses are available for either driving or riding.... A well laid out nine-link golf course will be a feature of the coming season. The morning band concerts and evening hop at the hotel are not to be overlooked."

J. G. Pangborn wrote of daily music concerts at Deer Park as early as 1883. In 1892 Professor Charles A. Zimmerman, director of the Naval Academy Band at Annapolis and composer of the popular "Anchor's Aweigh," began providing summer entertainment—waltz music, afternoon outdoor concerts—at the Deer Park Hotel each summer for a period of fifteen years. From 1895 until 1898 he also directed a small orchestra each summer at the Oakland Hotel. During this period he often combined his Deer Park and Oakland bands for special music productions and holiday entertainment.

Glory days, memories. A 1900 correspondent for the *Baltimore Sun* spoke well of the "comfortable and well-appointed folk who loaf luxuriously and cultivate the delights of an elegant ease and idleness on the porches" of western Maryland's highland resorts. Garrett County historian Felix G. Robinson wrote similarly in 1962 of the "exclusive social coterie" of Oakland and Deer Park in the late 1800s, and recalled that "from the start [the area] became one of the most exclusive summer colonies of that era. Its smart set was composed of industrial tycoons who knew how to persuade a President of the United States to board a train and in five hours, having escaped the sweltering heat of Washington, be comfortably seated on his front porch enjoying the mountain zephyrs."

Glory days, memories. Charles A. Jones, the young son of a Deer Park storekeeper in the 1890s, recalled years later that "the coming of the trains was a notable event in the village life. We enjoyed seeing the postal officials hang up the mail bags to be snatched by the 'big trains' and watching the arriving bags tossed out to roll in the dirt.... But the big train days were in the spring when the 'summer people' arrived, bringing what seemed to the normal citizens a momentous quantity of desirable goods.... The spuzzy carriages of the visitors were always a feature, with their gaily attired coachmen and footmen. Trips to Swallow Falls, Table

Rock, Eagle Rock, the Boiling Spring or to the county seat at Oakland were daily occurances.... After bicycles came to us, some of us boys developed the game of waiting until the 'big trains' were rolling through the village and then, jumping on our wheels, we would endeavor to get to the hotel station in time to put letters on the trains before they departed, which they usually did rather quickly."

Charles A. Jones wrote convincingly of the contrast between the year-round Garrett County mountain folk and their summer visitors. "The sputtering electric arc lights, from which we obtained discarded carbon 'candles,' " he recorded, "were the peer of any similar lighting in that region. The golf course [at Deer Park] furnished employment for village boys as caddies. Those who could not caddy were envious because of the spending money their playmates had. No villager thought of playing the game then; it was strictly for the rich."

And again: "One of my village associates, Earl Browning, obtained a position as coachman for one of the Watson families from Fairmont, W. Va. We asked him if we should speak to him, should he drive by in one of those splendid carriages. He took a day to find out and then said we were not to do so."

"Spuzzy carriages," "mountain promenades," "white-cravatted negro servants," "flocks of sheep and herds of cattle," "country rambles," "old aristocratic families," "gentlemen attired in flannel shirts," "delightful atmosphere," "invisible champagne," "dog-carts" and "tally-hos," "comfortable and well-appointed folk," "smart set," "industrial tycoons," "United States Presidents," "mountain zephyrs"—the Gilded Age. Deer Park, Oakland, glory days, memories. They lasted until the early twentieth century when the automobile innovation of Henry Ford began altering people's vacation habits, putting them on wheels and roads rather than trains and rails in pursuit of summertime pleasure. One of the last "glory days" visitors of note to the western Maryland mountaintop summertime playground was Mrs. Theodore Roosevelt, wife of the nation's president, and her son, Theodore, Jr., accompanied by the national conservationist

Gifford Pinchot. The party arrived in Oakland by train in early May 1902, and spent a weekend at the home of Gus W. Delawder, on Deep Creek, near McHenry.

The glory days of Oakland and Deer Park as renowned summer resorts—as the "Spa of Presidents"—lasted until the early years of the twentieth century and evaporated into memory with the advent of the Great Depression. The B&O Oakland Hotel was dismantled in 1911; its furnishings were sold at public auction. An Oakland newspaper article of October 8, 1908, revealed that "every public spirited citizen heaves a sigh of regret when he sees the historic old Glades Hotel being torn down." The Glades, having been unoccupied for several years, was dismantled that year for its lumber value.

The Baltimore and Ohio Company discontinued direct management of the Deer Park Hotel in 1910. The hotel's 1929 owner, Henry S. Duncan, lost title to the resort in the stock market crash of that year, and the resort itself never reopened after the 1929 season. A *Baltimore Sun* correspondent of 1941 reported that the Deer Park buildings had been boarded up, its grounds had been overgrown with weeds, its cottages had been abandoned. Local historian Felix Robinson wrote of Deer Park's "vacated mansions haunted by the most agreeable ghosts." The Deer Park Hotel was finally dismantled for lumber in 1944.

"The 'Glory Days' were over," noted Deer Park's Charles A. Jones, recalling the decline of the mountain resorts. "The Baltimore and Ohio very kindly stopped No. 1 to pick me up many times after [the train ceased making regular stops at Deer Park when] I lived elsewhere and returned to visit my parents. We would wait until we heard the train whistle at Altamont. Then Father and I would walk down to the beginning of the Hotel Station grounds. We would hear the sound of the train as it left Altamont, then all would become silent. In a moment or so, the headlight flashed upon us as the train came around the bend. . . . We would see the light stream out of the gateway. The train would draw up to where we were standing and a porter would get off with a step. I would shake hands with Father, step up into the car and the train would whirl on in the darkness, leaving him standing there watching it and thinking about us who had gone from Deer Park."

Oakland, Deer Park—glory days, memories.

The late nineteenth century glory days of Oakland and Deer Park were the glory days, also, of two new and unique Garrett County towns founded during the railroad resort days along the Baltimore and Ohio tracks in the Little Youghiogheny Glades just east of Oakland—Loch Lynn Heights and Mountain Lake Park. Both towns were organized chiefly as speculative land and resort enterprises; both were born of the late nineteenth century railroad resort mania.

Of the two neighboring towns, Mountain Lake Park was organized first—in 1881. In September of that year the Reverend J. M. Davis of Oakland, accompanied by four Wheeling, West Virginia, associates—Rev. C. P. Masden, E. W. Ryan, J. C. Alderson, and W. C. Snodgrass—rode by horseback east from Oakland to an open range area called Hoye's Big Pasture, "looking for suitable grounds to establish a summer resort founded upon Christian principles and designed to afford opportunities for religious and literary instruction and healthful recreation." All five men were Methodists. They liked the land they saw, and with Methodist friends they soon incorporated the Mountain Lake Park Association under Maryland regulations and bought 763 acres of Hoye's Big Pasture. Two of the incorporators—the Reverend John F. Goucher, and the Reverend John B. VanMeter—had been associated previously with the establishment of the Woman's College of Baltimore, later to be known as Goucher College.

The Mountain Lake Park incorporators of 1881 hired H. E. Faul, the Baltimore engineer who had designed that city's Druid Hill Park, to survey and plat the Mountain Lake Park grounds. They drew up regulations "regarding a due observance of the Sabbath day" in the park, and prohibited "the buying, selling, or using intoxicating liquor as a beverage, card playing, dancing and all immoral practices" there. They contracted with the Baltimore and Ohio for the establishment of a rail station near the Park, reserving the right to forbid Sunday train stops. On November 1, 1881, they authorized a special rail excursion to the park for the first public sale of lots. "A goodly number of lots were sold," according to a later corporation report.

The Mountain Lake Park Association was organized in late 1881 for the establishment of a "Religious and Educational Summer Resort" in the glade lands between Oakland and Deer Park. In 1882 the park's incorporators began construction of Mountain Lake Park's first public buildings. First they built a tabernacle, later an assembly hall (the Mountain Lake Park Auditorium, fifty feet by eighty feet in size), a restaurant, a store, a hotel (the Mountain Lake Park Hotel), a dam across Broad Ford Run, and an icehouse with a storage capacity of four hundred tons. The incorporators also initiated annual summer public programs at the Park in 1882, beginning with a religious camp meeting held in July under the direction of the Reverend Charles P. Masden, of Wheeling, accompanied by the railroad worker evangelist Jennie Smith and the Philadelphia Quaker, the Reverend John Thompson, of the *Christian Standard.* In August the park incorporators authorized the first session of the Mountain Sunday School Assembly, an annual production later developed and billed as the Mountain Chautauqua under the direction of the Reverend Wilbur L. Davidson, a leading contemporary Chautauqua director of national reputation. In the meantime, the incorporators continued selling town lots, until by late 1882 all the most desirable lots were labeled either "sold," "hold," or "reserved" for future sales.

In 1883 the Mountain Lake Park Association established a school of photography (conducted for the ensuing twenty summers by a Professor A. A. Line), and built a park office building. It also sold the park hotel that year to a relative of a member of its board of directors. The next year it authorized the Reverend John Thompson, one of its original stockholders known locally as "the Bishop of Mountain Lake," to hold annual Society of Friends camp meetings at the park. In 1885 it authorized the construction of a new assembly building. In 1888 it surrendered its ownership rights of park streets to the new community of Mountain Lake Park, established under Maryland law on July 18 of that year. The following year, encouraged by its successes, the park association "agreed to tender grounds to the Congress of the United States for [the construction of] the President's Summer Mansion" at Mountain Lake Park. Nothing came of the proposal.

The Mountain Lake Park Association, a private, religious, profit-oriented business, the founder of the community of Mountain Lake Park in western Maryland, took wing in the 1880s. For the next two decades it soared. It expanded and diversified its summer programs and cultural events. It erected new and improved buildings to accommodate its growing clientele; it sold more and more lots for summer and year-round housing; it made substantial park grounds improvements.

In 1894 the park association enlarged the Mountain Lake Park Lake to an area covering thirty-five acres of land. It also built a new boathouse that year. "The residents as well as the guests enjoyed swimming in the refreshing and invigorating cold waters of this delightful lake," recalled the local Leona M. Hardesty in 1968. "Boats were constantly ready for those who enjoyed a row in the cool evening beneath the soft moonlight." The association also enlarged the park tabernacle in 1894 to accommodate its expanding crowds of summer worshippers. "Over five hundred chairs were placed in the front of the building," the association recorded in a subsequent report, "and the remaining portion was supplied with new seats."

The Mountain Lake Park Association dedicated a Hall of Philosophy in 1896. Three years later it laid off an athletic field in the park and erected a grandstand. In 1900 it authorized the building of the park's first public golf links. By the turn of the century Mountain Lake Park had become such a popular summer resort that at least nine area hotels—The Mountain Lake Hotel, the Loch Lynn Hotel, the Columbian, the Chautauqua, the Dennett, the Allegany House, the Briar Bend, the Queenwood, and the Braethorn—had been erected nearby for the accommodation of its visitors.

The most popular attraction at Mountain Lake Park at the turn of the century was its annual summer chautauqua, a program featuring guest speakers of national fame, as well as renowned evangelists and musicians. In the spring of 1900 the park association dedicated a new amphitheater—the Bashford Amphitheater—on park grounds for the accommodation of crowds attracted to western Maryland by the chautauqua program. Resembling an inverted umbrella in structure, the auditorium was built of chestnut logs hauled from Backbone Mountain and shingles hewn at the sawmill of George T. Brew in the Shades of Death. Circular, 176 feet in diameter, the Bashford boasted a seating capacity of five thousand. "It is without question one of the finest and best equipped auditoriums in the land," the park association reported in 1902. The *Mountain Democrat* concurred. "The acoustics of the new Auditorium are perfect," it suggested in 1900—"a whisper can be heard in any part of the building. . . . The Auditorium is perfect in every particular and is beyond question the finest outdoor Auditorium of its capacity in the United States. The chief glory of the building is that no posts obstruct a view of the platform."

In 1902 the Mountain Lake Park Association issued a glowing report on the progress of its resort during its first ten years of growth. "The Mt. Lake Hotel has doubled its capacity," it revealed. "Hotel Dennett and Hotel Chautauqua have been enlarged; Hotel Columbia and Mt. View House have been built. The 85 buildings have increased to 200 or more . . . the alder and hazel bushes have about disappeared; the swamps that were almost impassable are now beautiful meadows. The thick forest of brush and trees have become delightful building lots; the cowpaths are no more. In their stead are magnificent roads and driveways. . . . An expenditure of $174,924.34 by the Association and a much larger sum by the community of Mt. Lake Park has made this once valueless and undesirable locality one of the most successful and popular religious summer resorts in the land with possibilities beyond the conception of man."

The association celebrated its "silver jubilee anniversary" on July 11, 1907, with a public reception in the Bashford. "Out of the wilderness of twenty-five years ago," the *Mountian Democrat* observed on the occasion, "has sprung up an ideal summer resort, combining worship and recreation, and giving an uplift to both mind and body."

Special summer programs at Mountain Lake Park around the turn of the century which provided "uplift to both mind and body" included interdenominational camp meetings, a school of liberal arts taught by various college teachers (with course offerings of Greek, Latin, German, French, English, American Literature, Natural Sciences, Mathematics, Music, Elocution, and Oratory), a school of photography, a kindergarten, a school of domestic science, Bible conference, and various other conventions and association activities. The big attraction, though, was the Mountain Chautauqua, under the direction of Wilbur L. Davidson, with its potpourri of nationally known speakers and musical personalities. Lecturers appearing at Mountain Lake Park prior to World War I included such celebrities as William Jennings Bryan, Sam Jones, Samuel Gompers, and William Howard Taft.

Deer Park's Charles A. Jones recalled in 1966 that "the Chautauqua each August gave Garrett County people much wider cultural opportunities than came to many sections of the country. So popular was the annual Chautauqua, in fact," he recalled, that "the excursion days were productive of long special trains on the Baltimore and Ohio. Many of these were crowded to their fullest capacity and it was often difficult to get on them at the stations nearest to Mountain Lake.... More than once I hung on to the lower step from Deer Park to Mountain Lake."

Thirteen Baltimore and Ohio passenger trains stopped daily at Mountain Lake Park throughout the regular summer season at century's turn; even more stopped during the chautauqua season. Each train carried from one to two thousand persons; often each was filled to capacity. The B&O itself encouraged travel to Mountain Lake Park by offering its passengers special ten percent rebates on ticket sales. Chautauqua Week excursion trains began arriving at the park as early as 6:00 a.m.; often they provided departure service as late as 1:00 at night. An Oakland newspaper of the late nineteenth century succinctly described the crowded conditions on chautauqua excursion coaches with the following article:

"The excursion train to Mountain Lake from the east was so badly crowded today that literally hundreds could not find seats. As a result a young woman was seated on the lap of an elderly veteran. They had a nice conversation ending when the young woman stood up at Mountain Lake. She thanked the veteran for his courtesy and added, 'I hope we shall meet again in Heaven.' 'Yes' replied the veteran, 'and I hope the train will again be crowded.'" The article itself created a small sensation.

"When the train arrived with guests," recorded the local Leona M. Hardesty in 1969, "people would flock to the station as a form of entertainment and passtime, greeting the newcomers. The ever-present horse and buggy, and hacks that had three to four seats were there to take people to their lodging places."

"Every morning, afternoon, and evening [of the big week]," recorded West Virginia's Mrs. Lloyd Logan Carr of the Chautauqua in 1898, "the Auditorium was crowded with people listening to the instructive lectures, fine concerts, and good music."

Deer Park's Charles A. Jones noted in 1966 that "the great day each year was 'Grand Army Day,' the closing day. Veterans were admitted free. They had a campfire, serving army fare.... The veterans marched, blue and gray, in alternate companies."

Jones related the following story pertaining to one of the annual GAR Days at Mountain Lake: "One of the speakers was General John B. Gordon [of Georgia] aide to General Robert E. Lee and afterwards United States Senator and Governor, with his fascinating address on 'The Last Days and Nights of the Confederacy.' There was no vacant space before him or around him on the stage. About halfway through his address, a Union veteran decided he must leave the room and the only way out he could see was to go up the steps to the platform and across close to the speaker. When General Gordon saw him coming up the steps he stopped speaking, reached out his hand and helped the veteran up the steps. As he passed, the General said: 'Good bye, Yank. I am sorry to see you going, but there was a day when I wouldn't have been.' The General's quip," Jones recalled, "was met with contagious and friendly laughter."

The Mountain Chautauqua at Mountain Lake Park at the turn of the twentieth century greatly enriched western Maryland culture with its public presentation of national dignitaries, poets, writers, and musicians. It lured thousands to the mountaintop. And through it all the Mountain Lake Park Association held a tight hand over the moral pulse of the growing community through a governing committee composed of five persons, two of whom were selected by the park residents, two by the park association itself, and a fifth selected by the first four or by the association in the event of tie votes. At all times the park association emphasized Methodist-oriented public manners and morals. In 1899 it announced "What Mountain Lake Park Is Not" in an issue of the *Mountain Chautauqua:* "Not a place for expensive dressing and meaningless idling.... Not a place given to social frivolities which enervate, and rob a vacation of its real purpose.... Not a place where hotel keepers get all your earnings of the year.... Not a place where exacting social requirements rob you of your strength, and you end your vacation more of a wreck than when you began." The park association strictly forbade such pastimes as dancing, gambling, card-playing, and drinking.

In spite of its successes, the Mountain Lake Park Association also began to experience some difficulties by the early twentieth century. As early as 1904 association member L. T. Yoder contended that "the Park as a summer resort is standing still ... unless new blood is brought in with brains and money it will soon be a thing of the past. ... The hide-bound laws must be loosened a little. Ones home is his castle and he should govern that household to his liking so far as he does not trample on the laws of God or man. ... Many good Christian people are averse to building in a community with such rigid regulations, and if we expect the Park to grow, they must be framed to meet the reasonable wishes of the people."

The park association was plagued by other problems throughout the first decade of the century. Chautauqua Week was a virtual failure some years due to poor weather. In addition, by 1907, one man—John F. Goucher, president of the Woman's College of Baltimore—owned more than a third of the association's 129 outstanding shares. With a few close associates, Goucher dominated the park association, and he was not the best of executives. The Woman's College was tottering on the brink of bankruptcy when he resigned from his position at its head in 1908. Auditors of park association accounts in 1909 made dreary announcements to association stockholders: "Unable to report on correctness of accounts owing to absence of vouchers . . . checks very indefinite as to purpose for which money was paid out. . . . 'Sundries' frequently entered amounting to hundreds of dollars without any means of ascertaining the particulars . . . books give little light on the financial condition . . . decided change in system of accounting certainly to be desired." Even the president of the park association painted a picture of gloom in 1909: "It is clear there is one of two ends to our present drift unless means be devised to turn the tide, via: BANKRUPTCY OR LIQUIDATION!"

Then in 1911, Wilbur Davidson resigned from his position of summer cultural director and chautauqua leader at the park, and the life began to drain from the park's summer programs. Dr. Goucher suggested the same year that the park be sold "with the definite stipulation that it shall be conducted as a religious, literary, and musical summer resort in harmony with the spirit of its original charter." The local 1958 historian of the park association, Jared W. Young, noted that "those in the saddle were attempting the difficult feat of keeping their cake and eating it too. They had a moribund corporation of which they had failed to make a success, yet wished to cop off a large personal profit on any sale, and at the same time dictate who could purchase, and how they were to operate. . . . That these sale efforts should come to naught was almost a foregone conclusion."

After 1920 the Mountain Lake Park Association searched in vain for summer programs to restore the park to some semblance of its former prestige and popularity. Though it worked with a variety of religious and business oriented groups toward this end, all its efforts seemed doomed to failure. The days of the Mountain Chautauqua—the great railroad excursion days of century's turn—faded rapidly with the advent of World War I, and the summer resort era at Mountain Lake Park vanished.

Citizens of the park in 1931 voted for town incorporation, and, meeting little resistance, succeeded. Then, in 1940, the park association announced the sale of all its remaining properties to a small private religious group engaged in orphanage and religious work. "The Park is Sold Down the River," a *Republican* correspondent bemoaned.

A fire in August 1941 destroyed a major portion of Mountain Lake Park's first building, the tabernacle. The following year the remaining original park association buildings were sold piecemeal to a variety of buyers. In 1968 the long empty shell of the Mountain Lake Hotel was razed. The local historian, Leona M. Hardesty, wrote the following that year: "Old foundation stones of the once great Auditorium [the Bashford], cobwebs in its circular and empty ticket office, a silt-filled lake, and traces of the romantic boardwalk remain to suggest great day's and exciting events." The town of Mountain Lake Park, with its Victorian homes and broad avenues, also lives on as a reminder of the gay nineties and a day when the rail resort business made the mountaintop bloom.

The history of Loch Lynn Heights, Mountain Lake Park's sister town, dates also from 1881, the year the Mountain Lake Park Association was first organized. One of the park association's original incorporators, Major Joseph C. Alderson, bought more than two hundred acres of farmland adjoining the Mountain Lake Park purchase that year. For thirteen years he farmed the land he had bought. Then he developed it.

The Mountain Home Company was organized in 1894. For the next couple of years the company laid out a prospective town on the Alderson farm and sold lots. Mrs. Alderson named the project Loch Lynn Heights. As lots sold, the town was extended to bordering farms. The Loch Lynn Hotel was erected in 1895.

The hotel, across the B&O tracks from the Mountain Lake Park rail station, "had a majestic setting on a knoll overlooking Mountain Lake Park," later recalled one of its contemporaries. "It was a large L-shaped building with a wing on each end. There was a cassino that stood about one hundred and seventy-five to two-hundred feet away from the hotel property. The cassino held a heated swimming pool which was fifteen by forty feet on both sides. There were bowling alleys and billiard tables to provide for ones pastime."

"The Loch Lynn Hotel," according to visitor Nanniene Thomasson Offutt, "was out of bounds for the (neighboring) Chautauqua and catered to an entirely different set of people." It burned to the ground in 1918. The town of Loch Lynn Heights, though, founded in 1894 as a speculative enterprise in the success shadows of Deer Park, Oakland, and Mountain Lake Park as highland rail resorts, incorporated by act of the Maryland legislature in 1896, survived the hotel's demise and continued to grow. Today it flourishes as a small, comfortable, gracefully aging residential community.

The late nineteenth century in America was an age of centralization, an age of diversification. Most of all it was an age of growth, an age of booming capitalization and industrialization. The age in western Maryland began with the construction of the Baltimore and Ohio Railroad over the Alleghenies in 1851. The railroad itself served the period as its most conspicuous symbol. It brought the Civil War to western Maryland. It provided new markets for the exploiters of natural resources and the manufacturers of industrial goods. By century's end it provided Garrett County with three industries around which the county's economy still revolves. It lured coal and timber specialists to the hills. (They founded new towns, laid new rails through once-virgin woods, stripped the land and ravaged the earth.) It encouraged money speculation in summer resorts and mountaintop recreation. It sealed the economic and social destiny of western Maryland for at least fifty years. (It even served as midwife in the birth of Garrett County itself.)

The industrial growth of the United States throughout the late nineteenth century was unprecedented. It was a wild growth, though, almost a presumptuous growth. It was a growth plagued again and again by recurrent repression, depression and doubt.

"During the panic of 1857," Oakland's J. M. Davis recalled in 1906, "my father and I sold several droves of cattle in Eastern Pennsylvania, and as there was no means of transferring funds through banks at that time, we carried home $2,270, which we drew direct from the Lancaster bank.... It required about ten days to reach home and make payment for stock bought to be paid for on return. In the meantime the bank failed and the money was almost a total loss."

Garrett County's namesake, John W. Garrett, was shot at during the rough times of the 1870s when railroad workers went on nationwide strike.

Deer Park's Charles A. Jones recalled the Cleveland Panic of the early 1890s as "a vivid memory" years later. "Thousands of so-called tramps moved along the railroad, asking for food at homes they passed," he recorded in 1966. "Mother kept a record and said that she fed one or more tramps every day for some seven hundred successive days. A part of Coxey's Army passed through our neighborhood out by Broad Ford [in 1894]. For months afterward the piles of straw on which the army had slept were pointed out to travelers along the road."

Grantsville's Ross C. Durst also recalled the tramps of the 1890s years later (in 1966). "They carried their entire worldly possessions in a bandana," he remembered. "They slept in the open or in haystacks wherever night overtook them. For the most part they were harmless, homeless wanderers. A request for a hand-out was never refused.... It was the code of the times never to refuse a hungry man." (Even by 1900 welfare was a thing of the future.)

Grantsville's Jacob Brown blamed the recurrent recessions and busts of the late nineteenth century on the rising capitalists of the age, and he was not alone in his opinions. "The practice is for millionaires to combine and form what they choose to call a trust," he noted in 1896, "assuming a popular and just name to deceive and impose on the many, that the rich few (the trustees) may be made still richer at the expense of the millions. These wicked men are in the habit of combining their vast capital to buy up and get control of articles that everybody must use.... They, by their monopolizing acts, soon become controllers of prices, which they will not allow to be controlled by the laws of trade, or supply and demand.... Monopolies instinctively destroy competition and even production, and then tell you when they have sent up prices that there has been a failure of crop or production. The fact is a great many good people believe that these enormously rich trust people have more power in legislative and governmental affairs than the millions who send their agents to the National Capitol."

In 1896 William Jennings Bryan, "the Great Commoner," championed the rights of "common men" such as Jacob Brown by seeking the office of the presidency and declaring to capitalist businessmen: "You shall not press down upon the brow of labor the crown of thorns; you shall not crucify mankind upon a cross of gold." Bryan demanded implementation of more effective power for the existing Interstate Commerce Commission, stricter enforcement of antitrust laws, establishment of a revenue tariff, and free coinage of silver. The coinage of silver was, indeed, the great issue of his campaign. "The silver question is now about the most lively and interesting national problem undisposed of," Jacob Brown had noted as early as 1886. "Dispense with gold and silver [the Constitution makes twins of them ...] and we will drop from enlightened civilization down to barbarism."

The 1896 campaign of William Jennings Bryan represented nationwide a rising discontent of the populace with the new large-scale capitalists and wasteful industrialists of the late nineteenth century. Among the most discontented of the era were the small-scale, family-oriented farmers. Farmers of the late nineteenth century increasingly felt the pinch in their pocketbooks created by high interest rates, recurrent depressions, unfair rail practices, the competition of large-scale capitalist farming. Beginning in the 1860s, they began organizing farmers' alliances and small-farm organizations to champion their interests. One Maryland historian of the late nineteenth century farmers' movement, Mary Jenkins, noted in 1974 that "the extent of the helplessness and discouragement of the farmer [of those times] can hardly be understood today. The rapid advancement of industry and the production of farm machinery that followed the Civil War changed the occupation of farming from self sufficiency to growing cash crops. This change required each farmer to be an efficient businessman as well as an efficient farmer, a complex job for which he was not trained. The cards were stacked against him. And to top it all off, the farmer and his family had little opportunity for social life. There was an urgent need for something which would 'educate and elevate the farmer.' That's why Oliver Hudson Kelly thought of a fraternal order for farmers."

Oliver Kelly and six associates organized the Patrons of Husbandry for discontented farmers in 1866. The following year he helped found the National Grange of the Patrons of Husbandry. By 1874, when the Maryland State Grange was organized, the national organization boasted a membership of nearly twelve thousand locals. On April 7, 1875, the first Garrett County local Grange—Cherry Creek No. 144—was organized. McHenry and Oakland locals were established in 1876. "Memberships in the Grange skyrocketed," Mary Jenkins believed, "because farmers found, for the first time, a national organization that would help them overcome their economic and social disadvantages." Among the 1874 declared purposes and goals of the Maryland State Grange itself was the promise to "advance the cause of education among ourselves, and for our children, by all just means within our power." Garrett County farmers, like farmers nationwide in the late nineteenth century, included the goal of self-education among their top priorities.

In the late 1880s and early 1890s some of these farmers joined discontented laborers and small businessmen in support of a major third political party—the Populists. Populists across the nation denounced unregulated concentration of industrial and business wealth and strongly advocated such programs as postal savings banks, the secret ballot, initiative and referendum, a graduated income tax, the confiscation of lands held by corporations and railroads in excess of their actual needs, civil service reforms, government ownership of railroads and telegraph and telephone services, and the free and unlimited coinage of gold and silver at a legal ratio of "sixteen to one." In 1896 the discontents of the day turned their support to William Jennings Bryan.

Deer Park, as well as other Garrett County communities, "had its share of the rousing McKinley-Bryan presidential campaign of 1896," recalled Charles A. Jones in 1966. "Silver and gold hats, silver and gold bug badges were in abundance. Never did men argue more about the issues involved. One night when I went to bed, four men were standing on the porch of the postoffice talking about 'sixteen to one,' etc. When I awoke the next morning they were still there. They had argued all night. Mr. Bryan's campaign party went west [through Deer Park] one morning about one o'clock. Although everyone knew the train would be traveling fifty miles an hour and there would be no glimpses of Mr. Bryan, fifty people, or more, were at the station yelling as the train went through."

Garrett County voted for William McKinley in 1896. William Jennings Bryan lost the election on a national level. His ideas of governmental reform in a growing, capitalistic, industrial society survived, though. They formed the core of the progressive spirit which swept the nation in the early twentieth century under the administrations of Theodore Roosevelt and Woodrow Wilson. They survived and triumphed, also, in Garrett County. (Their local resurgence and influence is explored in the following chapter.)

The late nineteenth century in America was an era of centraliziation, diversification, industrialization. Throughout the era Garrett County grew. She grew from a county of crude backwoods settlements and small self-sufficient farms to a county of coal towns, timber towns, resort towns, trade towns, and increasingly fertile fields and meadows. She grew from a county of barely ten thousand residents in 1872 to a county of over seventeen thousand residents by 1900. She grew from an isolated mountain region of unbroken woods and glades to a county pierced by an ever increasing patchwork of dirt roads and steel rails. Throughout the industrial era of the late nineteenth century, Garrett County grew.

In 1872, when Garrett County was formed, residents of the mountaintop could subscribe to only one local newspaper, the *Glade Star*. Within the next three decades, six more newspapers appeared in the county—the *Garrett County Herald* (1873), the *Republican Ensign* (1874), the *Republican* (1877), the *Mountain Democrat* (1878), the *American Star* (1897), the *Weekly Press* (1895), and the *Garrett Journal* (1897). Most of these publications, like the *Glade Star,* produced issues for only a few years. All, except the bi-monthly *American Star* of Bloomington, were headquartered in Oakland. Only two, the *Republican* and the *Mountain Democrat,* survived until the twentieth century. All, though, reflected county growth and strong feelings of local identification with that growth. (Only one of the seven nineteenth century Garrett publications, the *Republican,* is in print today. Its continued record of publication by the Sincell family since 1890 ensures its prestige as Oakland's longest-enduring private enterprise except for the Shirer Tin Shop, which was established eleven years earlier, in 1866.)

In 1872, when Garrett County was formed, residents of the mountaintop had no local banks at which to conduct their business. Then, in 1888, a group of local businessmen organized the Garrett County Bank, later known as the Garrett National Bank of Oakland. The bank opened with original assets of thirty-five thousand dollars; George W. Legge was its first director. The *Mountain Democrat* wholeheartedly supported the pioneer effort. "This town [Oakland] has ever since the county seat was established here, felt the need of banking facilities," it editorially noted in November 1888. "There are very few towns in the United States where so much business is done without a bank. Especially has this need been severely felt in the summer season when the town is filled with strangers.... Now that a bank has been organized and put in operation, let the merchants and others keeping bank accounts make their deposits at home."

The county was rapidly growing when the Garrett County Bank was established in 1888; the bank itself was soon a success. A second county bank, the First National Bank of Oakland, was organized twelve years later, in 1900. U. G. Palmer, secretary-treasurer of the Hutton Tannery, was its principal founder. A third county bank, the First National Bank of Kitzmillerville, was established under R. A. Smith in 1906.

In 1872, when Garrett County was formed, residents of the mountaintop could seek legal advice only from Cumberland-based attorneys-at-law. By 1895 more than a dozen lawyers resided in Oakland.

In 1872, when Garrett County was formed, residents of the mountaintop relied on a mere handful of doctors for medical assistance. More and more doctors—most of the "horse-and-buggy" type—located in the county after it attained political autonomy. (Some were retained by coal and timber companies for the care of their employees.) Then, on November 24, 1898, the *Mountain Democrat* took "pleasure in making the announcement that Dr. H. W. McComas has perfected arrangements for the opening of a private sanitarium in Oakland. . . . The establishment of this institution . . . is a step in the right direction and will furnish means of taking care of the sick never before existing here, as the sanitarium will be provided with the best of modern appliances and supplied with every facility necessary for the proper and scientific treatment of invalids, including that of an adequate and well-trained corps of nurses." The McComas Sanitarium was the mountaintop's first public health center.

In 1872, when Garrett County was formed, residents of the mountaintop relied solely on word-of-mouth and the United States mail for communication with the outside world. The railroad brought the telegraph line to western Maryland, though, and forty years after Samuel Morse installed his first telegraph line along the Baltimore-Washington tracks of the B&O in 1844, the first Oakland-based telegraph message was sent from the B&O station in Oakland to Baltimore. The year was 1884; the message sender was Patrick Garrett. By the end of the century Western Union telegraph stations had been established at Oakland, Mountain Lake Park, Deer Park, and Altamont.

When Garrett County was formed in 1872, residents of the mountaintop heated and lighted their homes almost exclusively with wood burning stoves, fireplaces, and candles. Recalling his childhood, Ross C. Durst of Grantsville noted in 1967 that he had "missed the candle-light era by one generation. All illumination (by the 1890s) was by 'coal oil' (kerosine) lamps and lanterns." Durst also recalled that by the nineties coal had replaced cordwood in his family's stoves.

In 1876 the town government of Oakland employed George Loughridge to light the town's coaloil lamps each evening at sundown. Charles A. Jones recorded in 1966 that "one of the most familiar figures [at Deer Park around the turn of the century] was the gruff but kindly old Union veteran, George Marley. Every evening he went around the town, trimmed the wicks, put oil in the street lamps, and lit them." Kerosine was used for both home and public lighting in America's industrializing era. Then, in the late 1880s, electricity became available in Oakland for the first time from sunset until midnight. (Oakland was the first town in Maryland to provide itself with such service.) The town's small powerhouse was located behind the railroad station. Electric lighting was introduced at Mountain Lake Park from the Oakland plant in 1895. The park established its own electric plant near Broad Ford Run in 1898. The Deer Park Hotel featured its own generator for lighting until the early 1920s. Around 1895 Leslie E. Friend repaired the old race of the Youghiogheny Iron Company forge and foundry at Friendsville and installed a small power plant for production of electricity in Garrett's oldest organized settlement.

In 1872, when the county was formed, residents of its seat of government, Oakland, walked on streets of dirt and sidewalks of gravel. By 1884 they walked on sidewalks of plank—boardwalks. In 1899 a contractor paved Alder Street with bricks. A 1900 Oakland news article noted that the county seat featured "paved streets of vitrified brick, elegant sidewalks, electric lights . . . banks and massive stores."

When Garrett County was formed in 1872, residents of the mountaintop sent their three thousand school-age children to fifty-seven schools taught by seventy-six teachers. School authorities in 1877 declared that "an average attendance of fifteen pupils shall be reckoned a school." New one-room schools were established throughout the county as its population grew. Garrett boasted 83 community school houses in 1880, 98 in 1889, 120 in 1895, and 133 in 1903.

Each Garrett County school in the late nineteenth century was governed by a local board of trustees elected by local residents. Trustees were responsible to a three-man county board of school commissioners selected by the circuit court prior to 1888; by the state governor thereafter. The commissioners themselves appointed the county's presiding school system secretary-examiner.

Late nineteenth century Garrett County teachers were usually appointed to their positions by the local boards of trustees, with the approval of the county board of school commissioners. Often they were poorly educated and overworked. Often they boarded with the parents of their students. More often than not, they were underpaid. (The average Garrett teacher salary as late as 1904 was only $157 per year.)

Leo J. Beachy taught at the Merrill School in Elk Lick Run in the 1890s. "This, my first experience tutoring in this large old cabin in a deep, narrow, lonely ravine were the most sere hours ever passed in my life," he later recalled. "My school opened with a membership of six children. The youngest was a boy of five, the oldest a girl of nineteen. The boys and girls were very kind [but] I could in no way help feeling unusually forlorn in my large old school house, used for a church at times, with its broken stove, its long benches and no desks. The badly worn floor allowed you to see out of doors through cracks in the boards. The wind sang me a sad song under the high pillars and I looked forward to suffering from the cold."

Ross C. Durst, 1967: "If the enrollment was large and all grades represented [in late nineteenth century Garrett County schools], the teacher had to rush through the work like mad in order to hear all the classes. Each class was allotted 10 or 15 minutes. The first graders fared worst of all, with two or three recitations per day. The rest of the day they had to entertain themselves as best they could—usually drawing pictures of the teacher. The Fifth Reader was about as far as the average student ever reached. Dropouts were frequent, as they were needed to help with the farmwork. The girls were allowed to remain longer than the boys, as they were not needed for farmwork."

Garrett County schools in the late nineteenth century, despite the county's overall growth, were plagued almost continuously by inadequate funding, poor teacher preparation, administrative conflicts, public scandal, and short terms. In 1875 the Garrett County School Board reduced the yearly school term from its previous seven and a half months to five months. (The five-month term remained in effect until 1905.) Two years later the county was rocked with scandals of School Board misuse of public funds. (Investigations failed to substantiate the charges.) An 1888 school board administrative conflict was solved only by resort to the Circuit Court of Appeals. (Jacob Brown, 1888: "The frequent remark here [Avilton] is 'why don't the double headed school board quit wasting the people's money in factious lawsuits?'") Garrett County schools in 1895 remained open a mere one and a half months due to a school board controversy over the construction of new buildings. (The schools closed when the board authorized construction of the Oakland Elementary School in lieu of a proposed public bond sale.) A conflict between incoming and outgoing Garrett County School Boards in 1900 again required circuit court intervention in county education matters.

Ross C. Durst, 1967: "Teachers [in the late 1800's] were judged by their ability to maintain order more than by their teaching ability. The large boys sometimes made life so miserable that the teacher gave up in despair."

Daniel P. Smouse (Grantsville), 1964: "Normal schools, held at various places in the county [in the late 1800's], were nothing more than cramming sessions for teachers and would-be teachers, in preparation for taking the examination that was given each year by the School Examiner. Regardless of the number of years that you had taught school in the county it was imperative that you take this examination [unless you held a diploma from some recognized educational institution] as, having taken and passed it, you were given a one year license, known as a Teacher's Certificate, showing that you had qualified as a teacher in Garrett County Public Schools. [Normal Schools, held at different county locations for a few weeks each summer] were rat races. I figured these examinations were just a sneaky way the School Board had of finding out how many applicants they would have for teaching jobs. Very few if any [applicants] ever failed to pass or get a certificate. Being a girl who had attained the age of 18 years or a boy of 19 years was the paramount requirement." (Married women were denied teaching positions at the time.)

Despite the county's overall late nineteenth century growth, the Garrett County school system of the late 1800s was periodically plagued by inadequate funding, poor teacher preparation, administrative conflicts, public scandal, and short terms.

When the county was organized in 1872, residents of the mountaintop attended a variety of churches of the Christian religion: Amish, Mennonite, Lutheran, Roman Catholic, Baptist, Presbyterian, Methodist, Episcopalian, and Brethren. Religion continued to be an important aspect of their lives throughout the century in spite of the nation's industrialization, and by 1900 they had built more than a score of new church buildings in the hill and glade country of western Maryland.

Oakland Methodists had built a church in 1852 on a lot donated by Edward McCarty. Oakland Lutherans built one in 1854; Oakland Episcopalians built one in 1874; Deer Park Catholics, Methodists, Presbyterians, and Brethren built a common meetinghouse—the Union Church—in 1873; Grantsville Lutherans built a church in 1874; McKenzie-Garlitz neighborhood Catholics on the National Road built one in 1874; Friendsville Methodists built one in 1879; Reformed and Methodist congregations each erected houses of worship at New Germany in the late 1870s.

By the 1880s Methodists, Brethren, and Amish had built churches near Grantsville. Also in the eighties, Methodists erected a church building at Selbysport (1882), Lutherans built one at Deer Park (1883), Mennonites erected one at Pleasant Valley (1886), Methodists built one at Kitzmiller (1887), Brethren built one at Swallow Falls (1888) and another near Accident (1889). Catholics and Brethren at Avilton had also erected meetinghouses by the late eighties.

In the 1890s, Methodists built a new church at Oakland (1891), Catholics built one on the National Road (1890), Lutherans built one in Accident (1895), Methodists and Brethren built a joint structure at Crellin (1896), and Union Congregationalists erected an interdenominational church at Gortner (1898). (This list of late nineteenth century Garrett County church construction is by no means complete. It does, however, substantiate the contention that religion continued to exert a major influence in the lives of county residents throughout the era.)

And what of social life and entertainment in Garrett County in these days—the "roaring eighties," the "gay nineties"?

C. C. Gnegy (1970): "Country school and community life offered much in entertainment and cultural development for us. There were games for growing youngsters, spelling bees, cyphering contests and debates. A debating society was organized at Horse Shoe Run School that met for many years on Friday evenings and was attended by large crowds. As a boy I [also remember] swimming in the Youghiogheny River where many excellent swimming pools had been gouged out from the practice of floating sawlogs to the Crellin mill."

Jacob Brown (1892): "A desire to see kindred and some old friends brought us to the vicinity of New Germany quite recently and [we] found the neighbors all anxious and busy in arranging for a picnic to be held on the 1st of July at the 'twin churches' [Reformed and Methodist]. The music, vocal and instrumental, the church organ being utilized, was very good. The choirs of the two churches sang as a unit and showed the effects of training and practice. The edibles were abundant; choice and of variety, indeed more like a banquet than a picnic. We had the satisfaction of greeting a number of old friends and acquaintances, and many young ones."

Bessie Ward Hinebaugh (1963): "Such good times as the young people had in dear old Oakland those days! What parties and dances they had! Usually a crowd of young people would pile into a big hay wagon and go to dances [or a sled in winter time]. They would drive to someone's home they knew in the country, taking their fiddles. It made no difference if the people knew they were coming or not. At one particular place, the people had gone to bed, but they were hailed with delight, and the family 'got up' and up came the carpets and rugs, and dancing began."

Dennis Rasche (1955): "The 'hay ride' was a firmly established tradition among the youthful. The liveryman furnished a team of horses. A dozen or more of boys and girls would take their places, and to the merry sound of jingling bells and joyous songs go hurtling along some snow-covered road at the headlong speed of nine or ten miles an hour. Mayhap some boy held some girl's hand.

"Nearly everybody then liked and admired a nice horse. Occasionally some unknown 'turn out' came into town, maybe a shiny new surrey drawn by a pair of spirited and well-groomed bays. This would excite as much attention as a jet plane circling at a low altitude over a town now does. That youthful gallant whose parents were affluent enough to provide him with a good trotter and a rubber-tired runabout enjoyed a favored social status, and an undue share of the smiles of the wasp-waisted, balloon-sleeved charmers of the time."

Charles A. Jones, 1966: "The great snows, with drifts in the upper part of the town [Deer Park] almost as high as houses, were almost a yearly occurrence. I recall days when the railroad trains could not get through. The chief sport of the snowy days was sled riding. The streets were relatively clear of horses, especially in the winter time. We would pour water over the street just before sundown. Then, later, we would take our sleds up near the Union Church, shoot down across the groove, jump the ditch and speed down the street. At night the larger boys would take part of a lumber bobsled, of considerable size, load it with ten or fifteen persons and go down the street at great speed, whooping and yelling.

"In my boyhood days, soldiers of the Civil War were in the height of their manhood days, filled with reminiscences of the 'Glory Days' in which they had participated. Men of both armies lived in and around Deer Park. On winter nights, as they gathered in the stores, often they ranged on the two sides of the counter, drawing maps of battles on sheets of wrapping paper torn off the rolls, and exchanging vivid reminiscences. The great clubrooms for men of the village were the stores. Almost nightly ten to twenty men gathered in each store to recite the incidents of the day and the stories they had heard. There was no limit to the type of stories that were related, nor to the tobacco smoke.

"There are memories of the election nights when there were big bonfires over local results, once a dry victory, once a wet one; the temperance parade, with all of us youngsters in line, gaily attired with a sash, and marching to war with lath swords equipped with tin points."

Garrett Countians of the late nineteenth century entertained themselves with political campaigns, school and church functions, horse talk, hayrides, sleighrides, dances, and storeroom gatherings. Timber and coal towns organized local bands and ball teams. Fiddlers' contests were common. Traveling shows were regarded as special treats.

"One day just as school let out," Ross C. Durst recalled in 1967 of his New Germany childhood, "a stranger appeared with a bear on a leash. Having no music box, the man sang a strange, weird song, an unintelligible chant. The bear shuffled about in an upright position in a crude imitation of a waltz. Since most of the children never had seen a real live bear, a dancing bear created quite a sensation and a conversation topic for months. When the supply of coins dried up, the stranger and the bear disappeared as mysteriously as they had appeared. Presumably they had walked all the way from old National Pike, a distance of four miles, but no one ever really knew whence they came or whither they went."

Deer Park's Charles A. Jones recalled in 1966 a "marked day" of his childhood which "began with the arrival of the eastbound accommodation. A stranger emerged from the smoker, came up to our store, opened a case and proceeded to set up a machine and its fixtures. Then he motioned for us youngsters to gather around and gave us long rubber tubes to put into our ears. A second later came the sounds of music and other features. It was Deer Park's introduction to the new talking machine—the graphophone. After the 'sample' we were charged a penny a number, and the business was rushing."

A four-ring circus arrived by rail in Oakland in 1889. Ten years later, John H. Sparks' New Railroad Show and Trained Animal Exposition, billed as the "largest, grandest and best 25 cent show on the road," exhibited in the county seat. Traveling railroad shows in those days were anticipated with great enthusiasm.

The late nineteenth century in America was an age of industrialization, an age of centralization, an age of diversification, an age of booming capitalism. The B&O Railroad brought all four major influences of the age to the mountaintop of Garrett County. Jacob Brown referred to the late years of the century as "exquisite times."

Years later Ross C. Durst offered a different view. "The early 1890s," he noted in 1968, "is often referred to as 'The Gay Nineties.' I do not recall much gayety in Garrett County. The county was young and backward and debt-ridden. Country living had not changed significantly since the days of the early colonies." Durst spoke succinctly for the farmer of the era.

Nevertheless, gay times or not, the late nineteenth century in America was a time of substantial and exciting social and economic change. Through it all Garrett County grew. And the single most important catalyst of her growth was the Baltimore and Ohio Railroad.

Narrow-gauge Climax. Although the Shay engine is better known and was valued for its higher traction, Climax engines were more commonly operated on the flimsy log roads during the "heyday" of lumbering in western Maryland, nearby Pennsylvania and West Virginia. The distinguishing feature of the Climax was its slanted cylinders. Photo courtesy Clyde VanSickle

Forestry operations. This is a typical early logging crew at the worksite. Men of this type were often referred to as "wood-hicks," but they were a hardy crew who worked hard and most bore the appellation proudly. Photo courtesy Clyde VanSickle

Woodsmen. This is a group of woodsmen gathered outside their living quarters. The young ladies are undoubtedly cooks. The corks (spikes) on some of the shoes suggest that the wearers were engaged in floating logs to the sawmill. Photo courtesy Clyde VanSickle

A sawmill. This was a Clark-McCullough sawmill located along Bear Creek at what is locally known as "Sam Jenkins Flat." The boiler is visible at the left of the mill and the carriage which carried the logs into the saw at the right. The mill crew is typical and the cant hooks they are holding were indispensable in moving logs. Photo courtesy Clyde VanSickle

Crellin Sawmill. This was one of the large sawmills of this county, a double mill, with sixty-four-inch circular saw and eight-foot band saw capable of producing 75,000 board feet of lumber per day. It operated until 1925 and was the second one on this site. The first mill began in 1892 and was destroyed by fire in 1902. These mills were supplied with logs by the Preston railroad which extended into Preston and Tucker counties, West Virginia. (See *History of Crellin* by Robert C. Shaffer; the *Glades Star*, vol. 2, p. 145.) Photo courtesy of Evelyn Wilt Clark

Autumn Glory Festival. Since 1967 the Autumn Glory Festival has been held each October to celebrate Garrett County's display of forest colors. Thousands come to see and to take part in the festival's colorful events. A highlight of the big Autumn Glory Parade is the passing of the lovely Autumn Glory queen and her court on their float through the streets of Oakland. The parade is held in Oakland on Saturday afternoon. Photo courtesy Tim Dugan

Garrett County Fair. After being discontinued for many years the annual fair was revived in the mid-fifties. It has become a very popular event and is held on the grounds at McHenry. In 1977 between twenty-five and thirty thousand people came to the fair. Photo courtesy B. O. Aiken

Garrett Community College. The college opened in 1971 on a beautiful site at McHenry overlooking Deep Creek Lake and the fairgrounds. It is rapidly becoming an attractive community center for advanced educational training. Photo courtesy Tim Dugan

U.S. Route 48—National Freeway. This view is near Friendsville of the modern four-lane limited access highway recently completed across Garrett County which gives the area unrivaled access to population centers to the East and West. Photo courtesy Ray McCullough

Coal mine at Steyer. This is a typical drift mine opening of which there were many in the county.
Photo courtesy Garrett Museum collection

Strip mine. For many years strip coal mines were not properly backfilled and little effort was made to restore the soil. New regulations on reclamation and the adoption of better methods are bringing about needed improvements in this method of coal removal. Photo courtesy Tim Dugan

Richter Tannery. John L. Richter started his tannery at Accident in 1872. It was continued in operation until 1928. The building still stands. Photo courtesy Mrs. Charles Strauss

Skiing. On the slope of the "Wisp" on Marsh Mountain, skiing is an excellent and popular sport in Garrett County. There are also cross-country trails in two state-owned parks, Herrington Manor and New Germany, where the trails are marked and maps are available. Photo courtesy the *Republican*

Boat building. An interior view of boats under construction in the Gordon Douglass Boat Company plant at Deer Park. This plant is new and built by its owners, Mr. and Mrs. Eric Ammann, who bought the company upon Mr. Douglass's retiring in 1972. Mr. Douglass designed a famous sailboat he named The Flying Scot and it is manufactured in this plant. Photo by Mrs. Eric Ammann

Old-fashioned winter. This scene in the 1920s identifies the locale as the junction of U.S. 219 and U.S. 40 at Keyser's Ridge. Note the elevation—2,881 feet. To open a drifted highway like this at that time was a tremendous task with available equipment and manpower. Photo courtesy B. O. Aiken

Boating. This is a Flying Scot sailboat in action on Deep Creek Lake. The largest fleet of this boat is found there. Boating enthusiasts across the nation revel in the sport of boating and the Flying Scot is a favorite among them. There are two yacht clubs at Deep Creek Lake. Photo by Eric Ammann

Golf. Oakland Country Club golf course is one of the loveliest settings anywhere in Maryland. There are rolling fairways, hilly fairways, as well as level ones. The course is not an easy one. Within the last few years another nine holes have been added making it eighteen holes and extending the beauty of the surrounding area. Photo by Robert J. Ruckert

Bausch & Lomb, Inc. This aerial photo shows the ophthalmic lens manufacturing plant built in 1971 with the Broad Ford Lake in the background. The plant driveway connects to Route 135 just out of sight in the foreground. The lake serves the triple purpose of flood control, recreation, and water supply for Mountain Lake Park, Oakland, and for lens manufacturing process. Photo by Ruthvan W. Morrow, Jr.

Altamont Spring Bottling House. This plant was located between Deer Park and Altamont on the B&O Railroad and engaged in bottling spring water for shipment to cities by the carload from 1908 to 1916.

The Altamont Spring Water Company was organized by the late Colonel George Truesdell and associated with him were Messers Woodward and Lothrop, prominent merchants of Washington, D.C.

In the picture foreground, *left to right*, are William B. Miller, George P. Marley, James Shaffer and John Robert Thrasher. In window are Grace Marley and Sadie Thrasher. (See also the *Glades Star*, vol. 3, p. 385.) Photo from company brochure in collection of Theodore Marley

Snow job. This scene at Keyser's Ridge in 1924 proves that back in the good old days it was a tough job to open a road with shovels and whatever trucks were available. Note the three levels from the roadbed to the top of the snowbanks. The picture is by courtesy of Robert Alexander who was a road supervisor in Garrett County for many years.

Garrett Memorial (Stone) Church. This church was built in 1869 by John W. Garrett as a memorial to his brother, Henry S. Garrett, to be used as a community church by the people of Oakland. Many prominent people have worshiped here, including Presidents Grant, Harrison and Cleveland. (See *Glades Star*, vol. 1, p. 356.) Photo from Dr. W. W. Grant collection by courtesy of Mrs. Patience Grant

One-room school. This typical one-room school is an example of more than a hundred schools built throughout Garrett County and provided a basic three-R education for children. With the advent of modern transportation and road improvements the schools were gradually consolidated. Photo courtesy B. O. Aiken

IV

THE TWENTIETH CENTURY

> The years flow by like water,
> and one day it is spring again.
>
> Thomas Wolfe

The Spanish came to North America in the sixteenth and seventeenth centuries looking for gold. The French came in pursuit of pelts. The English came for land.

The English prevailed.

They defeated the Spanish Armada in the English Channel in 1588. Nearly two centuries later they defeated the French in America in the Great War for the North American Empire.

In 1776 the American colonists of the Atlantic seaboard turned the tide on their mother country; they declared their own independence. The United States of America won political autonomy from England on September 3, 1783.

Garrett County in 1783 was still the extreme western fringe of Maryland's Washington County. Only a few dozen families then inhabited the highland Glade Country of the Maryland Alleghenies. The Maryland mountains west of Fort Cumberland on the upper Potomac in 1783 stood immense and silent and forested and still. Wild glade grass grew lush and tall in the Maryland highland valleys and swamps. Wild beasts roamed the woods at will. Fish swarmed in the streams. Spring blossomed into summer; summer peaked in the glory of fall. Fall fell to winter winds and snow, and then spring greened again. Garrett was very green, very clean, very pure in 1783.

Anglo-Saxon western civilization trod all over the mountains of western Maryland in the eighteenth and nineteenth centuries. Backwoods settlers came first. They established homesteads in the woods, cut the trees, farmed the land. They built sawmills and gristmills and pastured huge herds of cattle in the open glades. Then they fenced the glades, thinned the game, established schools, churches, communities. They tamed the frontier.

"Stand at Cumberland Gap," wrote the controversial historian Frederick Jackson Turner in 1893 of the American frontier movement of the eighteenth and nineteenth centuries, "and watch the procession of civilization marching single file—the buffalo following the trail to the Salt Springs, the Indian, the fur trader and hunter, the cattle-raiser, the pioneer farmer—and the frontier has passed by. The buffalo trail became the Indian trail, and this became the trader's 'trace'; the trails widened into roads, and the roads into turnpikes, and these in turn were transformed into railroads."

The railroad, the Baltimore and Ohio, introduced a new aspect of western civilization to Glade Country highlanders of nineteenth century western Maryland—industrialism. Industrialists of the late nineteenth century came to the Maryland mountains in pursuit of raw materials and fuels—timber and coal. They razed the forests of their virgin foliage and dug water-polluting mines deep into hillsides. In the meantime, resort financiers began arriving in the Maryland mountains in pursuit of the dollars generated by capitalists and industrialists in pursuit of summertime fun. Garrett County came of age by the twentieth century as a coal county, a timber county, a resort county, an agricultural county.

The twentieth century in Garrett County has been a time of change, of unprecedented change. Had George Washington returned to the Maryland Alleghenies after the Civil War, he could have adapted with ease to the mountaintop life-styles and economic structure of the time. Had he returned after World War II, he would have been baffled.

Twentieth century technology tied Garrett County to the world with a bond nearly unbreakable. Radio and television were popular twentieth century technical innovations; so were cars and trucks, telephones and electricity. As the innovations swept the nation, they swept Garrett County.

The first cars here appeared in the first decade of the century. They became popular in the twenties. In 1918 the three men chiefly responsible for putting the nation on wheels—Henry Ford, Thomas Edison, and Harvey Firestone—camped for a few days near Garrett County's Muddy Creek Falls. They were accompanied on their vacation by the naturalist writer John Burroughs. The trio returned to the campsite in 1921.

In 1976 Interstate Route 48—Garrett County's first divided two-lane freeway—opened for traffic between Cumberland, Maryland, and Morgantown, West Virginia. Route 48 followed the basic route of the 1816 Cumberland Road west to Devil's Half Acre, bypassing the towns of Frostburg and Grantsville. (It cost more than one million dollars per mile to construct. By way of comparison, the old Cumberland Road cost about ten thousand dollars per mile.) Route 48 today promises to return to the northern end of the county some of the former business volume drained from that area seventy-five years ago by the Baltimore and Ohio Railroad.

Telephones appeared in Garrett County homes with the dawn of the twentieth century. In 1899 W. A. "Billy" Smith, of Hoyes, organized the Garrett County Telephone Company with the support of M. Mattingly, Hoyes; Joseph McCrobie, Oakland; C. V. Guard, Friendsville; and William Miller, Accident. James M. Durst, of New Germany, joined the company in 1900.

The *Mountain Democrat* (April 20, 1899): "The new telephone line from Oakland to Paugh's, Thayerville, McHenry, Hoyes, Sang Run, M. J. Miller's Distillery, Accident, and Friendsville is now in full operation, connection having been made with the central office on Saturday last. This is by far the most important telephone line established in Garrett County."

Ross C. Durst (1962): "I believe it was in the summer of 1900 that we received the electrifying news that the Garrett County Telephone Company was building a telephone line across the mountain [to New Germany] from Bittinger. Previous to the coming of the telephone, we had virtually no contact with the outside world, not even a daily newspaper.

News had to be passed along from person to person. When President McKinley was assassinated in the fall of 1901, we received the news by telephone almost with in the hour."

The Chesapeake and Potomac Telephone Company established offices in Oakland in 1906. For sixteen years the Garrett Telephone Company waged war with the C&P for local exchanges and large party lines; then it sold out. In 1922 the C&P Company in Garrett County boasted 286 subscribers. Within three decades its Garrett membership more than quadrupled. Its membership more than doubled in a single decade following the Great Depression.

Electricity appeared in Garrett County in the late nineteenth century, but became popular in the twentieth. In 1921 Maryland's General Assembly granted the Youghiogheny Hydro-Electric Corporation, a subsidiary of the Pennsylvania Electric Corporation of Johnstown, exclusive rights to investigate the water power possibilities of the Youghiogheny river and its tributaries for the generation of electricity. For the next two years the Youghiogheny Corporation considered the construction of four major dams and three power houses in Garrett County at Deep Creek, Sang Run, Swallow Falls, and Crellin.

It finally decided to throw its corporate power behind initiation of the Deer Creek project, and in two years its agents purchased nearly eight thousand acres of Deep Creek watershed land from individual farmers and landowners. Buying through a company chartered as the Eastern Land Corporation, the Youghiogheny Corporation bought fifty buildings and one hundred forty Garrett County farms for purposes of flooding by 1923. The average price per acre? Fifty-five dollars.

The Youghiogheny Hydro-Electric Corporation began actual construction of the Deep Creek Dam less than two miles east of the confluence of Deep Creek and the Youghiogheny River on November 1, 1923. When completed in early 1925, the eighty-six-foot high dam created a lake twelve miles long covering forty-five hundred acres of land—Deep Creek Lake. Deep Creek Lake has produced electricity for thousands of western Pennsylvania residents for more than fifty continuous years.

Moving picture shows appeared in Oakland in the first decade of the century and so did phonographs. Radio started becoming popular in Garrett County in the twenties, television in the forties. The twentieth century in Garrett County has been a time of change, of unprecedented change.

The twentieth century in Garrett County has also been a time of advancing social awareness and a growing sense of public responsibility for the welfare of the natural heritage and society's individuals.

In 1906, in the Shadow of Theodore Roosevelt's concern with national conservation of natural resources, descendants of John W. Garrett granted nearly two thousand acres of cut-over Garrett County forestland in the Swallow Falls area to the state of Maryland, requesting only that the state, in return, create a special department for the proper administration and supervision of the new public holdings. Maryland accepted the gift, and, under the prodding of Garrett County State Senator McCulloch Brown, the General Assembly established the state's first Board of Forestry in 1906. The Garrett gift was expanded in ensuing years by public purchase and private donation to form the core of Garrett County's seven-thousand-acre Swallow Falls State Forest.

In 1929 the Maryland Forestry Department organized the fifty-thousand-acre Savage River State Forest of Garrett County; in 1931 the twelve-thousand-acre Potomac State Forest. Forests today cover an average of seven of every ten acres of land in Garrett County. The state itself controls seventy thousand acres of this land. Logging today in Garrett County is conducted chiefly on a sustained-yield basis. Wasteful practices of the past are now mere memories.

In 1905 the Garrett County School Board restored the seven-and-a-half month school term to the county school schedule. It established secondary schools in Grantsville in 1908, Oakland in 1909, Kitzmiller in 1911, Accident in 1915, Friendsville in 1923. A state school act of 1916 made school attendance compulsory for school-age children; another provided for tenure of teachers. A third provided that "the County Board of Education shall consolidate schools whenever in their judgment it is practical, and shall pay for the transportation of pupils."

Public bussing of Garrett County school children began in the 1920s. One-hundred-and-eighty-day yearly school terms were established in 1922. In 1924 the county supported 126 one-room schools; in 1934, 64; in 1941, 46. In the early 1950s, the county's five high schools were consolidated into two separate institutions—Northern High School, near Accident, and Southern High, near Oakland. Garrett Community College was officially organized by the county and state in 1966. Its first thirteen graduates celebrated commencement on the college campus near McHenry, with associate degrees, in 1973.

In 1910 the Maryland State Legislature passed an act providing for the first mandated public relief program for a special segment of the Garrett County populace—the Miners' Relief Fund. The act established for the first time a special fund for the relief and sustenance of Garrett and Allegeny County coal miners and their families in the event of mining injuries, disabilities, or deaths. The first awards to eligible miners were granted the same year the fund was organized.

The Miners' Relief Fund of 1910 was the first publicly mandated relief program ever established for the welfare of Garrett County citizens. More broadly based public welfare programs for Garrett citizens were instituted during the Great Depression under the influence of Herbert Hoover's belated response to the 1929 stock market crash and Franklin Roosevelt's New Deal of the 1930s.

In April 1933, in the early depths of the Depression, the Maryland state legislature earmarked $153,000 of Hoover Reconstruction Finance Corporation funds for relief purposes in seven Maryland counties, one of which was Garrett. A delegation of interested Garrett County citizens, including two coal company operators, the county superintendent of schools, a bank cashier, an attorney, a businessman, and a county commissioner, subsequently met with a representative of the Governor's Emergency Unemployment Commission for guidance in forming the county's first public-welfare board. The board was organized in April; its administrators were all volunteers.

The Garrett County Welfare Board of 1933 established a variety of public service work projects throughout the county to provide work for its dependents. Its first standards for relief compensation made no provision for single persons and provided maximums of $1.60 per week for eligible two-person families and $9.60 a week for families of twelve. All of its dependents were required to work. During a single week in late May 1933, the board received 746 applications from family heads for relief funds. By June it employed 1,134 Garrett citizens in twenty-three county projects. By year's end more than 25 percent of the county's total populace depended upon funds allocated through the county relief board for living expenditures. The Garrett County Welfare Board's own expenditures totaled almost $200,000 in 1933, the year the board was founded.

Other publicly funded work projects for the Garrett unemployed of the Great Depression also reflected a growing twentieth century concern of the American government on all levels for the welfare of society's individuals. The Civilian Conservation Corps, established by Congress in March 1933, provided work for as many as thirty Garrett County youths at a time in conservation projects. Garrett County itself hosted seven CCC camps during the depression. Camp residents in the county worked at reforestation projects on state-owned lands and drained the Swauger Grist Dam at New Germany to prepare for the construction of the thirteen-acre New Germany recreational dam. At the south end of Swallow Falls State Forest they constructed the fifty-three acre Herrington Manor Lake. For their services, CCC workers in Garrett County were paid thirty-two dollars per month, twenty-five dollars of which was earmarked by the program each month for the workers' families and parents.

In June 1933, the United States Congress passed the National Industrial Recovery Act, a major section of which authorized a vast program of public works under the administration of a new Public Works Administration. The PWA in

Garrett County employed county residents for about a year in road, sewer, street, park, school, and water projects. In the winter of 1934 the Civil Works Administration did the same. The Works Progress Administration, established by Congress in 1935 with funds of nearly $5 billion to provide work for the nation's unemployed, began construction of Garrett County's Savage River Dam as a flood control project in September 1939. (The Savage River project, Maryland's largest WPA project, was interrupted by World War II in 1942, but was completed in 1951.) The National Yough Administration, also created by Congress in 1935, employed various Garrett County students for several years in a variety of school related projects to aid in their secondary and college educations. The Social Security Act of 1935 established for the first time a national program providing massive government security against the problems of old age and work disability.

Franklin D. Roosevelt declared in 1935 that "government by the necessity of things must be the leader, must be the judge of the conflicting interests of all groups in the community." His words reflected a revolutionary twentieth century concern on the part of government with the welfare of society's individuals, the nation's natural heritage, and the national economy. His New Deal converted his words into action. His legacy today is a vast government bureaucracy which still touches the lives of Garrett County citizens daily. (Nearly one of every twenty Garrett residents today is employed in the government sector of the economy.)

The twentieth century in Garrett County has been a time of unprecedented social change, of surprising technical innovations, of advancing social awareness and a growing sense of public responsibility for the welfare of the nation's natural heritage and society's individuals. It has also been a time of remarkable scientific advancements and continued industrialization.

In 1933 Thomas Hunt Morgan, who had received his first schooling in an Oakland one-room building, won the Nobel Prize for discoveries in the field of biology. Twenty years later, Edwin McMillen, the grandson of an early Accident harness shop operator, received the Nobel Prize in the field of Physics for discovering Plutonium. Both Albert Einstein, proponent of the theory of relativity, and Jonas Salk, who developed the Salk Polio Vaccine, vacationed in Garrett County at Deep Creek Lake in the 1940s and 1950s. On July 20, 1969, Garrett County citizens joined millions of people around the world in watching the televised descent of astronaut Neil Armstrong as he stepped from the ladder of his spaceship to the surface of the moon. (The twentieth century has been a time of remarkable scientific advancement.)

Industry in nineteenth century Garrett County centered around the coal and lumber businesses. In the twentieth century the coal and lumber industries continued to play a major role in the mountaintop economic system. The coal business profited most during the two World Wars, but declined rapidly during the fifties and sixties. (In 1942 nearly a thousand persons were employed in the Garrett coal industry; in 1960 less than two hundred persons were so employed.) The energy crunch of the early seventies has dramatically revived the mountaintop coal business, however, and today numerous strip mines mark the Casselman and Savage River Valley coal basins. Deep shaft mining is being planned for the near future. The company-owned coal towns of yesteryear are now gone or fading, but thousands of tons of black gold remain buried deep in the ground in thick seams.

Lumbering today in Garrett County centers around the Westvaco Pulp and Paper Corporation of Luke, Maryland, in neighboring Allegany County. (The Westvaco Corporation was originally chartered as the Piedmont Pulp and Paper Company under William Luke in 1888, when the Garrett County lumber industry was still in its adolescence.) Today, Westvaco employs dozens of Garrett workers.

The natural gas industry came to Garrett County early in the century. In May 1907, the Yough River Oil and Gas Company which had organized the previous year with main offices at Oakland, began drilling a test well on a farm near Hutton. Geologists had predicted the company would tap a large oil field in the area. The *Mountain Democrat* noted that "about all the farms in the neighborhood have been leased by oil speculators and the outcome of the well being put down is awaited with much interest." The *Baltimore Sun* announced that an "oil fever" was "fast taking possession of a good many residents of Garrett County." The Yough Company drilled the Hutton oil shaft to depth of thirty-nine hundred feet, then abandoned the project, labeling the Hutton well a dry hole.

A drilling attempt conducted over forty years later by the Cumberland and Allegany Gas Company on a farm near Gortner was more successful. At a depth of forty-nine hundred feet the Cumberland company struck natural gas. The Gortner well produced almost a half million cubic feet of gas daily during its first weeks of production, and spurred drilling enterprises throughout the nearby Mountain Lake Park area. By the end of 1951, nearly two dozen gas drilling derricks dotted the Mountain Lake landscape. By the end of the decade, though, gas speculators had exhausted the fields there and moved on in search of greener pastures and more productive wells elsewhere.

In 1953 the Snee and Eberly Gas Company drilled a successful well near Accident. The company sold the Accident field to the Texas Eastern Transmission Corporation in 1962. Within a decade Texas Eastern drilled nearly seventy wells in the field, leased thirty-four thousand acres of underground storage space, and constructed a major pumping station on a hill northwest of Accident. Today, Texas Eastern uses the Accident gas field exclusively for storage purposes. The Accident field was the first completely automated storage field operating in the gas industry. Today, it is the second largest and perhaps the most modern in the world. Texas Eastern pumps natural gas into the Accident field every summer and withdraws it every winter for industrial and home use throughout the eastern United States. The average storage depth lies 7,375 feet beneath the surface of the ground.

Industrial manufacturing in nineteenth century Garrett County was limited almost exclusively to the production of timber products and the tanning of hides. Ten significant industries have established businesses in the county so far this century, however. The Union Fire Brick Company of

Pittsburgh constructed a brick manufacturing plant near Jennings in 1944. (The Union plant has since been acquired by Harbison-Walker Refractories, a division of Dresser Industries.) In 1953 the Flushing Shirt Manufacturing Company of New York opened facilities at Grantsville for the production of uniform shirts. The Greater Maryland Tool and Manufacturing Corporation began producing tools and machine parts at Accident in 1967. In 1969 the Garrett Manufacturing Company established facilities at Deer Park for the production of women's blouses. In 1971 Bausch and Lomb, Inc., a major manufacturer of glass lense products, opened a large branch factory near Mountain Lake Park. American HV Test Systems, Inc., constructed a factory for the production of high-voltage test equipment at Accident in 1975. The Sterling Processing Corporation operates an important plant for the commercial processing and freezing of poultry in Oakland. The plant was built and put into production in 1957. It uses an efficient aerated lagoon for treating the plant's large volume of processing water. The Gordon Douglass Boat Company, Inc., manufacturer of well-known sailboats, including the famous trophy-winning Flying Scot, started business in Oakland in 1958. The business is now located in Deer Park. Integrated Business Methods, Inc., purchased the data processing facility of the Glenn Engineering Company in June 1965. Glenn Engineering had started the business in Oakland in January of 1965. The enterprise transfers data onto cards and tapes. The twentieth century in Garrett County has been a time of continued industrialization.

It has also been a time—this century—of increased specialization and production in farming and of a resurging countywide interest in the tourism and resort business. Nineteenth century Garrett County farmers were practically self-sufficient, as had been their fathers. Farmers today in Garrett County produce enough food to feed thousands. A single dairy farmer today produces hundreds of pounds of milk each day; a single chicken farmer produces thousands of eggs. Other farmers produce tons of beef each year, and tons of vegetables. Maple syrup is still a favored early spring product. Other twentieth century Garrett County agricultural products include potatoes, turkeys, pork, corn, green beans, oats, wheat, buckwheat, and hay.

"They're getting weaker and wiser," an Accident-area farmer commented to his father at the turn of the century when a neighbor purchased the area's first grain binder. Twentieth century industry and technology enabled the nation's farmers each to do work that would have required dozens of farm hands the century before. Tractors were major twentieth century farm innovations; so were grain combines, silo fillers and unloaders, automatic barn cleaning and feeding systems, bulk milk tanks and automatic milking systems, hay balers and crop dusters. As individual farm productivity increased in the county throughout the century, with the aid of technical innovations, the number of actual farm workers here decreased. Eleven hundred farmers tilled Garrett County's 170 square miles of open farmland in 1950; in 1970 415 tilled the land. The twentieth century has been a time of specialization and increased population on Garrett County farms.

The resort-recreation business in twentieth century Garrett County has centered around the sixty-five miles of Deep Creek Lake shoreline. Tourists began to frequent the lake for vacation purposes in the 1940s and 1950s. By 1972 Garrett County tourism and recreation centering around Deep Creek Lake had become the county's most significant industry—in 1972 it comprised over 35 percent of the county's total economy; it provided over 20 percent of the county's labor force with jobs; it added nearly $20 million to the county's overall economy. The lake shoreline is sprinkled with summer vacation homes, restaurants, and marinas, campsites and cabins, bars, motels, and condominiums. Tourists today use the lake itself for boating, skiing, fishing, and skating. The Wisp Ski Resort on the northeast slope of nearby Marsh Mountain provides winter buffs with twelve miles of snow ski trails and slopes.

Other natural and man-made twentieth century Garrett County tourist attractions include the Swallow Falls State Park, the Herrington Manor State Park, the New Germany State Park, the Big Run State Park (at the head of the Savage

River Reservoir), the University of Maryland-owned Pleasant Valley Lake and Park (near Bittinger), the Youghiogheny Lake (built in 1943 north of Friendsville by the Youghiogheny River Flood Control Authority), the Deep Creek State Park, and the Broad Ford Dam near Oakland (built in 1970 by the town of Oakland).

Present-day annual pageants for the delight of both county residents and visitors include the Garrett County Fair (held each August at McHenry) and the countywide Autumn Glory Festival.

Oakland celebrated its centennial in 1949 with appropriate events during a week in August. The history of the town was written in verse form by Rev. Felix G. Robinson and entitled "The Ballad of Oakland." Mrs. Thekla Fundenberg Weeks wrote a one hundred-page history of Oakland and its environs with the title of "Oakland Centennial History." The town's centennial program was financially underwritten by a "Committee of 100."

The one hundredth year of Garrett County's existence was observed in 1972 and a number of programs throughout the county celebrated its pioneer history and the developments of the following years. Four centennial issues of the county's historical quarterly the *Glades Star* were published by the Garrett County Historical Society. Forty thousand people came to the county and thousands to Oakland in October to enjoy the Autumn Glory Festival.

The people of Garrett County participated locally and as a part of Maryland in the American Bicentennial. There were many community events developed to express the Bicentennial theme during 1976. Dr. Raymond O. McCullough, of Friendsville, was the vice-chairman of the Maryland Bicentennial Commission. He presented a Bicentennial flag and official certificate to the town of Bloomington that recognized it as the first official Bicentennial community in Garrett County. The people of Bloomington organized and published an illustrated one-hundred-page history entitled *The Bloomington Story*. The book was written by Miss Alice R. Howard and Mrs. Alice F. Howard. It was published by the Bloomington Bicentennial Committee.

Garrett County was represented in the Western Maryland Bicentennial Trail project which involved Washington and Allegany counties also. Site markers along the highways were put up to guide tourists to the landmarks of history. A Harvest Festival was held in September at McHenry. A historical musical drama entitled "Portrait of Liberty" was written and produced by people of Oakland community. More than one hundred people were involved and four performances in October were given at Southern High School.

B. O. Aiken, of Accident, was chairman of the Garrett County Bicentennial Committee. The committee also promoted the publishing of this county history.

The twentieth century has brought a resurging and ever-growing tourism and recreation business to the hills and valleys of western Maryland.

The economy of Garrett County today is much more complex, much more diversified than ever before. It is an economy in transition. In the nineteenth century the Garrett economy was based almost exclusively on lumbering, mining, agriculture, and resort-recreation. It is an economy fast becoming oriented to government, manufacturing, retail trades, and social services.

As the economy has so developed, its labor force has come to the fore in the public eye. In 1935 President Franklin Roosevelt signed a major labor act—the Wagner Labor Relations Act—which compelled employers for the first time to bargain in good faith with labor representatives, and prohibited management interference with labor activities. Thirty-five years later Garrett County public road workers conducted a seven-month strike—the longest public-employee strike in the nation's history—to attain county commissioner recognition of their newly formed AFL-CIO union local. The strike won local recognition for the first time of the right of Garrett County public workers to unionize in their own interests.

The twentieth century in Garrett County has been a time of change, of unprecedented change; a time of technical and scientific advancements; a time of government expansion and private industrialization; a time of economic diversification and unionization. It's been a century, also, interrupted by warfare on five occasions. Sixty-two Garrett Countians served in the armed forces of their nation during the Spanish-American War in 1898. Seven hundred four served in World War I, twenty-three hundred in World War II. Nineteen Garrett Countians died in Korea, fifteen in Vietnam. The twentieth century has been a time of international tension.

D. P. Smouse, 1963 director of Garrett County Civil Defense, speaking in the wake of the 1962 Cuban Missile Crisis (March 1963): "Our government, through the media of newspapers, radio, television, and an extensive Civil Defense program is warning us to prepare ourselves for the day the missile might be loosed. I pray you to heed this warning—build a shelter for yourself and family, a shelter with comfortable space, stock it with sufficient food and water to sustain you for a period of at least fourteen days. Always be on the alert for the alarm. Then, if you are fortunate enough to survive the heat and blast, your chance of a future life, in a greatly changed world, is possible."

The Ku Klux Klan organized for a brief period in Friendsville during the hysteria of the post-World War I Red scare. German-speaking church congregations throughout the county actually began to abandon the use of the German language in their services even before the close of wartime hostilities. During World War I itself, residents of New Germany considered changing the name of their community because of the negative connotations New Germany aroused at the time.

Garrett Countians of the late 1940s and early 1950s were shocked and dismayed by charges of Senator Joseph McCarthy, of Wisconsin, that the federal government was ridden with Communists and riddled with treason. In 1953, the American Central Intelligence Agency, experimenting with the use of LSD for biological warfare purposes, drugged the after-dinner drinks of civilian biochemist Frank Olson at a special weekend conference held at Deep Creek Lake. Olson, afterwards depressed, plunged to his death less than two weeks later from a tenth-floor New York City hotel room.

(Twentieth century international tension has had its Garrett County side effects.)

This century in Garrett County has also been a time for peace, though, a time for noble peaceful pursuits and peaceful individual contributions to the greater society. Three Garrett Countians of the twentieth century made especially notable peacetime contributions to the county: Charles E. Hoye, Ephriam E. Enlow, and George W. Loar.

Charles E. Hoye, the great-grandson of 1799 Sang Run settler William Waller Hoye, served with United States armed forces in the Philippines during the Spanish-American War of century's turn. After the war he remained in the Philippines for twenty-five years as an American educator. He taught in Los Angeles County schools for five years in the early 1930s, then returned to his native Garrett County.

Hoye was an amateur historian greatly interested in local history. In 1939 he suggested to the Garrett County Superintendent of Schools F. E. Rathbun that the educational facilities of the community be mobilized for the organization òf a Garrett County historical society. When the society was finally officially organized by members of the County Teachers' Association on February 27, 1941, "to discover, secure and preserve whatever relates to the history of this area, and to disseminate knowledge of our local history among our people," Captain Charles E. Hoye was elected its first regular president. He served as president of the organization until the end of 1943. He served as its guiding light until his death in 1951.

The Garrett County Historical Society began publication of its quarterly magazine, the *Glades Star* (named after E. S. Zevely's publication of 1871), in March 1941. Hoye himself wrote more than 75 percent of the historical material used in the thirty-six ensuing issues of the magazine's first volume. He also wrote two books, *The Hoyes of Maryland* and *A History of Garrett County Pioneer Families.* (His *History* was originally published in a series of local newspaper articles.) Hoye worked for ten years, spurring local interest in Garrett County history and historiography. When he died in 1951, the county's historical society boasted a membership of more than one thousand persons.

On Labor Day, September 1, 1952, Maryland's governor, Theodore K. McKeldin, proclaimed that Maryland's highest peak on Garrett County's Backbone Mountain be named Hoye Crest in memory of the founder of the Garrett County Historical Society. Forty persons attended the outdoor dedication program at the location, an elevation of 3,360 feet above sea level. Tableland historian Felix Robinson arranged the program. Years later Robinson spoke of Captain Charles E. Hoye as "a son of the oldest pioneers, a patriot-soldier, an educator who helped shape a culture of a new civilization in the Pacific, an historian who pioneered in cultural history," "Captain Hoye," he wrote in 1960, "will always be remembered as the Father of Garrett County history."

The Garrett County Historical Society itself is still strong. The *Glades Star* is in its fifth volume of continuous publication. In 1954 the historical society began sponsoring annual historical tours of the county; in 1964 it purchased the Episcopal Parish House on Oakland's Center Street for use as society headquarters and county museum. The Garrett County Historical Society Museum opened its doors to the public on November 9, 1969.

Charles E. Hoye is remembered in Garrett County today chiefly for his outstanding contributions in the establishment of the Garrett County Historical Society. Ephraim E. Enlow and George Loar are remembered for outstanding contributions in the establishment of the county library and the county hospital.

Garrett County's first libraries were established by community groups and organizations for the cultural enrichment of their members. The Garrett Literary Society in 1878 voted that most of its funds be used to buy books for the use of club members. In the 1890s a group of Deer Park residents established an evening reading room on the second floor of the town's schoolhouse for the use of the community. The Oakland Fire Company started an Oakland library around the same time with a subscription to the *Baltimore American* and purchase of the *Encyclopaedia Brittanica*. In 1906 Bittinger residents established a village reading room in Bittinger with a collection which expanded to a hundred and fifty volumes in three years. Then, in 1915, the Oakland Civic Club organized the Oakland Free Public Library. The Oakland Library became the Garrett County Free Library under state-authorized reorganization in 1946. Its facilities at that time were limited to three small rooms on the second floor of the Garrett National Bank Building in Oakland.

Then, on August 14, 1946, the Board of Trustees of the Garrett County Free Library received a letter from Ephraim E. Enlow, of Sebastopol, California, in which the Garrett County native offered to donate ten thousand dollars for the construction of a new Garrett library building. "As to my purpose," Enlow wrote, "I have two, the first of which is to cause a memorial to [be erected in memory of] my daughter, Ruth Christine Enlow. My second purpose is to help establish in my native county the best library, denied me in my boyhood, my contribution may help to secure. When a boy, looking out into the great wide world, what a boon to me would have been a fine Free Library!"

Ephraim E. Enlow's ten-thousand-dollar donation to the Garrett County Library Board in 1946 for the construction of a new county library spurred contributions from four additional sources. Calvin Crimm, of Cincinnati, native of Oakland, donated three thousand dollars to the fund; Charles E. Hoye donated one thousand; The Oakland-Mountain Lake Park Lions Club donated seventy-five hundred; the county itself donated four thousand. By 1950, Ephraim Enlow, still living in California, had increased his own original contribution to a total of thirty-five thousand dollars.

Construction of the Ruth Enlow Library on the corner of Oakland's Second and Center streets began in March 1950. The building was completed and accepted by the county in November. In 1959 the library opened a branch facility in Grantsville. Ten years later the Oakland building was remodeled and enlarged to its present size and shape. The Ruth Enlow Library of Garrett County functions as one of the county's foremost cultural assets. Its bookmobile serves the entire county.

The county's foremost health facility is the Garrett County Memorial Hospital, established in 1950 at the northern edge of Oakland with initial funding provided through the will of Garrett County native George W. Loar. Loar was the grandson of an 1815 Oakland settler; he made his career as a merchant and businessman in Grafton, West Virginia, before retiring to reside at his family home in Oakland.

In 1944 George Loar willed $125,000 for "the construction and equipping of a hospital building at Oakland, Maryland." He later increased his contribution to a total of $195,000. After his death, in 1946, the Garrett County Commissioners obtained $179,000 additional in federal aid for the use in the hospital fund. Other private contributors donated a total of $102,000 to the fund by 1948. Construction of the hospital began that year. The structure was completed in 1950. A bronze tablet at the entrance of the Garrett County Memorial Hospital immortalizes George W. Loar, the hospital's founder, as "a kind and understanding heart."

EPILOGUE: GARRETT COUNTY

The history of Garrett County, under white domination since John Friend's move here in 1765, is a relatively short one spanning little more than two centuries in time. Yet it is a phenomenal history, a history which reflects in large part the entire American experience.

It is a history with roots so deep in western civilization that they touch the Italian Renaissance of the fourteenth and fifteenth centuries. European man emerged from the darkness of the Middle Ages with striking attributes previously repressed by medieval customs and social structures; he emerged with a new self-awareness of his own unlimited capabilities, with a new sense of self-reliance, with a new self-confidence, with, in short, a new vision of mankind itself and of man's own potentials in a world ruled by men. William Shakespeare noted the transition joyously and succinctly in 1600. "What a piece of work is man!" he wrote for *Hamlet*. "How noble in reason! how infinite in faculty! in form and moving how express and admirable! in action how like an angel! in apprehension how like a god! the beauty of the world! the paragon of animals!"

European man brought his new self-identity born of the Renaissance to the Americas when he sailed west from Europe in the sixteenth and seventeenth centuries in the wake of the European Renaissance itself. He came to the Americas looking for gold and pelts and lands. He came, also, in pursuit of dreams. He sailed west in pursuit of the illusion of freedom; he came here looking for new life. And, more often than not, he sailed alone. The American immigrant of four hundred years ago was a man of extreme self-confidence and self-reliance. He was a man, in addition, nourished by grandiose dreams for himself and even grander hopes for his children and his children's children. He was two men in one; he was a man of God; he was a man of men.

White men first began to settle in Garrett County, Appalachian Maryland, in 1765. Within a hundred years they tamed the frontier. They worked hard, sweated much. Their only reliance was on themselves—on their own hearts, their own minds, their own muscles; their only dependence was upon the natural resources of their land. They were pragmatic men, and yet they were religious men. They built homes; they built churches; they established new communities on an old plateau. They were men of God, men of men. And they passed their ideals, their hopes, their dreams, and their ethics on to their children and their children's children.

Americans moved west in the early nineteenth century; they settled the land. In the late nineteenth century they industrialized. Men of capital organized large business corporations and trusts. In Garrett County they built railroads, stripped forests, and mined coal. They exploited raw resources at an ever-accelerating pace and often with reckless abandon. They exploited labor; they exploited the fruits of the earth. And they created the most powerful industrial empire the world has ever known.

In the twentieth century Americans began to correct some of the mistakes of their age of frantic industrialization. They passed federal, state, and local laws to regulate the activities of large-scale businesses. They set aside expansive lands for purposes of conservation. They granted laborers the right to organize and negotiate with employers. They began to create a welfare state for the care of society's individuals. Yet they retained their basic values of frontier life: hard work, self-reliance, independence, and freedom.

Today Garrett Countians live in a small world of nuclear bombs, neon signs, communication satellites, electric lines, and telephone poles. They drive internal-combustion-engine automobiles and live in comfortable suburban homes and house trailers. They work eight hours a day, five days a week and relax after work in armchairs pivoted to television sets. On Sundays most of them attend morning church services.

They educate their children in large public schools and universities; they bury their dead in community and church cemeteries. They seek medical advice in hospitals and community health centers; they seek recreation in bars, parks, woods, and commercial resorts. They sleep in warm coal, oil, gas, and electrically heated homes; they eat well.

Two hundred years ago the hand of Western Civilization had barely touched the mountain and glade country of the Maryland Appalachian plateau. Only a few dozen families of European origin then lived here. Today enough people of European descent inhabit the plateau to fill a major college football stadium.

Three hundred years ago Indians lived here.

Things change.

And yet, things remain the same.

Summer still follows spring here; autumn, summer; winter, autumn. The Indian saw it; we see it. The cycle is as old and as predictable and as true as the hills themselves. Some things never change. On such things rest the subtle foundations of history.

The years flow by like water here; every spring Garrett greens.

BIBLIOGRAPHY

I. Published Sources

Ashby, Iret. *The Ashby Story.* Terra Alta, W.Va.: Pioneer Press, 1975.

Bailey, Kenneth P. *The Ohio Company of Virginia.* Glendale, Calif.: The Arthur H. Clark Company, 1939.

Benet, Stephen Vincent. *Western Star.* New York: Farrar & Rinehart, Inc., 1943.

Billington, Ray Allen. *Westward Expansion.* New York: The Macmillan Company, 1950.

Bird, Harrison. *Battle for a Continent.* New York: Oxford University Press, 1965.

Bittinger, Wayne. *Generations: A History of the Biddinger, Bidinger, Bittinger, and Bittner Families of Garrett County, Maryland.* Parsons, W.Va.: McClain Printing Co., 1974.

Brown, Jacob. *Brown's Miscellaneous Writings.* Cumberland, Md.: J. J. Miller, 1896.

Browning, Meshach. *Forty-four Years of the Life of a Hunter.* Winston-Salem, N.C.: Winston Printing Co., 1942.

Cammack, John Henry. *Personal Recollections of Private John Henry Cammack,* Huntington, W.Va.: Paragon Printing and Publishing Co.

Chitwood, Oliver Perry, *A History of Colonial America.* New York: Harper & Brothers, 1948.

Cleland, Hugh. *George Washington in the Ohio Valley.* Pittsburgh: University of Pittsburgh Press, 1955.

Coleman, R. V. *The First Frontier.* New York: Charles Scribner's Sons, 1948.

Council of the Alleghenies. *Conference Bulletin No. 1.* Grantsville, Md.: Council of the Alleghenies, 1964.

———. *Journal of the Alleghenies.* Frostburg, Md.: Council of the Alleghenies, 1968, 1972, 1973.

Cresap, Joseph Ord and Bernarr. *The History of the Cresaps.* McComb, Miss.: The Cresap Society, 1937.

Davis, J. M. *The Hardware Bulletin.* Oakland, Md.: J. M. Davis & Sons, 1906-1908.

DeVoto, Bernard. *The Course of Empire.* Boston: Houghton Mifflin Company, 1952.

Enlow, E. E. *Recalling the Years of My Life.* Sebastopol, Calif.: (by the author), 1946.

Fansler, Homer Floyd. *History of Tucker County, West Virginia.* Parsons, W.Va.: McClain Printing Co., 1962.

Fitzpatrick, John C., ed. *The Diaries of George Washington.* Vol. 1. Boston: Houghton Mifflin Co., 1925.

Flexner, James Thomas. *George Washington: The Forge of Experience.* Boston: Little, Brown and Company, 1965.

Friend, D. A. *The Goodness of God.* Pittsburgh: Pittsburgh Printing Co., 1920.

Fuller, Kent B., and Frank, Paul S. *The Cranesville Pine Swamp.* College Park, Md.: Natural Resources Institute, 1974.

Garrett County Historical Society. *The Glades Star.* Vols. 1-4. Oakland, Md.: The Republican Press, March, 1941-Dec., 1976.

Garrett County Planning Commission. *A Close Look at Garrett County.* Oakland, Md.: Garrett County Planning Commission, 1973.

Garrett County Planning Commission. *A Development Plan for Garrett County.* Oakland, Md.: Garrett County Planning Commission, 1974.

Garrett, Robert Browning. *The Catholic Church in Garrett County.* Oakland, Md.: 1972.

Hahn, Thomas F. *Chesapeake and Ohio Canal Old Picture Album.* Shepherdstown, W.Va.: The American Canal and Transportation Center, 1976.

Hamilton, Charles, ed. *Braddock's Defeat.* Norman, Oklahoma. University of Oklahoma Press, 1959.

Hoye, Charles E. *The Hoyes of Maryland.* Oakland, Md.: The Sincell Printing Company, 1942.

Hulbert, Archer Butler. *Braddock's Road.* Cleveland, Ohio: The Arthur H. Clark Co., 1903.

———. *Washington's Road.* Cleveland, Ohio: The Arthur H. Clark Co., 1903.

Hungerford, Edward. *The Story of the Baltimore and Ohio Railroad.* New York: G. P. Putnam's Sons, 1928.

Jenkins, Mary and Eben. *The First Hundred Years: Maryland State Grange 1874-1974.* Baltimore: Maryland State Grange, 1974.

Jordan, Philip D. *The National Road.* Gloucester, Mass.: Peter Smith, 1966.

Josephy, Alvin M., ed. *The American Heritage Book of Indians.* New York: American Heritage Publishing Co., Inc., 1961.

Killough, Edward M. *History of the Western Maryland Railway Company*. Baltimore: Voluntary Relief Department Press of Western Maryland Railway, 1940.

Kline, Benjamin F. G. *Tall Pines and Winding Rivers: The Logging Railroads of Maryland*. Lancaster, Pa.: Benjamine F. G. Kline, Jr., 1976.

Knollenberg, Bernhard. *George Washington: The Virginia Period, 1732-1775*. Durham, N.C.: Duke University Press, 1964.

Lowdermilk, Will H. *History of Cumberland*. Baltimore: Regional Publishing Co., 1971.

Maxwell, Hu. *The History of Barbour County, West Virginia*. Reprint. Parsons, W.Va.: McClain Printing Company, 1968.

———. *The History of Randolph County, West Virginia*. Reprint. Parsons, W.Va.: McClain Printing Company, 1962.

Miers, Earl Schenck, Ed. *The American Story*. Great Neck, N.J.: Channel Press, 1956.

Morton, Oren F. *A History of Preston County, West Virginia*. Kingwood, W.Va.: The Journal Publishing Company, 1914.

Mulkearn, Lois, Ed. *George Mercer Papers Relating to the Ohio Company of Virginia*. Pittsburgh: University of Pittsburgh Press, 1954.

Olsen, Evelyn Guard. *Indian Blood*. Parsons, W.Va.: McClain Printing Company, 1967.

Pangborn, J. G. *Picturesque B. and O*. Chicago: Knight & Leonard, 1883.

Parkman, Francis. *The Conspiracy of Pontiac*. New York: Collier Books, 1962.

Passenger Department of the Baltimore and Ohio Railroad. *Book of the Royal Blue*. Vol. 2, nos. 1-12. Baltimore: Passenger Department of the Baltimore and Ohio Railroad, 1898-1899.

Rachel, William M., ed. *The Virginia Magazine of History and Biography*. Vol. 77, no. 3. Richmond, Va.: Virginia Historical Society, July, 1969.

Robinson, Felix G., ed. *Tableland Trails*. Vol. 2, nos. 2, 3, 4. Oakland, Md.: Tableland Trails Foundation, 1956, 1958, 1963.

Sargent, Winthrop, ed. *The History of an Expedition against Fort Duquesne*. Philadelphia: Lippincott, Grambo & Co., 1955.

Scharf, J. Thomas. *History of Western Maryland*. Vol. 2. Philadelphia: Louis H. Everts, 1882.

Schneider, Norris F. *The National Road: Main Street of America*. Columbus, Ohio: The Ohio Historical Society, 1975.

Searight, Thomas B. *The Old Pike*. Richmond, Ind.: M. Cullaton & Co., 1894.

Streaker, Margaret M. *Taming the Savage River.* Parsons, W.Va.: McClain Printing Company, 1968.

Swann, Don, Jr. *Colonial and Historic Homes of Maryland.* Baltimore: The Johns Hopkins University Press, 1975.

Taylor, George Rogers, ed. *The Turner Thesis Concerning the Role of the Frontier in American History.* Lexington, Mass.: D. C. Heath and Company, 1956.

Thoreau, Henry David. *Walden.* New York: Bramhall House, 1951.

Washington, George. *The Journal of Major George Washington.* Williamsburg, Va.: Colonial Williamsburg, Inc., 1959.

Williams, T. J. C. *History of Frederick County, Maryland.* Vol. 1. Baltimore: Regional Publishing Company, 1967.

Writers' Program of the Works Projects Administration in the State of Maryland. *Maryland: A Guide to the Old Line State.* New York: Oxford University Press, 1948.

II. Unpublished sources.

Bittinger, Wayne. *Bittinger History.* 1976.

Bowman, Charles and Mary. *McHenry Post Office.* 1976.

Browning, Verna DeWitt. *History of Garrett County Telephone.* 1976.

———. *Hoyes.* 1976.

Cooper, Pauline V. *The Fairview Church Area.* 1976.

Filer, Grace E. *Grace E. Filer's Ramblings.* 1976.

Fratz, Margaret, and Strauss, Mary. *Accident.* 1976.

Garrett, Robert B. *Deer Park.* 1976.

Hamilton, Wayne and Claudia. *The Red House Community.* 1976.

Harless, Margaret M., and Layman, Kathleen B. *Finzel.* 1976.

Howard, Alice R. *Bloomington History.* 1976.

Jarrett, Sara Stanton. *History of Grantsville.* 1976.

Kahl, Randall. *Garrett County Military Service Records.* 1976.

Lewis, Mrs. Asa. *Famous Pine Swamp.* 1976.

———. *The Town of Kempton.* 1976.

Pendergast, Ellena. *Hutton Switch.* 1976.

Reckner, Ida. *Beckman Post Office.* 1976.

Resh, Linda. *Jennings.* 1976.

Robeson, Zeloa L. *The National Pike Area.* 1976.

Salzmann, Emma and Mary. *Hutton.* 1976.

Shaffer, Lee B. *The Red House Community.* 1976.

Shaffer, Robert C. *History of Crellin, Maryland.* 1976.

INDEX

The spelling of proper names in the pioneer period varied considerably. In searching through the index, the reader should look under various forms.

Accident, 43, 44, 52, 72, 73, 74, 75, 77, 89, 92, 93, 109, 253, 258, 336, 343, 344
Accident Cove, 74
Accident doctors, 93
Accident Evangelical Lutheran English congregation, 107
Accident gas field, 343
Accident gristmills, 89
Accident Lutherans, 107
Accident Post Office, 74
Accident Valley, 33
Accident Zion Evangelical Lutheran Church, 107
Adams, John, 77, 78, 152, 192, 193, 212
AFL-CIO Union, local, 347
Agricultural products, 345
Aiken, B. O., xii, 320, 326, 333, 347
Alabama Creeks (Indians), 156
Alabama joins Union, 156
Alderson, Joseph C., 299
Alderson, Mrs. J. C., 299
Alexander, Robert, 331
All the Chances (homestead), 61
Allegany Ballistics at Cumberland, 4
Allegany County, 37, 50, 51, 52, 59, 60, 62, 78
Allegany County Convention, 164
Allegany County Court, 77
Allegany County District 3, 63
Allegany County District 10, 68, 74
Allegany County Levy Court on Roads, 116
Allegany forests and mountains, 83
Allegany Glades, 80

Allegany Grove, 121
Allegany House (Hotel), 293
Allegany Iron Company, 53
Allegany Mountains, 120
Alleghenies, 35, 37, 42, 117
Allegheny highlands, 46, 70, 79
Allegheny Mountains, 40, 45, 129, 130
Allen, Horatio, 194
Allen, John Prentice, 119
Allen, Polly, 119
Allen, Samuel, 129, 132
Allies, Indian, 2
Alpaca sheep, 67
Altamont, 16, 52, 200, 201, 245, 247, 249
Altamont Spring Bottling House, 330
Althers, W. A., 76
Althouse, 68
American Bicentennial in Garrett County, 346
American Central Intelligence Agency, 348
American colonists, 46
American Farmer, The, 80
American frontier history, 157, 158
American HV Test Systems, Inc., 344
American Republic, 49
American Revolution, 48, 49, 50
American Star (newspaper), 305
American Turf Register, The, 80
American West, roads to, 117
America's settlement, 334
Amish, 63, 64, 74, 310
Amish-Mennonite, 108
Amish settlers, 40, 72

361

Ammann, Eric, 326, 327
Ammann, Mrs. Eric, 326
Amsterdam, New, 2
"Anchors Aweigh," (music), 288
Anderson (John Brown), 208
Andes Mountains, Peru, 67
Animals, wild, 3, 94, 100, 101, 191
Annapolis, 30, 43, 121
Appalachian frontier, 118
Appalachian highlands, 32
Appalachian Mountains, 117, 121, 125, 134
Appalachian Plateau, 31
Appalachians, 2
Archer's Spring, 123
Arendt, Andrew, 261
Arkansas joins Union, 157
Armstrong, Edward, 61
Armstrong, Hanna, 61
Armstrong, Hannah, 60
Armstrong, James, 201
Armstrong, James D., 200
Armstrong, Neil, 342
Armstrong, Peter, 61
Armstrong, William, 47, 60, 61
Armstrong-Oakland settlement, 71
Armstrong tavern, 60, 126
Army Corps of Engineers, 17
Arnett, Daniel, 58
Arnold, John, 103
Arnold Run No. 1 (coal mine), 274
Arnos Vale estate, 39
Asbury, Francis, 108
Ashby Discovery tract, 41
Ashby, George, 40
Ashby, Henry, 40
Ashby, Jack, 40
Ashby, Jesse, 40, 216
Ashby, Nathan, 41
Ashby, Peter, 40
Ashby, Sarah, 41, 71
Ashby, Thomas, 61, 62
Ashby, William, 41, 45, 47, 86, 101, 266
Ashby, William Wilton, 40, 61, 71, 116
Ashby, Wilton, 119
Ashby gristmill, 88
Ashby Road, 116
Ashbys, 41, 83
Ault, George, 74
Ault, Kate, 75

Aurora Road, 61
Aurora, W.Va., 106
Auto, International Harvester, 181
Autumn Glory Festival, 320, 346
Avilton, 52, 62, 65
Ayres, Robert, 108

Backbone Mountain, 33, 35, 38, 39, 40, 43, 44, 67, 68, 69, 71, 72, 106, 116, 123, 125, 128, 200
Bad Is the Best of It (tract), 39
Baker, 62
Baker, Lloyd, 162
Baker, Lucius, 162
Baker, Peter, 232
Baker's (Lloyd) Tin Shop, 249
Ballot and Billmeyer, 272
Balls (dances), 163
Baltimore, 4, 30, 40, 43, 59, 62, 65, 77, 78, 81, 129, 194, 196
Baltimore American, 196, 350
Baltimore Boys' Home, 254
Baltimore Cathedral, 106
Baltimore Druid Hill Park, 254
Baltimore Gazette, 143
Baltimore and Ohio Blockhouse during Civil War, 210
Baltimore and Ohio Railroad, Frontispiece, 16, 61, 66, 70, 71, 146, 186, 193, 196, 198, 199, 201-10, 221-44, 252-58, 263-87, 290-95, 300-306, 314, 335
B&O Oakland Hotel, 290
B&O Station (Oakland), 61
B&O Viaduct, 16
Baltimore Sun (newspaper), 94, 288, 290, 343
Bancroft, George, 206, 250
Bandstand at Deer Park, 183
Baptists, 105, 106, 310
Barnards, 66
Barnstredder, Matthias, 51
Bashford Amphitheater, 294
Bassett, Thomas, 37
Bath (Berkeley Springs, W.Va.), 121, 122
Battle of Fallen Timbers, 156
Battle of Horse Shoe Bend, 156
Battle of Huamantla, 167
Battle of Tippecanoe, 156
Bauer, L. A., 261
Bausch and Lomb, Inc., 329, 344

Beachy, 72
Beachy, Leo J., 76, 112, 308
Beall, Aza, 58
Beall, Isaac, 146
Beall, Thomas, 43, 52, 145
Bear, 24-26, 96
Bear Camp, 39, 116, 144
Bear Camp Run, 39, 85, 88, 89
Bear Creek, 25, 28, 29, 31, 33, 44, 53-55, 89, 109
Bear Creek Glades, 25, 27, 77, 84
Bear Creek Iron Furnace, 182
Bear Creek Lumber Co., 270
Bear story, 73
Beegly, Jeremiah, 109
Bees, 26
Belasco, David, 180
Bell, Alexander Graham, 281
Belvoir household, 34
Benders, 63
Benet, Stephen Vincent, quote, 23
Ben-Hur, 180, 279
Berry, C. E., and Co., 249
Bibliography, 357-60
Bicentennial Calendar of Garrett County, xii
Bicentennial Committee, xi, xii
Bicentennial Community, first in Garrett County (Bloomington), 346
Big Boiling Spring, 36
Big Pool, 11
Big Run State Park, 345
Billington, Ray Allen, 118
Birds, 26
Birth of Republican party, 213
"Bishop of Mountain Lake," (Rev. John Thompson), 292
Bison, 3, 39
Bittinger, 33, 52, 62, 75, 76, 77, 81, 110, 336
Bittinger Election District, 76
Bittinger Glades, 75, 76
Bittinger, Henry, 75, 76
Bittinger, Joseph, 76
Bittinger Post Office, 76, 82
Bittinger, Wayne, 76
Bittner, Jere, 162
Black, Harry, 182
Black, Mrs. Harry, 182
Black, James, 150
Black people, first in county, 37

Blackwater River (W.Va.), 250
Blaine Coal Co., 275
Blair, F. P., 99
Blair, Montgomery, 279
Blocher, Andrew, 65
Blocher, Christian, 65
Blooming Rose, 23, 24, 25, 33, 43, 44, 52, 53, 95, 106, 116
Blooming Rose Ridge, 53, 107
Blooming Rose Roads, 53, 116
Blooming Rose School, 23
Bloomington, 16, 17, 33, 51, 52, 66, 67, 69, 126, 200, 245, 247, 249, 253, 267, 274, 275
Bloomington Methodists, 111
"Bloomington Story, The," 346
Bloomington Union Meeting House, 111
Blue, John, 232
Blue Lick, 89
Board of Commissioners of Public Schools, 113
Board of Forestry, state's first, 338
Board of Trustees Garrett County Free Library, 351
Boat building, 326
Boating, Flying Scot, 327
Boiling Spring, 33, 52, 57, 77, 78, 287
Bollman, Eric, 60, 68, 90, 102, 106
Bond Junction, 267
Book of the Royal Blue, 211, 284, 287
Boone, Daniel, 118, 155
Borig, A., 261
Bosley (George) House, 251
Boston, 48
Boucher, Jonathan, 43
Bower, Ele, 204
Bowman, 62
Bowser, Jake, 74
Boyd, Andrey Hunter, 262
Boyer, J. W., 75
Boyer, S. L., 283
Boyers, 236
Boyer's (S. L.) Central Hotel, 251
Boyer tannery (Accident), 92
Boyle, 59
Boyles, 66
Boyles, Charles, 51
Boyle's Sorrow, 59
Braddock, General Edward, 43

363

Braddock Road, 13, 36-40, 43, 44, 51, 52, 57, 62, 65, 80, 108, 118, 120-23, 128, 129, 134, 146, 172
Braddock Road taverns, 144
Braddock's British troops, 13
Braddock's defeat, 95
Braddock's expedition, 32
Braddock's fifth camp, 39, 62
Braddock's fourth camp, 37
Braddock's sixth camp, 39, 119, 129
Braddock's Trails, 58, 115, 116
Brady, Mathew B., 226
Brady, Samuel, 127
Braethorn (Hotel), 293
Bragg, Braxton, 235
Brain, James, 49
Brandt, J. B., Meat Market, 249
Brandt, Thomas J., 20, 214, 249, 279
Brandts, 66
Brant, Daniel R., 67, 247
Brant, John, 66
Brantsburg gun factory, 66
Bray, Daniel, 67
Bray, Philip, 68, 215, 216
Bray settlement, 116
Brenneman, Christian, 110
Brenneman, Clarence, 76
Brenner, Charles L., 109
Brethren, 74, 107, 310, 311
Brew, George T., 273, 294
Briar Bend (Hotel), 293
Briar Patch, 76
Bridges, four historic, 13
British, 50
British army, 40, 41
Britonic Majestic Colonies, 42
Broad Ford Dam, 346
Broad Ford Lake, 329
Broadwater, 65
Broadwater, Marion Viola, 146
Broadwater, Mrs. David (Marine), xii
Broadwater, Mrs. Maxine, 174
Brobst, John, 53
Brock, Miss Edith, xii
Brook, William J. R., 93
Brooke, Dr., 81
Brooks, James, 43
Brooks, Preston, 213
Brown, 65
Brown, Charles, 244
Brown, Elisha, 147

Brown, Jacob, xii, 46, 53, 54, 86, 89, 90, 93, 98, 100, 101, 105, 108, 109, 112, 114, 129, 134, 136, 139-44, 146, 148, 149, 151, 161-64, 167, 187, 214, 217, 243, 244, 255, 258, 273, 301, 302, 309, 311
Brown, John, 208, 213
Brown, McCulloch, 338
Brown, Ridgely, 227-29
Brown, Samuel, 108
Brown, William, 129, 130
Browning, Allen, 30
Browning, Dorcas, 25
Browning, Earl, 289
Browning, Edward R., 241
Browning, James, 30
Browning, Jane, 30
Browning, Jeremiah, 30
Browning, John, 95
Browning, John Lynn, 29, 232
Browning, John T., 284
Browning, Joshua, 95, 130
Browning, Maria Louise, 232
Browning, Mary, 23, 25, 28, 29, 30, 92, 98, 166
Browning, Meshach, 20, 22-25, 28, 30, 52, 57, 59, 65, 72, 77, 83, 88-91, 94-104, 107, 115, 129-32, 160, 164, 166, 186, 201, 207, 255, 257
Browning, Meshach's Cabin, 21
Browning, Meshach's gristmill, 88
Browning, Meshach's poem about his wife, 30, 31
Browning, Nancy, 30
Browning, Rachel, 26
Browning, Richard T., Frontispiece, 255, 257, 284
Browning, Sally, 30
Browning, Thomas, 30
Browning, William, 26, 95
Browning House, 251
Browning House (Hotel), 284
Browning Roadside Marker, 22
Brownsville, Pa., 54
Bruce, Norman, 39, 68
Bruce, Upton, 54, 68
Brunley Inn, 146
Brydon, (Commissioner) William A., 255, 261

Bryan, William Jennings, 295, 302, 304
Buckel, Joseph, 75, 76
Buckle, Catherine, 76
Buckle, Henry, 76
Buffalo, 3, 31, 57, 77, 120
"Buffalo Bill" (William F.) Cody, 180, 243, 279
Buffalo Marsh, 33, 36, 52, 57, 77-79, 81, 83, 90, 95, 100, 110, 115
Buffalo Run, 33, 39, 44
Bunting, Mr. ("old Red"), 150
Burkhart, George, 75
Burkhart, Leonard, 75
Burns, 66
Burns, Patrick, 51
Burroughs, John, 9, 11, 12, 336
Burton, a Mr., 250
Butler, Jim, 182

Cade, Mortimer D., 146, 216
Calderwood, Paul T., 17, 87, 181
Calendar, Garrett County Bicentennial, xii
Calhoun, John C., 188, 190, 212, 246
California, first white wagon train, 157
California joins Union, 157
Calmes, 104
Calmes, George, 70, 71
Calmes, George, residence, 125
Calvert, Cecilius, 2
Calvert, George, 38
Cambria County, Pa., 72
Camden Station, Baltimore, 254
Camp, 65
Campbell, William, 77, 80, 81, 86, 89, 100, 101, 102
Campbells, 80
Camp Charlotte Treaty, 46
Canada, 67
Canal, C&O, 121, 242
Canal (C&O), study of proposed, 190
Canal purchase (C&O), 1938, 193
Canal use, 193
Candles to electricity, 307
Carlisle, Alexander, 147
Carolinas, 32
Carr, M. A., 93
Carr, Mrs. Lloyd Logan, 296
Carr, R. F., 93

Carroll, Charles, 193
Carroll County, 68
Carrollton Viaduct, 195
Carter, Ephraim, freed, 163
Casselman Bridge, 13, 14, 135
Casselman Hotel, 148
Casselman Railroad, 272, 276
Casselman River, 13, 33, 37, 40, 62, 76, 121, 135
Casselman Valley, 40
Casteel, Thomas, 47
Casteel William, 261
Castle Hill, 43, 68, 125
Castle Hill Inn, 126
Catholic church at Blooming Rose, 107
Catholic, first settler, 53
Catholicism in Western Maryland, 106
Catholic priests, 106
Catholics, Roman, 310, 311
Caton, 66
Cattle, 26, 103
Census, first federal, 52
Central Hotel, 283
Central Pacific Railroad, 207
Chaffee, 275
Chaffee Coal Company, 276
Chance, 44
Chaney, 65
Chaney, Jesse W., 89
Chaney's Wagon Stand Inn, 145
Changes brought by B&O Railroad, 199, 200
Charity, Miss, 167
Chase, Salmon P., 206, 209
Chase, Samuel, 43
Chautauqua (Hotel), 293, 294
Chautauqua at Mountain Lake Park, 296, 297
"Cheap John" Michael's Toy and Candy Shop, 249
Cheat River, 31, 32, 41, 46, 47, 49, 77, 124, 125, 250
Cheat Valley, 118
Cherokees, 118, 120
Cherry Creek, 33, 40, 41, 45, 78, 86
Cherry Creek Meadows, 77
Cherry Creek No. 144 Grange, 303
Cherry Hill, 44
Chesapeake Bay, 2

365

Chesapeake and Ohio Canal, 121, 190, 193, 242
Chesapeake and Ohio Canal Company, 189
Chesapeake and Ohio Railroad Station at Friendsville, 171
Chesapeake and Potomac Telephone Company, 337
Chevoit, Dale, 81
Chief Cornstalk, 45
Chisholm, Daniel, 260
Chisholm, P. A., 239, 240
Chisholm, W. Wallace, 241
Chisholm's (Daniel) Drug Store, 249
Christian Standard, 292
Christmas in Garrett County, 162
Church of the Brethren, 107
Church events, 162
Churches in Garrett County, 310, 311
Cincinnati Enquirer, 253
Circuit riders, 104, 107
Civil Defense program, Garrett County, 348
Civilian Conservation Corps (CCC), 340
Civil War, 208, 211-38, 241, 243
Civil War effects in Garrett County, 217-20
Civil Works Administration, 341
Clark, Evelyn Wilt, 319
Clark, H. E., 271
Clark and McCullough Lumber Company, 270
Clarksburg, 60, 125
Clarksburg Academy, 115
Clay, Henry, 246
Cleveland, Grover, 281, 332
Cleveland, Mrs. Grover (Frances Folsom), 281
Cleveland honeymoon in Garrett County, 282
Cleveland Panic of 1890s, 301
Cleveland wedding, 282
Clifton, 33
Clover Bottom, 62
Coach lines through Garrett County, 140
Coal, 274-78
Coal mine at Steyer, 322
Cocklefield tract, 43
Coddington, Benjamin, 47, 51

Coddington, Samuel, 59
Coddington, William, 47, 51, 55, 261
Coddingtons, 38
Cody, "Buffalo Bill," 243, 279
Cohongoroota River, 31
Colardeau, St. Felix, 249
Colardeau's Woolen Mill, 249
Colemine Lick, 44
College, Garrett Community, xii
Colonial troops in Ohio County, 46
Colonies, 48
Columbian (Hotel), 293, 294
Columbus, 37
Columbus, Christopher, quote, 1, 2
Combs, William, 200
Commercial House Hotel, 283
Communications in Garrett County, 306
Community Park (Friends' Delight), 57
Compromise of 1850, 213
Compton Schoolhouse, 174
Concord coach, 139
Concord, N.H., 139
Confluence and Oakland Railroad, 270, 272, 274, 276
Connecticut, 129, 133
Connell, John A., 266
Connelly's, 66
Connestoga Wagons, 144
Conneway, Joseph M., 284
Conrad, Jacob, 147
Consolidation of schools, 339
Constitutional Convention, 78
Continental army, 50
Continental Congress, First, 48
Continental Divide, 2, 35, 68
Convention or Counsel of Safety, 47
"Coon" Michael's General Store, 249
Cooper, Peter, 194, 195
Corcoran, W. W., 283
Cord, H., 272
Cornucopia, 39, 43, 62, 63
Cove, The, 8
Covent Garden, 44
Covered bridges, 116
Coxey's Army, 301
Crabtree (Crab Tree) Bottom, 44, 57
Crabtree Creek, 67
Cranberry Glade Marsh, 33
Cranberry Swamp, 65, 66, 134
Cranesville Road, 44

Cranesville Swamp, 9, 19
Crawl, Peter, 51
Creighton (A. B.) Coal Company, 276
Crellin, 33, 43, 45, 52, 61, 62, 86, 101, 274, 275, 277, 337
Crellin, Rolland P., 62, 266
Crellin Sawmill, 319
Cresap Company formation, 48
Cresap, Michael, 47
Cresap, Thomas, 47, 128
Cresaps, 117
Crimm, Calvin, 351
Croghan, George, 117
Crook, George, 240, 241, 243
Cross, 146
Cross, Lemuel, 217
Crowe, 65, 66
Crozet, Claude, 126
Crystal's (Margaret) Dress Shop, 249
Cumberland, 26, 50, 52, 57, 73, 79, 90, 108, 116, 131, 133
Cumberland, Allegany Ballistics at, 4
Cumberland and Allegany Gas Company, 343
Cumberland Daily News, 264
Cumberland Gap, Ky., 118, 155
Cumberland's growth, 197
Cumberland News, The, 256, 257
Cumberland-Ohio Road Bill, 133
Cumberland Road, 63, 117, 134, 135, 153, 154, 336
Cumberland Times, 58
Cunningham, James, 77, 81
Cuppett, Jacob, 55

Dailey, John, 230, 251, 279, 280
Daily, Charles, 241
Dan Mountain, 131
Davidson, Wilbur, 292, 295, 298
Davis, Bishop and Townshend's General Store, 249
Davis, "Black Jack," 228
Davis, Henry Gassaway, 246, 264, 266, 268, 280-83
Davis, Jefferson, 180, 242, 278, 279
Davis, John (free black), 68
Davis, John, 215, 250
Davis, J. M., 90, 188, 248, 255, 291, 301
Davis, John M., 103, 110, 111
Davis, John W., 275

Davis, Joseph, 51
Davis, Mrs. Lillian, 183
Davis, Phoebe (free black), 68
Davis Coal and Coke Company, 269
Davis and Elkins College, 247
Davis House, 251
Davises, 66, 67
Deakins, Francis, 38, 43, 50, 60, 125, 260
Deakins, William J., 73
Deakins Line (Old State Line), 50
Dean, Levi, 148
Declaration of Independence, 43
Deep Creek, 33, 38, 85, 98, 337
Deep Creek Bridge, 7
Deep Creek Dam, 80, 337
Deep Creek Glades, 35, 44, 79-81, 101
Deep Creek Lake, 77, 190, 246, 337
Deep Creek State Park, 346
Deer, 26, 86
Deer Park, 17, 43, 52, 69, 70, 71, 88, 125, 201, 245, 247, 249, 252, 257, 258, 265, 267, 284-91, 300, 304, 307, 344
Deer Park Distillery, 71
Deer Park Hotel, Frontispiece, 44, 178, 253, 280, 281, 285, 290
DeHaven, William, 148
Deidricks, 70
Delaware, 133
Delaware River, 83
Delawares (Indians), 32
Delawder, G. W., 261
Dennett (Hotel), 293, 294
Dennis (Negro dancer), 145
Dennison, James, 51
Dennisons, 66
Destiny—Part III, 186
Devecmon, Peter, 58, 61
Devil's Half Acre, 134, 336
DeWitt, Henry, 57
DeWitt, John, 58
DeWitt, Joseph, 161
DeWitt, Peter, 85
Dickson, George, 68
Dietrich, Andreas, 75
Dill, W.Va., 268, 269
Dinwiddie, Governor, 119
Distillery, M. J. Miller's, 336
Dixon, Jeremiah, 41, 42, 259
Dixons, 66

Dobbin, W.Va., 268, 269
Doddridge, Joseph, 46
Dodson, 276, 277
Dorsey, James, 216
Dorsey, Patrick, 65
Douglas Run, 40
Douglas, Stephen A., 213
Douglass, Frederick, 213
Drane Grave, 179
Drane House, 73, 178
Drane, James, 27, 178, 179
Drane, James, Jr., 47, 73
Drane, Mrs., 93
Drane, Susan, 196
Drane, Tommy, 161
Drane, William, 74, 162
Dranes, 74
Dred Scott Case, 279
Dred Scott decision, 213
Drees, 66
Dresser Industries, 344
Droege, Emil, 71, 245
Droege, John Albert, 245
Druid Hill, 127
Druid Hill Park, 291
DuBois and Bond Brothers Lumber Corporation, 265
Duckworths, 66
Dudley, Eileen, 146
Duel: Francis Thomas and William Price, 64
Dugan, Tim, 17, 320, 321, 323
Dumfries tract, 43
Durst, John "Lightfoot," 89, 100
Durst, Ross C., 65, 104, 136, 244, 264, 301, 307, 308, 313, 314, 336
Dutch, 2
Dutch Reformed, 106
Duvall, Absalom, 258
Duvall, Benjamin, 47
Duvall-Browning fight, 258

Eagle Rock, 17
Early, Jubal A., 240
Eastern Land Corporation, 337
Eastern Seaboard, 2
Eckhart, John, 74
Economy of Garrett County, 347
Eden's Paradise Regained, 44
Edison, Thomas, 9, 11, 12, 336
Edwards, Harry C., 135

Eger, 68
Einstein, Albert, 342
Eisenhower, Dwight D., 193
Elder Hill, 44
Elections, 58, 164, 165
Electricity in Garrett County, 337
Elkins, W.Va., 247
Elk Lick Creek, 33
Elliott, John S., xii
Empire Mine, 274
Encyclopaedia Brittanica, 350
Endsley, 146
Engle, 62
Engle, Will, 76
Englehardt, Frederick, 74
Englehardt, Michael, 74
Englehardt, William, 75
Engle's gristmill, 89
Engle's Mill, 271
Engle's Mill Road, 75
English, 2, 48, 76
English Crown, 46
English king, 34
English Trinity Congregation, 107
Enlow, 87
Enlow, Ephraim E., 349-51
Enlow, John, 53
Enlow, Ruth Christine, 351
Enlow, William Frazee, 85
Enterprise Tanning Company, 267
Entertainment in Garrett County, 312, 313, 314
Epilogue: Garrett County, 353-55
Episcopal Parish House, 350
Episcopalians, 254, 310
Europe, 124
Evangelical Lutheran Church, 110
Expansion and settlement 41, 42

Fadely, 66
Fair Hill, 44
Fairall, 146
Fairall, Richard, 73, 74, 98
Fairall, Truman, 149
Fairfax, William, 34
Fairfax Stone, 15, 34, 35, 41, 50, 260
Fairmont, W.Va., 289
Fallen Timbers, 46, 53
False Alarm, 44
Farmer's Hotel, 148
Farming, 86, 303, 344, 345

Farragut, David G., 240
Father Slattery's Cathedral, 111
Faul, H. E., 291
Faulkner, Mr. and Mrs. Joe V., 176
Fay, John Baptist, 241, 243
Fazenbaker, George, 51
Fazenbakers, 66
Fear, Daniel, 149
Fear, George A., 55
Federal forces, 16
Federal highway, 14
Federalists, 164
Fenwick, Edward, 106
Figgie, 62
Fike, 65
Fike, John, 160
Finzel, 52, 66
Finzel, Annie Margaret, 66
Firestone, Harvey S., 9, 11, 12, 336
Firestone, Harvey S., Jr., 11
Firestone, Russell, 11
"First Church of Jesus Christ in the Youghiogheny Glades," 106
First National Bank of Kitzmiller, 306
First National Bank of Oakland, 306
Fischer, Leonhard, 75
Fish, 3, 101
Fishing, 86
Fitzwater, Florence, 229
Fizer, George A., 277
Flat Woods, 93
Flatwoods, 44
Flintstone, 131
Florida joins Union, 157
Flour mills, 87
Flowery Vale, 44, 68, 73, 74
Flushing Shirt Manufacturing Company, 344
Flying Scot (boat), 344
Folsom, Frances (Mrs. Grover Cleveland), 281
Forbes, John, 40
Forbes Road, 40, 118
Ford, Edsel, 11
Ford, Henry, 9, 11, 12, 289, 336
Forest Service, Maryland, 10
Forestry Operations, 316
Forests, 9
Forsyth, Gabriel, 55
Fort Ashby, 40
Fort Cherry Creek, 40

Fort Cumberland, 3, 13, 35, 37-39, 41, 42, 50, 121, 128, 130, 136, 188
Fort Delaware, 239
Fort Donelson, 224
Fort Duquesne, 37, 40, 95
Fort Frederick, 128
Fort Henry, 48, 224
Fort McHenry, 78, 81
Fort Morris, 46, 47
Fort Pendleton, 222, 236
Fort Pitt, 41, 117, 120
Fort Stanwix Treaty, 118
Fort Sumter, 208
Forts, 45
Forty-Four Years of the Life of a Hunter, 20, 95
Fouch, Samuel, 167
Fountain Inn, 62
Four-H (4-H) Center, 81
Fourth of July, 79
Fowl, 26
Fowler, James A., 11
France, 79
Franklin House, 145
Frankville, 200, 245, 247, 249, 253
Frantz, Jackson, 55
Frantz, Jonathan, 74
Frantz, Joseph, 92
Frantz, Thomas, 55
Frantzes, 45
Fratz, Leonhard, 75
Fratz, Mrs. Wayne, xii
Frazee, Ephraim, 159
Frazee, H. M., 261
Frazee, Hiram, 58
Frazee, Isaac, 55
Frazee, Jeremiah, 39, 51
Frazee, Jonathan, 39, 51
Frazee, Richard, 55
Frazees, 38, 45
Frazee's Ridge, 53, 106
Fraziers, 117
Frederick, 29, 30
Frederick County, 3, 37, 38, 47, 48, 50, 64, 67, 73, 76, 77, 130
Frederick Town, 48
Fredericksburg, 120
Freehold, N.J., 129
French, 2, 32, 48
French Huguenot, 73
French and Indian War, 117, 120

Frey, William, 55
Freys, 45
Friend, Andrew, 35, 36, 55
Friend, Augustine, 36, 44, 47, 57, 77, 80, 83, 95, 99, 100, 160
Friend, Charles, 36, 52, 59, 77, 96, 103, 122, 123, 125
Friend, Cornelius, 85
Friend, D. A., 54, 55, 83, 92, 102, 105, 162, 217
Friend, D. H., 261
Friend, Elijah Hoye, 230
Friend, Mrs. Elizabeth, 230
Friend, Gabriel, 35, 43, 47, 53, 101
Friend, Gabriel's Grave, 177
Friend, Grave of John, Sr., 177
Friend, Jacob, 55
Friend, John, 3, 23, 28, 31, 35, 36, 37, 40, 47, 51, 56, 69, 77, 91, 95, 99, 160
Friend, John, Jr., 57
Friend, John G., 55
Friend, John S., 55
Friend, Jonathan, 55
Friend, Joseph, 107
Friend, Joshua, 55
Friend, Leslie E., 307
Friend, Nicholas, 36, 77
Friend, Stephen Willis, 216
Friend, Teen, 100
Friend, William E., 55, 91
Friend settlement, 39, 59, 107
Friend stockades, 49
Friends, 36-38, 45, 83, 101
Friend's Choice, 44, 107
Friend's Cove, 56
Friend's Delight, 57
Friend's Fenced Graveyard, 177
Friend's Fortune, 36
Friend's Graveyard, 177
Friend's Post Office, 53
Friendsville, 7, 36, 43, 52, 53, 54, 56, 72, 74, 75, 91, 101, 253, 270, 336
Frog Harbor Manor, 57
Frog Hollow, 126
Froman, Jacob, 39, 47, 88
Froman gristmill, 89
Froman Mill, 88
Fromans, 38
Frost, Meshach, 86, 145
Frostburg, 86, 336

Frye, William, 93
Fuchs, Andreas, 74
Fuchs, Gottfried, 74
Fuller, Henry, 148
Fuller-Baker Log House, 171
Funds for Roads (Maryland General Assembly), 125
Furguson, R. F., 164

Gainors, 66
Gainor's Inn (Brien), 126
Galloway, Phoebe, 215
Garlitz, 146
Garlitz, Christian, 65, 100, 101
Garlitz, Henry, 167
Garrett, Charles A., 247
Garrett, Harrison, Frontispiece
Garrett, Henry, 208, 209, 254
Garrett, Henry S., 110, 332
Garrett, John Work, Frontispiece, 110, 186, 208, 226, 235, 247, 251-54, 258, 267, 280, 281, 301, 332, 338
Garrett, Patrick, 306
Garrett, Robert, 199
Garrett, Mrs. Robert B. (Nelle), Frontispiece, 21, 174
Garrett, Robert B. (Browning), xii, 201, 209
Garrett, Robert (son of John W.), 282
Garrett Community College, xii, 321, 339
Garrett Cottage, Deer Park, 174
Garrett County, 3, 4, 8, 24, 31, 32, 34-38, 40, 43, 47, 48, 50-52, 59, 62, 65, 66, 72, 74
Garrett County Apprenticeships, 160
Garrett County Bank, 305
Garrett County Bicentennial Committee, 347
Garrett County Boundaries, 257, 260, 261
Garrett County churches, 106, 107, 109, 110
Garrett County Coal Company, 275
Garrett County commissioners, 352
Garrett County Community College, xii, 321, 339
Garrett County continued growth, 104

370

Garrett County conventions, early, 261
Garrett County Court House, 184
Garrett County courthouse and jail, first, 262
Garrett County doctors, 93
Garrett County early churches, 105
Garrett County, eighteenth century, 334, 335
Garrett County Fair, 320, 346
Garrett County firsts: courthouse and jail, 262; industry, 54; library, 350; public officers, 261; school secretary-examiner, 261; state representatives, 261; Sunday school, 110; town, Selbysport, 39; water-powered up-and-down-sash sawmill, 85
Garrett County formation, 254, 258, 259
Garrett County game, 95
Garrett County genesis, 186, 259
Garrett County Grange, 303
Garrett County gristmills, 88, 89
Garrett County growth, early, 52
Garrett County Herald (newspaper), 305
Garrett County Historical Society, 15, 179, 180, 346, 349, 350
Garrett County history, early, 263
Garrett County history book, xii
Garrett County hunters, 96
Garrett County industries, early, 54, 263
Garrett County Memorial Hospital, 60, 352
Garrett County Museum, 183, 350
Garrett County nineteenth century, 335
Garrett County Panic of 1857, 301
Garrett County pioneer life, 90, 91, 92, 93
Garrett County pioneers, 83, 84, 159, 160
Garrett County population 1870, 255
Garrett County public roads work, 347
Garrett County religious groups, 111
Garrett County Revolutionary War Rangers, 47
Garrett County sawmills, 86
Garrett County schools. *See* Schools.

Garrett County School Board, 338
Garrett County settlers, 82, 85
Garrett County teachers, 114, 349
Garrett County Telephone Company, 336
Garrett County Welfare Board, 340
Garrett Journal (newspaper), 305
Garrett Literary Society, 350
Garrett Lumber Company, 272
Garrett Manufacturing Company, 344
Garrett Memorial Church, 110, 254, 332
Garrett mountains, 3
Garrett Museum, 183, 322, 350
Garrett National Bank of Oakland, 305
Garrett Star (Glade Star), 256
Garrett Telephone Company, 337
Garrett's Road. *See* B&O RR
Garrison, William Lloyd, 212
General Assembly, 51
Genoa, 2
Georg, Johann, 75
George, Earl, 247
George, John, 66
George's Creek, 37, 120
Georgetown, 30, 38, 50, 68, 125
Georgia, 133
German, 76
German stowaway (Joseph Buckel), 75
Germany, 71
Getty, William R., 258
Gibbons, James, 282
Gibbons' reception at Deer Park, 283
Gilbert, 68
Gill, Samuel, 238
Gillus, Samuel, 147
Gingerichs, 63
Ginseng Hill, 56, 57
Gist, Christopher, 42, 101
Gists, 117
Glade Country, 78
Glade Run, 31, 35
Glade Star, 256 305
Glades, 3
Glades Hotel (Oakland), 180, 250, 251, 257, 278-80, 290
Glades Indian Path, 70, 125
Glades Path, 32, 43
Glades Road, 126

371

Glades Star, The, 4, 6, 11, 15, 16, 82, 319, 330, 332, 346, 349, 350
Glades weather, 79
"Glory days, memories," (C. E. Jones), 287-91
Glotfelty, E. H., 93, 261
Glotfelty, Joseph, 63
Glotfelty, William, 82
Glotfeltys, 237
Gnagey, 63, 72
Gnagey, John, 75
Gnegy, C. C., 311
Gnegy, Elizabeth, 84, 92
Gnegy, Samuel, 84, 92
Gnegy Church, 44
Godwin, Joseph M., 222
Goehringer, Adam, 74, 75
Goehringer, George, 74
Golf, Oakland Country Club, 328
Gompers, Samuel, 295
Gonder, W. A., 184
Good Hope, 44, 62
Good Intent Stage Company, 139, 145
Good Spring, 44
Good Will tract, 37, 39
Gordon, John B., 296
Gordon Douglass Boat Company, 326, 344
Gorman, 68, 71, 92, 123, 126, 127, 276, 277
Gorman, Daniel, 145
Gorman, Senator Arthur Pue, 69
Gormania, 69
Gortner, 38, 40, 41, 72, 343
Gortner, Barbara, 72
Gortner, Peter, 72, 92, 103, 107
Goucher, John F., 291, 298
Goucher College, 291
Gould, George W., 167
Governor of Maryland, 4
Governor of Virginia, Lord Dunmore, 45
Governor's Emergency Unemployment Commission, 339
Gower settlement, 44
Grace Creek, 133
Grafton, 128
Grain field, 8
"Grand Army Day" at Mountain Lake, 296
Grant, Daniel, 62

Grant, Elizabeth, 62
Grant, Mrs. Patience, 332
Grant, Ulysses S., 64, 67, 235, 236, 240, 242, 281, 332
Grant, Mrs. Ulysses S., 281
Grant, W. W., 231, 232
Grant Settlement, old, 63
Grantsville, 13, 33, 43, 44, 46, 52, 53, 62, 63, 64, 65, 74, 75, 76, 86, 88, 89, 94, 108, 130, 135, 142, 253, 258, 336, 344
Grantsville Amish-Mennonite and Brethren, 109
Grantsville Charge of St. John's Evangelical Reformed Church, 109
Grantsville doctors, 93
Grantsville gristmills, 88, 89
Grantsville Lutherans, 109
Grantsville Methodist Church, 108, 109
Grantsville taverns, 147
Grass, 26
Grassy Cabin tract, 37, 63
Grave of Meshach Browning, 22
Great Crossings, 120
Great Depression, The, 274, 284, 290, 339
Great Glades Manor, 38, 40, 60
Great Meadows of Pennsylvania, 121
Great Pine Swamp, 19
Great Warrior Trail (Path), 31, 35, 37, 40, 43, 59, 68
Greater Maryland Tool and Manufacturing Corporation, 344
Green, John, 49
Green, Sarah, 49
Green Glades, 33, 52, 69, 70, 105
Green Glades Manor, 38
Green Glades Run, 38
Green of Sang Run, The, 57
Greenwood, 246
Griffith, Benjamin, 85
Grimes, Mrs. June Dunnington, 182
Gristmills, 89
Groemiller, Leonard, 75
Groenmiller, Michael, 74
Groundhogs, 23
Grouse, Ferdinand, 75
Grove, Piney, 146
Groves, Elwood S., 82
Grower, Frederick, 75
Guard, C. V., 336

Gulf of Mexico, 2, 36, 67
Guthrie, Leroy, 274
Guthrie Mine, 274
Guynns, 66
Gwynn's Tavern (Evan), 121
Gwyns Tavern, 130

Haenftling, Alexander, 75
Hagerstown, 30, 64, 69
Halderman, John, 148
Halderman Tavern, 148
Hall, Richard, 44, 51, 116
Hall of Philosophy, Mountain Lake Park, 292
Hallar, L. S., 241
Halls, 38
Hamill, Gilmor S., 261
Hamill, P., 22, 255
Hamill, Patrick, 66, 232, 258
Hamill Coal and Coke Company, 275
Hamills, 67
Hampshire County, 125
Hanover, Va., 129
Harbison-Walker Refractories, 344
Hard Labour Treaty, 118
Hardesty, Jim, 247
Hardesty, Leona M., 293, 296, 299
Harding, Rebecca, 99, 203, 283, 284
Harding, Warren G., 11
Hare, 62
Hare, Philip, 85, 273
Harman, Asher, 227-29, 231
Harper, R. G., 190
Harpers Ferry, 34, 66, 67, 210, 213
Harper's Magazine, 203, 205, 206, 250, 283, 284
Harriet's Laundry, 249
Harrison, General and Mrs. Benjamin, Deer Park, 283
Harrison, William Henry, 156, 165
Harshes, 70
Hartman, John, 55
Hart's (Owen) Dry Goods Store, 249
Harvest Festival, 162, 347
Harvesting, 86, 87
Harvey, Huldah, 229
Harvey, John L., 241
Harvey, Nathaniel B., 229
Harvey, Rachel Olive, 229
Harvey, William, 261
Harveys, 67
Haye's Place (John), 126

Head, John, 39
Heck, Yost, 70
Helbig, Peter, 231
Helbig's (John) Tannery, 249
Hench, Dromgold and Shull Company, 269
Henry, W.Va., 268, 269
Herders, 104
Herman, Dr., 93
Hermitage at Nashville, Tenn., 138
Herring, Jacob, 55, 91
Herrington, Abijah, 47
Herrington Creek, 104
Herrington Manor, 43
Herrington Manor Lake, 340
Herrington Manor State Park, 345
Hershberger, 63
Hershberger, Daniel, xii
Hershberger gristmill, 88
Heyden, Thomas, 106
Heyer, C. F., 107
Highest point on B&O RR., Altamont, 200
Highland Hall, 145
Highways, U.S., 8
Hinebaugh, Alfred, 162
Hinebaugh, Bessie Ward, 312
Hinebaugh, Dan, 247
Hinebaugh, Daniel, 92
Hinebaugh, William, 75, 255
Hinebaugh's (Jonathan) General Store, 249
Hiram College, Ohio, 115
History of Crellin, 319
History of Cumberland, 197
History of Garrett County Pioneer Families, A, 349
Hobach, Michael, 75
Hoblitzell, Dennis, 148
Hoblitzell, J. H., 86
Hoff, Abram, 55
Hoffman, 68
Hoffman, David, 59, 85, 88, 160
Hoffman, H. W., 258
Hoffman, William, 75
Hog Run, 46, 47
Holiday entertainment, 162-64
Holland, 53
Home building, 26
Home chores, 27
Home heating, 307
Home remedies, 93

Homestead, 28
Hook, John L., 55, 91
Hoopole Ridge, 33, 59
Hoover, Herbert, 339
Hoover Reconstruction Finance Corporation, 339
Hopkins, Gerald, 132
Hopkins, Gerald T., 129
Hopkins, Johns, 199
Horse Shoe Bend, 46, 49
Horses, 26
Hostility between Americans and Indians, 45
Hotel owner, A. B. Reis, 75
"Hotell, The," 145
Hotels and Inns, 142-49
House, Andrew, 57
Houston, Sam, 246
Howard, Mrs. Alice F., 346
Howard, Miss Alice R., 346
Howard, Mrs. Charles, 278
Howard, Frances Key, 278
Howard, John Eager, 278
Hoye, Charles E., 15, 57, 74, 81, 159, 214, 349-51
Hoye, John, 54, 190
Hoye, Samuel, 241
Hoye, William, 190, 241
Hoye, William W., 27, 160
Hoye, William Waller, 57, 216
Hoye Crest, 15, 350
Hoyes, 22, 44, 58, 253, 336
Hoyes of Maryland, The, 349
Huddleson, 146
Hughes' Drug Store and General Merchandise, 249
Humberson, Noah, 55
Hungerford, Edward, 194, 197, 208, 251, 253
Hunting, 97, 98, 99, 100, 102
Hutton, 43 44, 265, 267, 342
Hutton Tannery, 306

Ice Age, 19, 66
Illinois joins Union, 156
Imboden, John D., 227, 233
Imboden, G. W., 237
Independence Day celebration, 163
Indian allies, 2
Indian grave mound, 35
Indian Old Fields, 38
Indian relics, 33

Indian Removal Act, 157
Indian Rocks, 33
Indian trails, 43, 126
Indiana joins Union, 156
Indians, 2, 3, 31, 32, 36, 40, 45, 49, 53, 118, 129, 137, 156
Indians: Cayugas, 48; Iroquois, 32, 118, 120; Mingo, 45; Mohawks, 41, 48; Ohio, 37; Oneidas, 48; Onondagas, 41, 48; Ottawa, 45; Senecas, 48; Shawnee, 45; Six Iroquois Nations, 41, 118; Tuscaroras, 48
Indians' description, 32
Industrialism, 335
Industry, nineteenth and twentieth century, 342
Ingman's Inn, 59
Ingman's Inn (Henry), 126
Integrated Business Methods, Inc., 344
Interstate road, 126
Interstate, 48, 135, 336
Iowa joins Union, 157
Irish, 76
Irish laborers, 200
Irons, 47
Irvine, Colonel, 221
Irwin, 60

Jackson, Andrew, 138, 152, 153, 156, 157, 221
Jackson, Juliana, 160
Jackson, Stonewall, 235
Jamestown, Va., 95
Jankey, John, 247
Jarboe, J. M., 183
Jefferson, Peter, 34
Jefferson, Thomas, 133, 156, 189
Jenifer, Daniel, 70
Jenkins, Mary, 303
Jennings Brothers Railroad, 270, 272, 274, 276
Jennings, Cord H., 77
Jennings, 76, 277, 344
Jennings, Worth B., 272
Johns, Thomas, 45
Johnson, Cornelius, 230
Johnson, David, 147
Johnson, Joshua, 86, 146
Johnson, Thomas, 43, 70, 71, 116, 122, 145, 146

Johnstown (Hoyes), 107, 253
Johnstown, Pa., 337
Johnstown Catholic Church, 107
Johnstown Coal and Coke Company, 276
Johnstown Methodists, 107
Johnstown Planing Mill, 271
Johnstown Post Office, 58
Jonas, John, 47, 51
Jones, Charles A., 283, 288-90, 295, 296, 301, 304, 307, 312
Jones, David, 129
Jones, Mrs. Lewis R., 11
Jones, Sam, 295
Jones, Samuel, 227
Jones, W., 232-34
Jones, William E., 227-29
Jordan, Philip D., 135, 153, 223, 226, 234
Judges, Western Maryland Circuit Court, first, 216
Junction Ohio and Mississippi Rivers, 119, 120
June Bug Line, 139
Juniata Lumber Company, 273
Junkinses, 67

Kaese, Henry, 89
Kaese gristmill, 89
Kaeses, 45
Kahl, Henry, 75
Kahl, Val, 75
Kahl, Valentine, 74
Kanawha River, 118, 120, 123
Kansas-Nebraska Act, 213
Keller, Bayard T., 93
Kelley, Benjamin F., 180, 200, 222, 234, 236, 240, 243
Kelley, General, 241, 242
Kelly, Oliver Hudson, 303
Kempton, 276, 277
Kendall, 270, 272
Kendall Lumber Company, 266, 271, 272
Kennedy, John, 193
Kennedy's Grog Shop, 200, 249
Kent, David, 55
Kentucky, 40, 41, 45, 118, 129, 133
Kentucky valleys, 45
Kepner's Cobbler Shop, 249
Kerr, Elias, 85
Kerr, Joseph, 133

Key, Francis Scott, 81, 278
Keyser, 16, 115
Keyser's Ridge, 8, 36, 51, 109, 134
Keyser's Ridge tavern, 149
Kildow, Michael V., 88
Kilgour, William, 99
Killams, 120
Kindness, 43, 44
King, Dr., 284
King, English, 2
King's Tavern, 249
Kingwood Tunnel, 205
Kinsingers, 63
Kiser, John, 51
Kite, Henry, 51
Kites, 66
Kitzmiller, 33, 52, 67, 88, 267, 269, 270, 275, 276, 277
Kitzmiller, Ebenezer, 67, 88
Kitzmiller gristmill, 88
Kitzmiller Methodists, 111
Kitzmiller woolen mill, 67
Kitzmillerville, 67
Klipstine, Lewis, 164
Knabb, A., and Company, 271
Kolb, Frederick, 75
Kolb, Heinrich, 75
Korean War, 348
Kreebs, 86
Krug, Henry, 272
Krug Lumber Company, 271
Ku Klux Klan, 348

Lackey, Mr., 115
Lafayette, 78, 80
LaMar, William, 73
Lamont, 281
Land, The; Part I, 1
Land Flowing with Milk and Honey, 62
Land jobbers, 45, 123
Landlord's Line, 139
Latrobe, Benjamin, 198, 199, 206
Laughlin, Robert, 109
Laurel Hill, 130
Laurel Run, 85
LaVale, 73
Layman, 63, 146
Layman, George, 258
Layman, John, 89
Lee, Dudley, 47, 51
Lee, Richard Henry, 189

Lee, Robert E., 226, 234, 235, 240, 242, 296
Legal advice in Garrett County, 306
Legge, George W., 305
Legge's (George) General Store, 249
Legislation for free schools, 113
Lehman House, 148
Lehman, John, 148
Lewis, Daniel, 49
Lewis, Thomas, 34
Lewis and Clark Expedition, 156
Liberator, 212
Library, Ruth Enlow, xii
Lichty, 72
Lichty, M. P., 236
"Lightfoot" John Durst, 89
Lincoln, Abraham, 209, 210, 213, 214, 224-27
Lincoln, Joseph, 284
Line, A. A., 292
List, Mrs. L. C. B., 185
Liston, John, 55
Little Bear Creek, 107
"Little Brown Church," 107
Little Crossings, 13, 63, 64, 80, 85, 131, 132, 135
Little and Great Crossings, 129
Little Savage Mountain, 145
Little Shades of Death, 130
Little's (Tom) Store, 249
Llangollen (Bloomington), 66, 245
Llangollen Mining Company, 245, 274
Lloyd, Edward, 45
Loar, George, 60, 110, 350, 352
Loch Lynn Heights, 291, 299
Loch Lynn Heights Hotel, 185, 239, 299, 300
Lochiel, 265
Lock Haven Lumber Company, 271
Locust Tree Bottom, 43, 78, 81, 110
Logsdon, Joseph, 123
Lohr, Catherine, 76
Lohr, Peter, 76, 110
Lomax, Colonel, 228
Look Sharp, 43
Loom and the Anvil, The, 80
Lord Baltimore, 2, 37-41, 50, 60
Lord Dunmore, 45, 46
Lord Fairfax, 34, 41
Loughridge, George, 307
Louise (town), 275, 276, 277

Louisiana joins Union, 156
Louisiana Purchase, 156
Lowdermilk, Walter, 59
Lowdermilk, Will H., 197, 243
Lower, Catherine, 71
Little Meadows, 37-39, 43-45, 63, 85, 88, 101, 108, 120, 134, 135, 138, 142
Little Thunder gristmill, 89
LSD in Garrett County, 348
Luke, William, 141
Luman, Samuel, 141
Lumber shipping areas, 265
Lumbering, 86, 263-74
Luraw, W. A., 266
Lutherans, 74, 106, 107, 310, 311
Lutherans at Bittinger, 110
Lutherans at the Cove, 107
Lutherans at Oakland, 110
Lyle, Perry, 251, 278, 279
Lyles, Virginia, 278
Lynn, David, 73
Lynn, John, 29, 77, 78, 103, 166
Lynn mansion, 81
Lynns, 26, 27

McAdam, John L., 151
McAndrews, Philip, 272
McCarty, Edward, 201, 310
McCarty Hill, 59
McCarty house (Isaac's), 61
McCarty, Ingabe, 61, 201
McCarty, Isaac, 60, 68, 86, 102, 115, 119, 201, 215, 216, 247
McCarty's Mill, 61
McCartyville, 201
McCleary, John, 85
McCleary, Samuel, 167
McClellan, 221
McClellan, George B., 220, 226
McComas, H. W., 306
McComas, J. Lee, 222, 223, 250
McComas Sanitarium, 306
McCrobie, Joseph, 336
McCulloch's Path, 15, 19, 43, 121-23
McCullough, J. W., 271
McCullough, James, 70
McCullough, Raymond O., xi, 22, 177, 321, 346
McCulloughs, 117
McCurdy, Samuel, 147, 167

McCurdy's Little Crossings Hotel, 138
McDonald, Captain, 230
McDonald-Dangerfield Detachment, 229
McDowell, Governor of Virginia, 64
McDowell, Sallie, 64
McFadden, Frank, 75
McGoffin, James, 53
McGraw, 146
McHenry, 7, 29, 43, 52, 82, 258, 336, 347
McHenry, Daniel, 81, 103
McHenry, Daniel William, 78
McHenry, James, 77, 78, 79, 81, 110
McHenry, John, 54, 77, 81, 90, 94, 100, 109, 115, 190, 216
McHenry,/Martha, 81, 196
McHenry Glades, 190, 303
McHenry homestead, 82
McHenrys, 80
MacInnes, Alexander, 231
McKaig, Thomas I., 258
McKane, John, 39
McKeldin, Theodore K., 15, 350
McKenzie, Helen, and sister, 243
McKenzie, John, 243
McKenzie, Leo, 65
McKenzie Settlement, 65
McKinley-Bryan campaign, 304
McKinley, William, 180, 243, 279, 283, 336
McMillen, 75
McMillen, Edwin, 342
McMullen, James, 23, 24, 51
McMullen, Mary, 24, 77, 107
McMullen, Rachel, 23
McNeill, Captain, 238
McNeill, Jesse, 240
McNeill, John, 16
McNeill, John H., 227, 229
McNeill, John Hanson, 240
McNeill, Lieutenant, 241
McNeill's rangers, 239, 240
Macon, Nathaniel, 152
McPipe, James, 51
Magruders, 66
Mahaney, 146
Mahaney, David, 147
Mail, 306
Mail stages, 140
Main joins Union, 156

Manhattan Hotel, 251
"Manifest Destiny," 133
Manor Land, 271, 272
Manors in Maryland, 38
Mansfield, J. K. F., 150
Marbury, 78
Marbury, William, 77
Margroff, Edward, 75
Markell, Jacob, 200
Marley, George, 307, 330
Marley, Grace, 330
Marley, Theodore, 330
Marsh Hill, 81
Martin, Peter, 226
Martin's Cove, 37
Martin's Livery, 249
Mary Ann Furnace (Iron), 55
Maryland, 2, 15, 26, 38-42, 46, 48, 50, 51, 72, 80, 133
Maryland Advocate, 93, 164, 190-92
Maryland Assembly, 4
Maryland Bicentennial Commission, 346
Maryland Forestry Department, 338
Maryland Forestry Service, 10
Maryland General Assembly, 50, 57, 68, 112, 116
Maryland Historical Society, 250
Maryland Journal, 70
Maryland militia, 43
Maryland Revolutionary Convention, 47
Maryland senate, 78
Maryland Sons of Liberty, 47
Maryland State General Assembly, 54
Maryland State Grange, 303
Maryland State House, 64
Maryland state legislature, 52, 64, 193
Maryland state routes, 135-39, 126
Maryland-Virginia Commission, 190
Maryland-Virginia Interstate Road, 124, 126, 154
Maryland-West Virginia Boundary, 19
Masden, C. P., 291, 292
Mason, Alexander, 261
Mason, Charles, 41, 42, 259
Mason, D. M., 239, 240
Mason, James W., 241
Mason, Jno. Thomson, 6
Mason-Dixon Line, 41, 85, 260
Massachusetts, 70, 71

Massacres, 157
Mateer, Paul, 10
Matthews, Aza, 261, 262
Matthews, George, 59, 159, 160
Matthews, Lydia, 159
Matthew's (P. A.) General Store, 249
Mattingly, M., 336
Maust, 62
Mayer, Brantz, 205, 206, 250, 251
Mayo, William, 34
Mayo, Winslow surveys, 260
Maysville Turnpike, 153
Meadow Mountain, 33, 42, 138
Meadow Mountain Coal and Coke Company, 276
Meadow Mountain Lumber Company, 271
Meadow Run, 85
Media, 348
Medication, 29
Meeting House on Sandy Creek, 116
Menhorn, George, 75
Menhorn, Michael, 74
Menhorn, Mr., 236
Mennonite settlers, 40
Mennonites, 63, 72, 74, 82, 310, 311
Merrill, 65
Merrill's Meat Market, 249
Methodists, 53, 107, 108, 110, 310, 311
Mexican-American War (1846), 165, 166, 167
Meyers, Father (Rev.) Henry, 107
Meyers, Joseph, 63
Michaels, 66
Michigan joins Union, 157
Migrants, 119
Military land grants, 51
"Milk and Honey," 44
Mill Run, 39, 85, 88
Miller, 62, 65, 72
Miller, Abraham, 85
Miller, Benedict, 109
Miller, Carl, 181
Miller, Fred, 181
Miller, George, 181
Miller, Ivan J., 82
Miller, Melchoir, 74, 75
Miller, Paul, 181
Miller, Rose, 181
Miller, S. M., 283
Miller, William, 181, 336
Miller, William B., 330

Millers, 63
Miller's (S. M.) Commerical Hotel, 251
Mills (Oakland), 86, 88
Mimma, James, 114
Minear, John, 46
Minear, Jonathan, 49
Miners' Relief Fund, 339
Mining, early, 263
Mining techniques, 277
Miscellaneous Writings by Jacob Brown, xii
Mississippi Company, 119
Mississippi joins Union, 156
Mississippi River, 2, 124
Mississippi River Valley, 69
Mississippi Valley, Roads to, 116
Missouri Compromise, 211
Missouri joins Union, 156
Mitchael's (John) Tavern, 249
Mitchell, T. R., 151, 152
Mobley, Mr., 151
Mogart, William A., 276
Mogart Coal Mining Corporation, 276
Monongahela County, 124
Monongahela River, 42, 117, 128
Monroe, James, 152, 153, 156
Moore, Thomas, 133, 189
Morgan, Thomas Hunt, 341
Morgantown, 115, 125
Morgantown Road, 39
Monte Vista, 284
Montgomery County, 30, 50
Morris, John B., 193
Morrison, Gross and Company, 269
Morrow, Ruthvan W., Jr., 9, 13, 329
Mound Builders, 32
Mount Airy, 44
Mount Chautauqua, 292, 299
Mount Clare Reading Room, 254
Mount Nebo, 44
Mount Pleasant, 44, 145
Mount Savage Ignatius Catholic Church, 109
Mount Vernon, 120, 121, 122
Mount Zion, 106
Mountain, Joseph, 51
Mountain Democrat (newspaper), 284, 294, 305, 306, 336, 342
Mountain Home Company, 299
Mountain Lake Park, 38, 291, 293-300, 344

378

Mountain Lake Park Amphitheater, 169
Mountain Lake Park Association, 291-94, 297-99
Mountain Lake Park Association Silver Jubilee, 294
Mountain Lake Park athletic field, 293
Mountain Lake Park Boathouse and Icehouse, 169
Mountain Lake Park gas field, 343
Mountain Lake Park golf links, 293
Mountain Lake Park grandstand, 293
Mountain Lake Park Hotel, 183, 293, 294, 299
Mountain Lake Park Lake, 293
Mountain Lake Park summer programs, 295
Mountain Lake Park tabernacle, 293
Mountain Lake Park tabernacle fire, 299
Mountain Sunday School Assembly, 292
Mountain View House (Hotel), 294
Mountain's (Joseph) Inn, 121
Moving pictures in Garrett County, 338
Muddy Creek, 12, 246
Muddy Creek Falls, 9, 18, 336
Museum, Henry Ford, 11, 12
Muskets with bayonets manufactured at Bloomington, 66

Narrow-gauge Climax, 315
Narrows, The, 138
National Democratic Convention 1844, 65
National Freeway, 13, 321
National Grange of the Patrons of Husbandry, 303
National Hotel, 148
National House, 148
National Industrial Recovery Act, 340
National Park Service of Department of Interior, 193
National Pike, 86
National Railroad Strike 1870, 301
National Road, 13, 14, 54, 59, 63, 85, 86, 134-36, 138-46, 149, 154, 188, 243, 244, 248
National Road Stage Company, 139

National Turnpike, 136
Natural Gas in Garrett County, 342
Naval Academy Band in Garrett County, 288
Negro Hannah, 160
Negro Mountain, 65, 121, 130, 134
Neil, Mrs. Selma, 171
Nemacolin Path (Trail), 31
Nemacolin Trail (Path), 39, 119
Nemacolin-Braddock Trail, 37
Nevill, Joseph, 125
New Creek, 16
New Deal, 341
New Germany, 52, 62, 64, 65, 67, 86, 89, 92, 336, 340
New Germany Recreation Dam, 340
New Hampshire, 133
New World, 40
New World settlement, 38
New York, 32, 74
Newman, 63
Newman, George, 217
Newman, George B., 215
Newman, Patty, 147
Newspaper, Maryland's first west of Cumberland, *Glade Star*, 256
Nobel Prize winners, 341, 342
Norris and Steedman, 221
North America, 2, 19, 31
North American Mine, 275
North Branch Coal Company, 274
North Branch Mine, 274
North Carolina, 118
Northern High School, 339
Northern Maryland and Tidewater Company, 276
Northern Neck land tract, 34
Northwestern Trail, 31
Northwestern Turnpike, 68, 117, 126, 142, 155

Oakland, 4, 6, 11, 33, 38, 41, 44, 52, 59, 60, 61, 71, 88, 93, 110, 122, 127, 201, 248-51, 253, 257, 258, 265, 267, 274, 275, 284, 286-91, 300, 305, 336, 344, 347
"Oakland, The Ballad of," 346
Oakland, first county seat, 262
"Oakland Centennial History," 346
Oakland Civic Club, 351
Oakland Coke and Coal Company, 274

Oakland Episcopalians, 110
Oakland Fire Company, 350
Oakland Free Public Library, 351
Oakland Glades Hotel, 255, 259, 261, 262
Oakland Grange, 303
Oakland Hotel, 15, 179, 253, 281, 288
Oakland Methodists, 110, 111
Oakland mills, 88
Oakland Presbyterians, 110
Oakland Railroad Station, 173
Oakland streets, 307
Oakland's first burgess (mayor), 249
Oakland-Friendsville Road, 85
Oakland-Mountain Lake Park Lions Club, 351
Ocean, Atlantic, 2
O'Connor, Father, 111
Offutt, Nanniene Thomasson, 300
Offutt, Thorton, 66
Offutt Mining Company, 274
Offutt's General Store, 249
Ogle, Charles, 165
Ohio, 27, 28, 53, 55, 133
Ohio Company, 31, 42
Ohio Company of Virginia, 119
Ohio Constitutional Convention of 1803, 133
Ohio Country, 52
Ohio Forks, 119
Ohio Indians, 129
Ohio joins Union, 156
Ohio River, 2, 31, 117, 120, 121, 123, 133
Ohio Valley, 32, 40, 42, 44, 45, 69, 118, 119, 120, 121, 129, 132
"Oil Fever" in Garrett County, 343
Old Dutch Settlement, 64
Old Grantsville, 134
Old Hickory, 139
Old Morgantown Road, 58, 88, 115
Old Shelby's Port, 58
Old State Line, 50
Old Warrior Indian Path, 99
Old-fashioned winter, 326
Oldtown, 35, 37, 47, 128, 131
Oliver, John, 78
Oliver, Robert, 78
Olivers, 80
Olives (Olivers), 80
Olson, Frank, 348

One-room school, 333
Opel, Mrs. Earl, xii
Orme, Robert, 43, 172
Orme's Whim, 43, 45
O'Sullivan, Father, 114
O'Sullivan, John L., 155, 156
Otto, C. J., 272
Owens, William, 245

Paca, William, 43, 45
Pacific Railroad, 207
Palatines, 122
Palmer, John W., 225
Palmer, U. S., 306
Palo Alto, 81
Palos, 2
Pangborn, J. G., 203, 285, 287, 288
Panthers, 26
Parker, Aaron, 39, 47, 144
Parks, 345, 346
Parsons, L. B., 235
Parsons Pulp and Paper Company, W.Va., 269
Part IV, Twentieth Century, 334
Partisan Rangers, 227
Passage to west, 3
Patrons of Husbandry, 303
Patterson, John H., 93
Paugh, Johanes, 51
Paugh, Michael, 47, 51
Paugh, Tom, 94, 227
Paughs, 66, 67, 336
Paul, James, 167
Payton, Benjamin, 114
Peabody Institute Art Gallery, 254
Peace and Plenty, 44, 70, 71, 247
Peerce, John T., 238, 239
Pee Wee Mine (coal), 275
Peirsol, Jesse J., 148
Pelf, Professor, 115
Pendleton, Philip, 222
Penn, William, 40
Pennington, Josias, 176
Pennington Cottage, 176
Pennsylvania, 24, 38, 40, 49, 50, 55, 63, 80, 118, 120, 133, 248
Pennsylvania army, 60
Pennsylvania Dutch, 74
Pennsylvania frontier, 117
Perils of early settlers, 94, 95
Peru, 67
Petersburg, Pa., 93

Petersheim, 72
Petersville, 67
Pews, 67
Pfeil, 72
Philadelphia, 124, 139
Philadelphia Centennial World Fair, 67
Philanthropy of John W. Garrett, 254
Phonographs, 338
Picturesque B&O, 203
Piedmont (W.Va.), 16
Piedmont Coal and Iron Company, 274
Piedmont Pulp and Paper Company, 342
Pierson, Stephen, 51
Pilot, B. S., 215
Pilot Line, 139
Pinchot, Gifford, 290
Piney Bottom, 41, 44
Piney Grove, 146
Pink of the Alleghanies, 81
Pinkney, William, 4
Pioneer entertainment, 160-63
Pioneer settlers, 149
Pise, Charles C., 106
Pittsburgh Post Office, 117
Pleasant Valley, 33, 52, 69, 71, 72
Pleasant Valley Glades, 123
Pleasant Valley Recreation Park, 81
Pleasant Valley State Park, 346
Plough, The, 80
Pontiac, Chief, 117
Pontiac's Conspiracy, 46
Pontiac's uprising, 3
Poole, William H., 241
Poole shirt, 67
Pope Leo XIII, 283
Poplar Lick Run, 89
Populists, 303
"Portrait of Liberty" (Oakland), 347
Post offices, early, 140
Post, William, 58
Potomac Canal Company, 189
Potomac and Piedmont Railroad, 268, 275
Potomac River, 2, 3, 16, 31-36, 38-40, 42, 52, 57, 66-69, 94, 105, 116, 121-28, 133, 188, 189, 250
Potomac State Forest, 338
"Potomac tributaries" by Winslow, 34

Potomac Valley, 33
Pott's Adventure, 44
Presbyterians, 24, 254, 310
President Grant, 65, 67
President Harding, 332
President-elect Harrison, William Henry, 138
President-elect Jackson, Andrew, 139
President-elect Polk, James K., 138
President-elect Taylor, Zachary, 138
President Washington, George, 49
Preston County, W.Va., 19
Preston Lumber and Coal Company, 266, 274
Price, Ed, 14
Price, Walter W., 115, 117
Price, William, 64
Price's Choice, 44
Prince Georges County, 73
Pringle brothers, 41
Pritchard, John, 58
Pritchard, Thomas, 58
Pritchards, 66
Proclamation, King's (England 1763), 117
Proclamation by Governor Whyte, 5, 6
Proclamation of King of England, 37
Proclamation by President George Washington, 49
Proctor, Percy, 284
Progue, Mr., 162
Promised Land, 44
Promised Land Camp, 33
Public relief program, 339
Public service work projects, 340
Public Works Administration, 340
Puzzley Run, 46
Pysell, Jacob, 109

Queen, Charles, 51
Queen City Hotel (Cumberland), 253, 257
Queens, 66
Queenwood (Hotel), 293

Radio, 338
Rafters, 67
Railroad, B&O, Frontispiece
Railroad history, 195
Railroads, 268

Rambles in the Path of the Steam Horse, 204
Ramsey, Aaron, 161
Rangers, 16
Rappahanock River, 34
Rasche, Dennis T., 47, 85, 87, 88, 161, 283, 312
Rathbun, F. E., 349
Rattlesnake, 25
Rawlings, William L., 261
Reckner, John, 145
Recreation, 312-14
Red House, 44, 126, 127, 144
Red House Inn, 146, 178
Red Ridge Hotel, 216
Red Run, 86, 246
Redmond, James, 106
Redstone, 130, 132
Reeside, James, 139
Reinhart, George, 47
Reinhart, Susanna, 106
Reinhart, William, 245
Reinhart Tavern, 127
Reis, A. B., 75
Reis, John, 74
Relief applications, 340
Religion, 310, 311. *See* Churches
"Religious and Educational Summer Resort," (Mountain Lake Park), 291, 292
Religious fervor, 2
Religious liberty, 40
Renaissance, 1, 2, 38
Republican, The (newpaper), 11, 299, 305, 325
Republican Ensign (newspaper), 305
Reserved lands released, 51
Resort business, 344, 345
Resort recreation, early, 263
Rest, The (Hotel), 284
Resurvey of Shawnee War tract, 76
Revere House, 241
Revolutionary army, 60
Revolutionary War, 43, 121, 129
Revolutionary War veterans, 71, 73, 77
Reynolds, James, 149
Rhinehards, 70
Rich Glade, 44
Rich Mountain, 220
Richlands, 81
Richter, Adam, 92

Richter, Albert, 178
Richter, Edward, 75
Richter, Henry, 75
Richter, John, 92
Richter, John L., 75
Richter Tannery, 324
Ridder, 68
Ridder, Henry W., 241
Ridenours, 70
Ridgely, Eli, 76
Ridgely, William, 76
Ridgely Hill, 76
Ridgely's, 109
Riley, George W., 247
Riley, Stephen, 55
Rinehart, George, 71, 72, 106, 163, 164
Rinker, 68
Rivers: Blackwater (W.Va.), 250; Casselman, 13, 33, 37, 40, 62, 76, 121, 135; Cheat, 31, 32, 41, 46, 47, 77, 124, 125, 250; Cohongoroota, 31; Delaware, 83; Kanawha, 118, 123; Mississippi, 2, 69, 124; Monongahela, 42, 117, 125, 128; Ohio, 2, 31, 117, 120, 121, 123, 133; Potomac, 2, 3, 16, 31-42, 52, 57, 66-69, 94, 105, 116, 121-28, 133, 188, 189, 250; Rappahanock, 34; Savage, 2, 17, 32-35, 51, 65, 66, 69, 88, 101, 111, 124, 125; Wild Geese, of (Cohongoroota), 31; Yockie Geni (Casselman), 42; Youghiogheny (Yough), 2, 3, 7, 18, 23, 25, 28, 29, 31, 33, 35-39, 41, 43, 45, 47, 49, 51-62, 69, 71, 85, 86, 88, 101, 107, 116, 121, 123, 246, 250, 251, 337
Road feasibility study, 128
Roads, 3, 116, 125-28, 132-39, 149-56, 336
Robertson, David, 51, 58
Robinson, Felix G., 55, 56, 65, 74, 245, 246, 288, 290, 346, 350
Rock Lodge Road, 44
Romney, 115
Roosevelt, Franklin D., 341, 347
Roosevelt, Franklin's New Deal, 339
Roosevelt, Theodore, 338
Roosevelt, Mrs. Theodore, 289
Roosevelt, Theodore, Jr., 289

Roseby's Rock, 205
Rosecrans, William, 235, 236
Rosenberger, 66
Ross, Moses A., 59
Route 40, 13
Route 42, 22
Route 48, 13, 336
Route 219, 7, 8, 89
Rowlesburg, W.Va., 31
Royal British Army, 188
Ruckert, Mrs. Robert J. (Adeline), 15, 72, 178
Ruckert, Robert J., xii, 8, 18, 19, 170-75, 328
Rumbarger, J. L., 268, 269
Rush, James H., 55
Russell, Adam, 139
Rutan, Jesse, 160
Rutan, John, 51
Rutans, 38
Ruth Enlow Library, xii
Ruth Enlow Library branch, Grantsville, 351
Ryan, E. W., 291
Ryan, John, 39, 51
Ryans, 66
Ryan's Glade, 35, 39, 52, 67, 68, 72, 123
Ryland, Sylvester, 51, 55

Sabbath regulations in Mountain Lake Park, 291
Sac Chief Black Hawk, 157
Saint Clair, 52, 188, 189
Saint George (W.Va.), 46, 248, 266
Saint Mary's Roman Catholic Church, 107
Saint Paul's church, 107
Saint Peter, 26
Saint Peter's Roman Catholic Church, 110
Salisbury, Pa., 108
Salk, Jonas, 342
Salt Lick, Va., 41
Sand Spring Tavern, 145
Sandy Creek, 47, 51
Sandy Creek Glades, 38, 46, 88, 105, 122
Sandy Creek Hundred, 52, 59
Sandy Creek rangers, 47
Sandy Gap, 134

Sang Run, 21, 28-30, 33, 52, 56-58, 85, 88, 89, 101, 107, 336, 337
Sang Run Methodists, 107
Sanging Ground, 57
Sanging Ground Bridge, 116
Sanging Ground Roads, 116
Savage, John, 34
Savage, Robinson, 51, 114, 116
Savage, Robinson T., 57
Savage Creek, 69
Savage Mountain, 41, 42, 51, 65, 129, 130, 134
Savage River, 2, 17, 32-35, 51, 65, 66, 69, 88, 101, 111, 124, 125
Savage River Dam, 17, 341
Savage River Valley, 81
Sawmill, first water powered up-and-down-sash, 85
Sawmills, 85, 318
Scales, Mrs. J. P., 272
Schaeffer, Jacob Rhodes, 92
Scharf, J. Thomas, 136, 139, 210, 247, 251, 286
Scharf, Thomas, 137, 138, 140-42
Schartzer, Jacob, 75
Schedule of Stages, 140
Schley, J. M., 255
Schley, James M., 258
Schlossnagel, Charles, 44
Schlossnagle, Christoff, 75
Schlossnagle, Karl, 75
Schlosnagle, Steve, xi
Schneider, Frederick, 74
School of Photography, 292
School requirements, early, 112
School terms, early, 115
Schoolhouse description, early, 112
Schoolhouse, first Garrett County, 114
Schools: Accident, 114; Asher's Glade, 114; Blooming Rose Ridge, 114; Bray's, P. H., 114; Buffalo Marsh, 114; Catholic, private, 114; Clifton, 114; Crab Tree Bottom, 114; Custer's, 114; 1872, 57 in Garrett County, 307; Frantz's, Jonathan, 114; German Settlement, 114; Grantsville, 114; Hazlet's Mill, 114; Little Crossings, 114; Little Meadows, 114; Little Youghiogheny, 114;

Lower's, Henry, 114; Mars Hill, 114; Normal Schools, 310; One-room established, 308; Ryan's Glade, 114; Sanging Ground, 114; Schockley's, Abraham, 114; Secondary, 338; Selbysport, 114; Susan's Church, at, 114; Tomlinson's, 114
Schools, administration of, 309
Schools, consolidation of, 339
Schools, districts, 114
Schools, early Garrett County, 112, 114, 115
Schrock, 72
Schroyer, Adam, 55
Scotland, 43
Scott, George, 70
Scott, James, 160
Scott, Thomas, 108, 129
Scott, Winfield, 167
Scott's Road (Tom), (Pennsylvania Railroad), 253
Searight, T. B., 145, 165
Seibert, David, 47
Selbysport, 39, 51, 52, 58-60, 74, 85, 88, 92, 116, 118, 126, 253, 270
Selbysport doctor, 93
Selbysport gristmill, 88
Selbysport Post Office, 59
Selder, 72
Sembower, 89
Sembower, Adam, 85
Seneca Trail, 32
Senecas (Indians), 32
Settlement following Revolutionary War, 50
Settlements, early, 52
Settlers, 12
Seven Hills, 68
Shades of Death, 86, 134, 141
Shaeffer, Jacob, 68
Shaefferville, 68
Shaffer, James, 330
Shaffer, lumber town, 266
Shaffer, Robert C., 319
"Shake-guts," 139
Shakespeare—quote, 1
Shallmar, 276, 277
Sharp, Horatio, 38
Sharp, Joseph, 279
Sharp Shooters, 137
Sharpe, Edmund, 188

Shaw, Sidney, 210
Shawnee Indians, 32
Shawnee War, 44, 46
Sheets, William, 148
Sheetz, William, 148, 149
Sheetz Tavern, 148
Shelby, 39
Shelby, Evan, 39, 58, 118
Shelby, Isaac, 58
Shelby's Station, 118
Sherman, William T., 240, 242, 281
Shirer, Peter, 127
Shirer's (Scott) Oak Hotel, 251
Shirer's (Peter) Tin Shop, 249, 305
Shriver, David, 135
Shriver, James, 190
Shuck, George, 150
Shultz, Adam, 109, 147
Shultz, Perry, 88, 147
Shultz tavern 148
Sideling Hill, 130
Sides, 146
Simkins, Elie, 160
Simkins, John, 47, 51, 116, 119, 129, 145, 160, 163
Simmons, Mr. and Mrs. W. Blair, 185
Simpson, John, 41
Sines, Henry, 57, 100
Sines, John, 100
Sines, Solomon, 231
Skiing at "Wisp," 325
Skinner, F. G., 100
Skinner, Frederick E., 80, 81
Skinner, John Stuart, 80
Skipnish, 265, 267
Skipnish Railroad, 272
Skipton Company, 47
Slabtown, 61
Slaubaugh, 72
Slavery, 214
Slaves, 215, 216, 217
Slicer, John, 55, 148
Slicer, Samuel, 150
Sloan, John, 63
Sloan's Ville, 63
Small Meadows, 43, 45, 61
Smith, Alexander, 68
Smith, Edmund Kirby, 242
Smith, Jacob, 61
Smith, Jennie, 292
Smith, John, 61, 108
Smith, Mason, 247

Smith, R. A., 306
Smith, W. A. (Billy), 336
Smith Farm (John's), 61
Smith House (Alexander), 127
Smithman Hotel, 251
Smithsonian, Washington, D.C., 96
Smooth Valley Inn and Store, 147
Smouse, Daniel, 59, 148, 309, 348
Snakes, 94, 101
Snee and Eberly Gas Company, 343
Snodgrass, W. C., 291
Snow, 331
Snows, Oakland, 57
Snowy Creek, 41, 49, 61, 62, 86
Snowy Creek Falls, 251
Snyder, Christian, 75
Snyder, Fred, 76
Social changes, twentieth century, 341
Social Security Act, 341
Society of Friends camp meetings, 292
Somerset County, Pa., 40, 72
Southern High School, 339, 347
Southern Literary Messenger, 202
Spa of Presidents, 282, 290
Spain, 2
Spanish-American War, 349
Specht, Samuel, 232
Spedden's Store, 249
Speelman, John, 85
Speelman, Peter, 89
Speicher, Kathryn A., 74
Spiker, 62
Spiker, Adam, 74
Spiker, Joseph, 74
Spoerlein, Konrad, 75
Spruce Spring, 44
Spurgeon, John, 52, 83
Spurgeons, 38, 45
Squatters, 25, 39, 50, 51, 71, 117
Stabler, Edward, 20
Stackpole, James, 126
"Stage box," 148
Stagecoach robberies, 141
Stagecoaches, 139
Stallings, Lish, 161
Standards for relief, early, 340
Stanley Steamer (auto), 181
Stanton, 62
Stanton, Edward M., 209
Stanton, Eli, 88

Stanton, Thomas J., 106, 107, 215
Stanton, William, 88
"Star Spangled Banner, The," 81
Stark, Adam, 75
Stark, Francis, 76
Stark, George, 75, 76
Stark, William, 76
Starner, Archibald, 148
Starner, Solomon, 63, 148
Starner House, 148
State Department of Forests and Parks, 135
State Road Commission, 135
States road improvement, 154
Stauch (Stouch), John, 69, 70, 105, 106
Stemples, 70
Stephens, Alexander H., 208
Stephenson, George, 195
Sterling Processing Company, 344
Stewart, Charles, 70
Stewart's Delight, 60
Stewart's Delight tract, 248
Steyer, 123, 267, 269
Stockade life, 46
Stockton, L. W., 150
Stockton, Lucius W., 150
Stockton Line, 145
Stockton and Stokes Stage, 196
Stoddard, 78, 146
Stoddard, Benjamin, 77
Stoddard, James, 149
Stoddard Tavern, 149
Stone House Inn, 63, 138, 146, 147, 175
"Stonewall Jackson's Way," (poem), 225
Storm, John, 51
Strauss, Mrs. Charles, 179, 324
Streets, 66
Streets, John, 51
Strip mine, 323
Strong, David, 167
Strong, Joseph, 140
Sugar Maple Camp, 170
Sugar Point, 44
Sugar Tree, 44
Summitville (Altamont), 245, 253
Sunnyside, 52, 69, 71, 72, 84, 92, 106, 107, 127
Sunshine (Crellin), 52, 62, 86, 88
Surmount (boarding house), 284

Surveying expedition, 34
Surveys, 39
Susan's Church, 106
Swallow Falls, 11, 18, 19, 36, 37, 44, 96, 99, 122, 246, 337, 338
Swallow Falls State Forest, 338, 340
Swallow Falls State Park, 9, 12, 18, 345
Swan, John, 43, 70, 71
Swan, John, Sr., 71
Swan, Robert, 71
Swann, John, 283
Swann, Thomas, 200, 206
Swansylvania, 43
Swanton, 59, 88, 200, 253, 265, 267, 271
Swanton gristmill, 88
Swartzentruber, 72
Swartzentruber, Jacob, 89
Swauger, John, 86, 89
Swauger Grist Dam, 340

Table Rock, 128
Taft, William Howard, 295
Tasker, Richard, 47, 51
Taskers, 67
Tavern business, 142-45
Taverns, 146-49
Taxation for public schools, 113
Taylor, John, 105, 159
Taylor, Richard, 240, 242
Taylor, Walter S., 271
Taylor, Zachary, 138, 139
Teacher tenure, 339
Teachers, 307, 308, 309
Teacher's Certificate, 310
Technology, twentieth century, 335, 336
Tecumseh, Shawnee chief, 156
Telegraph Company, Garrett County, 336
Telegraph stations, 306
Telephone service, first, 381
Telephones, 336
Templeman, John, 111
Tennessee, 118
Tenskwatawa, Indian Prophet, 156
Terra Mariae, 38
Texas Eastern Transmission Company, 343
Texas joins Union, 157
"Thank-you-marm," 244

Thayer, 70, 71
Thayer, Ann, 14
Thayer, F. A., 216
Thayer, Murray, 61, 86, 88
Thayer, Nancy, 72
Thayer, Ralph, 55, 58, 59
Thayer, Ralph T., 164
Thayer, Stephen, 71, 114
Thayer, Walter, 216
Thayer, Wright, 85
Thayer (John) Tavern, 251
Thayer-Browning settlement, 246
Thayerville, 336
Thistle, 146
Thistle, Thomas, 148
Thistle Tavern, 148
Thomas, Francis, 64, 65, 67, 73, 165, 200, 218
Thomas, George H., 236, 240
Thomas, Philip E., 194
Thomas, William, 216
Thomas and Ann, 43
Thompson, 70
Thompson, Isaac, 229
Thompson, Israel, 68, 71, 103, 199, 255
Thompson, John, 292
Thompson, John R., 202
Thompson, Josias, 133
Thompson, Katie, 229
Thompson, Lewis, 71
Thompsons, 71
Thoreau, Henry David, quote, 186-88
Thrasher, Harry, 247
Thrasher, Robert, 330
Thrasher, Sadie, 330
Three Fork Coal Company, 275
Three Fork Lumber Company, 270
Tichenal, Moses, 88
Tillson, E. C., 247
Timber towns of West Virginia, 268
Tobacco, 55
Tollgate, 68
Tolliver Run, 246
Tomlinson, Jesse, 47, 51, 85, 88, 146, 160, 163, 175, 216
Tomlinson, Joseph, 37, 39, 144, 146
Tomlinson's Inn, 108, 120
Tomlinson's post office, 63
Tomlinson's Tavern, 121
Tom Thumb locomotive, 195
Totten, Ezekiel, 51

Tower, E., 127
Tower, William H., 261
Townshend, J. L., 247
Trading, 248
Trail, Great Warrior, 31
Trail, Northwestern, 31
Trail, Seneca, 32
Treaties, 118
Treatise on Law of Ejectments..., 79
Treaty of Camp Charlotte, 46
Treaty of Fort Stanwix, 120
Treaty of Hard Labour, 120
Trees, 25
Trenton, N.J., 139
Trout, 24
Troy, N.Y., 139
Troy coach, 139
Trubees, 66
Truesdell, George, 181, 330
Turf, Field and Farm, 80
Turkey Foot, 123
Turkeyfoot, Pa., 36, 52
Tumblestone (Tomlinson, Jesse), 119
Tumblestones (Little Meadows), 130
Turner, 65
Turner, Frederick Jackson, 157, 158, 188, 335
Turner, Nat, 212
Turney, Abram, 75
Turney, Tom, 76
"Turtle-backs," 139
Twentieth Century, Part IV, 334
Tyler, John, 152
"Typecanoe and Tyler, Too," 165

Underwood Hill, 61
Union Bank of Maryland, 63
Union Church, 106, 310
Union Fire Brick Company, 343, 344
Union Pacific Railroad, 207
Uniontown, Pa., 134
United States Department of Interior, 19
United States Magazine and Democratic Revue, 155
United States railroad history, 194
United States Route 48 (National Freeway), 321
United States Route 50, 126

Vagdon, George, 75
Vale, Arnos, 39
Vale of Avoca, 81
Van Buren, Martin, 165
Vandalia, Ill., 136
Vanderbilt's road (New York Central Railroad), 253
Vandiver, C. H., 233
VanMeter, John B., 291
VanSickle, Clyde, 315-18
Van Sickle, Zachariah, 51
Van Sickles, 38
Vesey, Denmark, 211
Veterans, 348
Vietnam War, 348
Vindex, 267, 269, 275-77
Virginia, 35, 38, 40-42, 46, 48, 69, 71, 77, 80, 118, 133
Virginia Glades, 69
Virginia House of Burgesses, 120, 189
Virginia-Maryland Interstate Road, 116
Virginia military troops, 45
Virginia's Hampshire Coal Mines, 255

Wagner Labor Relations Act, 347
Wagners, 70
Wagon stand, 149
Walcott, Major, 221
Walker, Samuel H., 167
Wallace, Lew, 180, 218, 219, 279
Wallman, 267, 269, 272, 276, 277
Wallman Mill, 269
Walnut Bottoms, 44
War for Great Empire, 2, 35, 37
War of 1812, 165-68
Ward, J. T., and Sons Cabinet Shop, 249
Warner, 66
Warner's Glade, 39
Warnick, Joseph, 51
Warnicks, 66
Wars, 165-68
Washington, Bushrod, 122
Washington, D.C., 127, 138
Washington, George, 4, 13, 15, 48, 49, 78, 95, 119-26, 189
Washington, Pa., 115
Washington County, 50, 51

Washington County, Pa., 46
Washington Spring, 15, 253
Washington Town, 52
Water Street, Oakland, 86
Water Street gristmill (Oakland), 88
Watsons (Fairmont, W.Va.), 289
Wayne, "Mad Anthony," 46, 53, 156
Webster, Daniel, 246
Wedding, 70
Weekly Press (newspaper), 305
Weeks, Mrs. Thekla Fundenberg, 346
Weimer, 62, 65
Welch, Abraham, 55
Welch, Joseph H., 169
Welfare, 339
Welfly, David R., 93
Weller's Flour Mill, 89
Wesley's Chapel, 107
West, Corbin, 116
West, Richard J., 261
West, Truman, 73, 237
"West Union Towne," 149
West Union Towne, 116
West Virginia, 15, 35, 55
West Virginia Central and Pittsburgh Railway, 268, 269, 275
Western Maryland Bicentennial Trail, 347
Western Maryland Railway Company, 268, 269, 270, 274, 275
Westernport, 58, 75, 116
Westernport Catholic Church, 111
Western settlers, 124
Weston-Dodson Company (Coal), 275
Wests, 74
Westvaco Pulp and Paper Corporation, 342
Westward expansion, 156, 157
Westward movements, 118
Wheeling, 49, 133
Whetzel's Blacksmith Shop, 249
Whigs, 165
Whiskey, 143
Whiskey, Melkey Miller Rye, 75
White House, The, 198
White Oak Level, 44
White, Richard, 55
White, Rowan, 250
Whites, 45
Whitzell, Eli, 65
Whyte, Edward C., 4

Whyte, William Pinkney, 4, 257, 259
Widow Ward, 145
Wiland, William, 92
Wild animals, 3, 94, 100, 101, 191
Wild Cherry Tree Meadows, 44, 77, 78
Wild Cherry Tree tract, 82
Wild game, 26, 102
Wilderness Road, 155
Wilderness Shall Smile tract, 61, 247
Wiles, William, 101
Wiley, Holmes, 100
Wiley, John, 115
Wilhelm, 65
William James Hotel, 251
Williams, Eli, 133
Williams, T. J. C., 48
Williams, William, 103
Williams family, 119
Williamsport, 57
Wills Creek, 31, 32, 52, 134
Wilson, 267
Wilson, George W., 268
Wilson, J. H., 245
Wilson, Jonathan, 103
Wilson, Thomas, 67, 88
Wilson, William, 61
Wilson Lumber Company, 268
Wilts, 66, 70
Winchester, Va., 125, 132
Wind Ridge, 130
Winslow, Benjamin, 34
Winston Tavern, 127
Wirsing, John, 84
Wisconsin joins Union, 157
Wisp Ski, Marsh Mountain, 345
Wolf, 66
Wolfe, Thomas, 334
Wolves, 25
Women's College of Baltimore, 291, 298
"Wood hicks," 273
Wooden, William, 147
Woodland Farm, 73, 74
Woods, John, 149
Woodsmen, 317
Woodward and Lothrop, 330
Works Progress Administration, 341
World War I, 17, 348
World War II, 274, 276, 341, 348
Wotrings, 70
Wright, 86

388

Yaldwin, Master John, 115
"Yankee" Miller's Notion Store, 249
Yaulding, 80
"Year without summer (1816), 94
Yeast, Peter, 147
YMCA—Baltimore, 254
Yockie Geni (Casselman River), 42
Yoder, 62
Yoder, L. T., 297
Yost, Mae, 127
Youghiogheny Dam, 58
Youghiogheny Glades, 32, 33, 40, 45, 52, 61, 71, 88, 101, 102, 110, 115, 116, 122, 124-26
Youghiogheny Glades Post Office, 60, 61
Youghiogheny Hydro-Electric Corporation, 337
Youghiogheny Iron Company, 54, 55, 182, 307
Youghiogheny Lake, 346
Youghiogheny Manor, 270
Youghiogheny Manor Land Company, 270
Youghiogheny Manor Land Lumber Company, 271
Youghiogheny River, 2, 3, 7, 9, 18, 23, 25, 28, 29, 31, 33, 35-39, 41, 43, 45, 47, 49, 51-54, 56-62, 69, 71, 85, 86, 88, 101, 107, 116, 121, 123, 125, 246, 250, 251, 337
Youghiogheny River Flood Control Authority, 346
Youghiogheny River Oil and Gas Company, 342, 343
Youghiogheny River Valley, 32, 33, 118
Young, Jared W., 298
Yutzy, 72

Zanes Trace (Ebenezer), 154
Zeptner, Bernard, 75
Zevely, E. S., 255-57, 349
Zimmerman, Charles A., 288
Zinkin, Henry, 75
Zion Lutheran Cemetery, 179